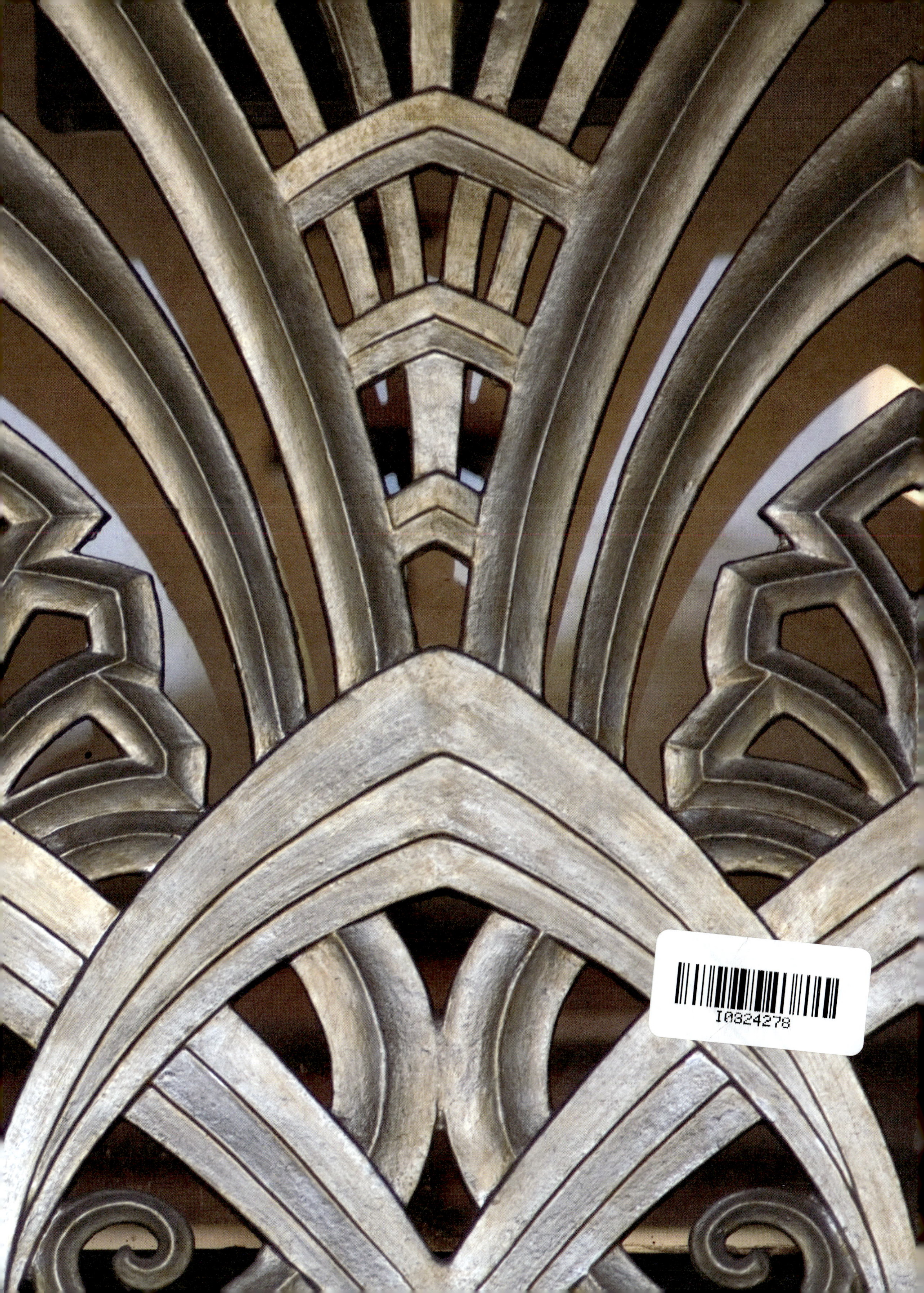
I0324278

ART DECO | LOS ANGELES

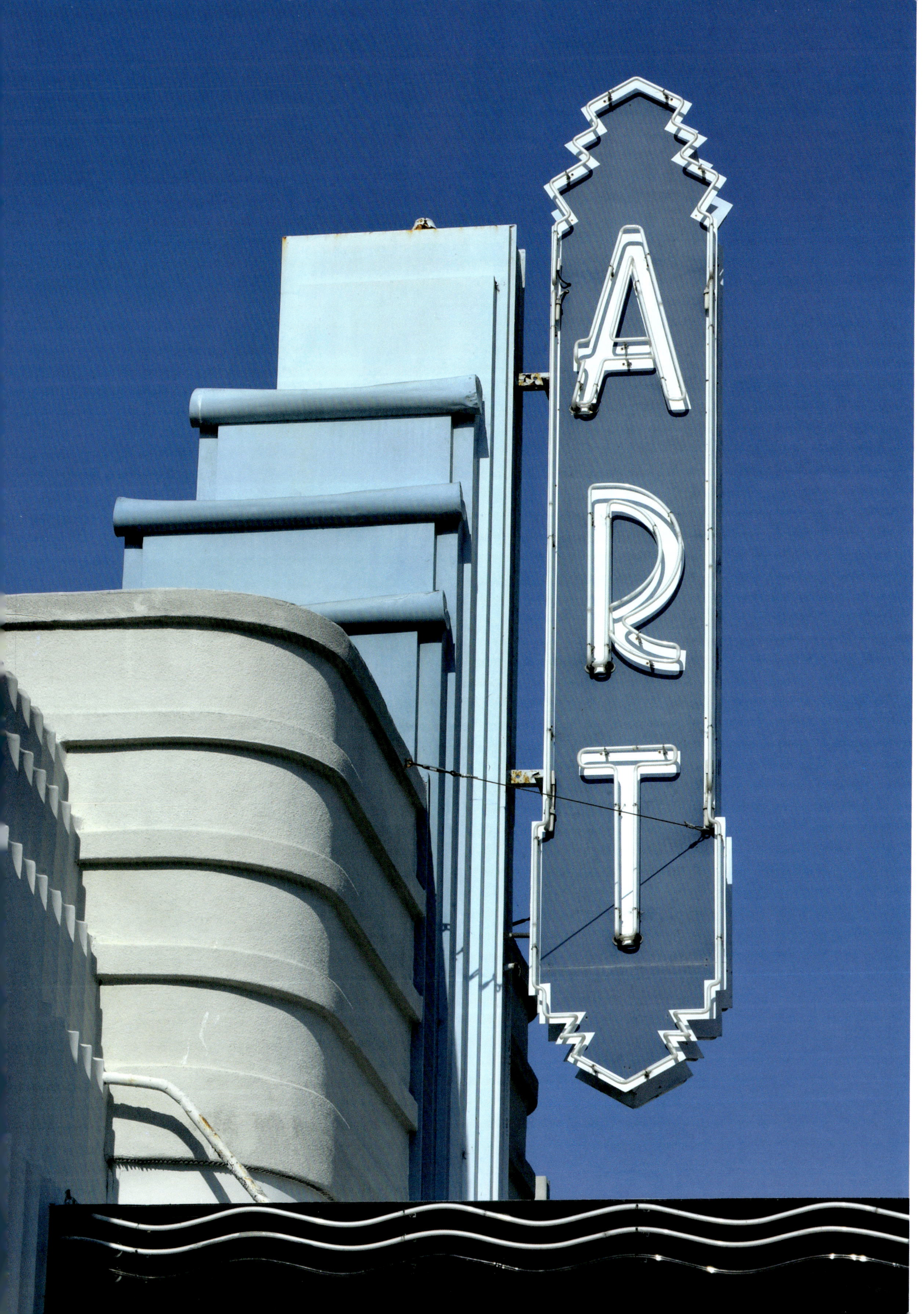
ART

ROBERT LANDAU

ART DECO | LOS ANGELES

Essay
ALAN HESS

Book Design
FRANS EVENHUIS

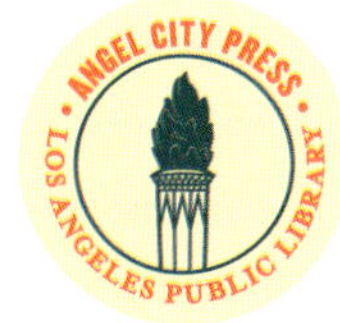

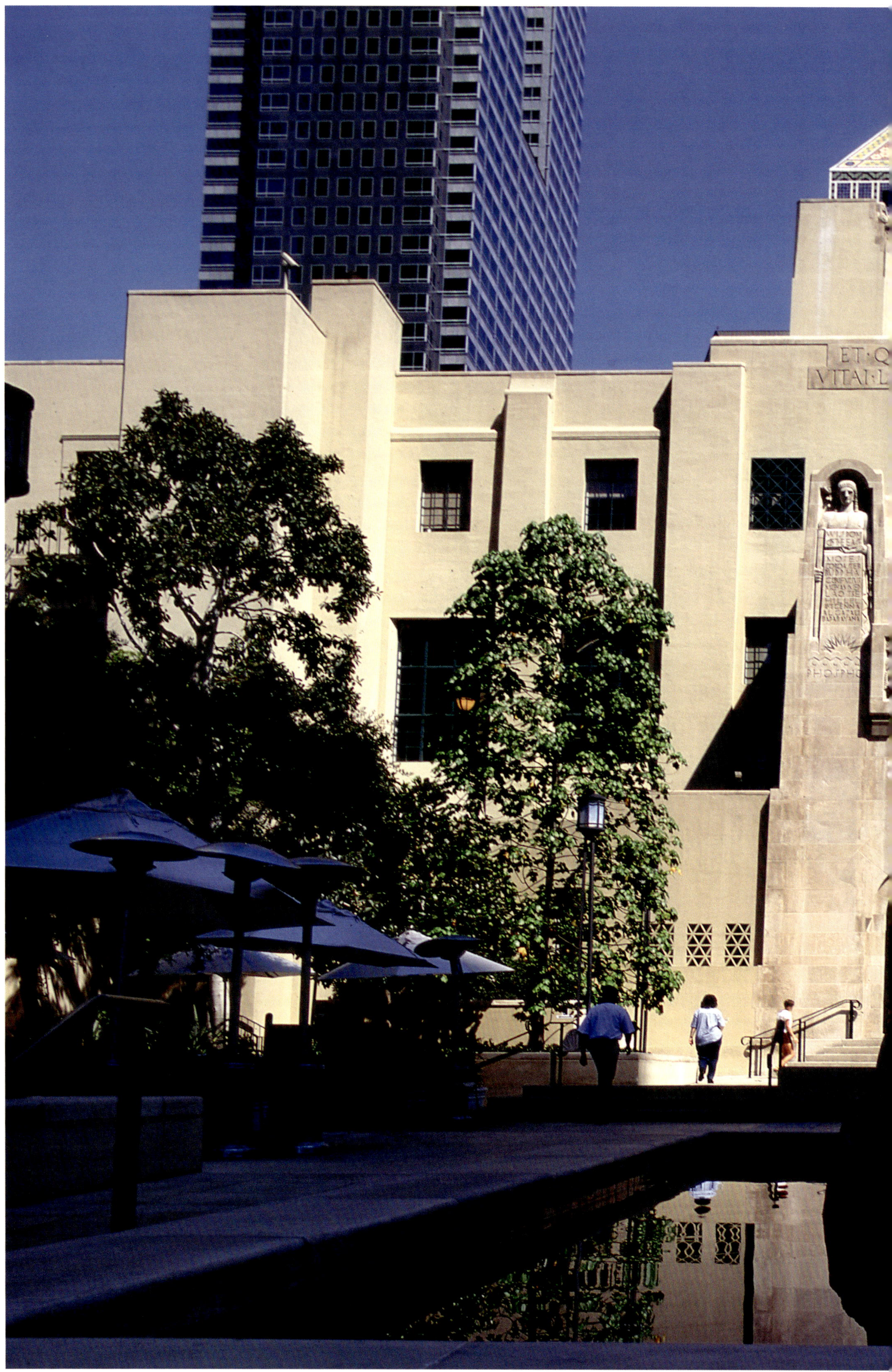
ET·Q
VITAI·L

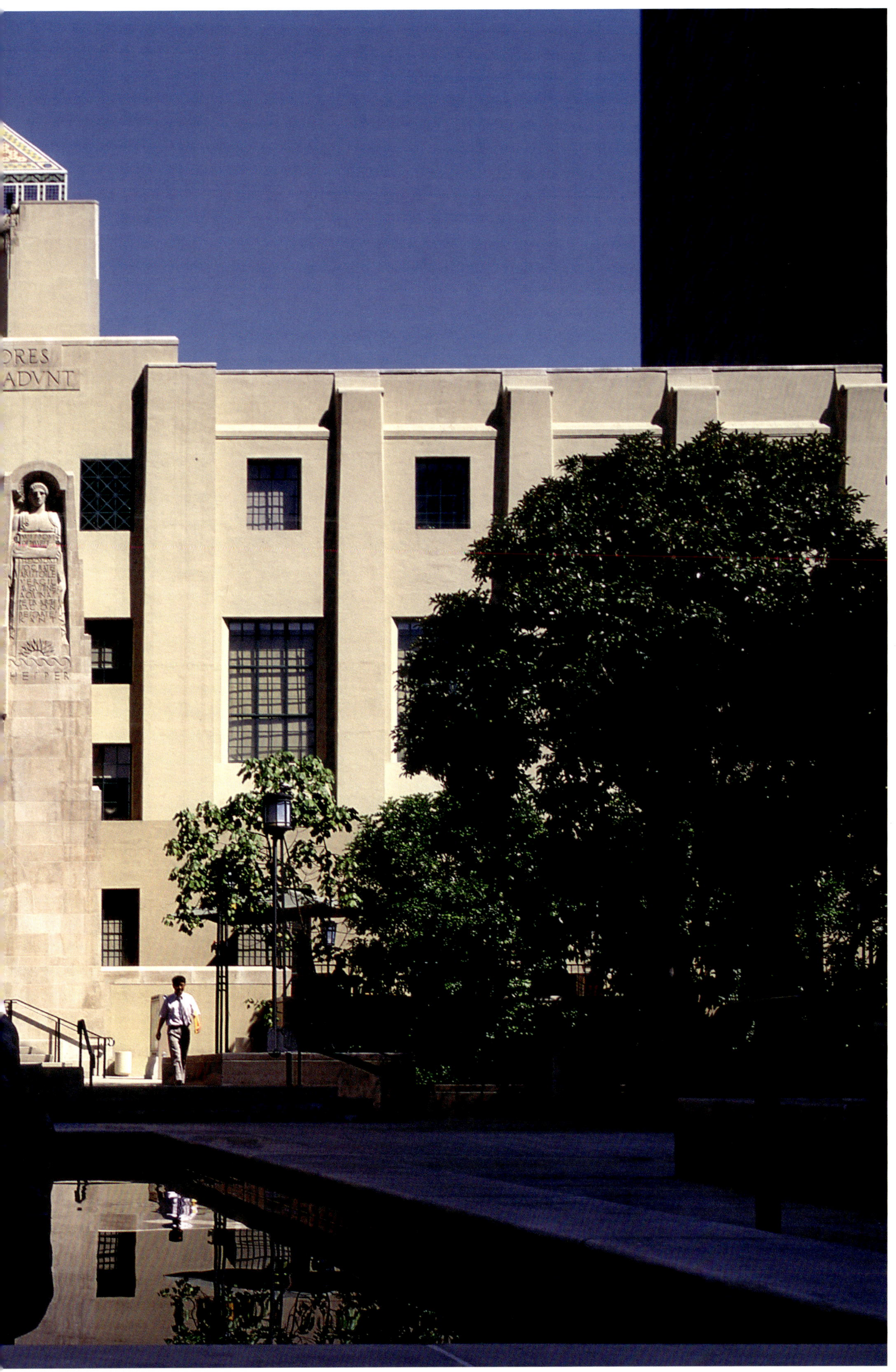
ORES
ADVNT

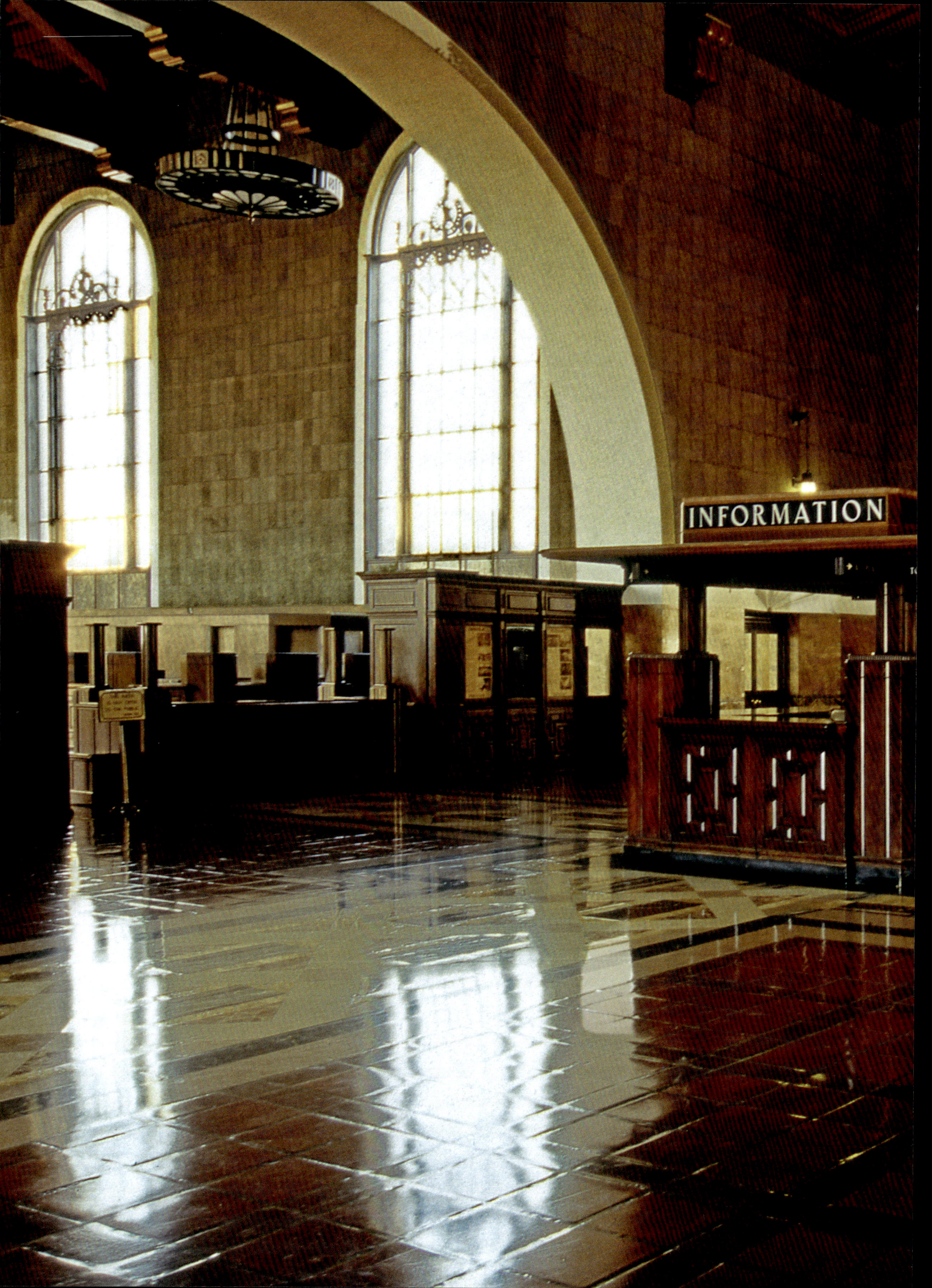
INFORMATION

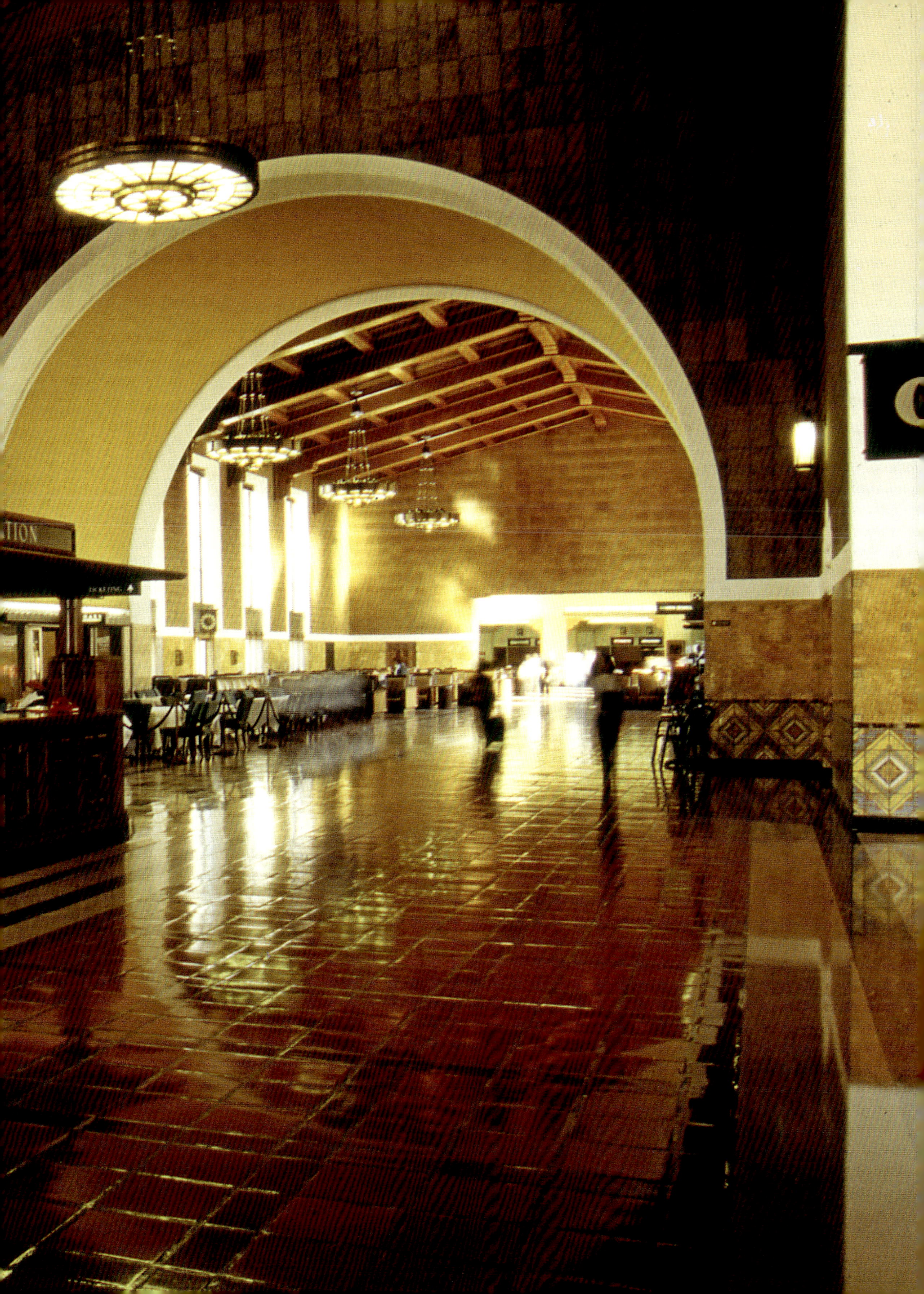
TION
TICKETING

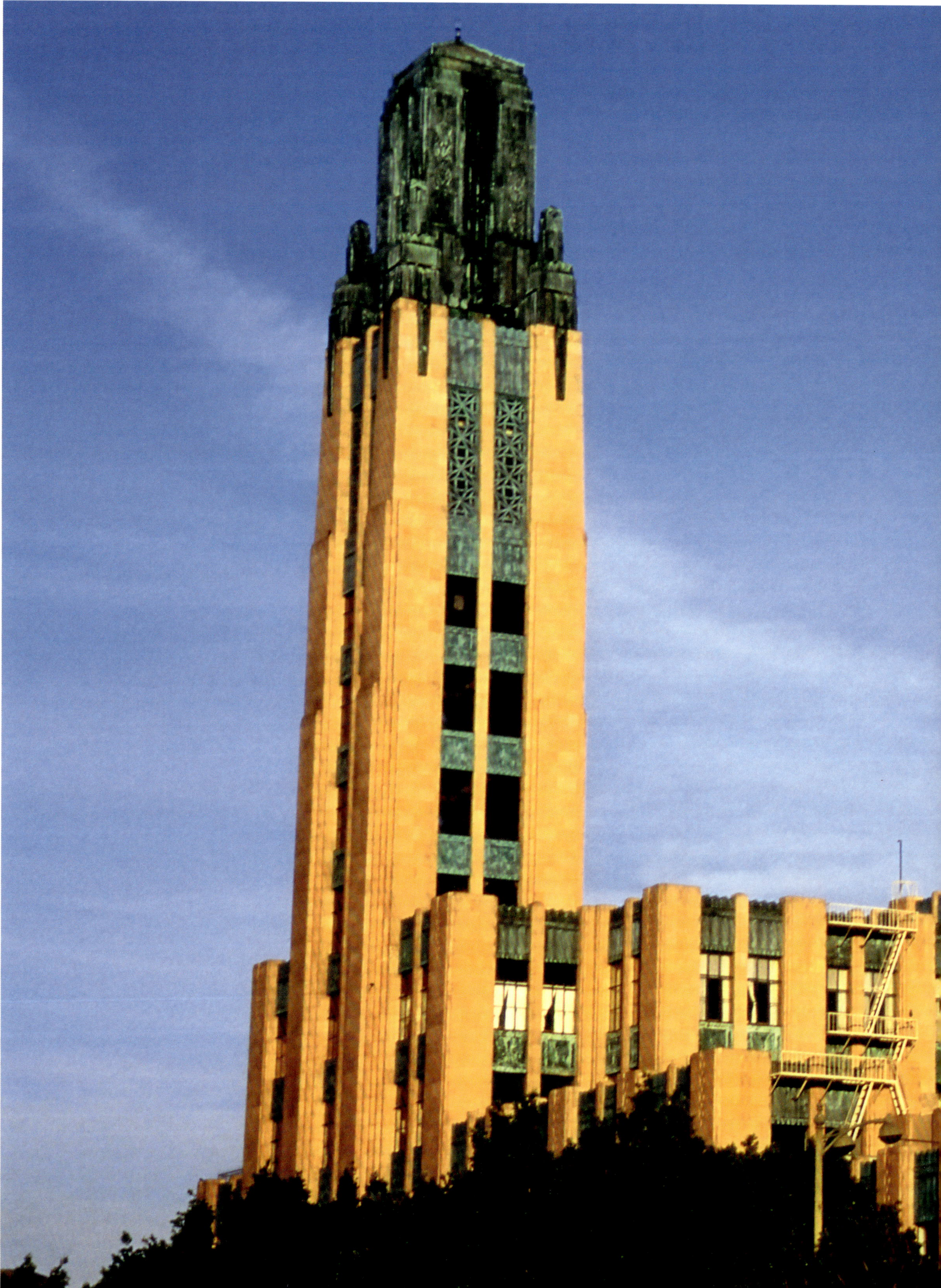

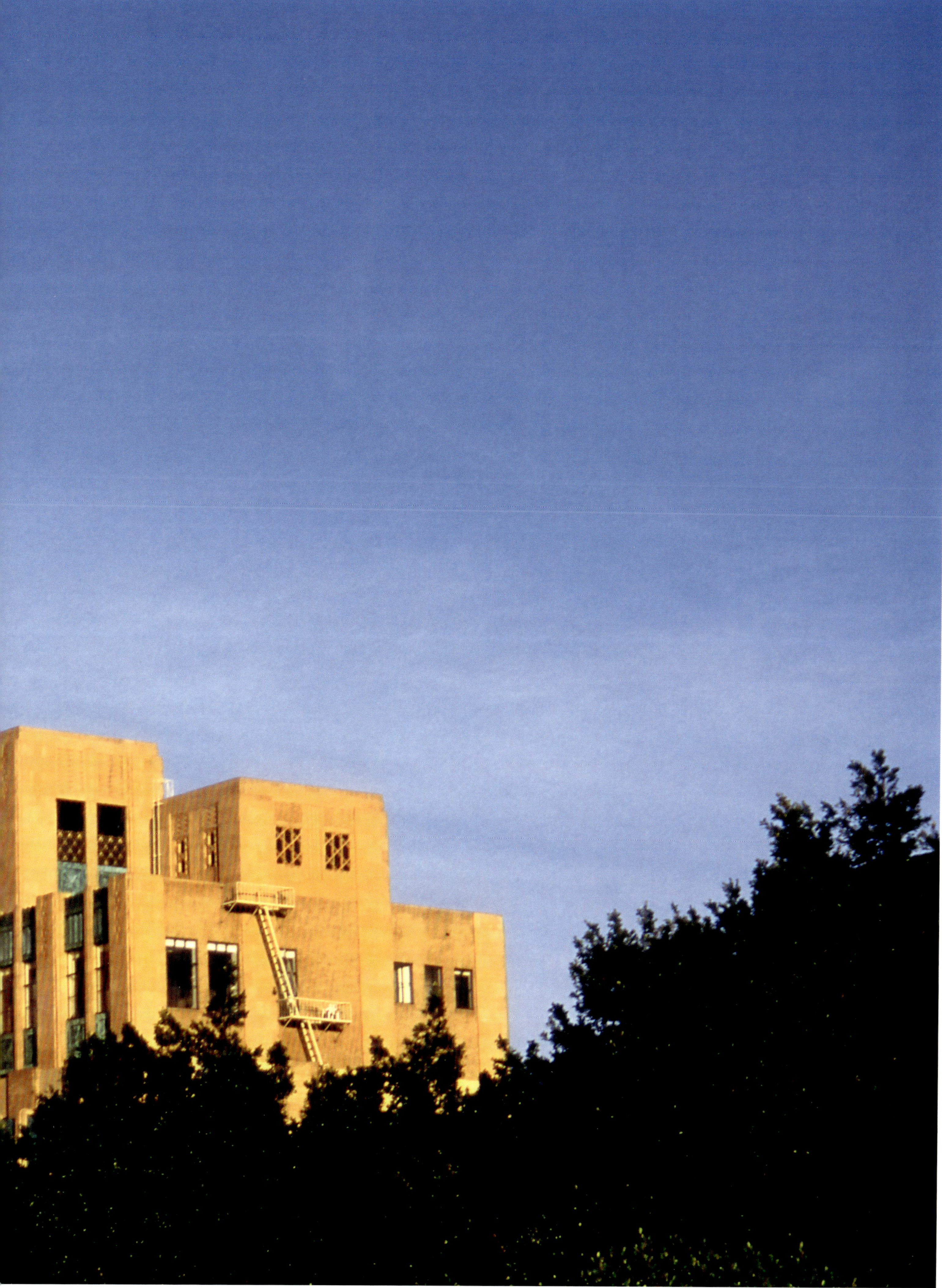

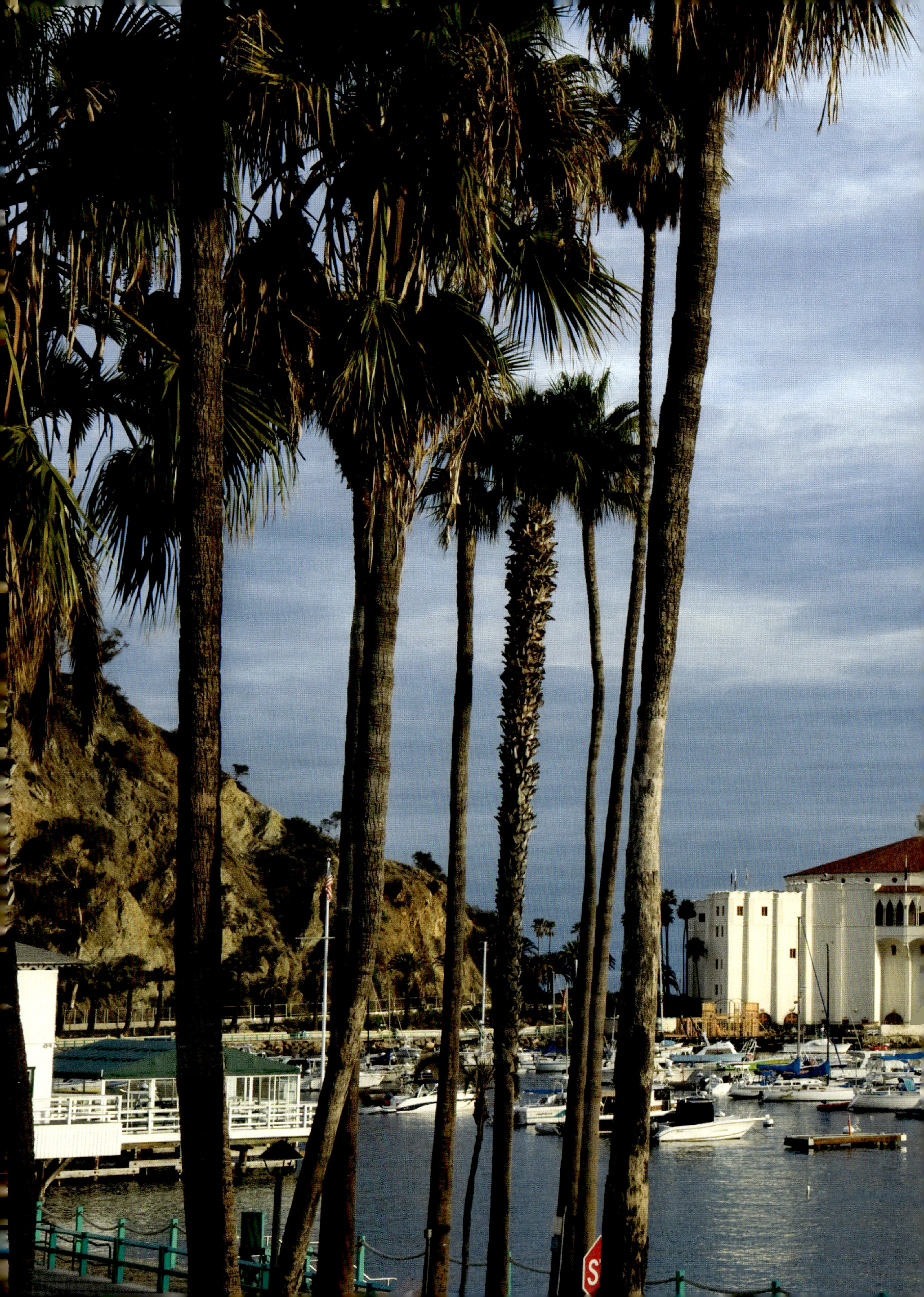

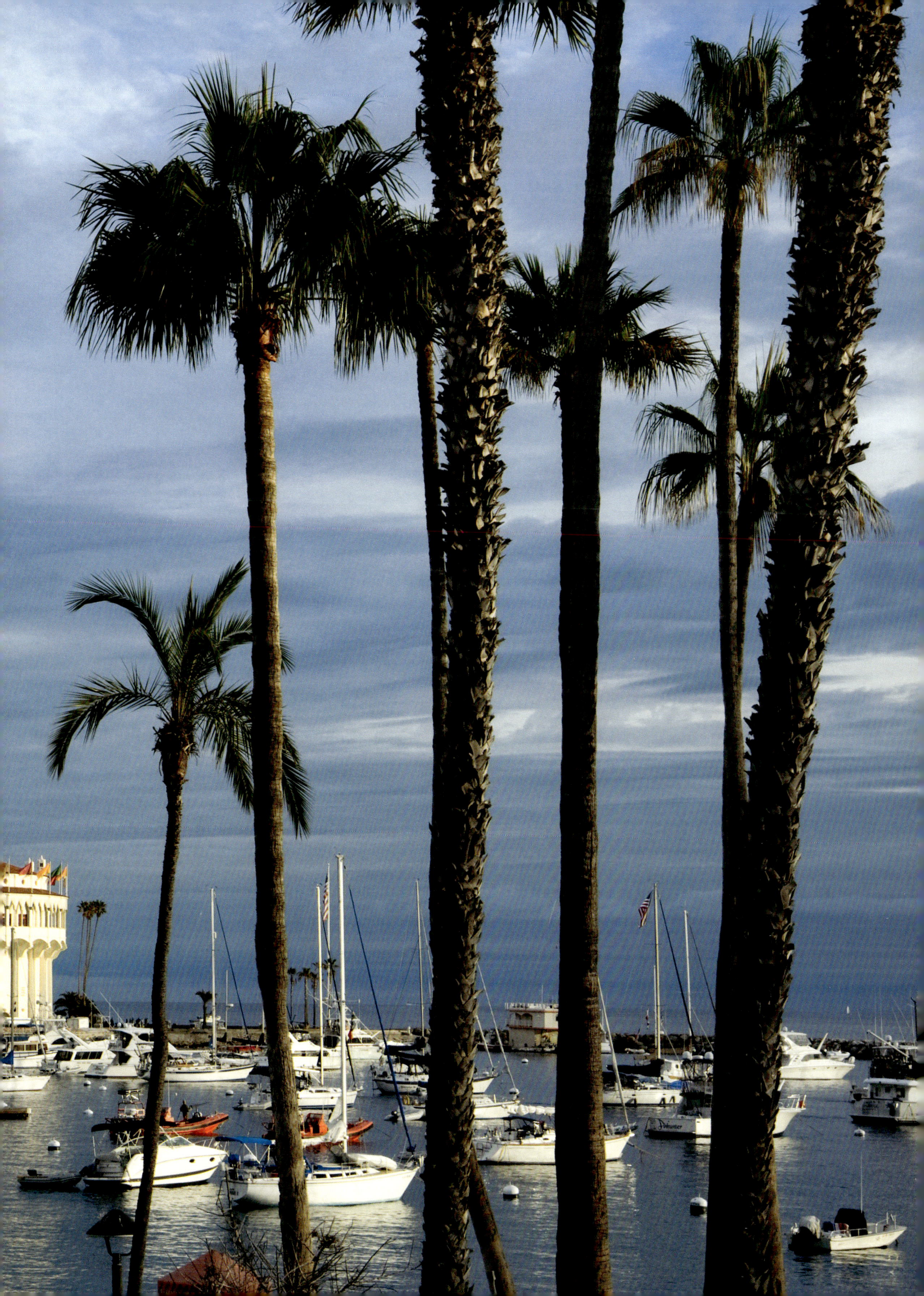

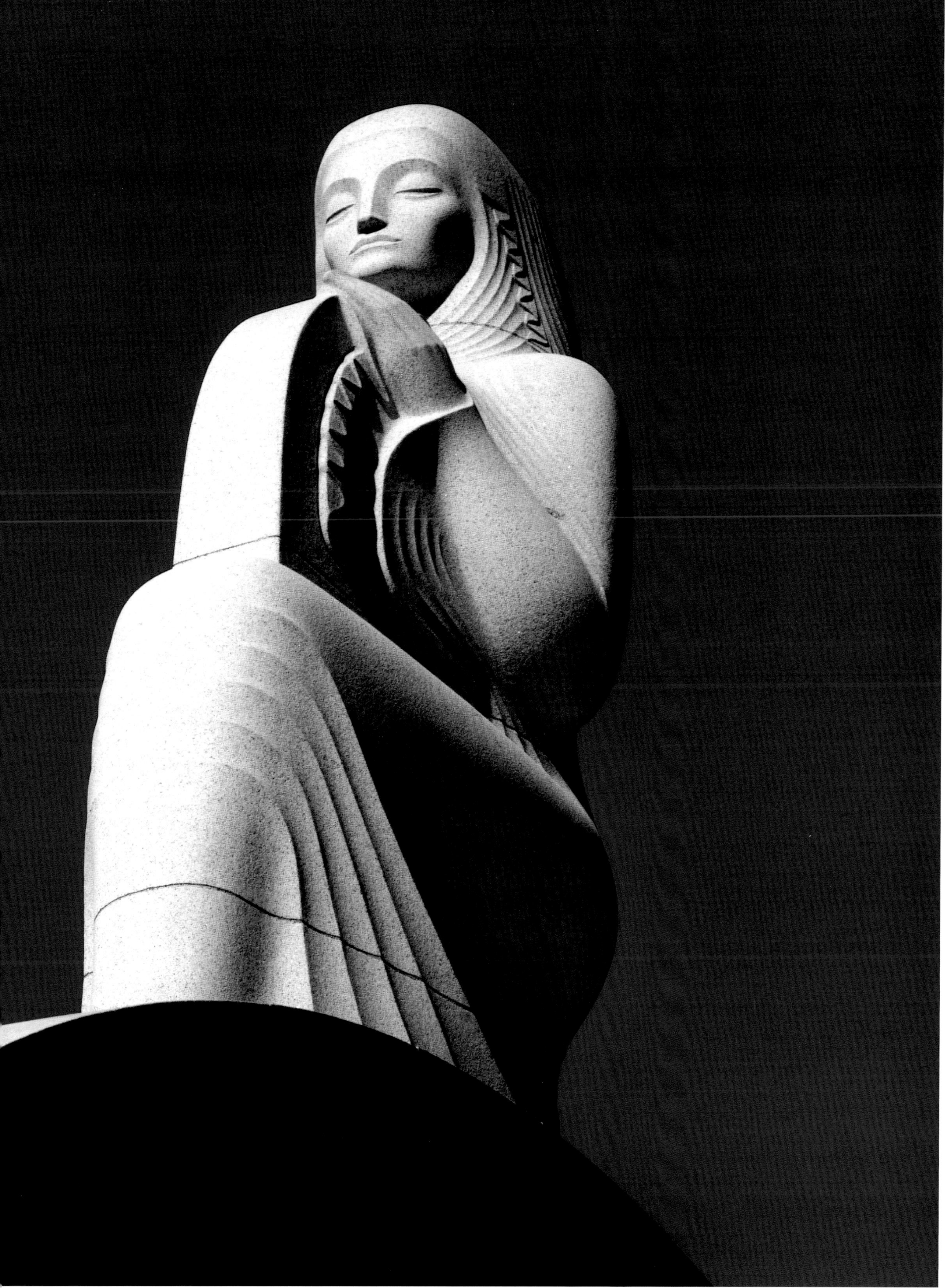

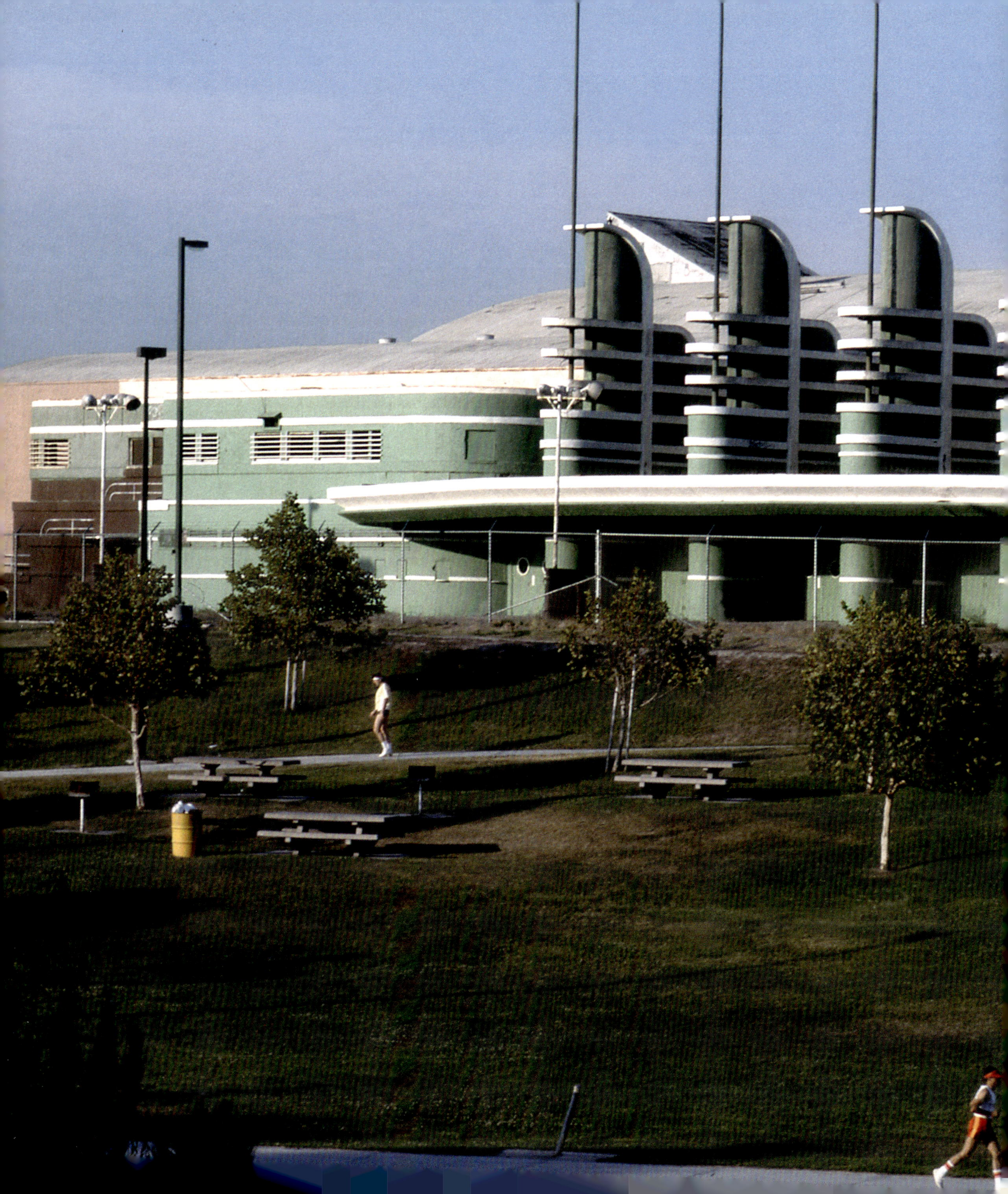

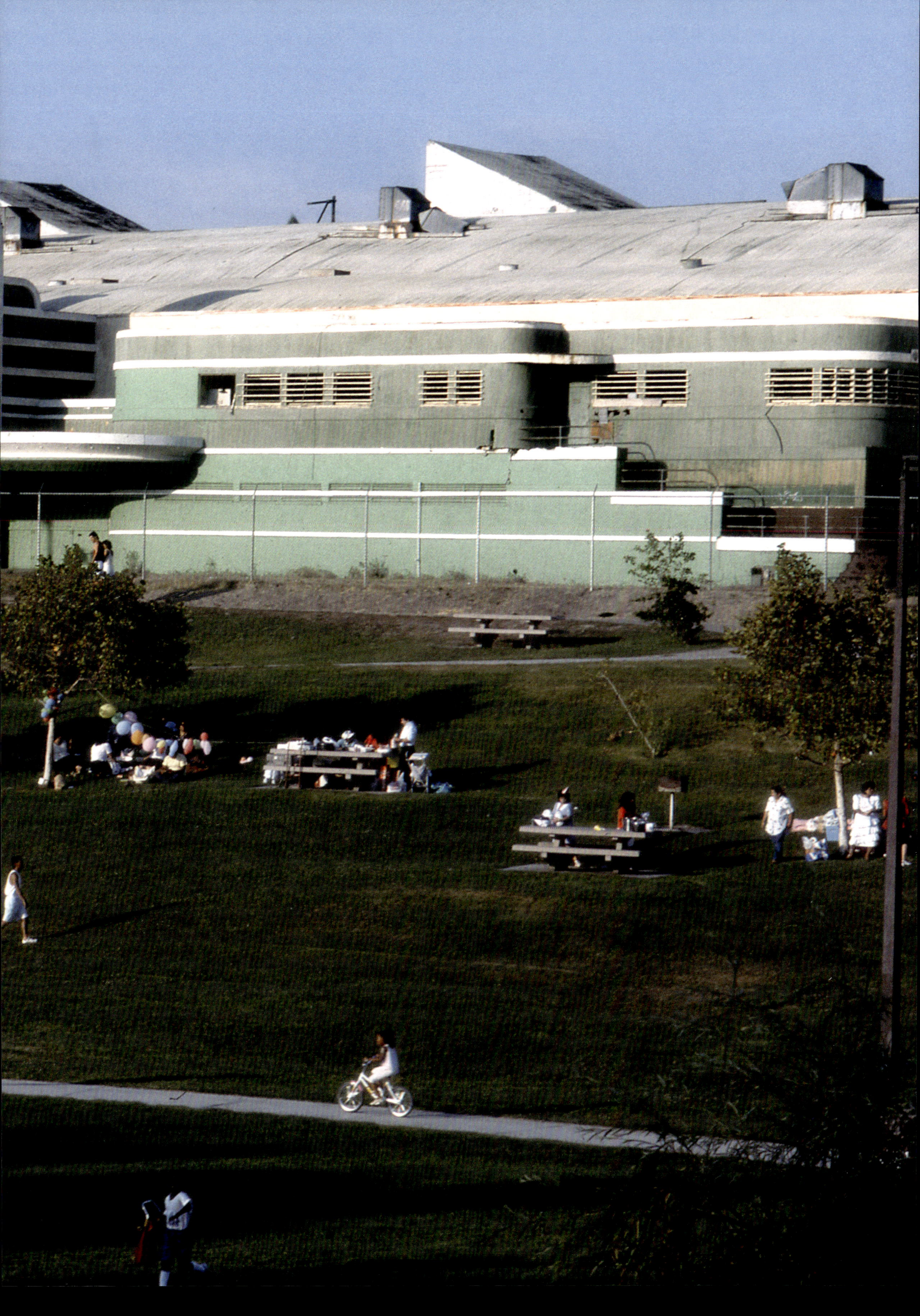

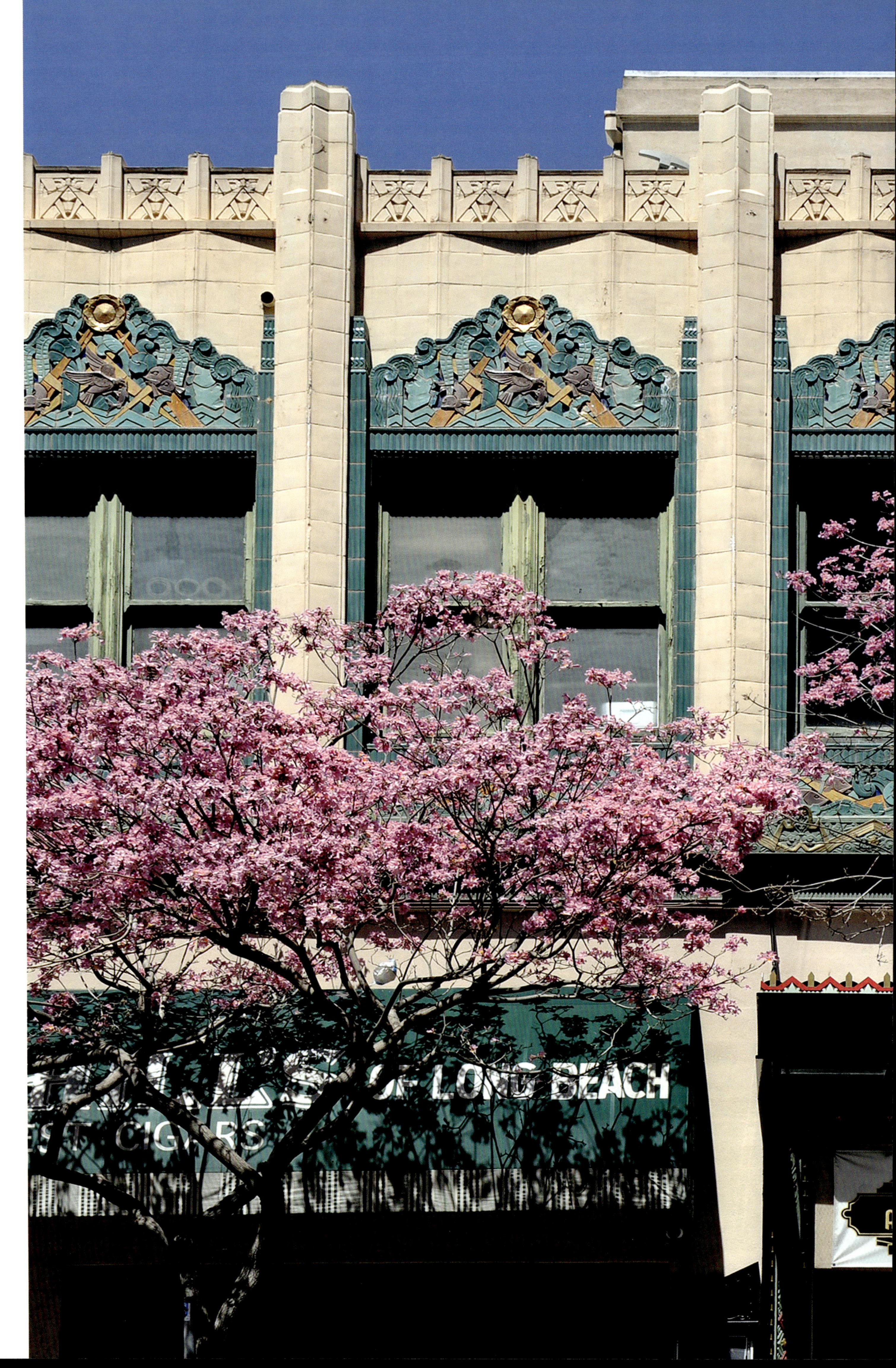
OF LONG BEACH

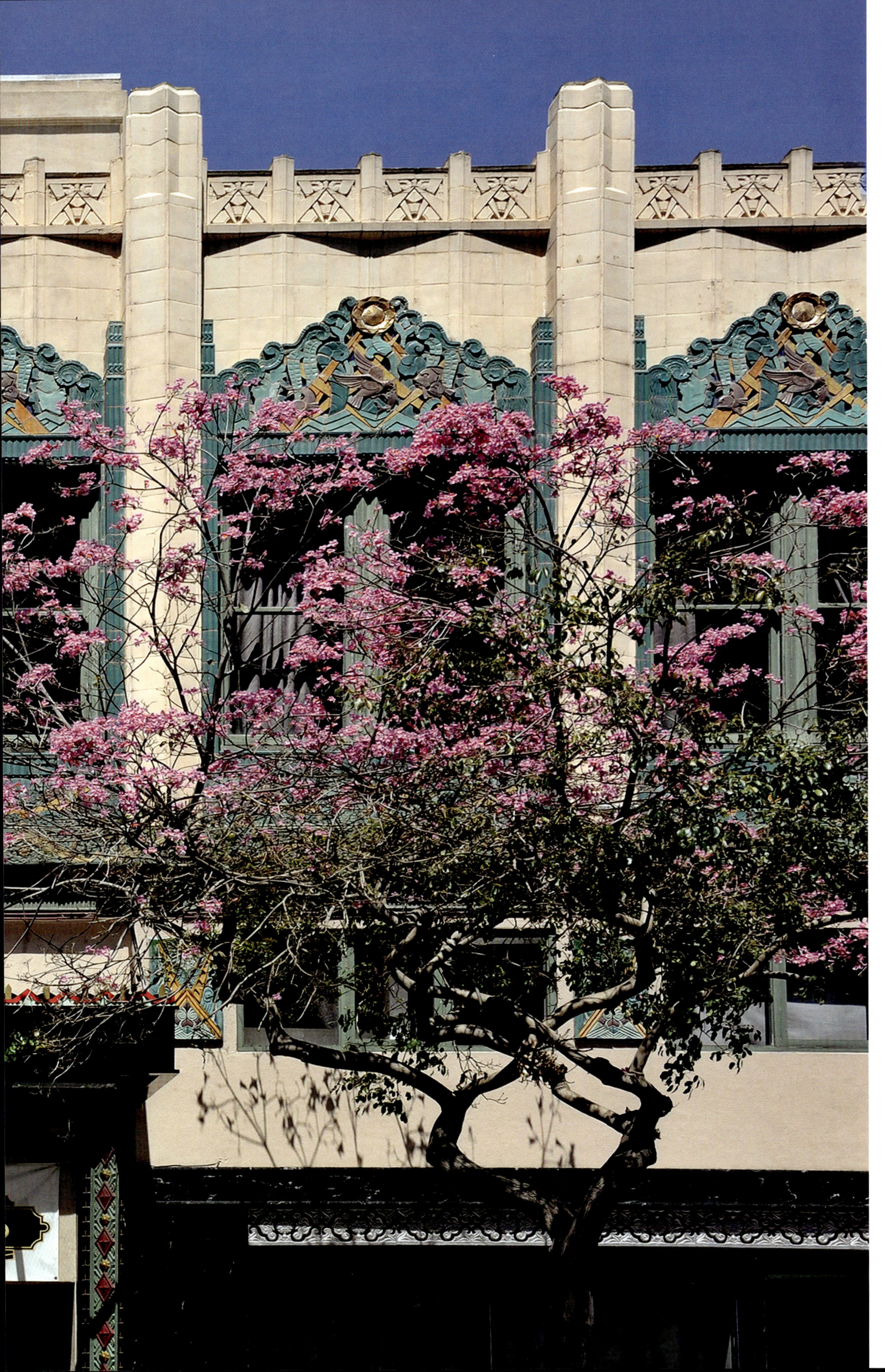

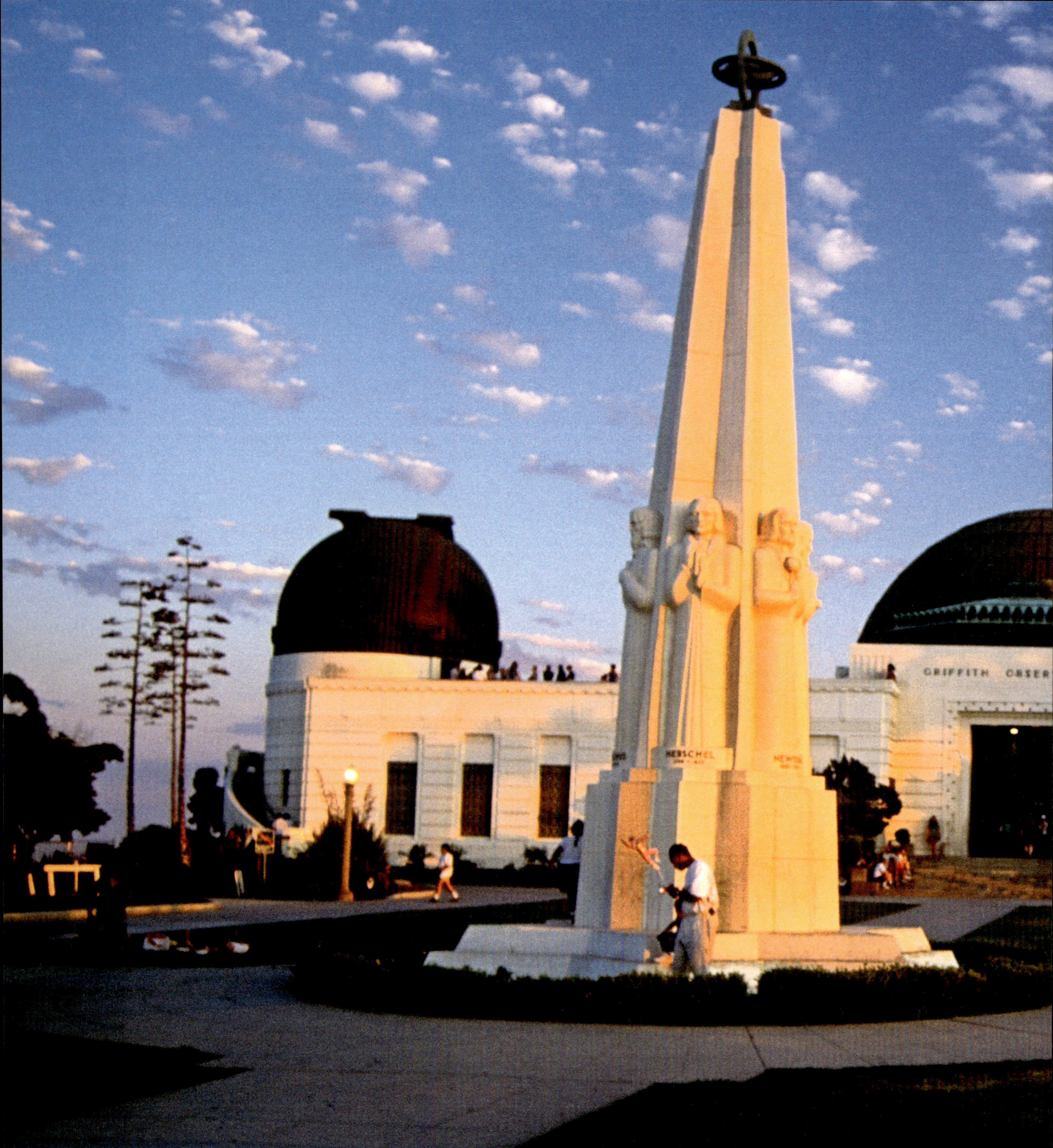
HERSCHEL
GRIFFITH

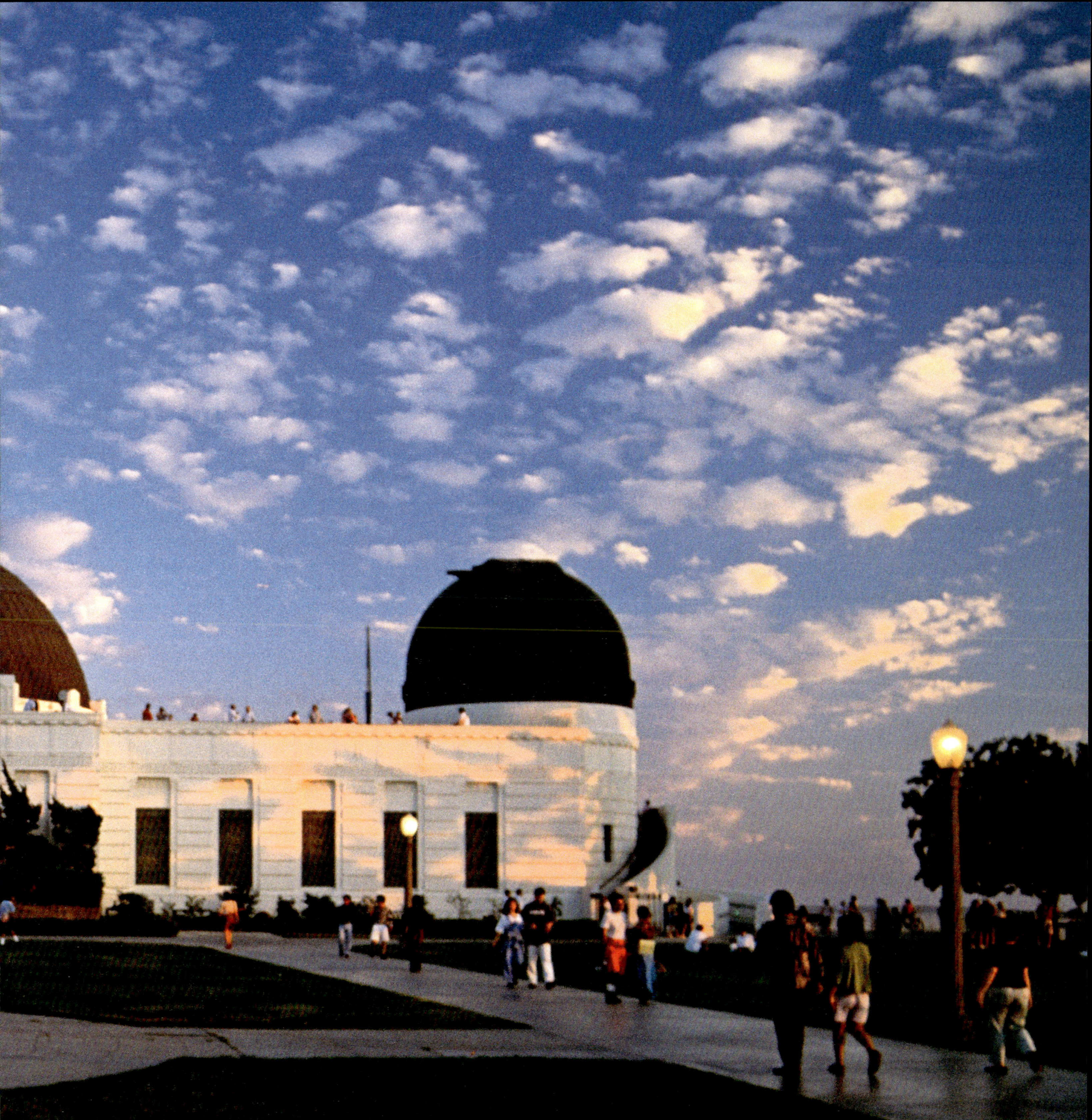

For Hulya, my soul mate in this life.

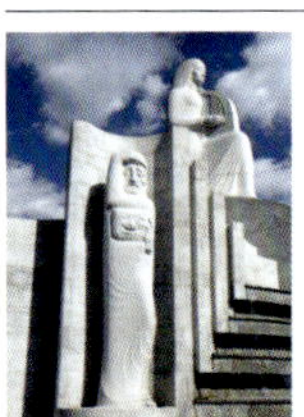

COVER: Muse of Music, Dance, Drama *at the Hollywood Bowl (sculpture by George Stanley, 1940) 2301 Highland Ave., photographed 2008.*

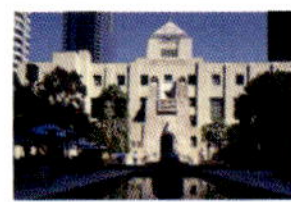

Los Angeles Central Library (Bertram G. Goodhue and Carleton Winslow, 1926) 630 W. 5th St., photographed 1988.

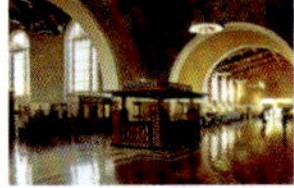

Union Station (John Parkinson and Donald B. Parkinson, 1939) 800 N. Alameda St., photographed 2003.

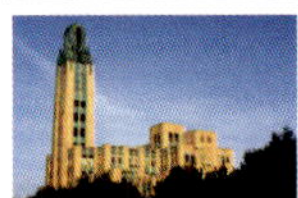

Bullock's Wilshire, now Southwestern Law School (John Parkinson and Donald B. Parkinson, 1929) 3050 Wilshire Blvd., photographed 2003.

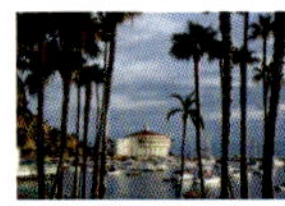

Catalina Casino (David Malcom Renton, 1929) Avalon, Catalina Island, photographed 2016.

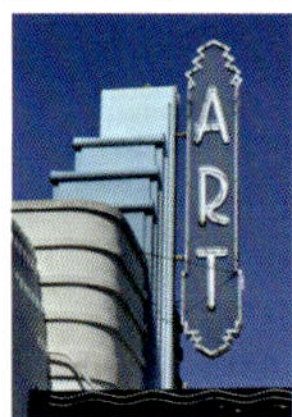

TITLE PAGE: *Lee Theatre, now Art Theatre of Long Beach (Schilling and Schilling, 1933) 2025 E. 4th St., Long Beach, photographed 2024.*

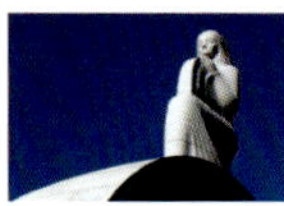

Muse of Music, Dance, Drama *at the Hollywood Bowl (sculpture by George Stanley, 1940) 2301 Highland Ave., photographed 2008.*

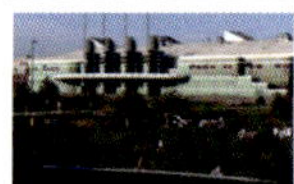

Pan-Pacific Auditorium (Wurdeman & Becket, 1935) formerly at 7600 Beverly Blvd., photographed 1988.

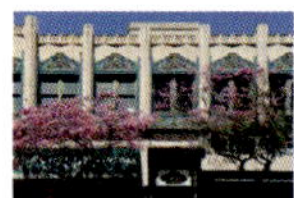

Rowan-Bradley Building (Krempel & Erkes, 1930) 201-209 Pine Ave., Long Beach, photographed 2024.

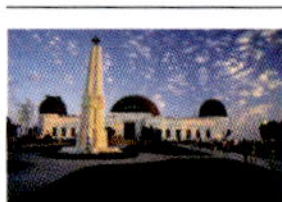

Griffith Observatory (John C. Austin and Frederick M. Ashley, 1935) 2800 E. Observatory Rd., photographed 1994.

→ *Los Angeles City Hall (John C. Austin, John Parkinson, and Albert C. Martin, 1928) 200 N. Spring St., photographed 2003.*

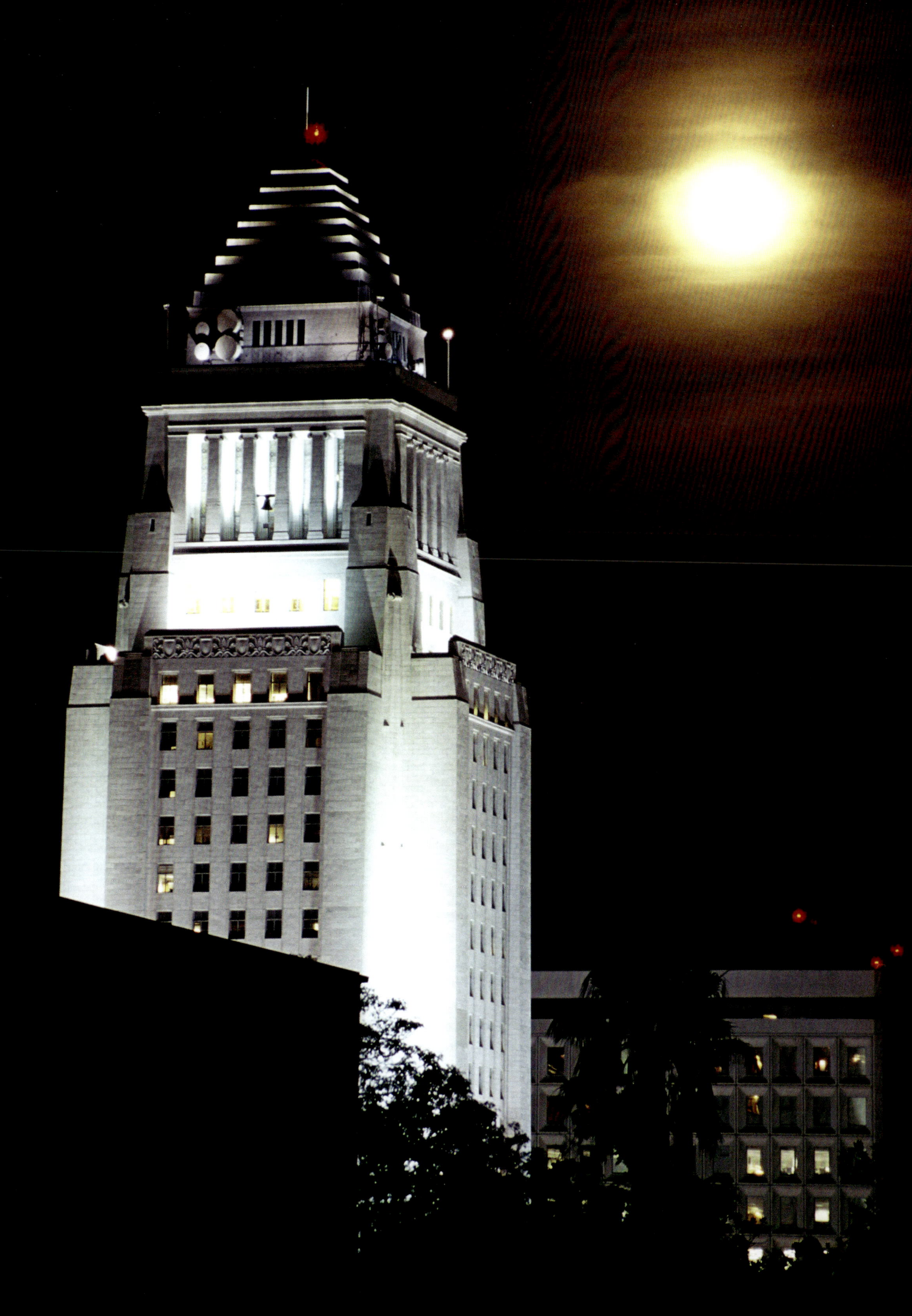

Essay | **ALAN HESS**

RECONSIDERING ART DECO

During the decades of the 1940s through the 1960s, no aspect of architecture was held more in disdain than that of the Art Deco of the '20s and '30s. Art Deco, the popularized modern of these decades, was either ignored by our major architects and writers, or it was dismissed as an unfortunate, obviously misguided effort; the sooner it was forgotten the better. – David Gebhard, 1980[1]

David Gebhard knew what he was talking about. As one of the few scholars to take Art Deco seriously, Gebhard saw that most critics separated Art Deco architecture (too popular, commercial, and ornamental) from "high art" Modern architecture ("approved" by academic critics). Art Deco was more like decoration than architecture, they claimed. High art architecture such as the International Style was elegant, austere, and certified as important by any number of learned manifestoes.

Yet as Gebhard pointed out, Art Deco's characteristics have proven over time to be its strengths, not weaknesses. Art Deco was not a lesser Modernism; it was another manifestation of the wide-ranging global experimentation to discover an architecture that would reflect the astonishing changes in technology and culture ushered in with the twentieth century.

The term "Art Deco" itself is actually a latecomer, introduced decades after its heyday; in its time it might have been called "moderne," "modernistic," "modern," or (more exotically) "Egyptoid." As we use it today, Art Deco encompasses a variety of styles, each growing out of the search by architects and designers for an architecture that reflected a new era in human history, supercharged by airplanes, automobiles, and scientific advances. There was no single answer to how to express this dynamic, ever-changing world, and Art Deco explored many ideas and directions.

Art Deco could be a newly invented ornamental style based on geometry or nature, today dubbed Zigzag Moderne. It could mirror modern machines and speeding vehicles, today labeled Streamline Moderne. Inspired by amazing archeological discoveries, it could reach back to reinterpret historic styles through sleek simplification and abstraction, as in Art Deco's Hollywood Regency and WPA Moderne variations. Malleable and adaptable, Art Deco responded quickly to changing social conditions, leading to the distinctive Late Moderne style.

All of these phases can be seen in Los Angeles, which, as arguably the most modern city in the world, played a unique role in Art Deco's evolution. In the 1920s and 1930s, its population exploded as people surged to work in its nascent industries: oil, Hollywood, media, aeronautics, automobiles—industries that would reshape the coming century. Los Angeles was particularly open to new possibilities, new uses, and new materials, such as glassy Vitrolite and glowing neon.

This environment produced two of Art Deco's definitive landmarks: Bullock's Wilshire by Parkinson & Parkinson (1929) and the Pan-Pacific Auditorium by Wurdeman & Becket (1935). Each defined the rapidly

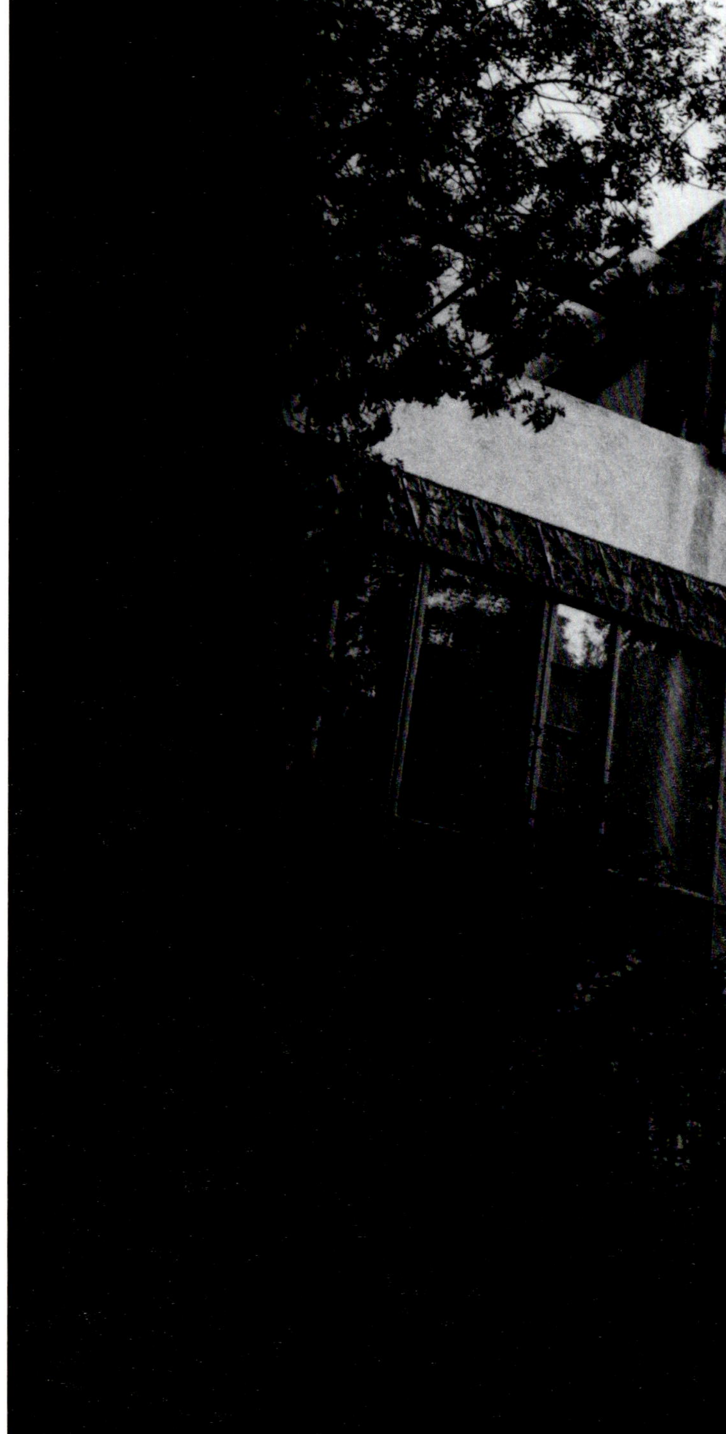

changing appearance of a rapidly advancing epoch. Bullock's Wilshire captured the jazzy, syncopated geometries of Art Deco's early Zigzag Moderne phase. A few years later, Art Deco evolved the sleek curves and smooth horizontal lines of its Streamline Moderne phase seen at Pan-Pacific Auditorium.

Bullock's Wilshire's soaring, tapering tower linking the bustling city streets to the blue sky above was a direct response to Los Angeles: the city in the 1920s was reshaping itself for the automobile. As the first major department store established outside downtown, Bullock's Wilshire was designed to attract modern car-mobile customers along the new Wilshire Boulevard that would stretch all the way to the Pacific Ocean. Its architecture's angular, rhythmic sculpture, ornament, lettering, and signage owes little to previous historical periods. It grew from the new era of machines, speed, and science improving the lives of citizen-motorists. When a design competition selected an architect for another prominent project, the Pan-Pacific Auditorium, across town a few years later, Wurdeman & Becket's design captured the kinetic energy of that city in motion. Its centerpiece displayed four flagpoles rising from four sculpted streamline towers. They somehow evoked a phalanx of modern ocean liners plowing through the ocean waves. Instead of the rich geometric detail of Zigzag Moderne ornament, this building's curved horizontal and vertical planes suggestively put the building in motion.

Samuel-Novarro House (Lloyd Wright, 1928) 5609 Valley Oak Dr., photographed 1984.

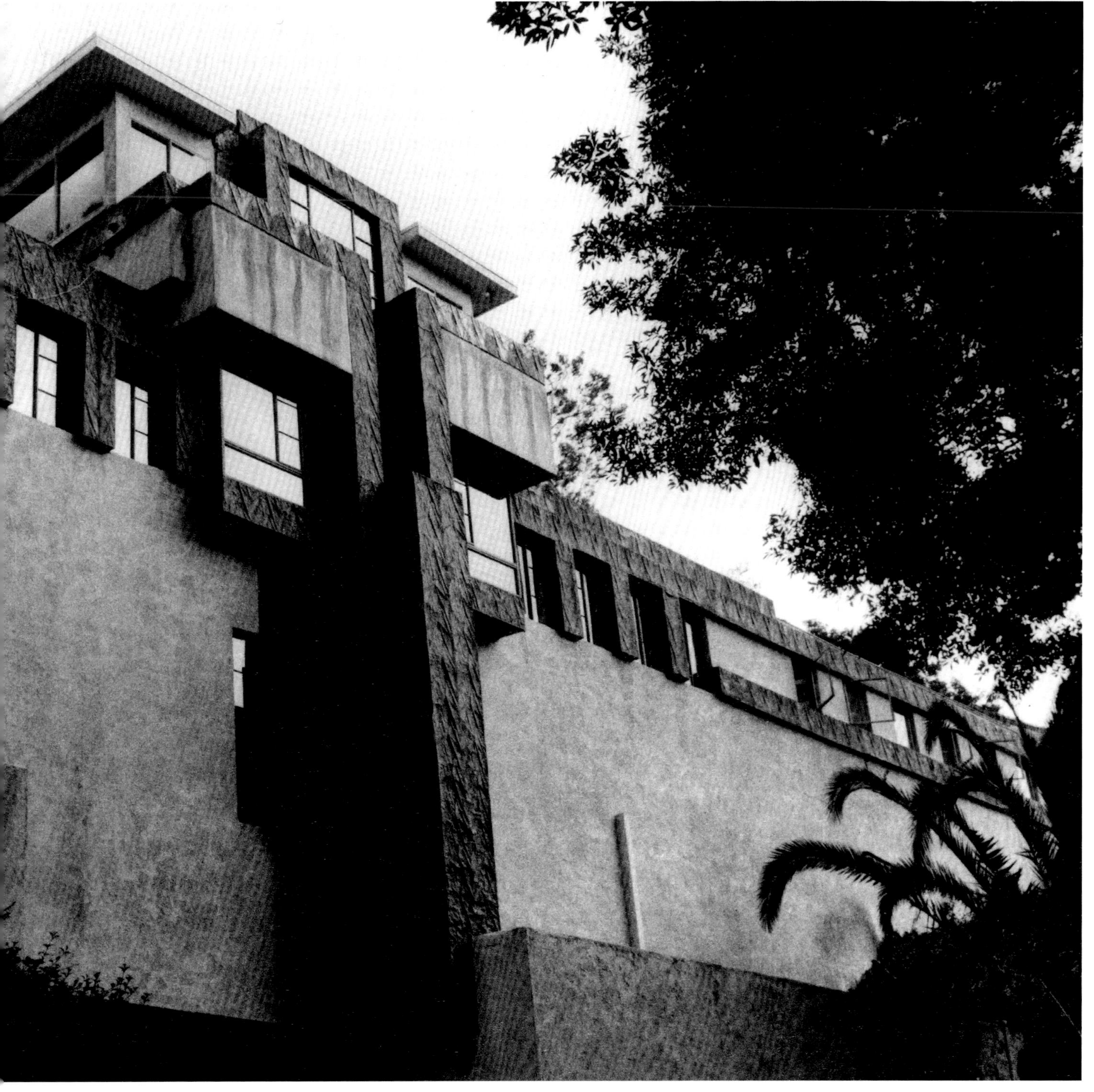

The Pan-Pacific Auditorium's lines also echoed the auto show displays held there annually. This cross-cultural connection between Art Deco and autos was already clear to observers, especially in Los Angeles: "The very extraordinary beauty of your Chrysler or Nash or Ford is due to the honest decorativeness out of materials, efficient disposal of parts, massing, stream lines, with a dedicated warmth through color and the flash of metals," wrote historian Sheldon Cheney[2].

Bullock's may have been the quintessential department store of Los Angeles's upper class, but along its streets, Art Deco would be for everyone. It was becoming the visual signature of the city. Only three blocks away from the Bullock's Wilshire tower, one of many Streamline Moderne Simon's drive-ins by architect Wayne McAllister boasted its own neon-lined tower and circular canopy. Its form followed its automobile function, making it one of the most modern buildings anywhere in the world.

Los Angeles was creating its own unique version of Art Deco. Where the office towers of Chicago or New York's dense traditional cities created vertical Art Deco towers, Los Angeles perfected a horizontal Art Deco. The style was conceptually limber and much more than a decorative fad.

Yet in Europe and New York, high art critics were already promoting the stripped-down International Style as the correct look of the modern technological age. Tellingly, one of the International Style's best examples in Los Angeles, the Lovell Health House by Richard Neutra, was completed the same year as Bullock's Wilshire. Los Angeles, the city of experiment, welcomed multiple ways to be modern.

THE ROOTS OF ART DECO

The term "Art Deco" derives from the "Exposition Internationale des Arts Décoratifs et Industriels Modernes" in Paris in 1925. It was not invented there, though.

Historians may pigeonhole Art Deco in the Roaring Twenties and the Depression Thirties, but it was in fact part of an ongoing international search for a new architecture that started before and extended beyond those decades. The 1925 Paris exposition successfully focused the international spotlight on a style that was already established in Amsterdam, Paris, Shanghai, New York, Detroit, Miami, Tulsa, and Los Angeles.

Los Angeles architect Lloyd Wright, for example, had engaged in this exploration since moving to California in 1911; his ideas were rooted in those his father, Frank Lloyd Wright, and his father's mentor, Louis Sullivan, had been building for more than thirty years: a fresh architecture based on the modern age and its technology pointing to the future. It could draw on a wide range of unconventional sources, including nature, geometry, and history. Ornament was integral to their concept of architecture.

Critic Lewis Mumford recognized these roots in 1929: "The attempt to found a modern system of ornament was undertaken a generation ago by Louis Sullivan and Frank Lloyd Wright…[with] a powerful influence upon subsequent designers, not merely in the skyscraper itself, but in every other department of architecture."[3]

At the Taggart House in Los Angeles (1922) and Palm Springs's Oasis Hotel (1925), Lloyd Wright created original ornament that foresaw the Paris Exposition itself—as had his father in the textile block houses he built in Los Angeles at the same time. Continuing in the Samuel-Novarro House (1928), Lloyd Wright's home and studio (1927), the Sowden House (1927), and the Yucca Vine Market (1928), Lloyd Wright showed the sophistication of the ideas that would also underlie Art Deco.

INSPIRATION AND SOURCES

Art Deco's use of ornament on Los Angeles streets made it a mass medium broadcasting the latest trends in culture to the public. The design of airplanes, cars, ocean liners, locomotives, machinery, as well as the world's exotica were all fair game. Art Deco's early Zigzag Moderne phase showcased a lush, angular ornament of crystals, cogs, chevrons, fins, tetrahedrons, stylized flora, gazelles, borzois, and unfurling ferns.

Yet as transportation technology advanced in the 1930s,

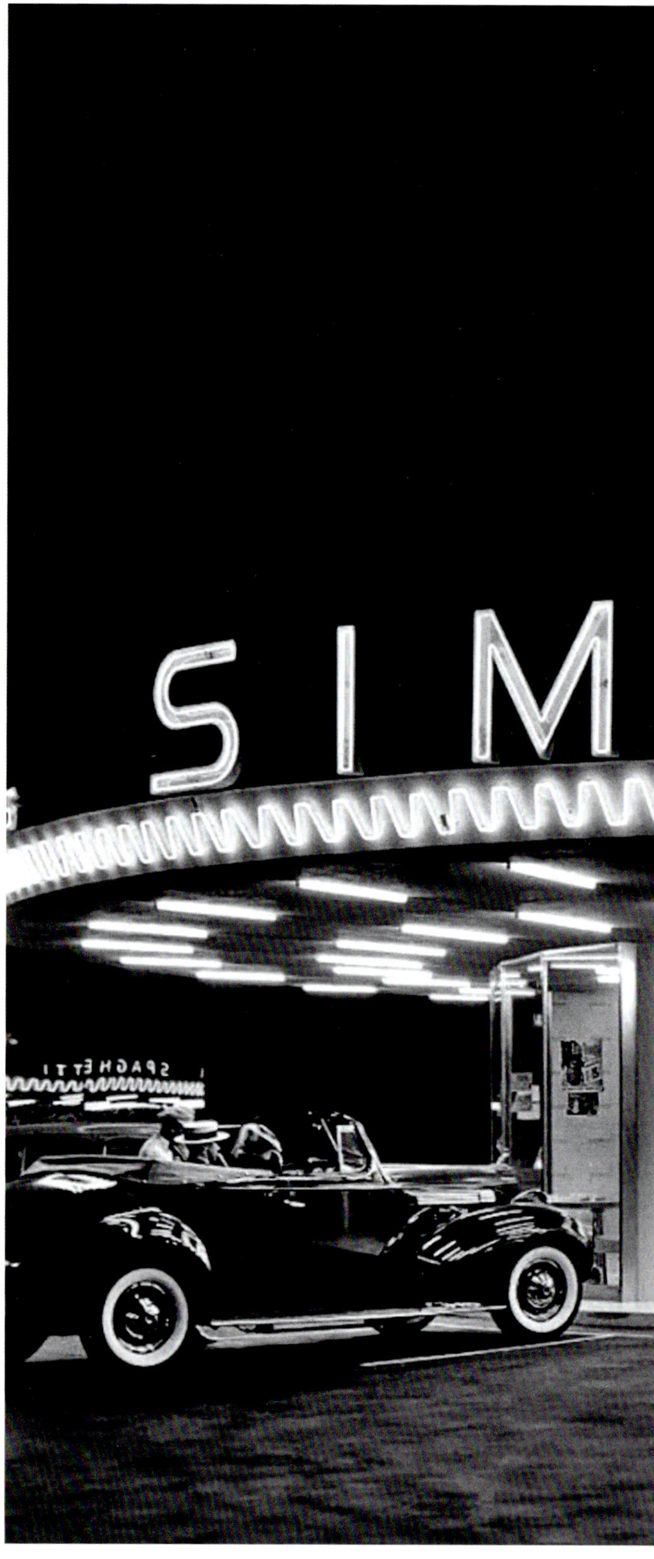

Art Deco reflected that progress. Airplane design traded gangling biplanes for the DC-3's sleek aerodynamic monocoque. The boxy Model T gave way to the sleek Chrysler Airflow. Art Deco rapidly responded with its Streamline Moderne phase, emphasizing flowing horizontal planes resolving into dynamic asymmetrical curves. The Depression's austerity called for a sober style of efficiency as a hopeful guide to a better future. Architects reflected these changes to communicate the modern era to the public with murals, bas-reliefs, and sculpture integrated into the architecture.[4]

Art Deco ornament proved to be broadly democratic and popular across classes. The crystalline Oviatt Building (Walker and Eisen 1928) in downtown Los Angeles may have housed the swank haberdasher where Clark Gable and Gary Cooper shopped, but Newberry's five-and-dime on Hollywood Boulevard served the general public just as stylishly.

Simon's Drive-In Restaurant (Wayne McAllister, 1939) 5171 Wilshire Blvd., photographed 1939.

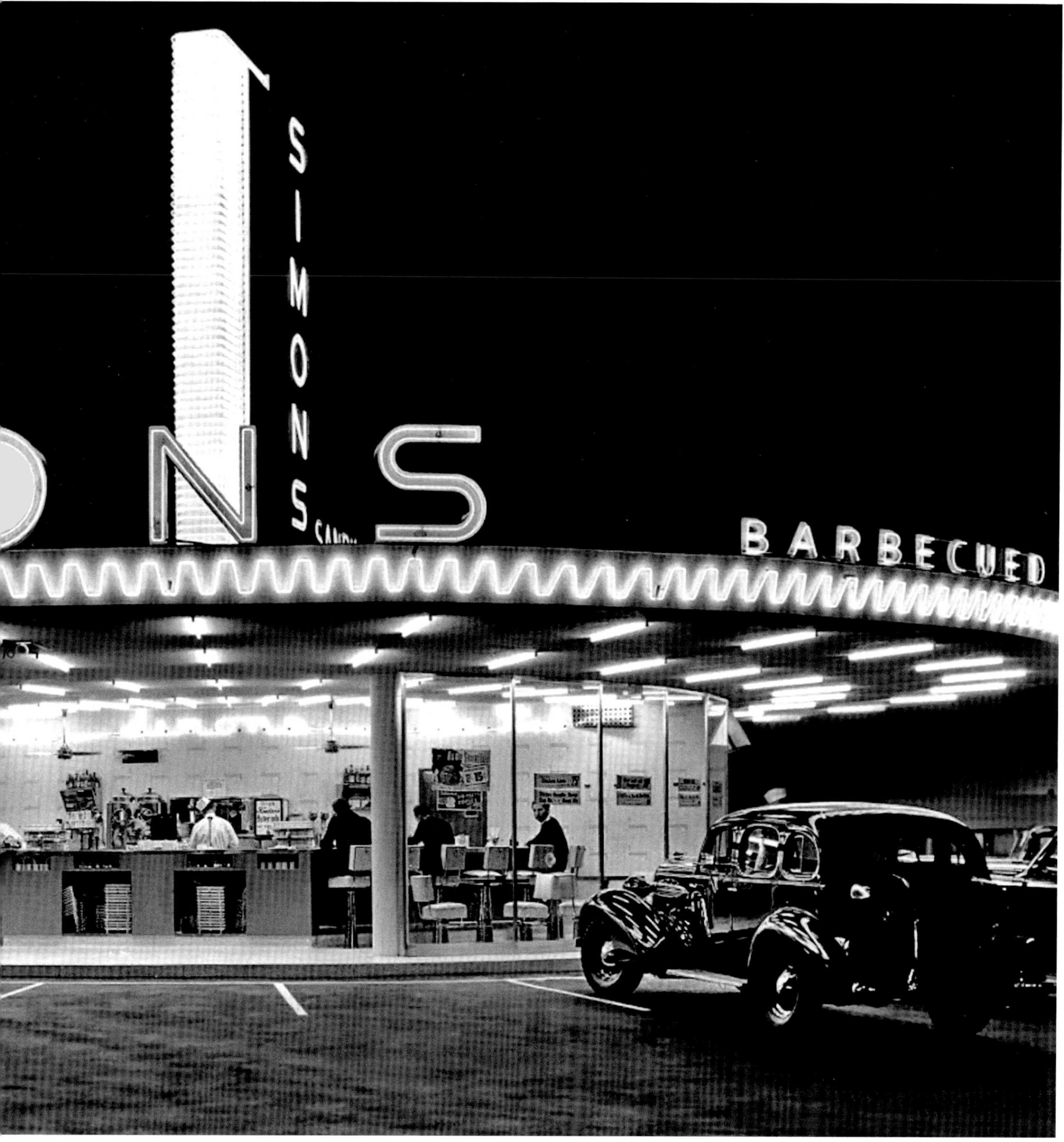

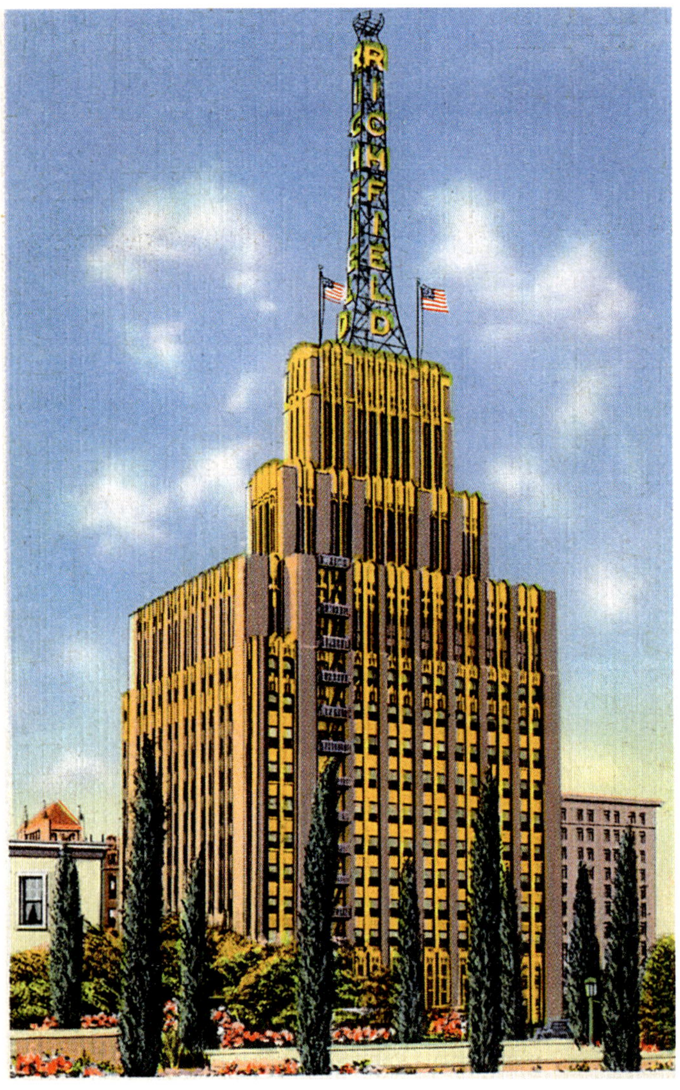

Modern technology inspired architect Robert Derrah to translate the flowing forms of transatlantic steamships into the Coca-Cola Bottling Factory (1939) and Crossroads of the World (1936). Airport control towers (an entirely twentieth-century invention unknown to previous history) as at Glendale's Grand Central Air Terminal (Henry L. Gogerty, 1930) drew on airplane motifs to proclaim its vision of a new age.

These geometric or mechanistic inspirations for Art Deco's Zigzag and Streamline Moderne phases were not the only aesthetic sources that architects tapped. Intriguing Indigenous cultures and the latest archaeological finds also inspired Art Deco; the glittering discoveries in King Tut's tomb in 1922 suited Grauman's Egyptian Theater (Meyer & Holler), opening the same year. Contemporary digs at Mayan temples in the Yucatan lead to Robert Stacy-Judd's Aztec Hotel (1924).

While Art Deco's embrace of vivid ornament often misled critics into seeing it as more fashion than architecture, these new transgressive images actually liberated architects from Classical Western architectural precedents in the same way as did Cubism and Surrealism did in Modern art.

Even the establishment's Classical architecture provided a source for Art Deco when passed through the lens of modernist simplification. In the 1930s, Art Deco broadened into the WPA Moderne; the name derives from the large number of federal government commissions for post offices or governmental buildings built during the Great Depression by the Works Progress Administration (WPA).[5] With Washington DC's Roman Republic formality (decreed by architect Thomas Jefferson) as an initial template, WPA Moderne (also called Stripped Classicism) artfully abstracted and modernized fluted columns, Ionic capitals, and formal symmetry in buildings for Griffith Park Observatory (1933) by John Austin and the Hollywood Post Office (1937) by Claud Beelman.

The Hollywood Regency style offered yet another variation of Art Deco's appropriation of Classical imagery—specifically the attenuated eighteenth-century Regency designs of British architect Robert Adam. Art Deco architects refined, elongated, flattened, and modernized Adam's Neoclassical ornament for houses, Hollywood's Max Factor building (S. Charles Lee, 1928), upscale department stores such as Saks Fifth Avenue, and public places of recreation; at Santa Anita Racetrack (1934), Gordon Kaufmann festively and fancifully included Hollywood Regency tented pavilions and exotic palm trees.

California's own Hispanic history also came under the modernizing influence of Art Deco design. Parkinson & Parkinson's Union Station (1939) abstracted the bell tower, broad plastered walls, and arcades of California's historic Franciscan mission buildings for the grand scale of a public monument. Stylized Moderne light standards blended comfortably with Spanish ironwork. Likewise, the Regency Village Theatre (originally Fox Westwood Theater, Percy Parke Lewis, 1931) evokes a Spanish Renaissance church's bell tower with corbels, columns, and cartouches, but stretched and modernized so it would be a visible landmark to the cars driving on Wilshire Boulevard three blocks away.

CITY PLANNING

The Fox Westwood tower reveals yet another dimension of Art Deco as architecture: its impact on urban design and planning. Art Deco concepts offered a fresh strategy for composing tall buildings. Downtown office buildings and department stores usually followed the Beaux Arts model, conceiving them as boxy Florentine palazzi. Art Deco proffered an alternative: a prominent tapering central tower rising above lower flanking wings. Gordon Kaufmann's *Los Angeles Times* Building (1935), Bertram Goodhue's Central Library (1926), George Simmons's Sears warehouse (1927), and Claud Beelman's Elks Lodge (1925) offered this model, along with prominent Art Deco sculpture and bas-reliefs.

This new architectural sensibility also shaped an entire urban district in Los Angeles. The Miracle Mile is an innovative stretch of Wilshire Boulevard roughly between Fairfax and Western avenues, conceived by developer A. W. Ross beginning in the late 1920s at the height of Art Deco's popularity. His vision for a linear downtown mixing office towers, theaters, residences, and shops reflected the modern automobile era in contrast to the traditional pedestrian-oriented downtown.

The twelve-story Pellissier Tower (Morgan, Walls, and Clements, 1931), for example, is the linchpin for the streets and neighborhoods around two major thoroughfares, Wilshire Boulevard and Western Avenue. Clad in unmistakable turquoise terra-cotta and set on a diagonal, the Pellissier building demands attention from near and far. Its asymmetrical tower, rising and stepping in as it reaches into the sky, embodies the Art Deco aesthetic; it is something new in the world, experienced as a modern landmark in four-dimensional space by motorists in motion around its base.

Along with four other Art Deco office towers punctuating the Miracle Mile visually and functionally, the Pellissier Tower with its Wiltern Theater is a vision of a modern city. The E. Clem Wilson Building (Meyer & Holler, 1929), the Wilshire Tower (Gilbert Stanley Underwood, 1929), the Dominguez-Wilshire Building (Morgan, Walls, & Clements, 1930), the Wilshire Professional Building (Arthur E. Harvey, 1929), and the Pellissier bring a rhythmic order and a suite of powerful urban landmarks to the new district.

DECLINE AND REBIRTH

As David Gebhard noted, however, the inclusive and innovative designs which we now call Art Deco were dismissed by a large number of high art critics focused on the minimalist International Style from Europe. New York's Museum of Modern Art mounted its "Modern Architecture: International Exhibition" in 1932 with strategic curation by the influential historian Henry-Russell Hitchcock and critic Philip Johnson. It attempted to codify what qualified as Modern architecture, rejecting any ornamented, popular, or commercial Art Deco examples. It gave its name to the International Style. The influence of this exhibit caused Art Deco to be largely written out of serious architectural history. Yet at least one observer did note the many alternatives to the International Style throughout Europe and North America. Sheldon Cheney collected these examples in his book *New World Architecture* in 1930. Like Mumford, he traced their roots to Frank Lloyd Wright; he included Art Deco examples from the 1925 Paris Exposition, Willem Dudok in the Netherlands, streamlined examples by Erich Mendelsohn in Germany, and Lloyd Wright, R. M. Schindler, and Frank Lloyd Wright in Los Angeles. Cheney's book is a window into the unheralded variety of possibilities of Modern architecture at the time.

Yet even without official blessing, Art Deco continued to thrive, giving rise to yet another variation, the Late Moderne. Though cut short by World War II, Late Moderne incorporated elements of the International Style, but without its doctrinaire minimalism. Examples such as Bullock's Pasadena (Wurdeman & Becket, 1947) continued Streamline Moderne's flowing, kinetic shapes, but rendered more free form with kidney-shaped canopies and curving corners. Straying from International Style austerity, Late Moderne introduced its own ornamental motifs, including egg-crate screens and bold bezel frames for windows. At Wayne McAllister's Bob's Big Boy in Burbank (1949), strong irregularly shaped volumes (paralleling the modern art of Alexander Calder and Joan Miró) complemented a strong vertical rectangular signboard, decorated with neon.[6]

Claud Beelman's Mutual-Don Lee Television Studio (1948) used bold columns pierced with circular openings as a sculpted, structural expression. While its large planar wings and flat roofs echoed the International Style, its use of decorative screens flanking its entry and jewel box sidewalk display cases place it in the Late Moderne category.

The New York and San Francisco World's Fairs of 1939 boosted Late Moderne's popularity, and it continued for a while after World War II when new domestic building began after years of economic depression and war. It did not become the favored face of post-war Modernism in Los Angeles, however; the Case Study Program of *Arts & Architecture* magazine riveted the attention of most critics after the war. Those powerful, minimalist forms expressing the elegance of their structural skeletons paralleled the International Style's rectilinear forms, then rising in influence and backed by a brigade of

← *Postcard of Richfield Oil Building, 1929*

↙ *Fox Village Theatre (Percy Parke Lewis, 1931) 959 Broxton Ave., photographed 2013.*

↓ *Bullock's Wilshire, now Southwestern Law School (John Parkinson and Donald B. Parkinson, 1929) 3050 Wilshire Blvd., photographed 1989.*

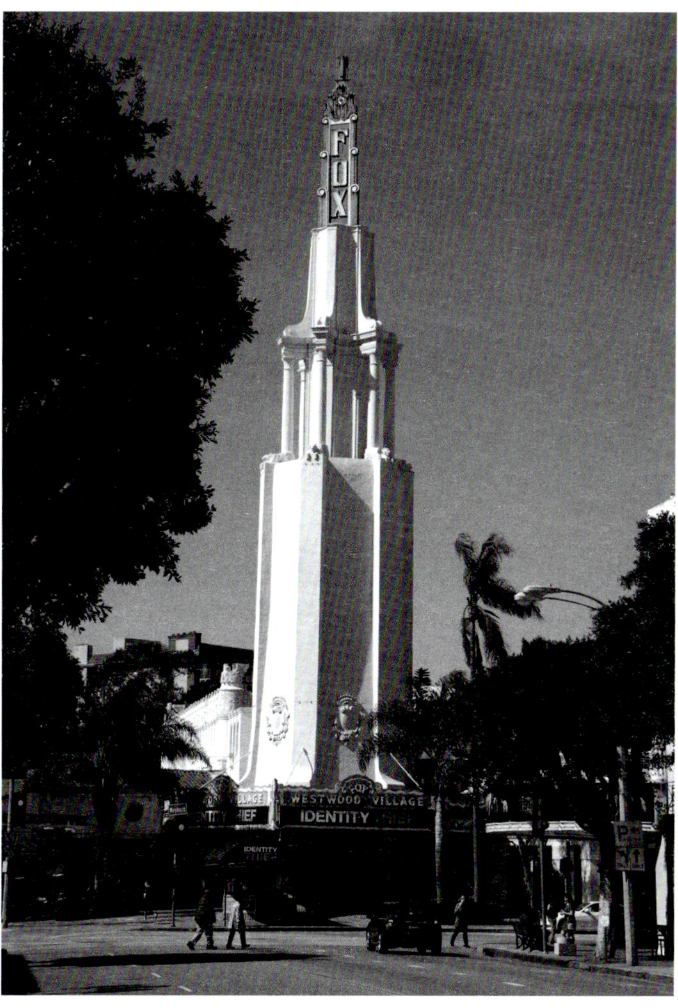

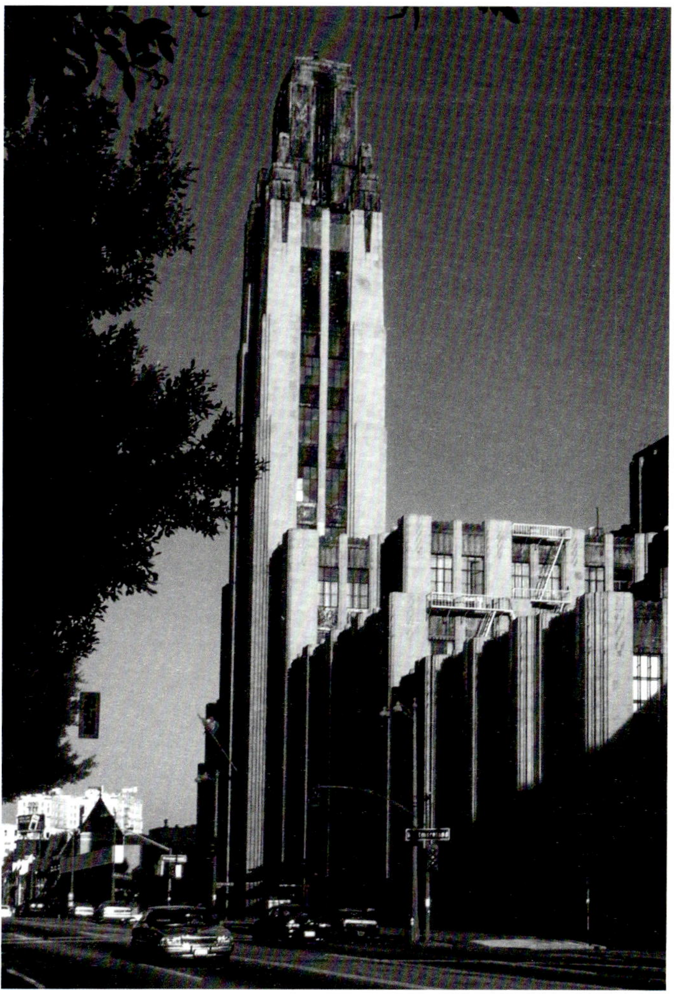

high art critiques promoting the International Style's inevitability as the true look of the future.

In spite of Sheldon Cheney's convincing catalog demonstrating the diversity of Modern ideas, the prevailing academic opinion of Art Deco as a second class Modernism held on into the 1960s. Even the respected urban observer Kevin Lynch pointedly described Los Angeles's Richfield Tower (Morgan, Walls and Clements, 1929) as the "ugly, black and gold Richfield Building"—though today it is acknowledged as one of the city's greatest Art Deco designs.[7]

Nevertheless, by the 1960s Art Deco was ripe for revival. Flea markets, thrift shops, and used furniture stores discovered a market for Art Deco jewelry, toasters, cocktail shakers, cigarette cases, vanities, and Erté posters. Sheldon Cheney had anticipated this broad, culture-wide influence thirty years before: "Some of the most exciting industrial craftsmanship and decorative art of today is to be found in automobile fittings, electric refrigerators, cash registers, and the like."[8]

A second Paris exhibit, "Les Années '25: Art déco. Bauhaus. Stijl. Esprit nouveau" at the Musée des Arts Décoratifs, reassessed Art Deco in 1966, followed soon by author and *Los Angeles Times* journalist Bevis Hillier's book *Art Deco of the 20s and 30s*, which helped to popularize the term Art Deco. David Gebhard followed with his 1975 book *L.A. in the Thirties* with *Tulsa Art Deco: An Architectural Era 1925 to 1942* in 1980. Martin Greif's 1975 book *Depression Modern: The Thirties Style in America* and Laura Cerwinske's 1981 *Tropical Deco: The Architecture and Design of Old Miami Beach* demonstrated the renewed interest in Art Deco across the country.[9]

PRESERVATION

A sad cycle afflicts our architectural judgment: a style is well-received when introduced in one decade, but inevitably becomes old-fashioned in the next. If it is lucky it is later rediscovered and revered—if enough examples remain to be appreciated.

Art Deco has thankfully reached the third stage for a number of its remaining examples. Los Angeles has lost major monuments: the magnificent Richfield Tower with its oil-black terra-cotta cladding bedecked with gold terra-cotta ornament was demolished in 1969, the neglected Pan-Pacific Auditorium burned in 1989.

Recently, however, a few smaller Art Deco monuments have found new uses: a Zigzag Moderne gas station is now a Starbucks. But the entire set of Streamline Moderne drive-in restaurants, once found on nearly every major corner, has been wiped out in Southern California.

Bullock's Wilshire is no longer a department store, but its building survives and was enthusiastically restored as a law school in 1994. The Eastern Columbia building, built as offices, is now residential. Even the vanished Pan-Pacific Auditorium remains indelible in popular memory, and was rebuilt at Disney theme parks on the East and West Coasts.

Histories of Modern architecture honor many of Los Angeles's innovative architects, including Richard Neutra, R. M. Schindler, Charles and Ray Eames, Craig Ellwood, Pierre Koenig, and Frank Gehry. Los Angeles's Art Deco architects, however, are rarely mentioned. They should be. They were also creative contributors to the broad search for a dynamic new era of technology, transportation, and society.

Though traditionally trained, notable Art Deco architects Stiles O. Clements, Claud Beelman, Paul R. Williams, Gordon Kaufmann, and Parkinson & Parkinson brought original perspectives to the use of modern materials and engineering. Though primarily commercial architects, S. Charles Lee, Wayne McAllister, and Wurdeman & Becket brought their intimate understanding of modern life in modern Los Angeles to their buildings. Los Angeles itself encouraged the freedom to experiment, and perfected new building types to suit its citizens' modern lifestyles: drive-in movies, drive-in restaurants, suburban department stores, suburban office towers, airports. Art Deco was their defining style. Unlike the International Style coming out of Europe, Art Deco did not reject history, but saw itself continuing the long tradition of

architecture, where ornament had always been an essential part of buildings. As a mass medium, Art Deco architecture embraced the popular culture and symbols of its times (and ours) to unify a growing and diverse city. Conceptually rich, Art Deco evolved from Zigzag to Streamline to WPA Moderne to Late Moderne; its aesthetic DNA enabled it to generate new forms and create new building types as society and technology evolved.

With the hundredth anniversary of the 1925 Paris Exposition, the role of Los Angeles and other cities in inventing Art Deco should be spotlighted. For more than forty years Robert Landau has documented Art Deco Los Angeles. His photographs guide us through the entire urban fabric, from major civic landmarks to everyday gas stations and camera stores. With Landau's photographic proof, Art Deco can be clearly seen as a significant chapter in the long history of Modern architecture. ■

Sunset Tower Hotel (Leland A. Bryant, 1931) 8358 Sunset Blvd., West Hollywood, photographed 2020.

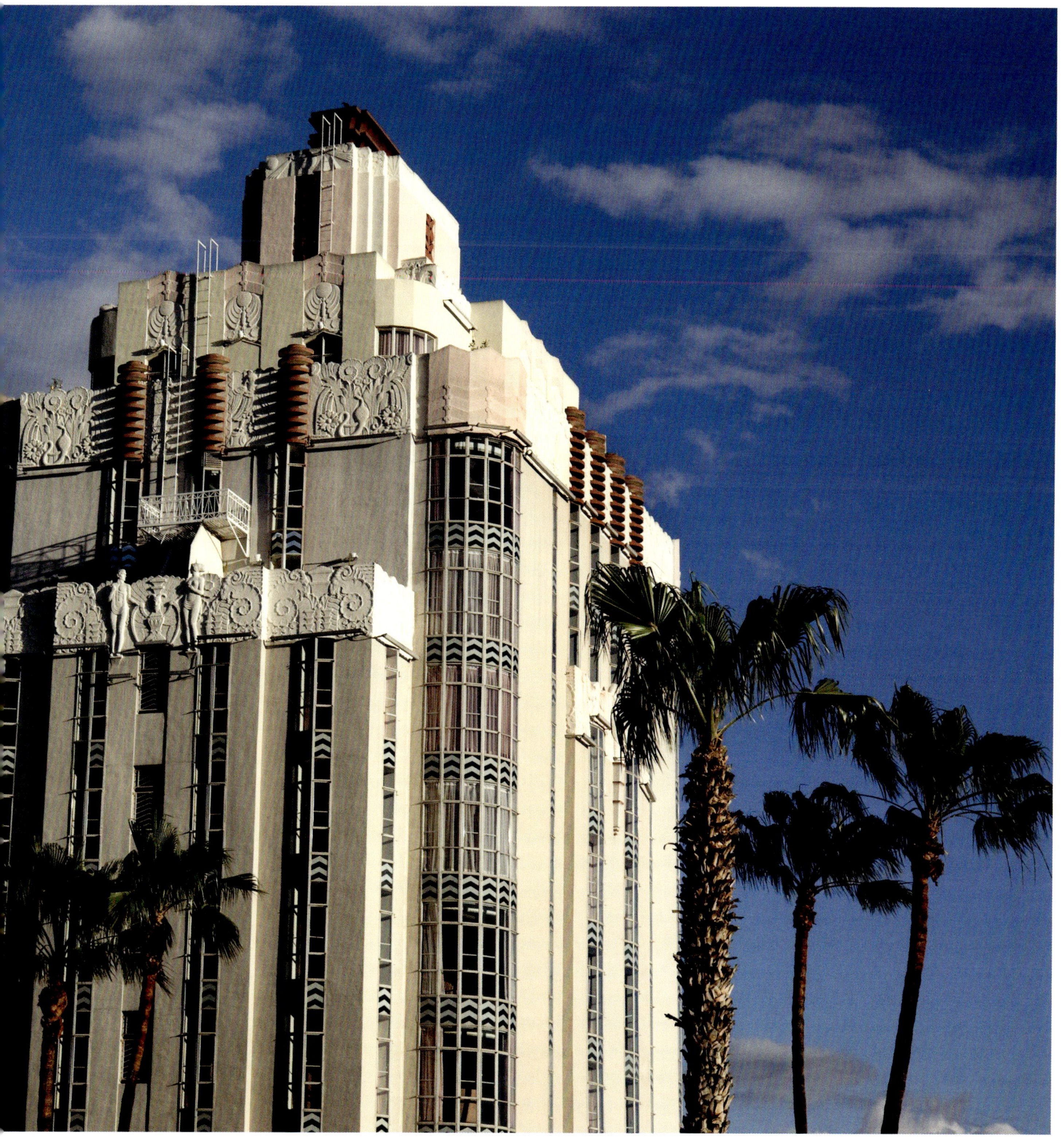

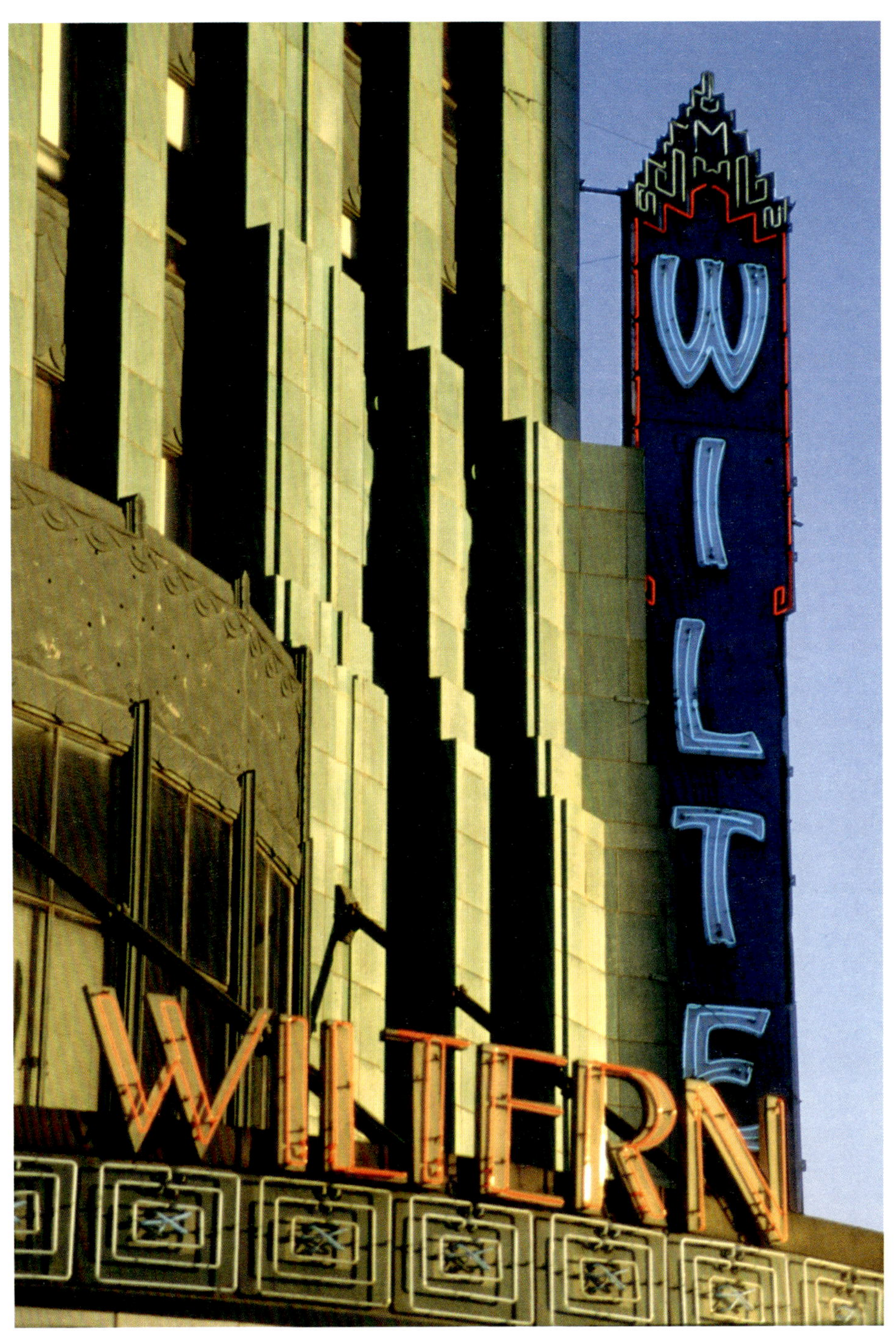

↑ *Wiltern Theatre and Pellissier Building (Morgan, Walls, and Clements, 1931) 3790 Wilshire Blvd., photographed 2002.*

→ *Eastern Columbia Building, now Eastern Columbia Lofts (Claud Beelman, 1929) 849 S. Broadway, photographed 1996.*

OVERLEAF: *Newberry Company, now Hollywood Toys and Costumes (Newberry Company, 1928) 6600 Hollywood Blvd., photographed 2006.*

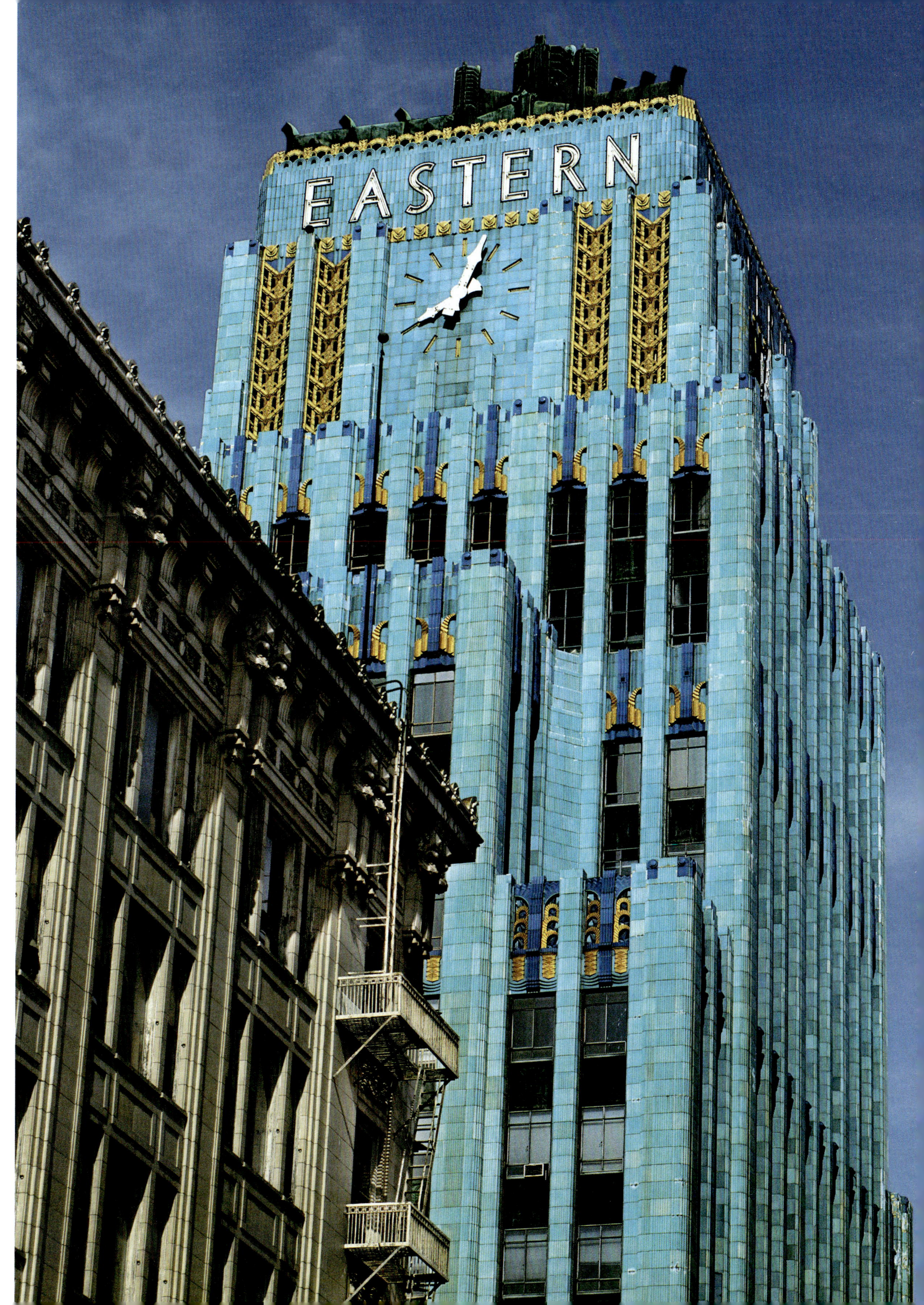
EASTERN

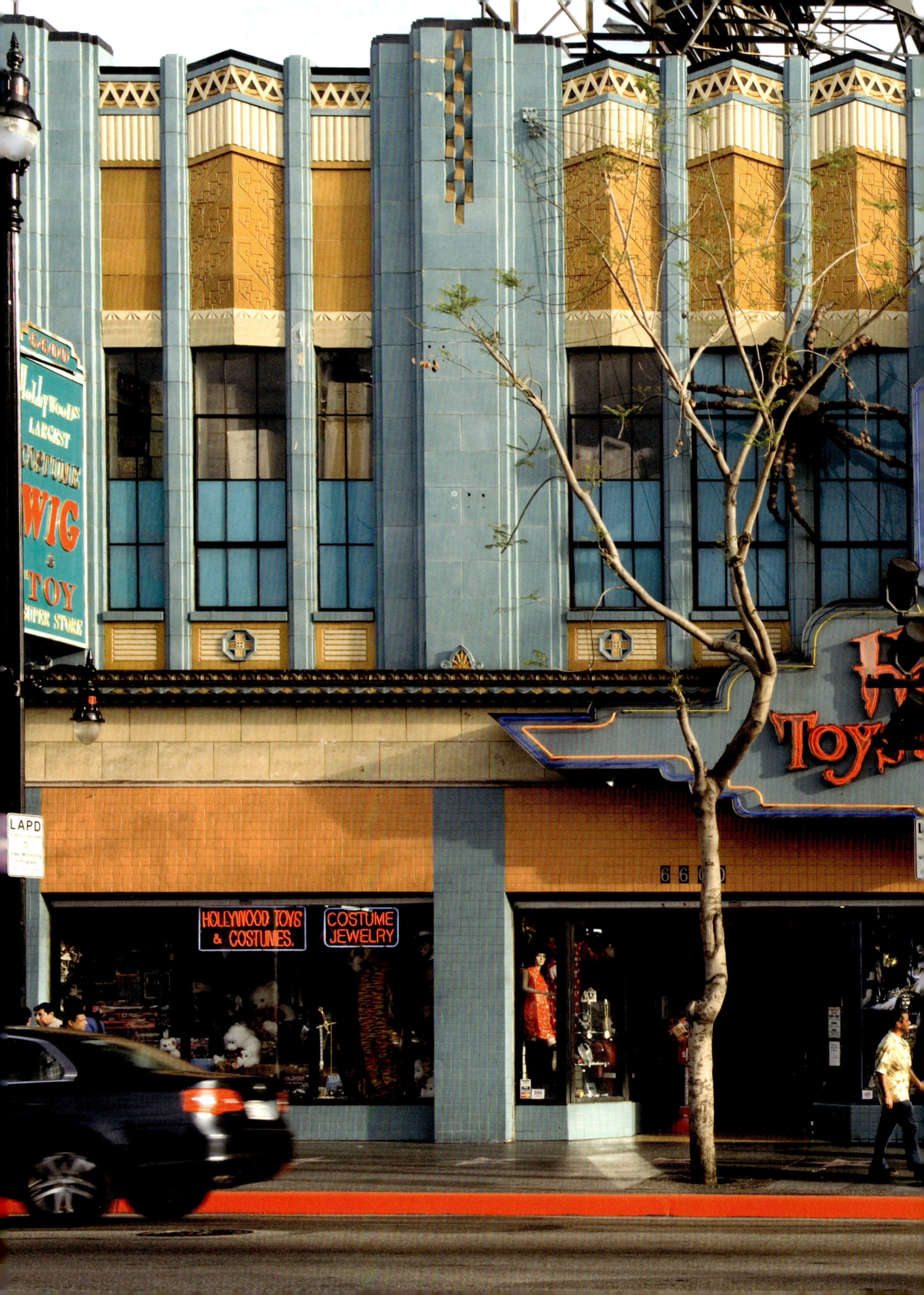
6600
HollyWoods
LARGEST
COSTUME
WIG
&
TOY
SUPER STORE
LAPD
Toys
HOLLYWOOD TOYS
& COSTUMES.
COSTUME
JEWELRY

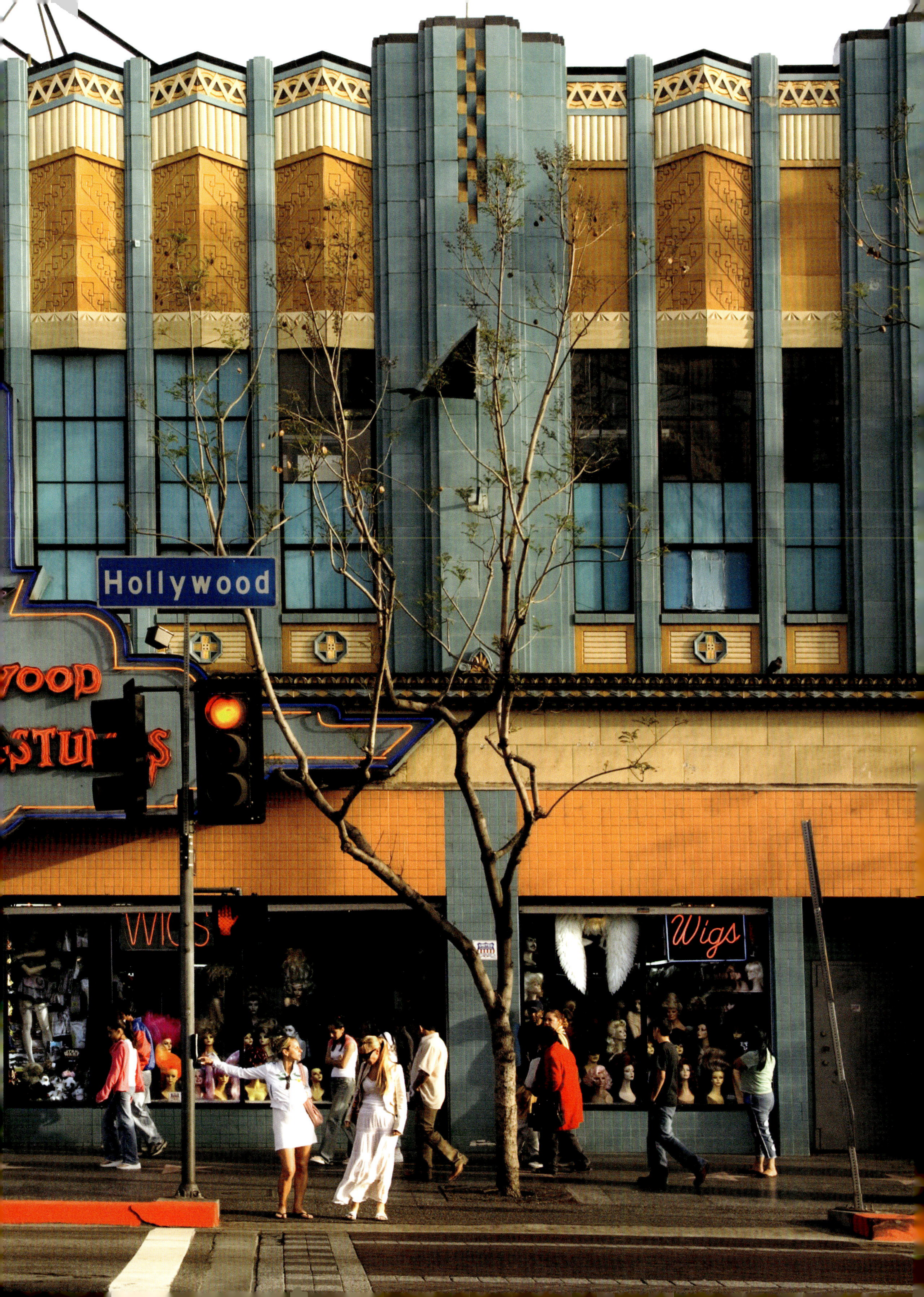
Hollywood
WIGS
Wigs

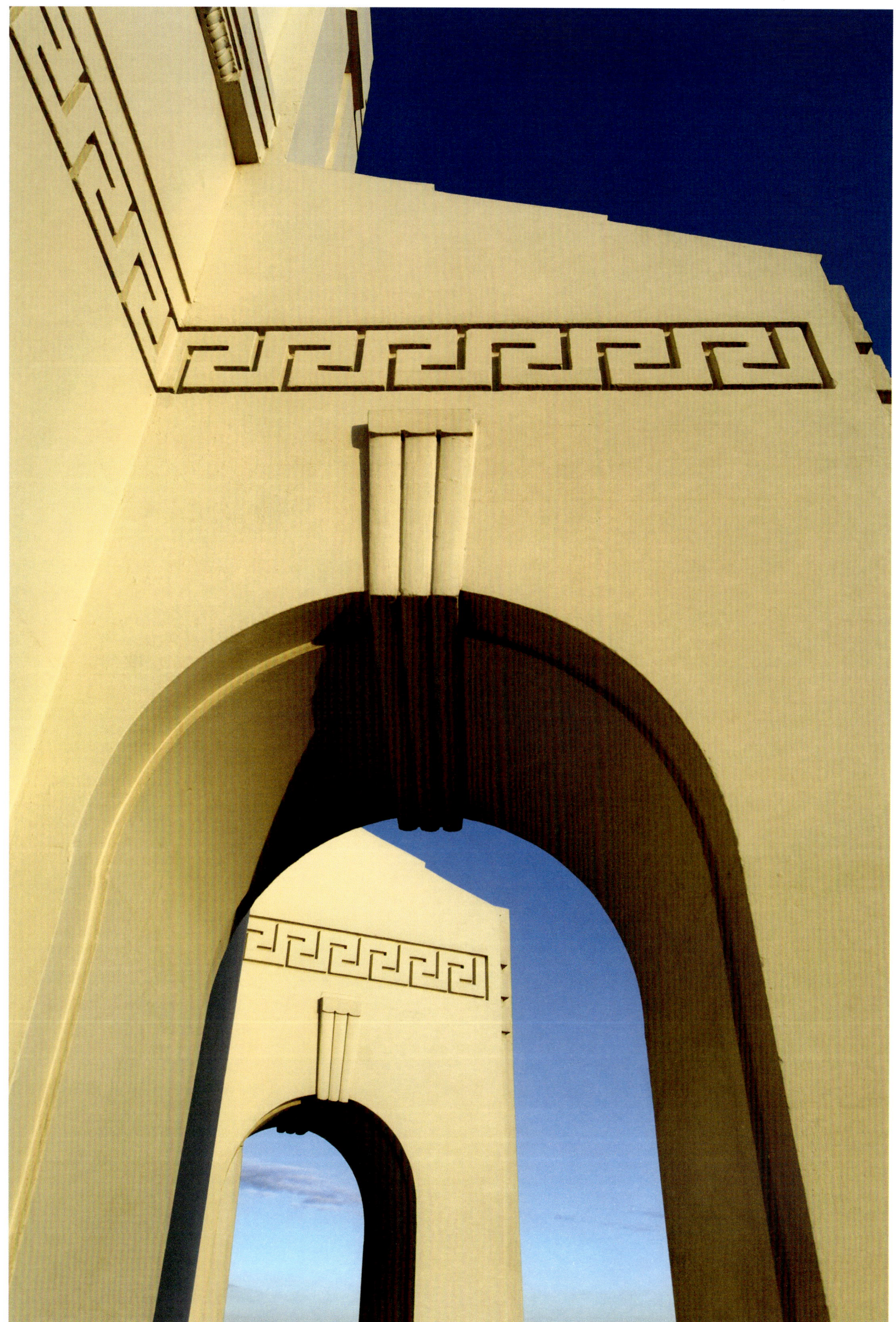

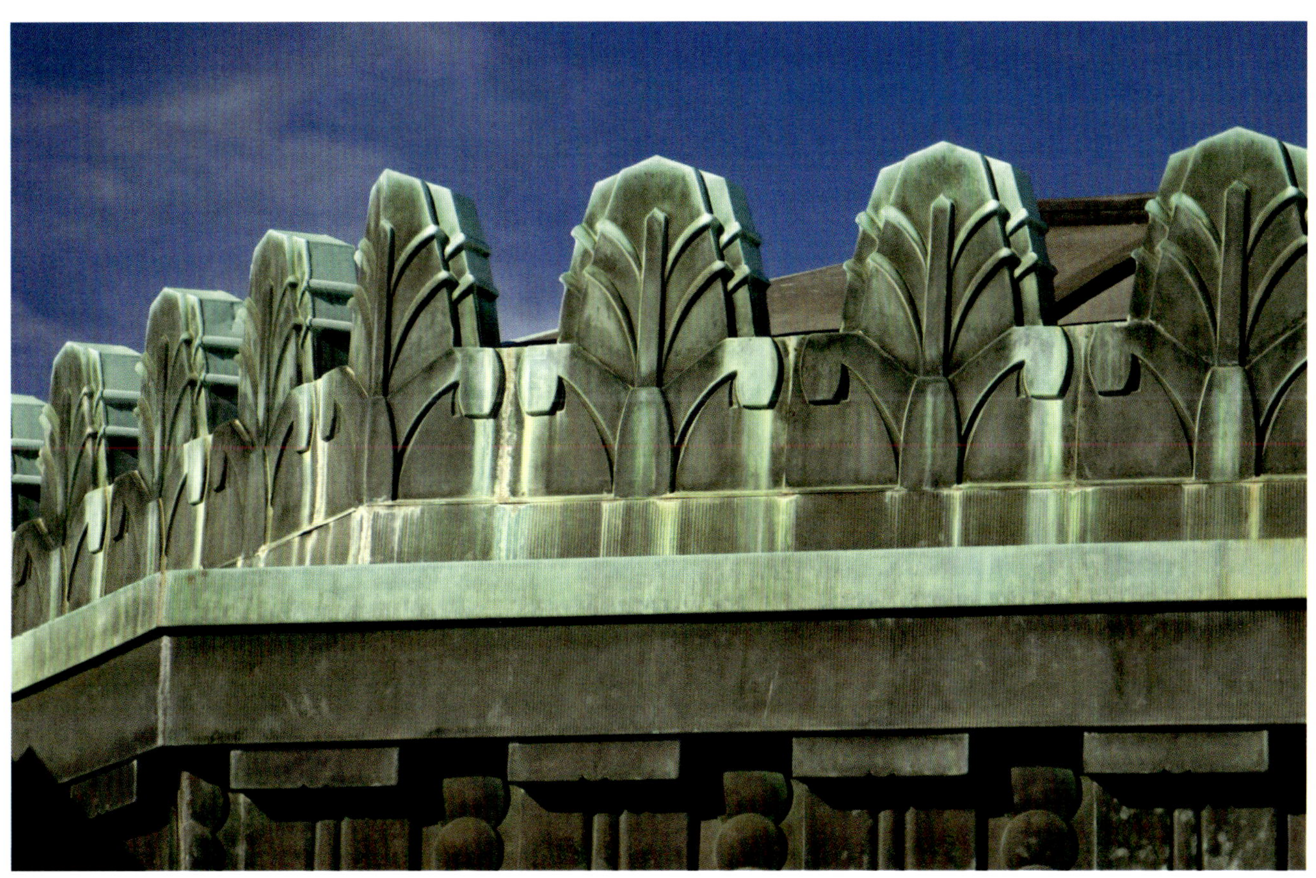

← *Griffith Observatory, detail of archway (John C. Austin and Frederick M. Ashley, 1935) 2800 E. Observatory Rd., photographed 2010.*

↑ *Griffith Observatory, detail of leaf pattern (John C. Austin and Frederick M. Ashley, 1935) 2800 E. Observatory Rd., photographed 1992.*

OVERLEAF: *Hollyhock House (Frank Lloyd Wright, 1921) 4800 Hollywood Blvd., photographed 2024.*

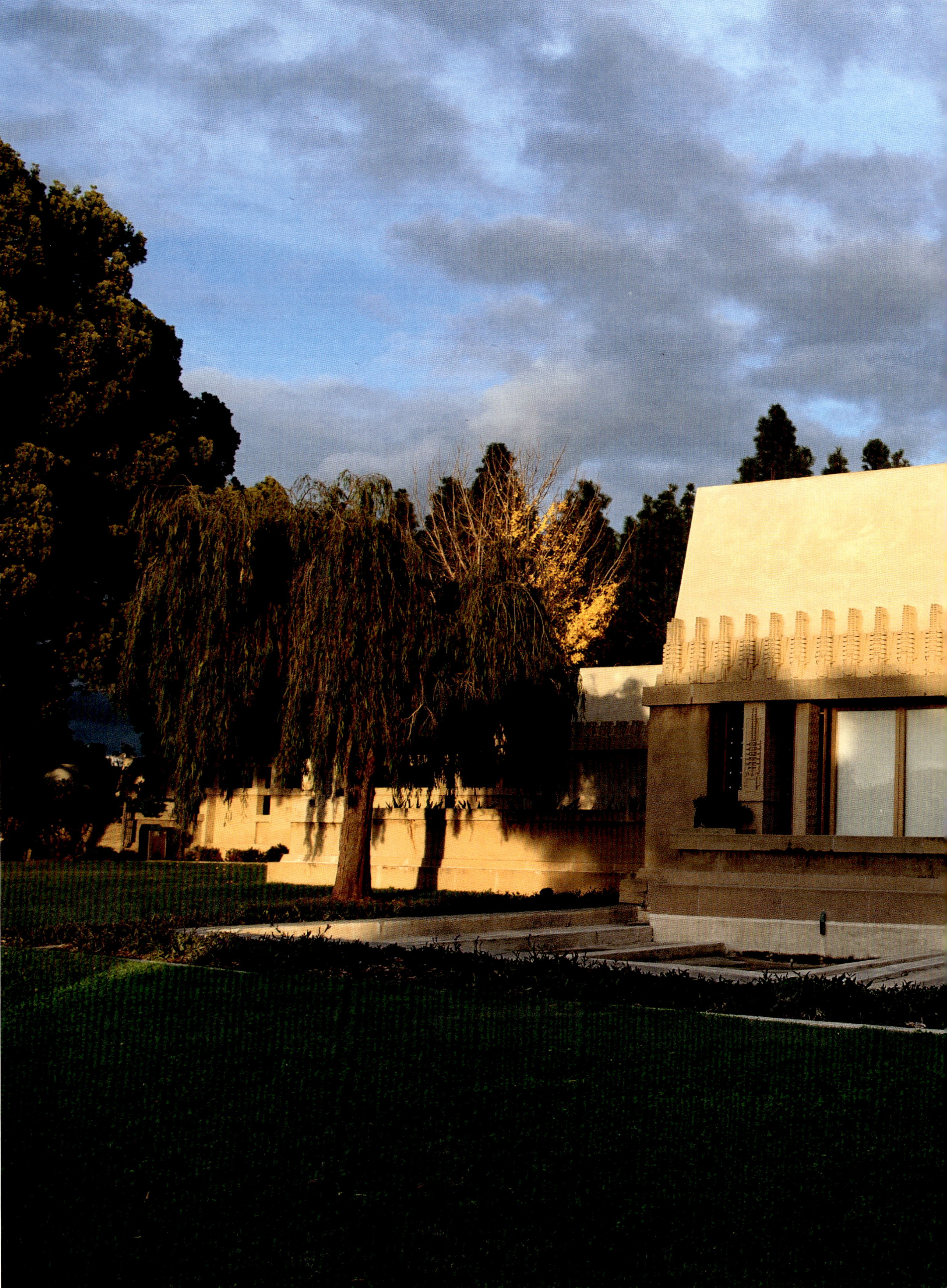

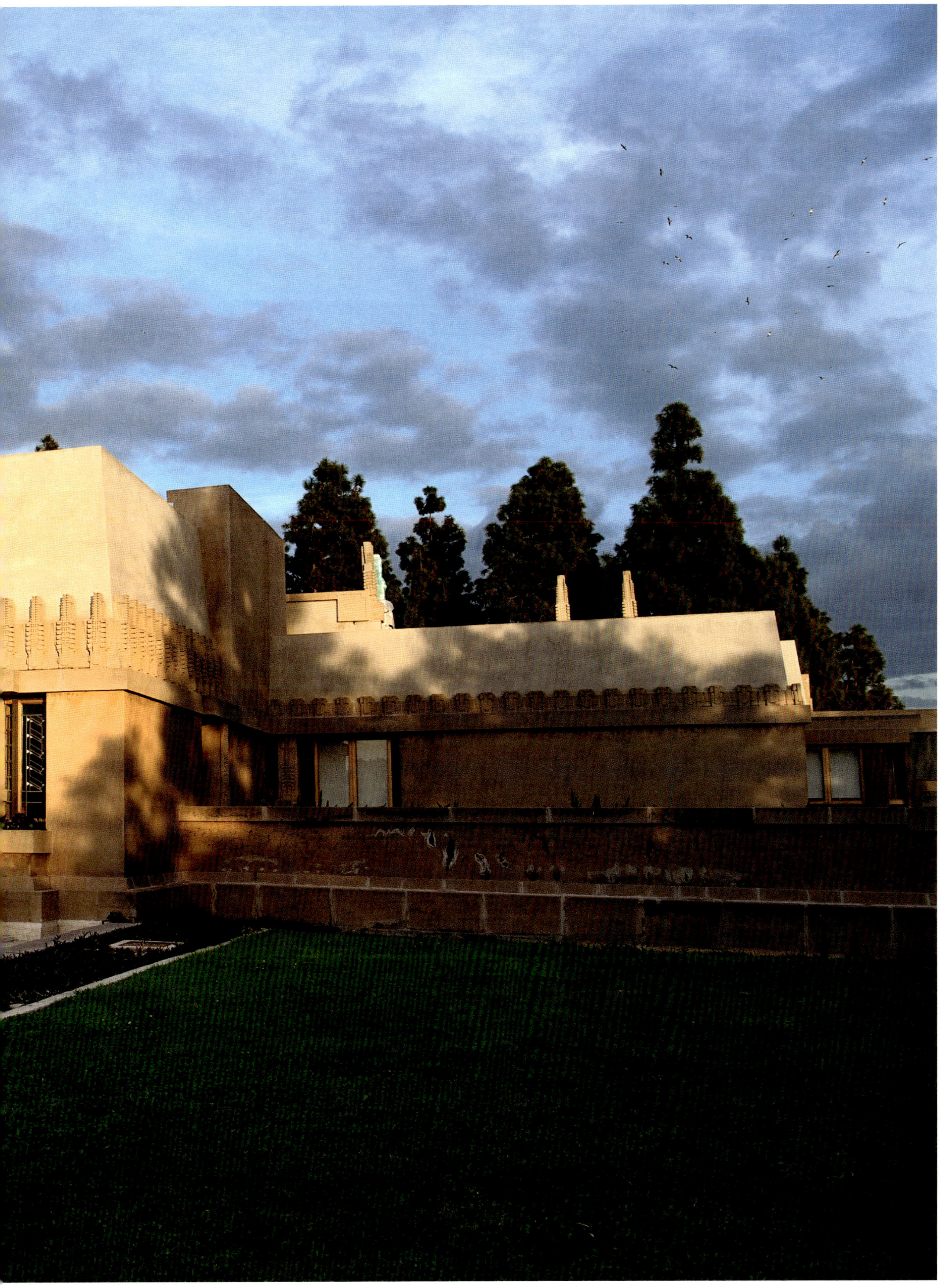

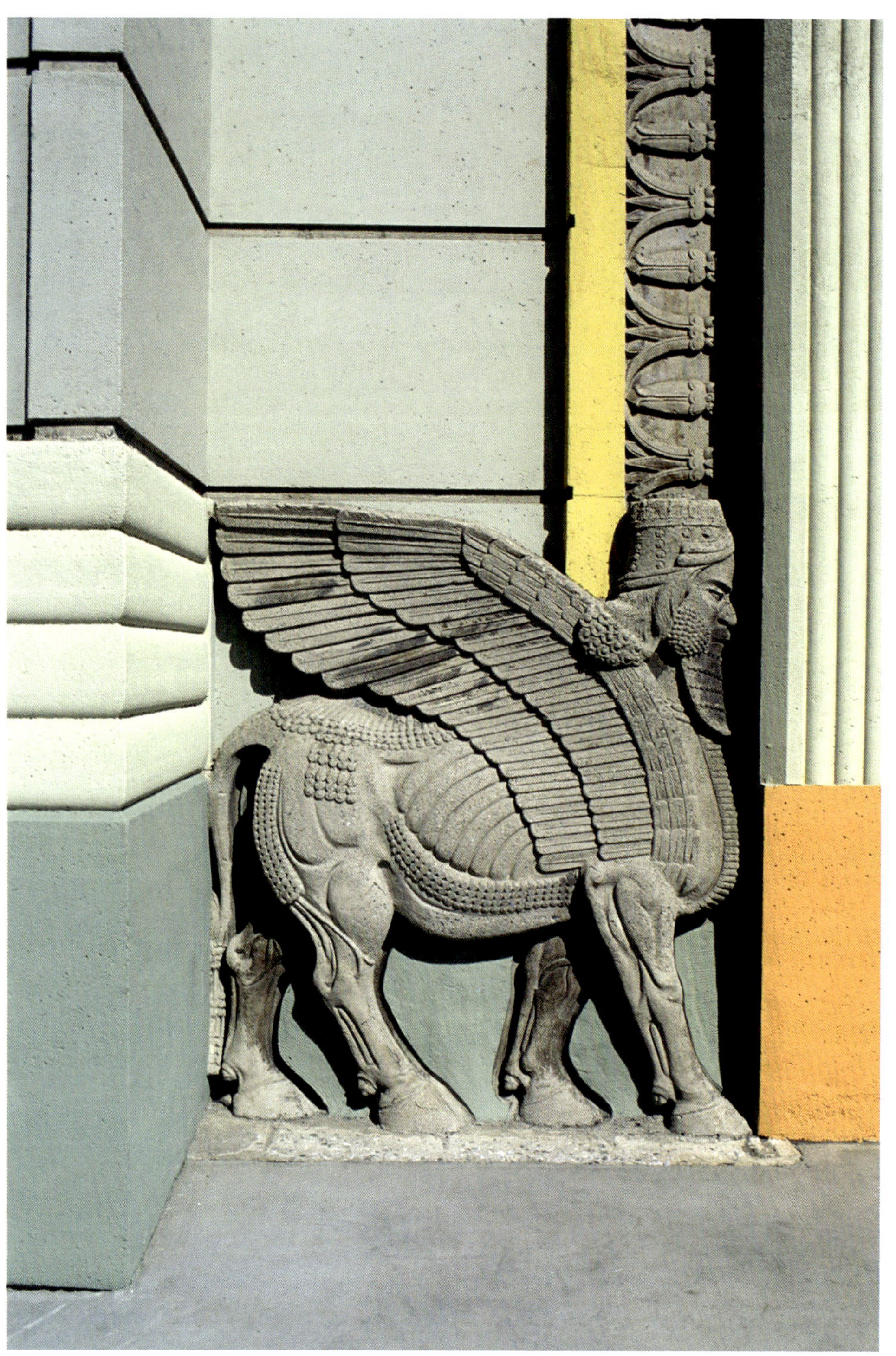

↑ *Samson Tyre and Rubber Company, now Citadel Outlets (Morgan, Walls, and Clements, 1929) 5675 Telegraph Rd., Commerce, photographed 1991.*

→ *Elks Lodge, now The MacArthur, exterior detail (Curlett and Beelman, 1924) 607 S. Park View St., photographed 2008.*

OVERLEAF: *Union Station (John Parkinson and Donald B. Parkinson, 1939) 800 N. Alameda St., photographed 2024.*

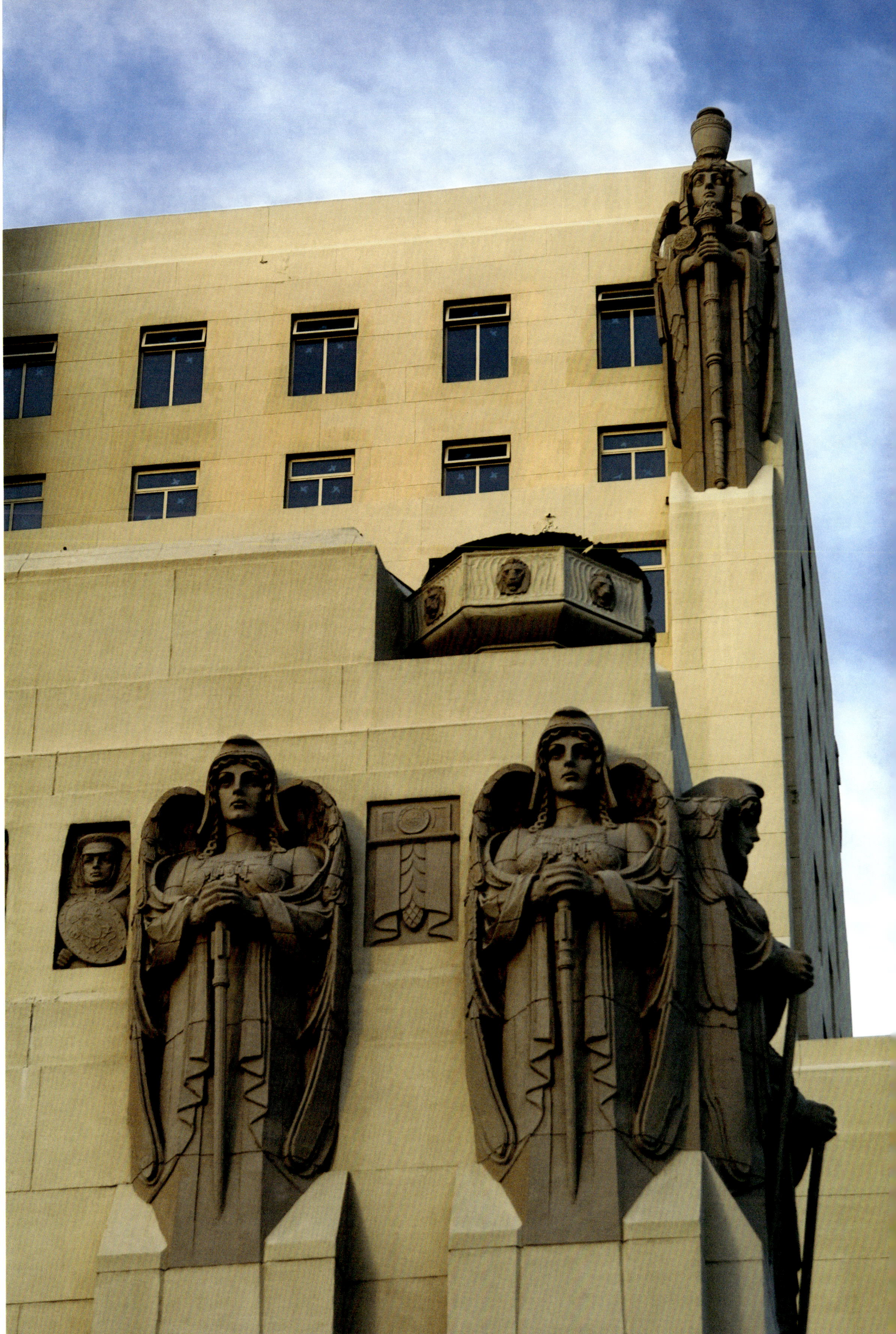

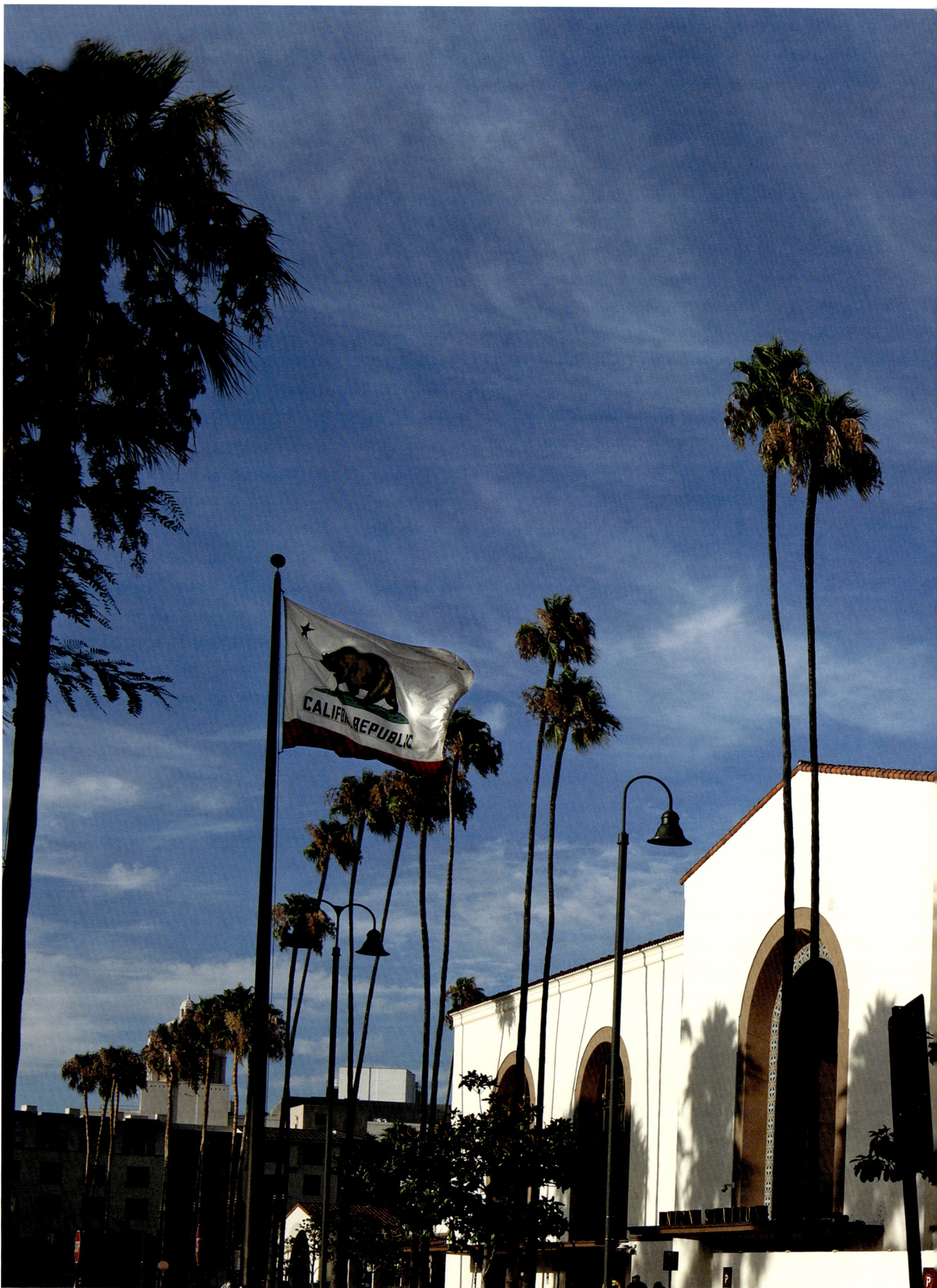
REPUBLIC

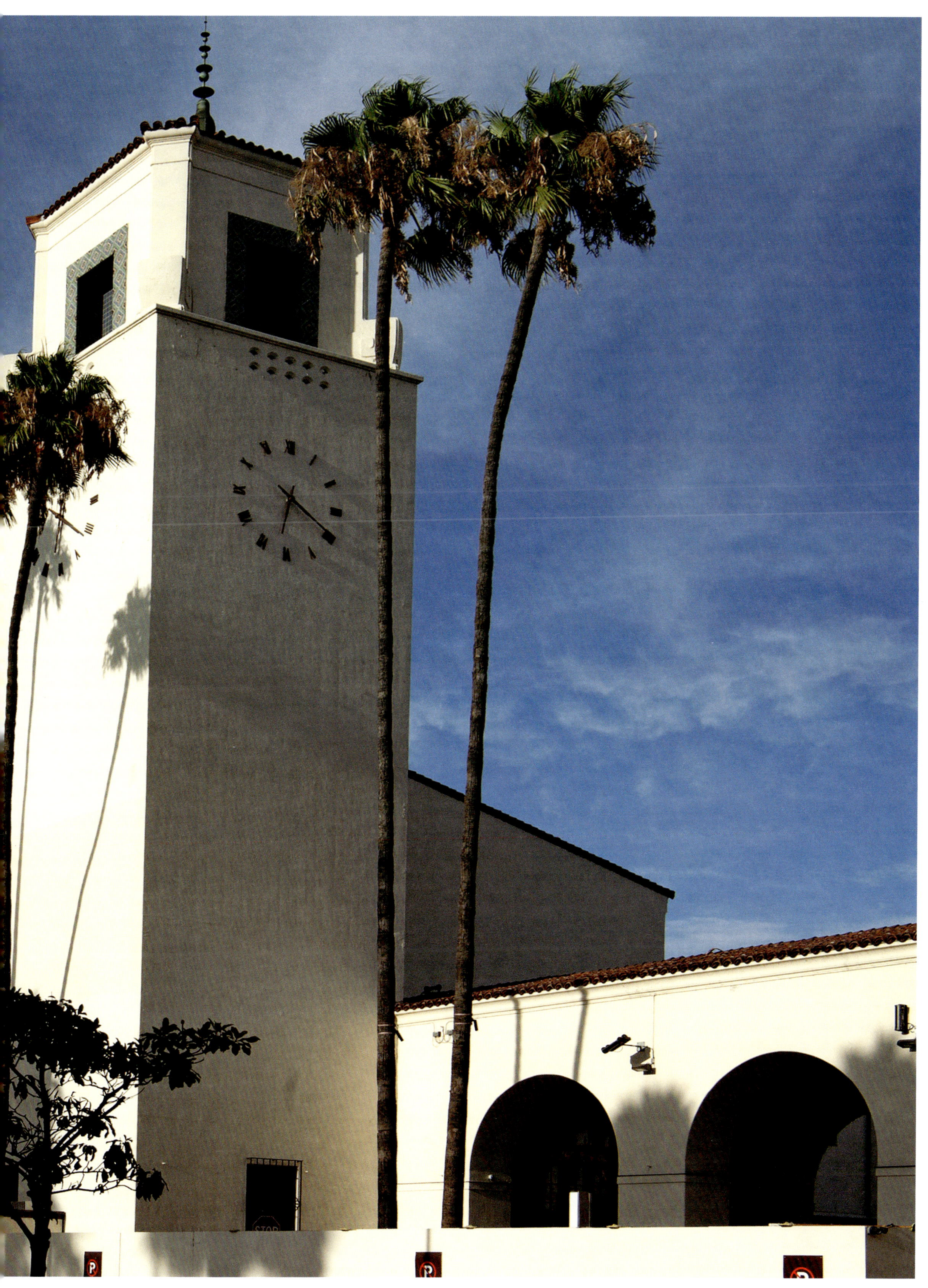

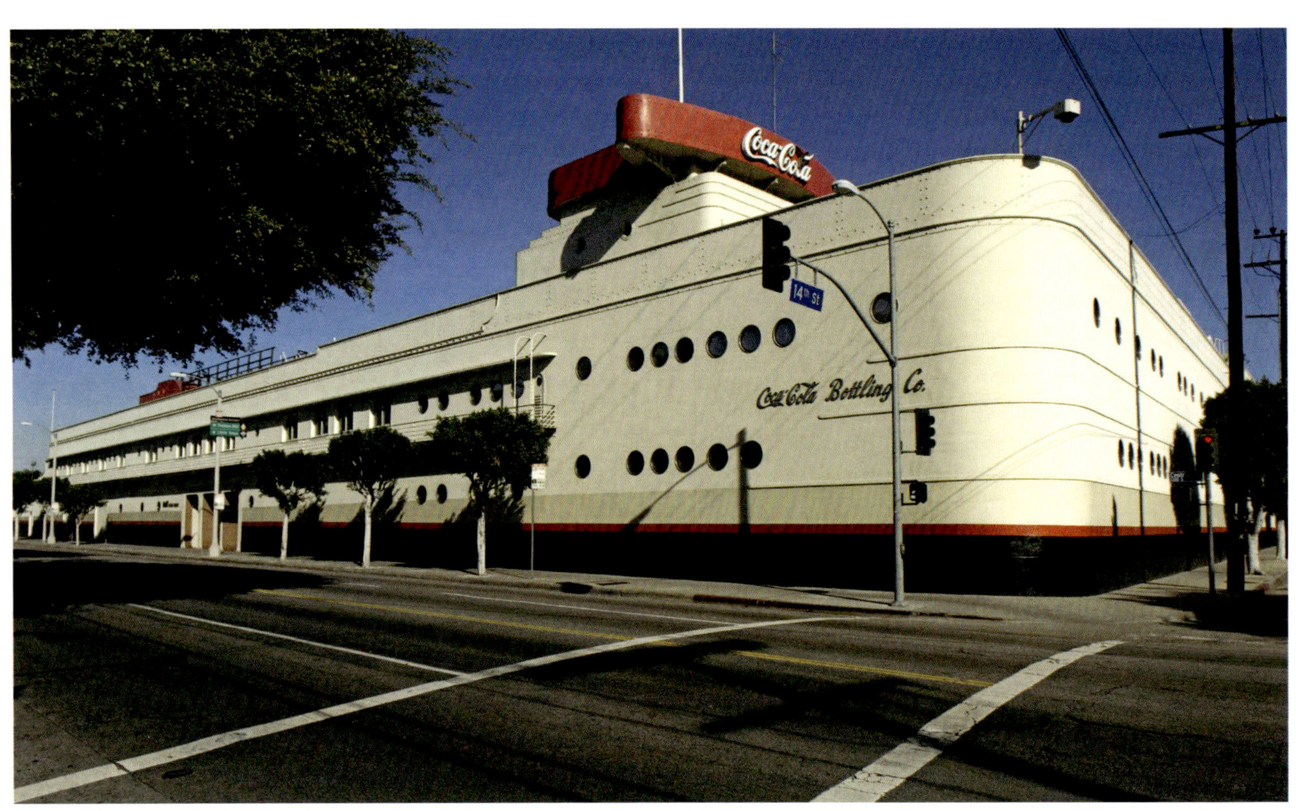

↑ *Coca Cola Bottling Company (Robert V. Derrah, 1937)*
1334 S. Central Ave., photographed 1985.

→ Queen Mary *(Built by John Brown and Co., Ltd, 1934)*
1126 Queens Highway, Long Beach, photographed 1981.

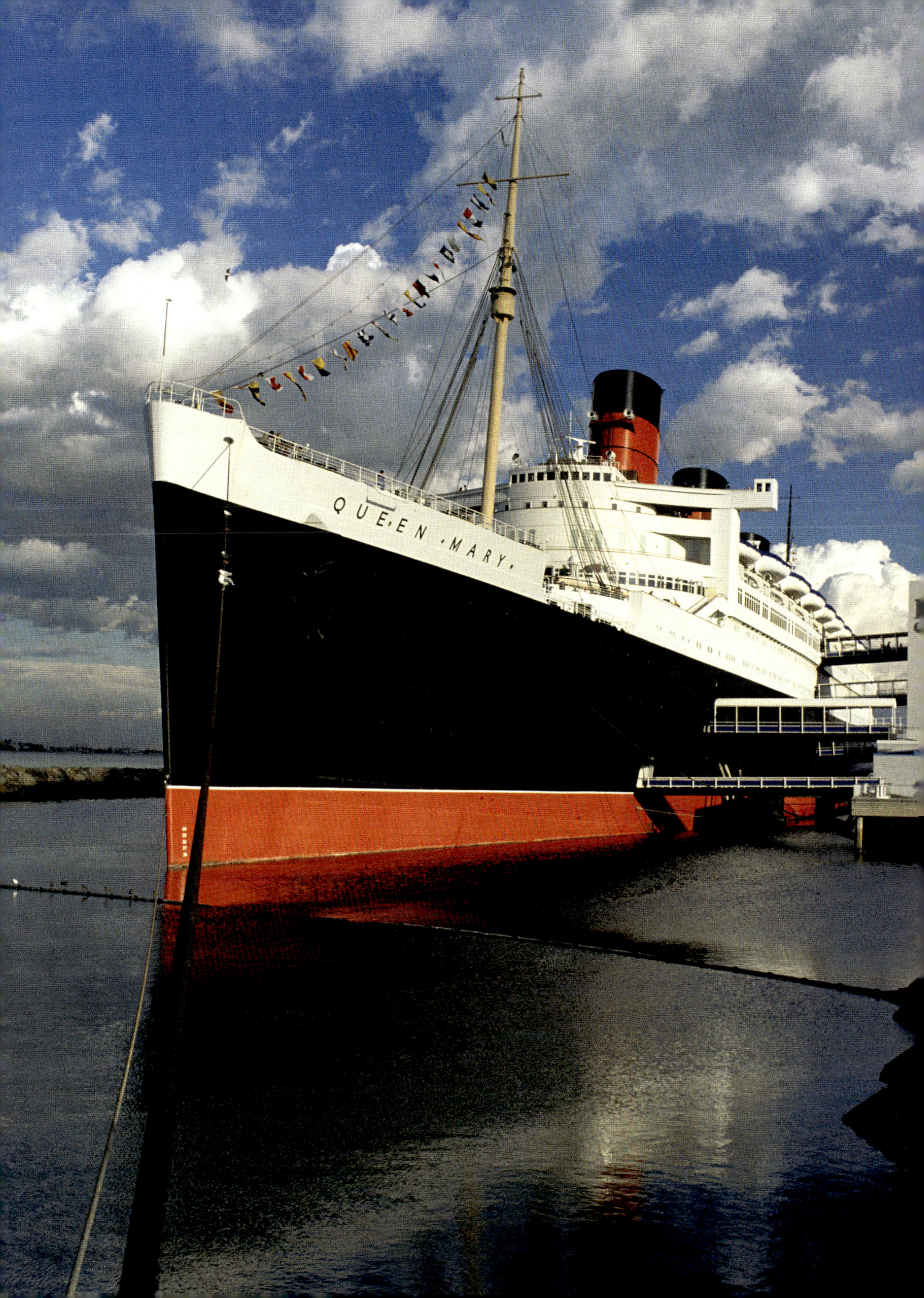
QUEEN MARY

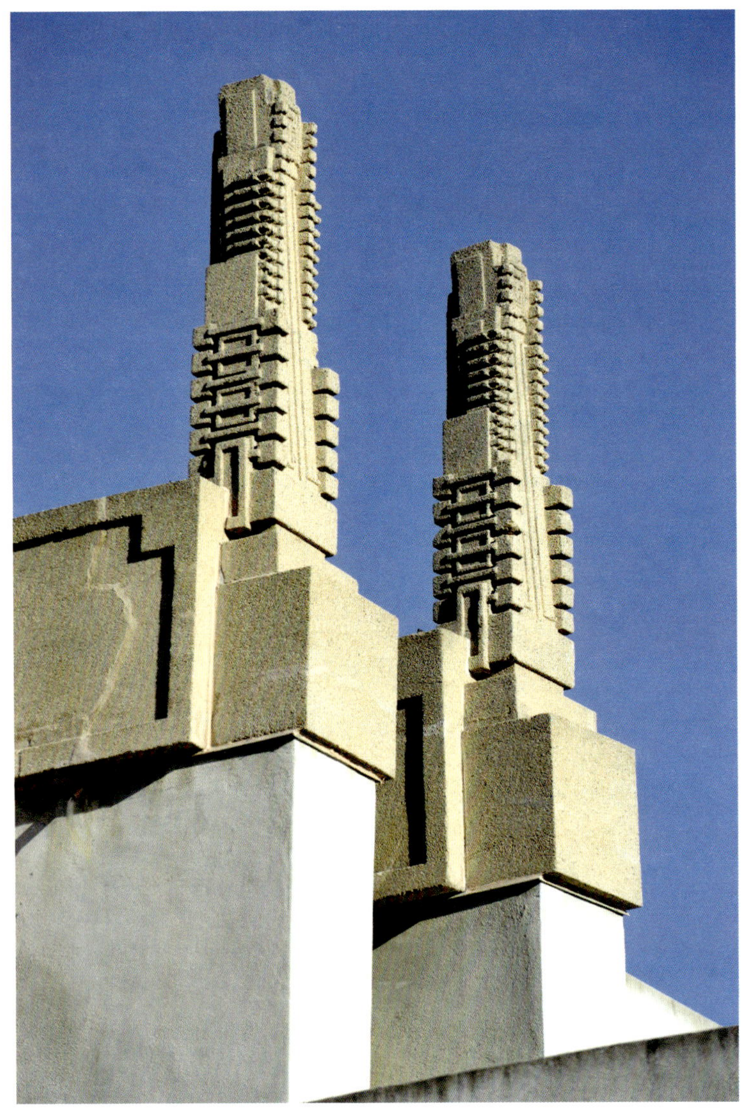

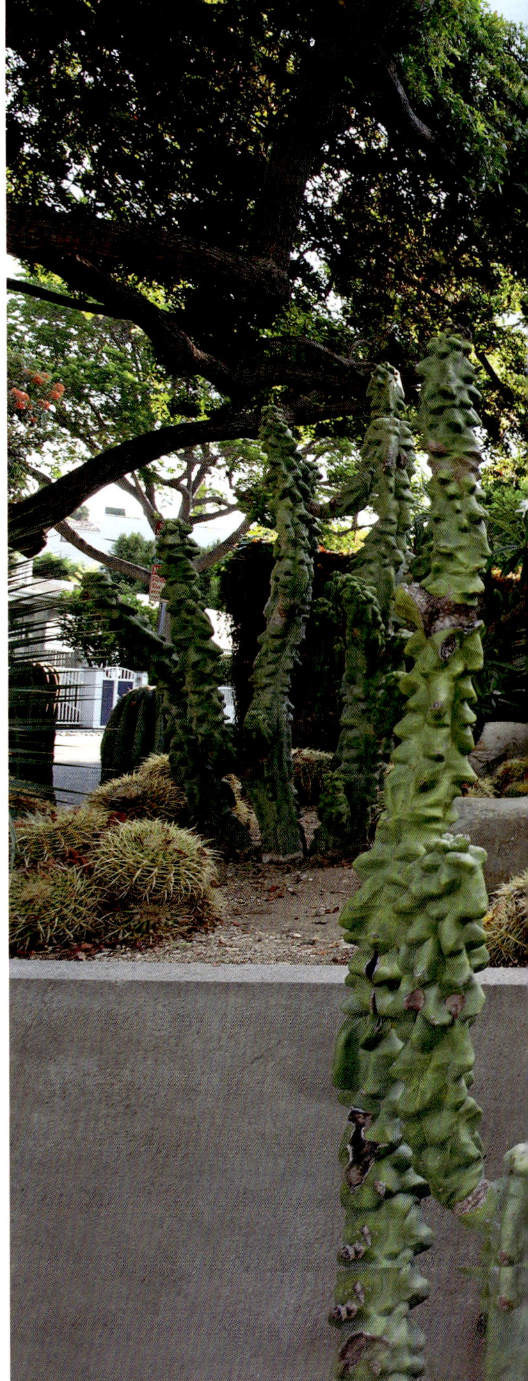

↑ *Hollyhock House, exterior detail (Frank Lloyd Wright, 1921) 4800 Hollywood Blvd., photographed 2024.*

→ *Lloyd Wright Home and Studio (Lloyd Wright, 1928) 858 N. Doheny Dr., photographed 2024.*

OVERLEAF: Los Angeles Times *Building (Gordon B. Kaufmann, 1935) 202 W. 1st St., photographed 2024.*

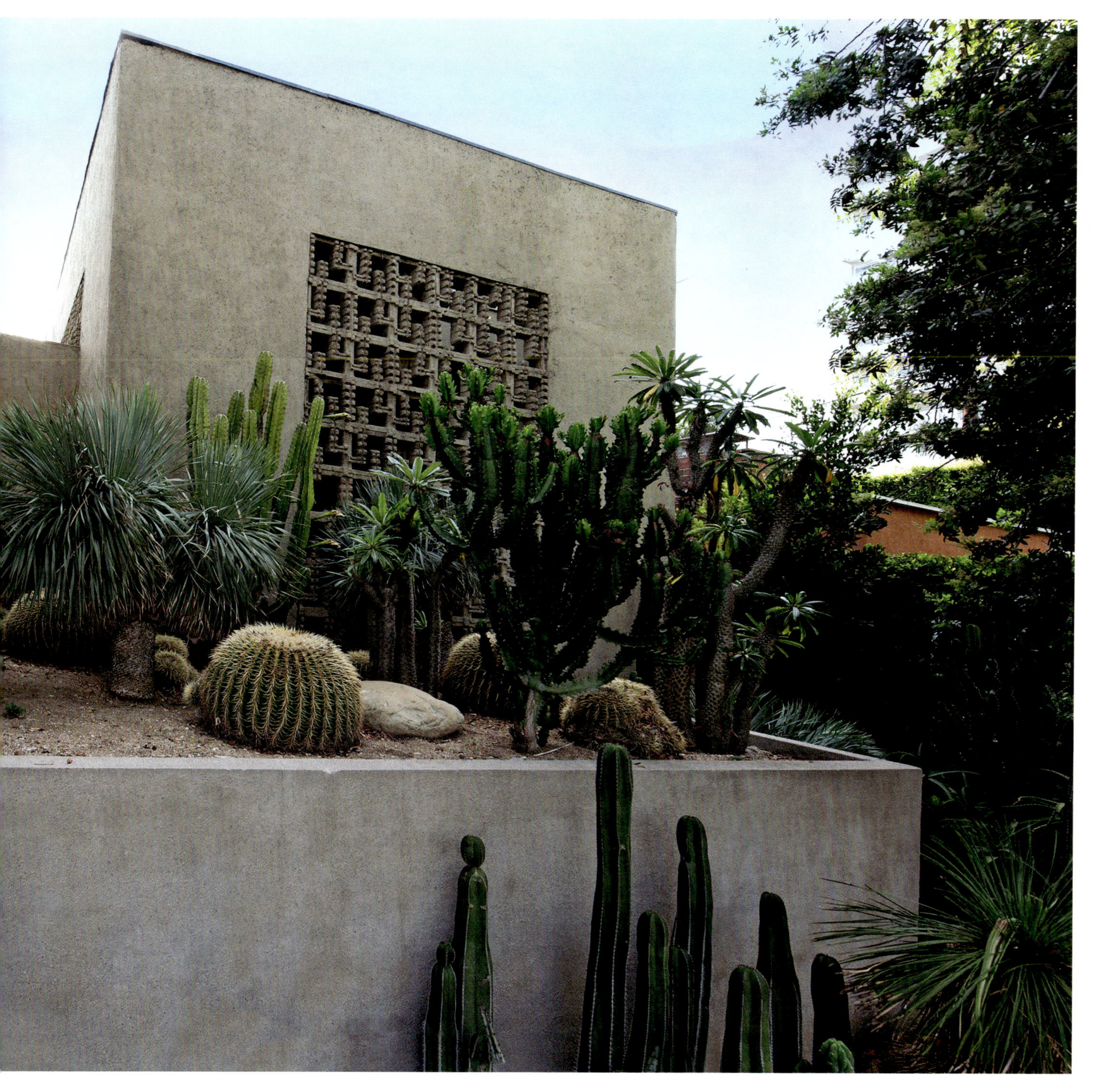

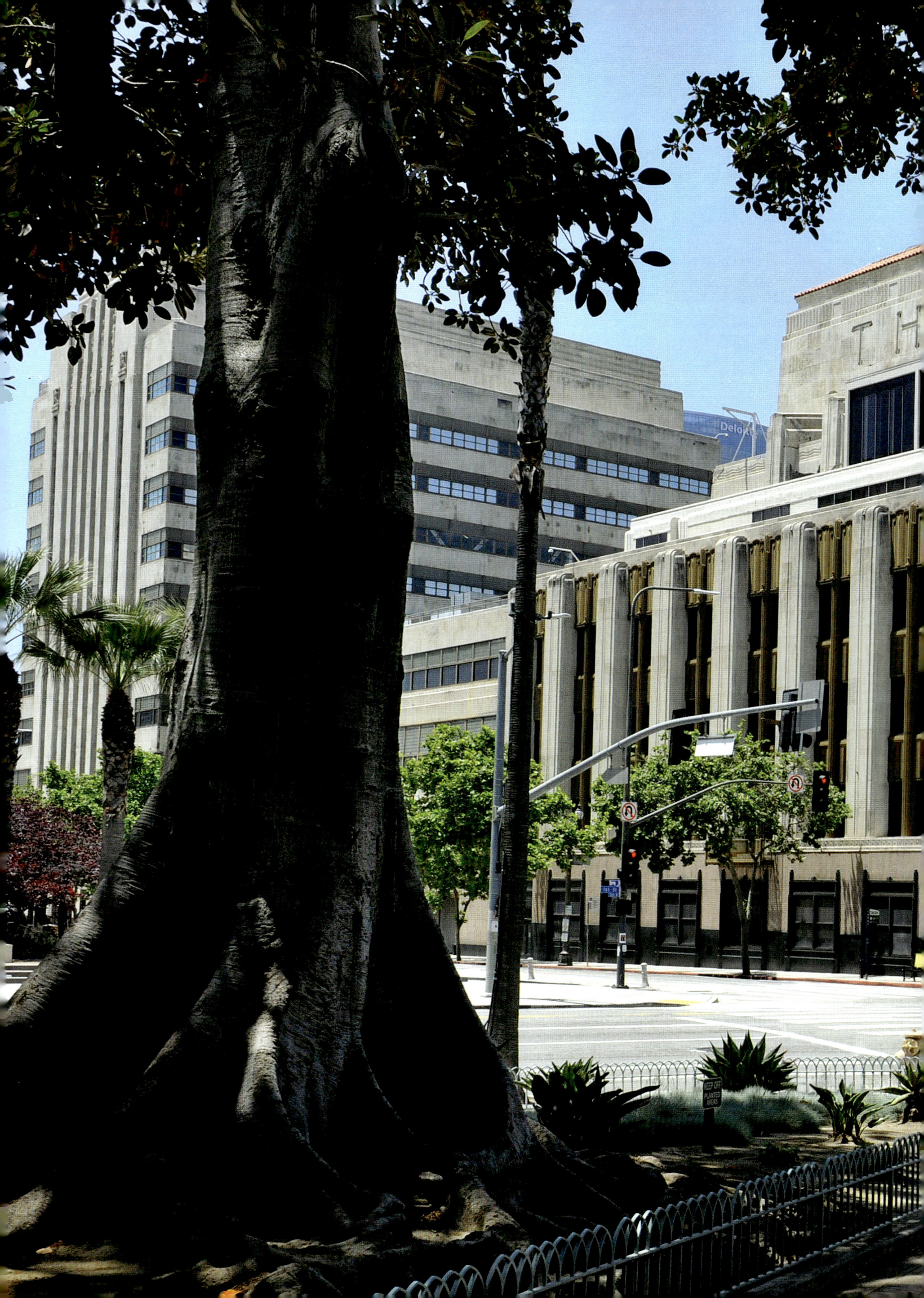

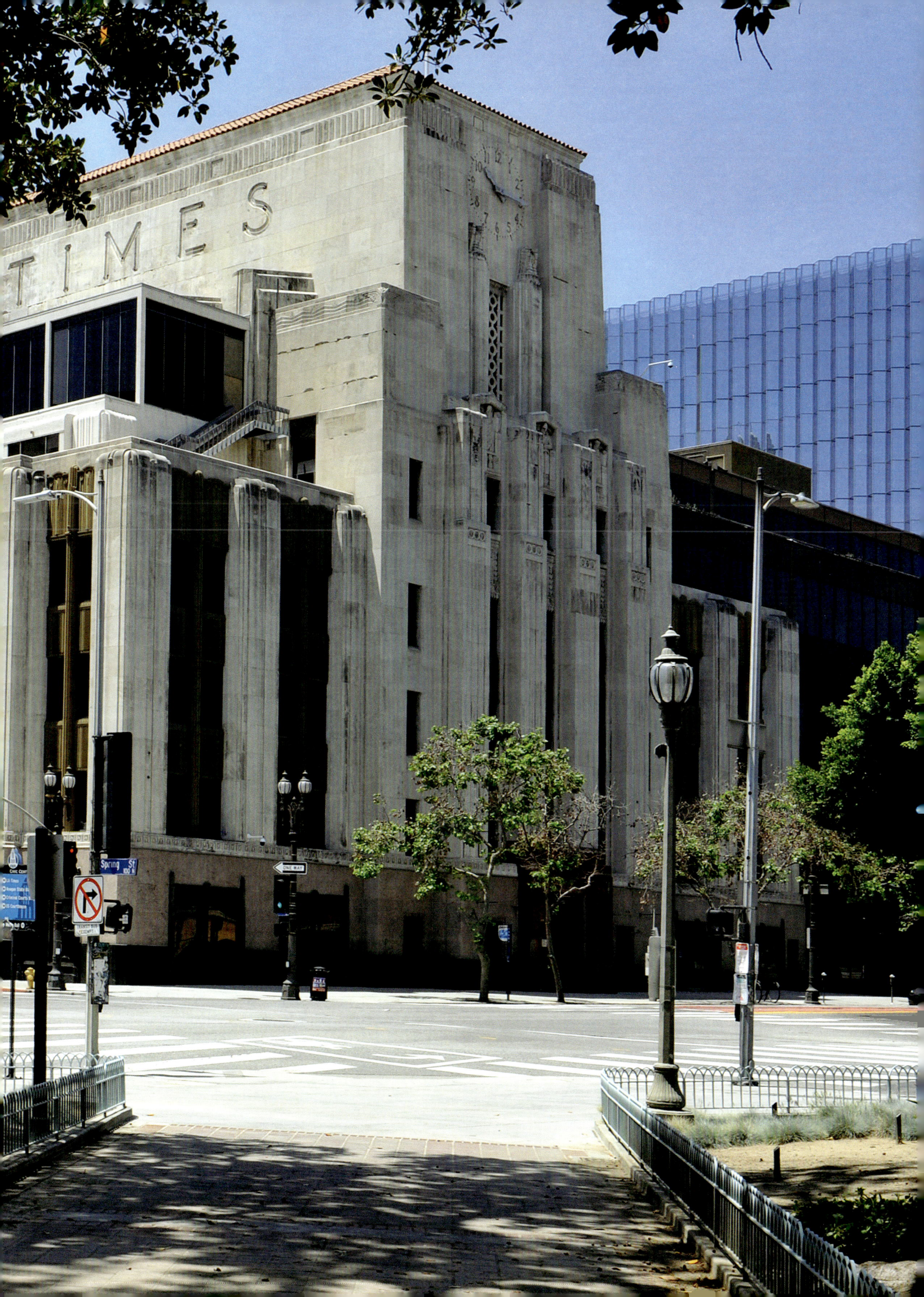
TIMES
Spring St
ONE WAY

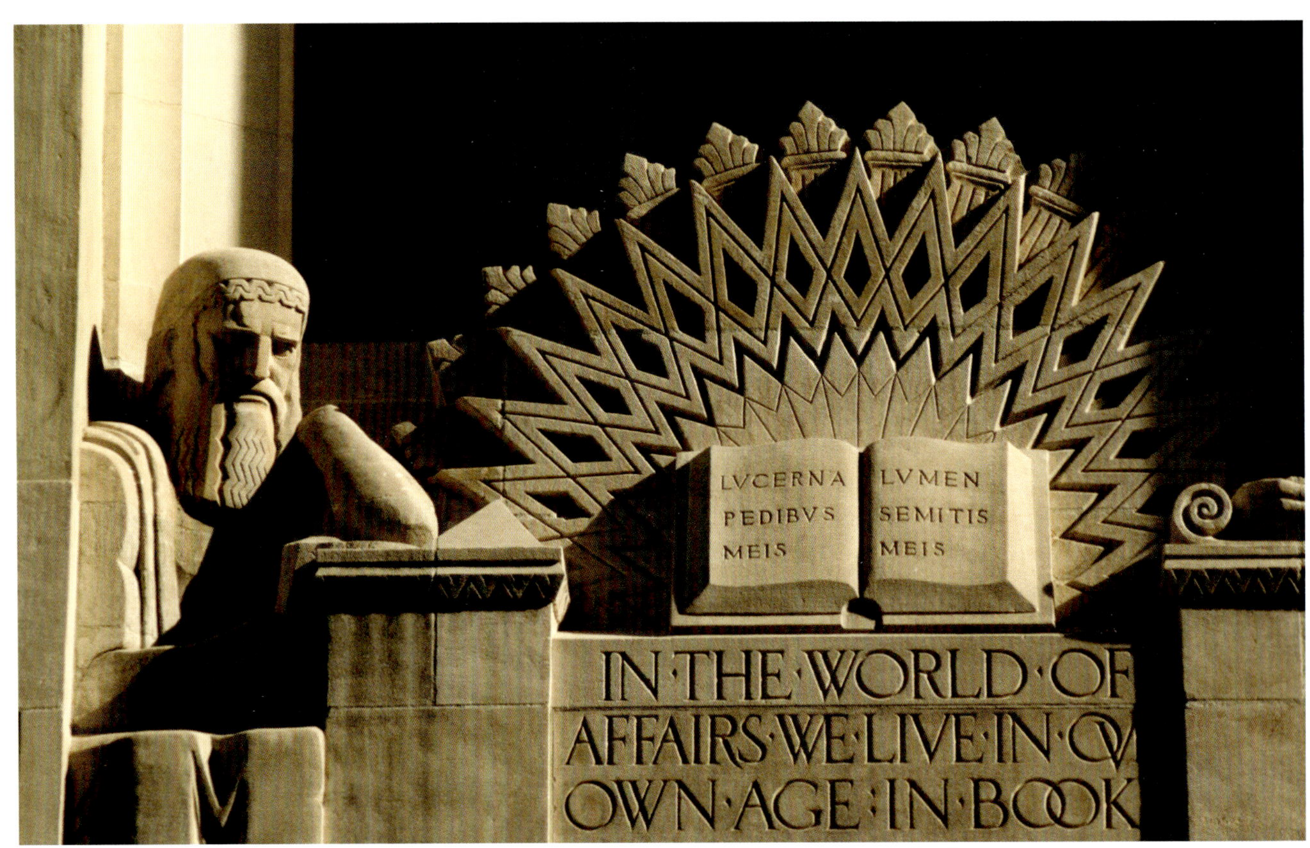

↑ *Los Angeles Central Library, exterior detail (Bertram G. Goodhue and Carleton Winslow, 1926) 630 W. 5th St., photographed 2008.*

→ *Griffith Observatory, Astronomers Monument (monument designed by Archibald Garner, 1934) 2800 E. Observatory Rd., photographed 2008.*

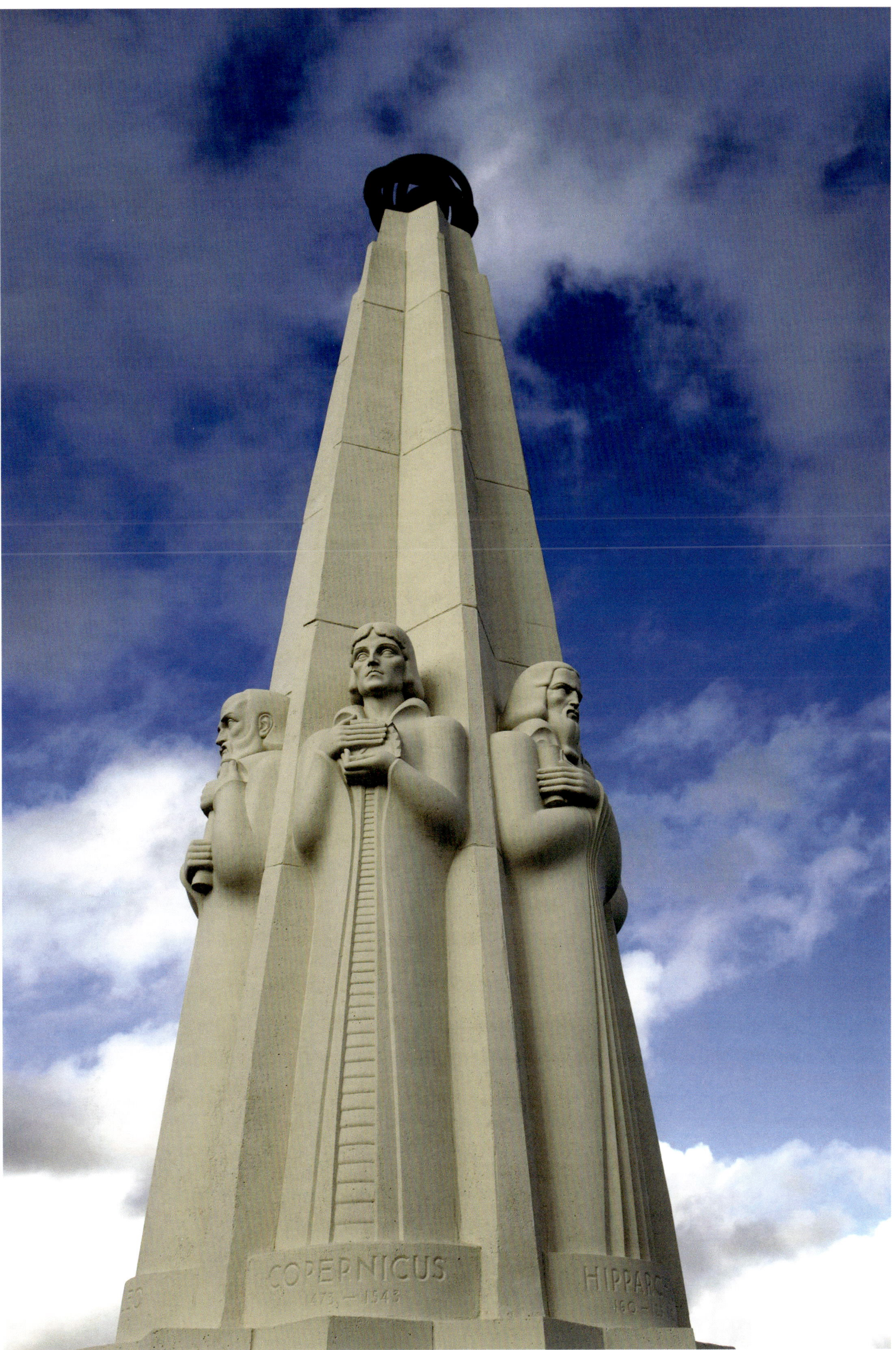
COPERNICUS
1473 — 1543

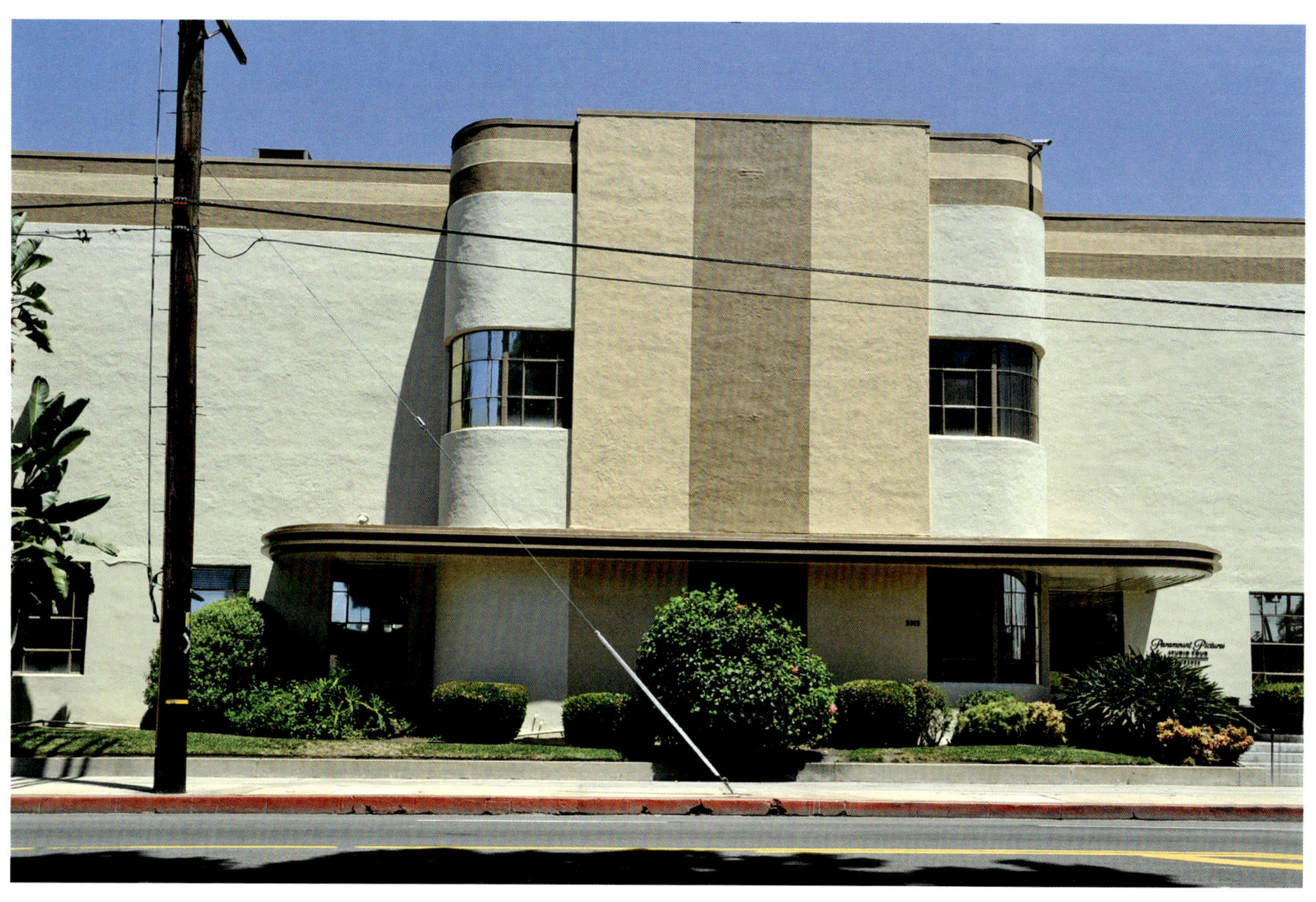

↑ *NBC Radio Studio, now part of Paramount Studios (Austin Co., 1937) 5515 Melrose Ave., photographed 2024.*

→ *H.A. McMurphy (Architect Unknown, 1937) 6424 Santa Monica Blvd., photographed 2003*

OVERLEAF: *Oviatt Building (Walker and Eisen, 1928) 617 S. Olive St., photographed 2024.*

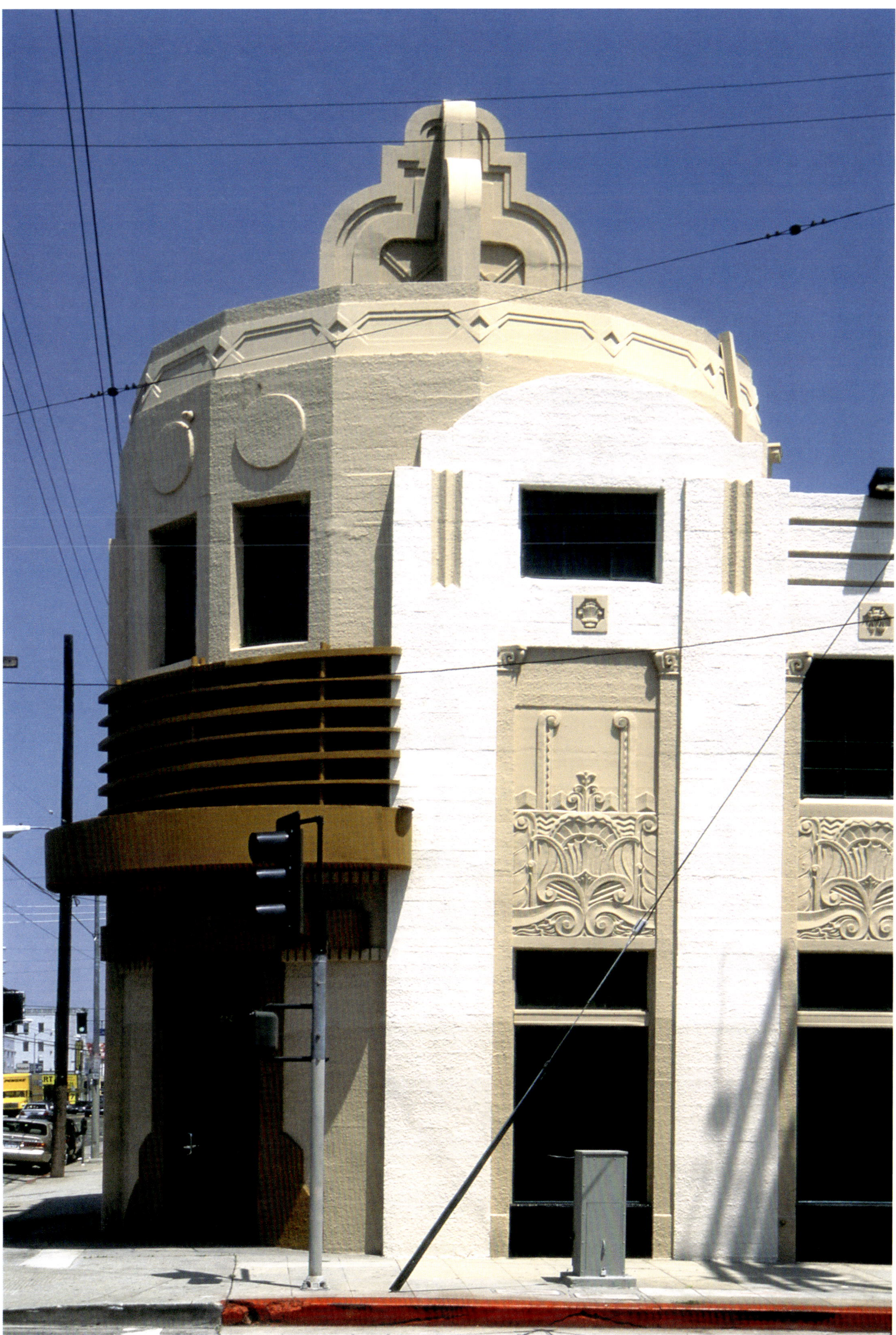

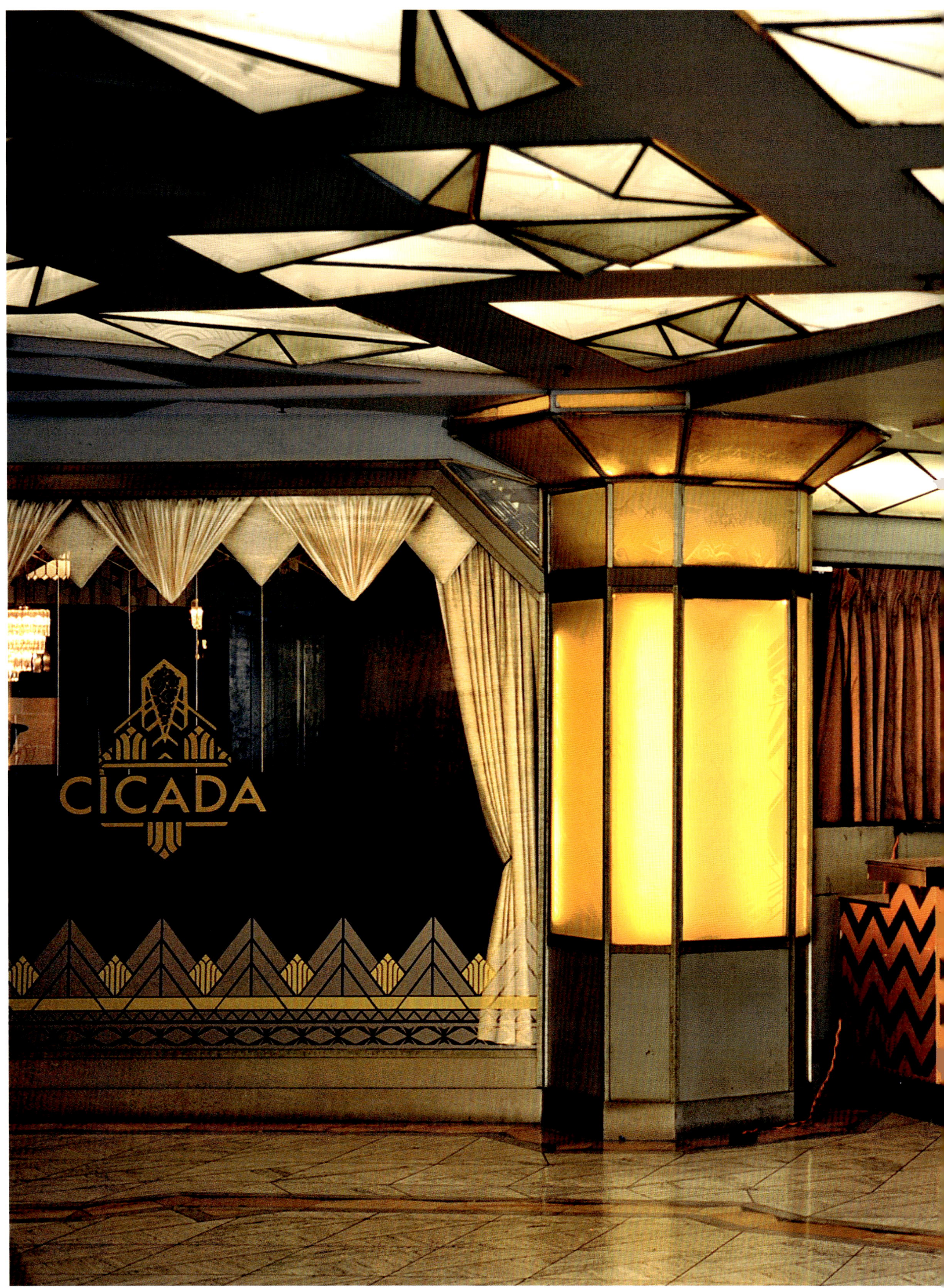
CICADA

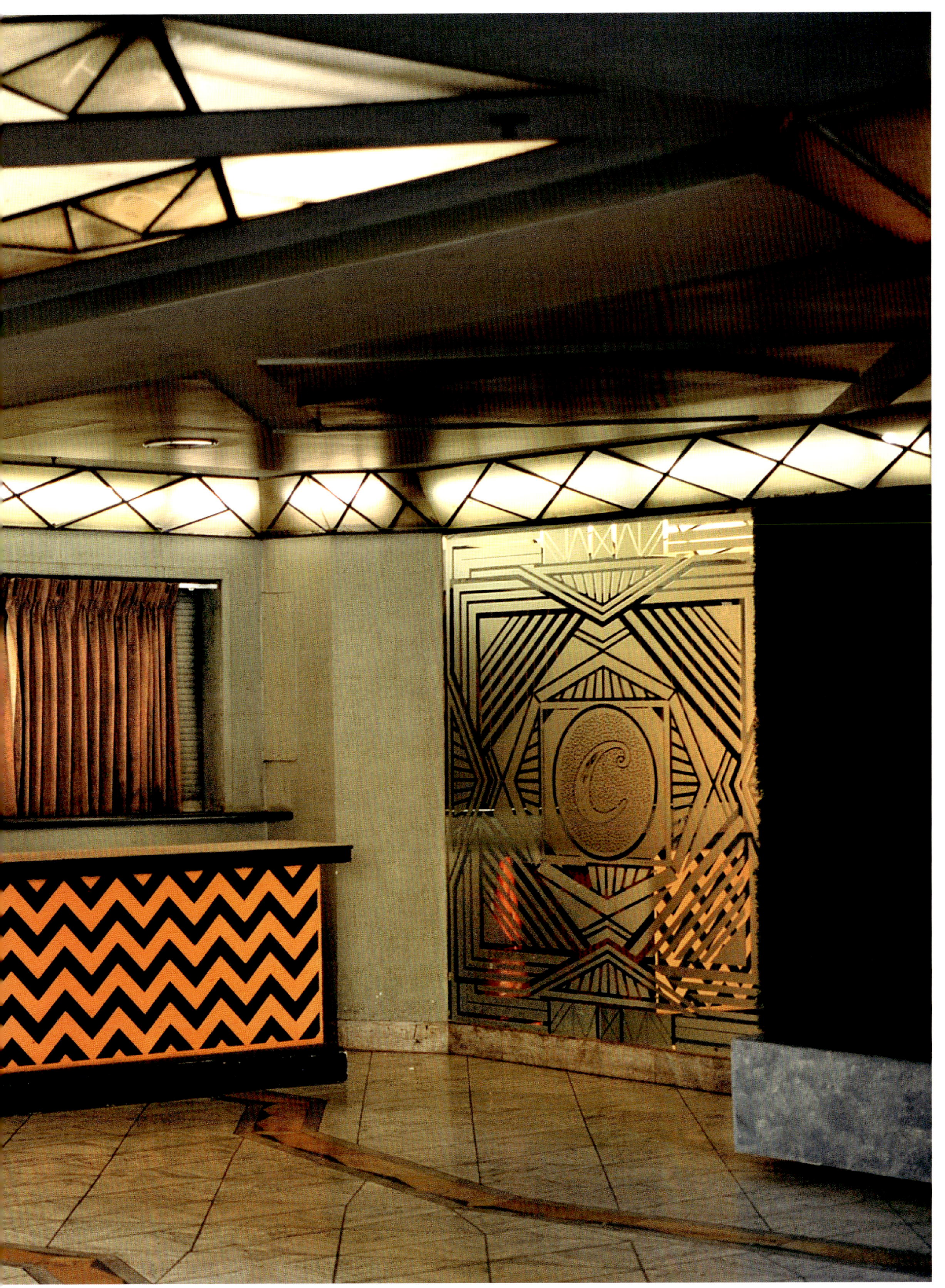

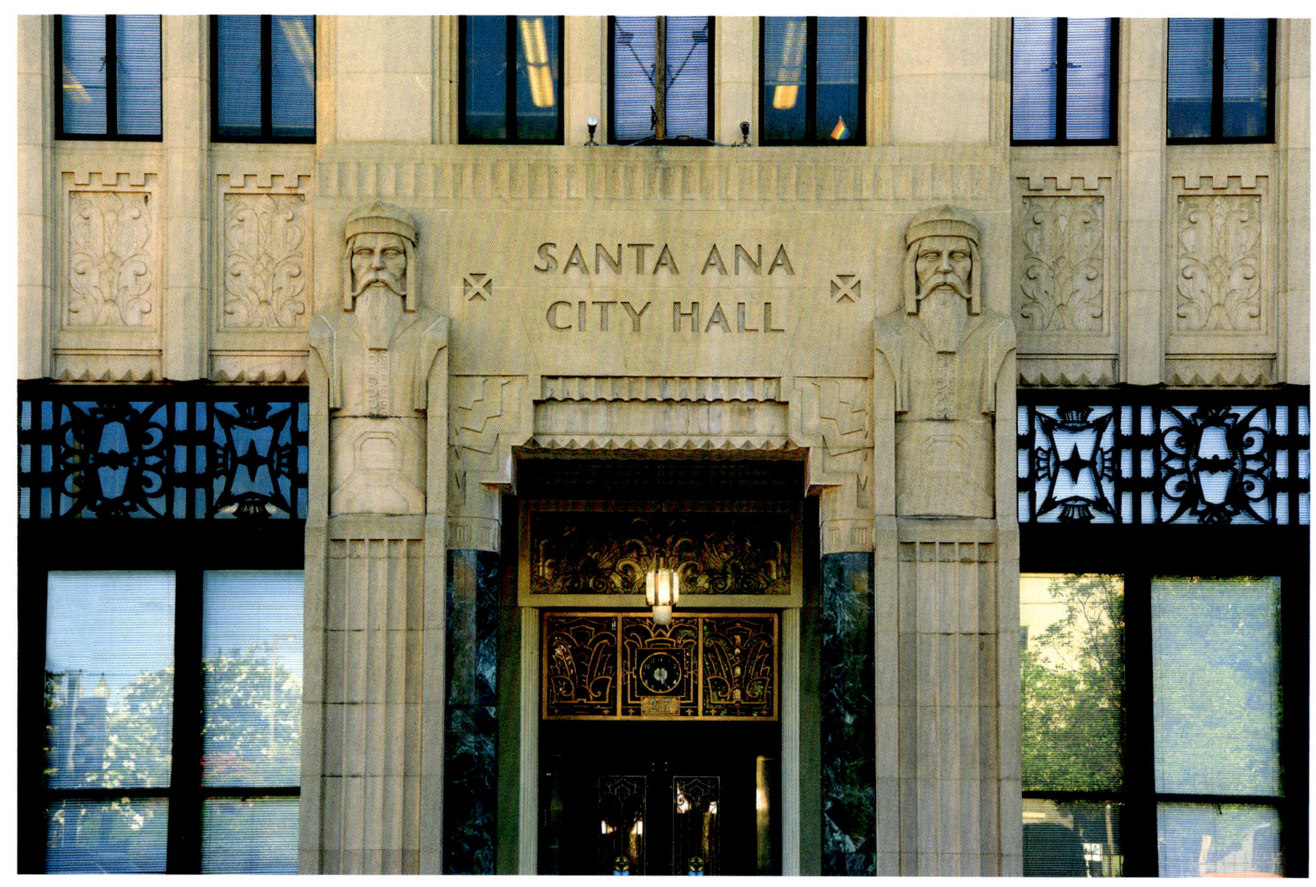

↑ *Former Santa Ana City Hall, exterior detail (W. Horace Austin, 1935) 217 N. Main St., Santa Ana, photographed 2024.*

→ *Los Angeles County/USC Medical Center (Allied Architects, 1933) 1200 N. State St., photographed 2024.*

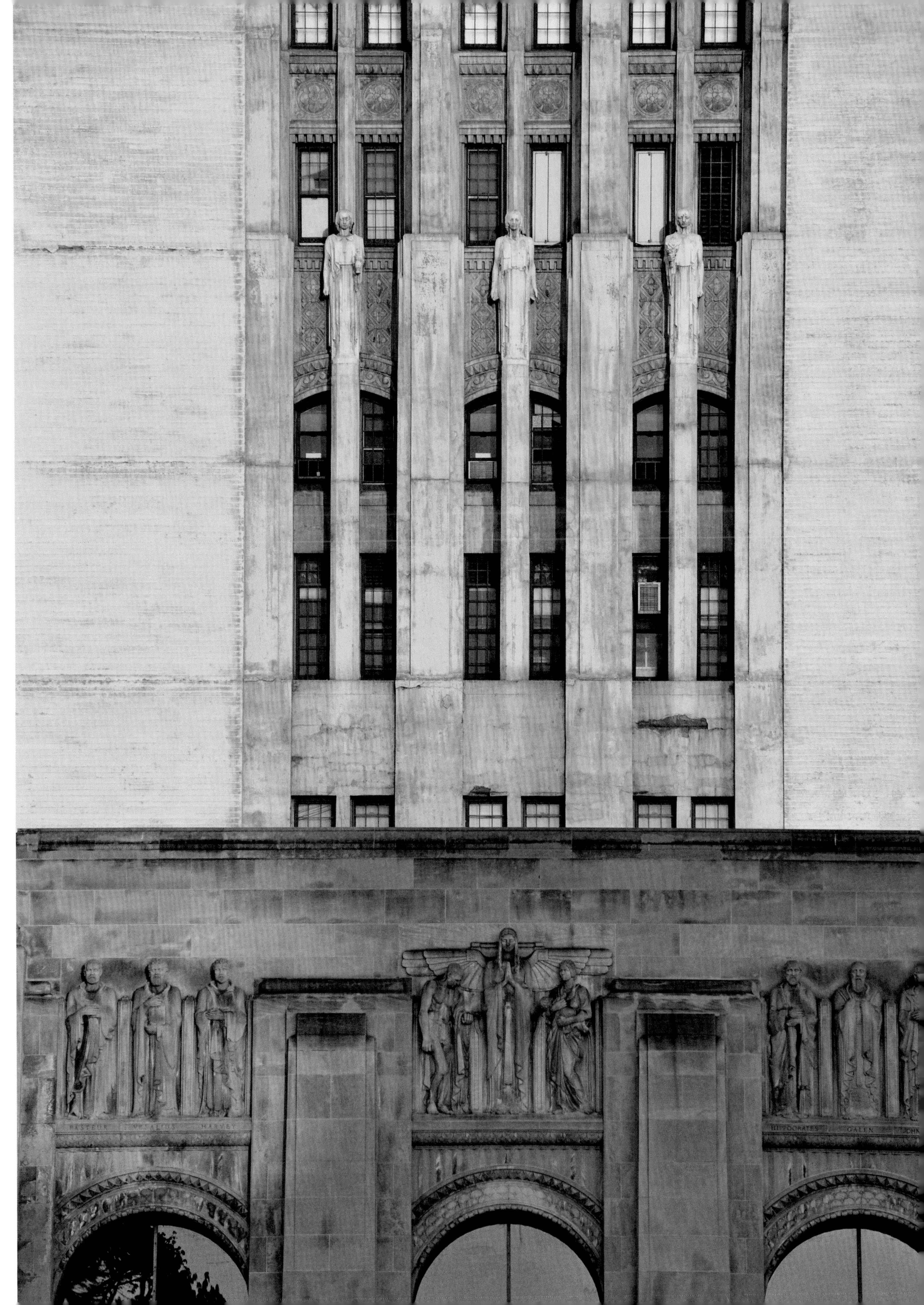
PASTEUR
VESALIUS
HARVEY
HIPPOCRATES
GALEN

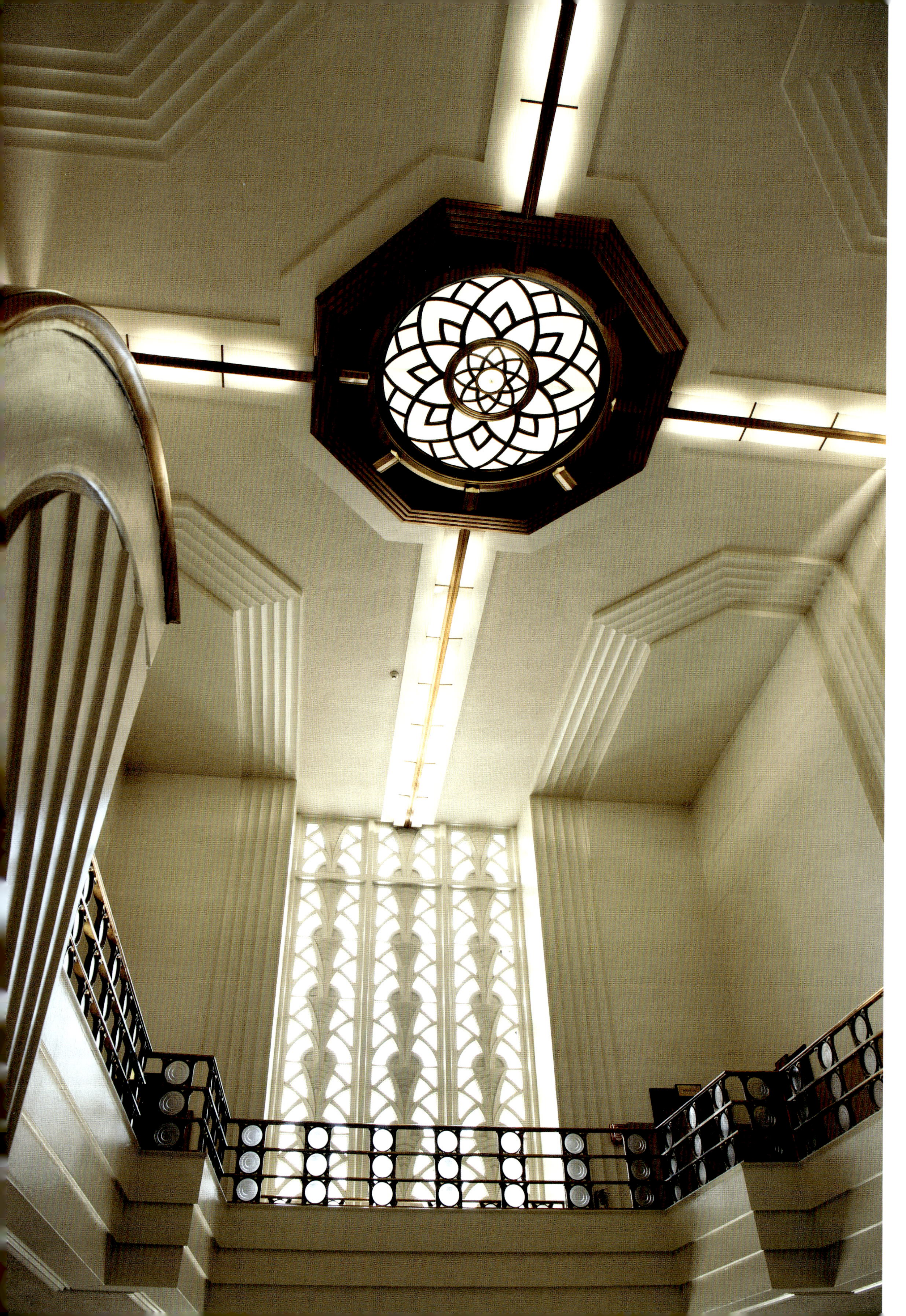

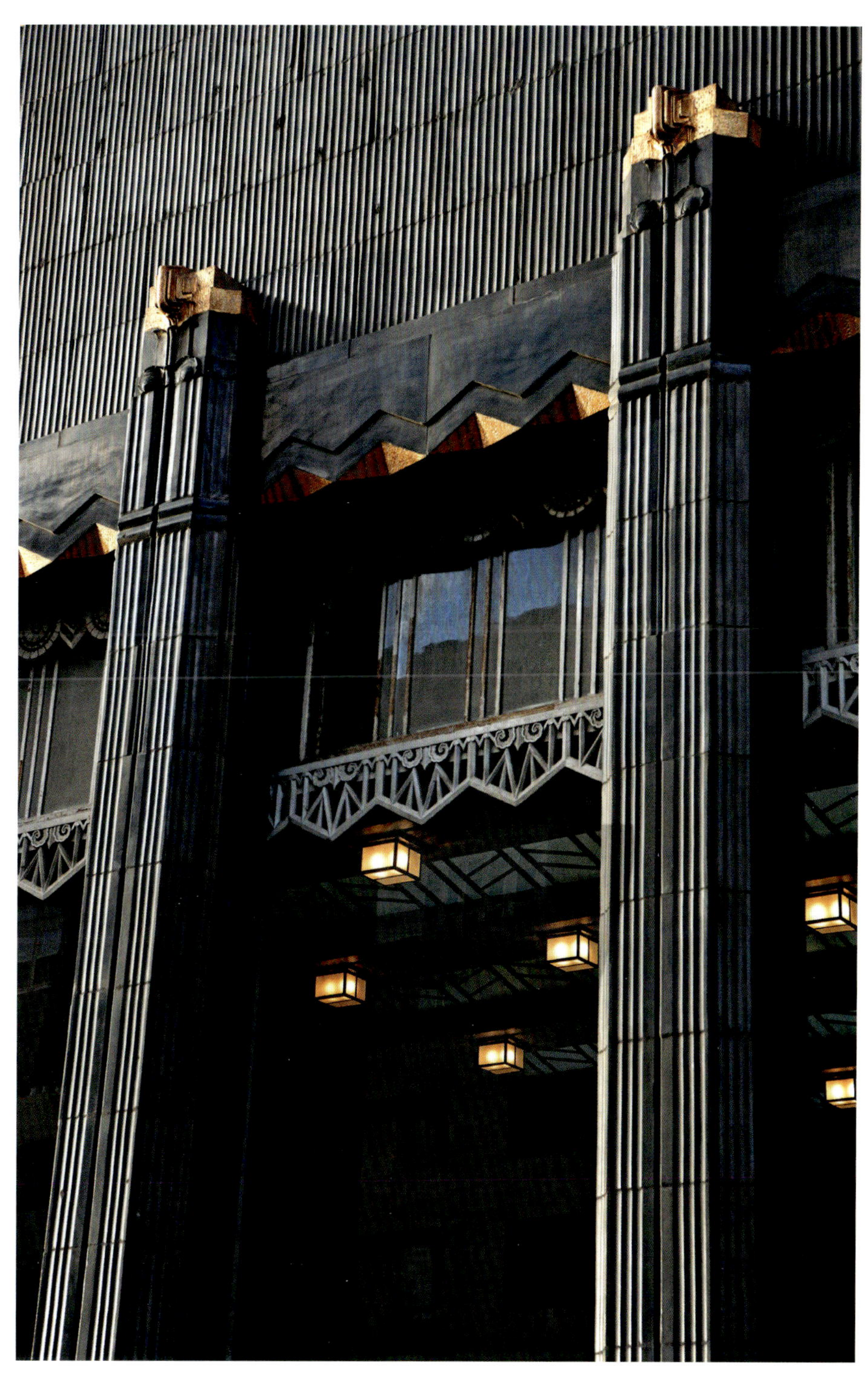

← *Burbank City Hall, interior detail (William Allen and George Lutzi, 1943) 275 E. Olive Ave., photographed 2024.*

↑ *The Deco Building (Morgan, Walls, and Clements, 1929) 5209 Wilshire Blvd., photographed 2024.*

OVERLEAF: *Lafayette Apartments, exterior detail (Shilling and Shilling, 1928) 140 Linden Ave., Long Beach, photographed 2024.*

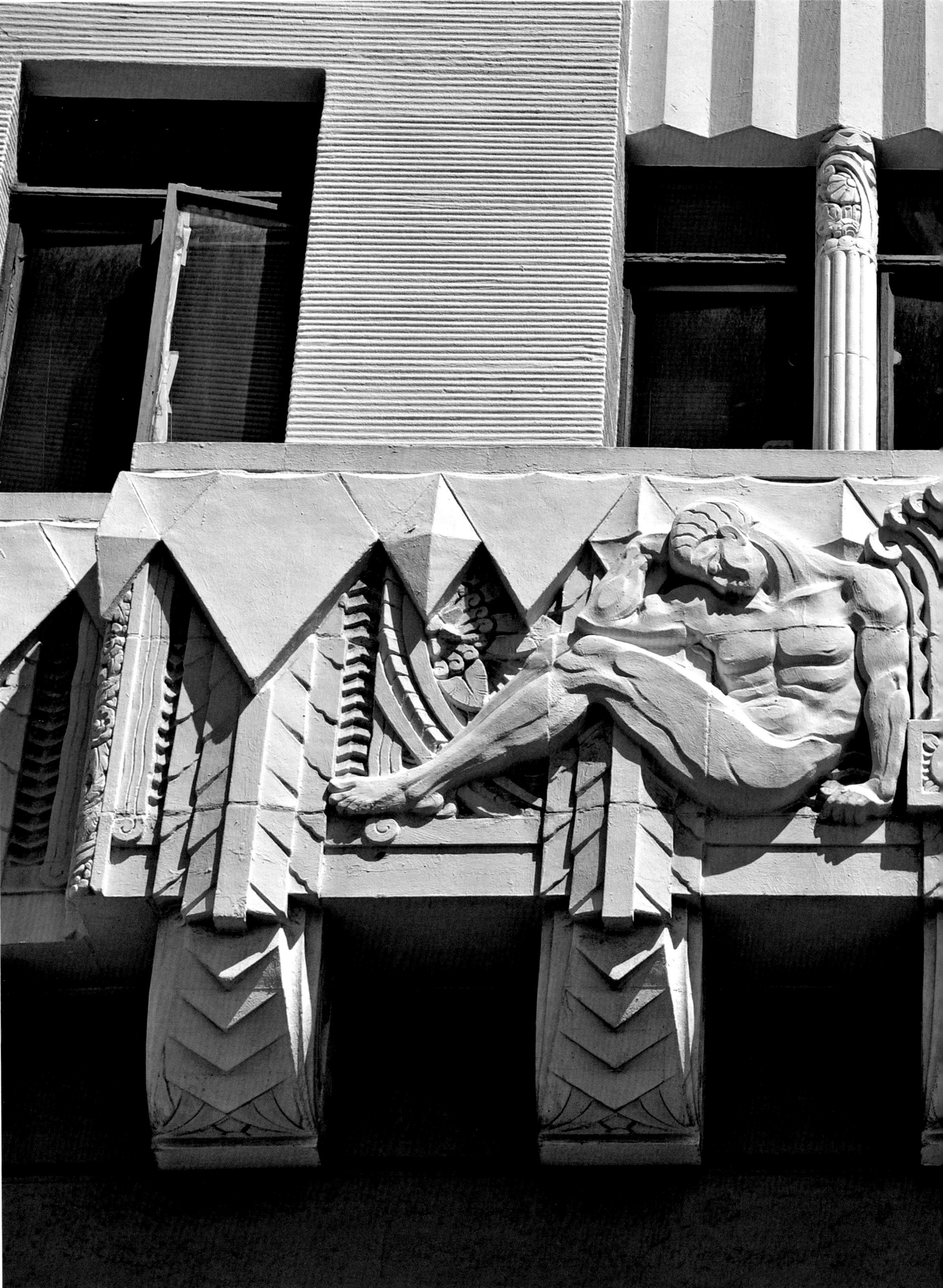

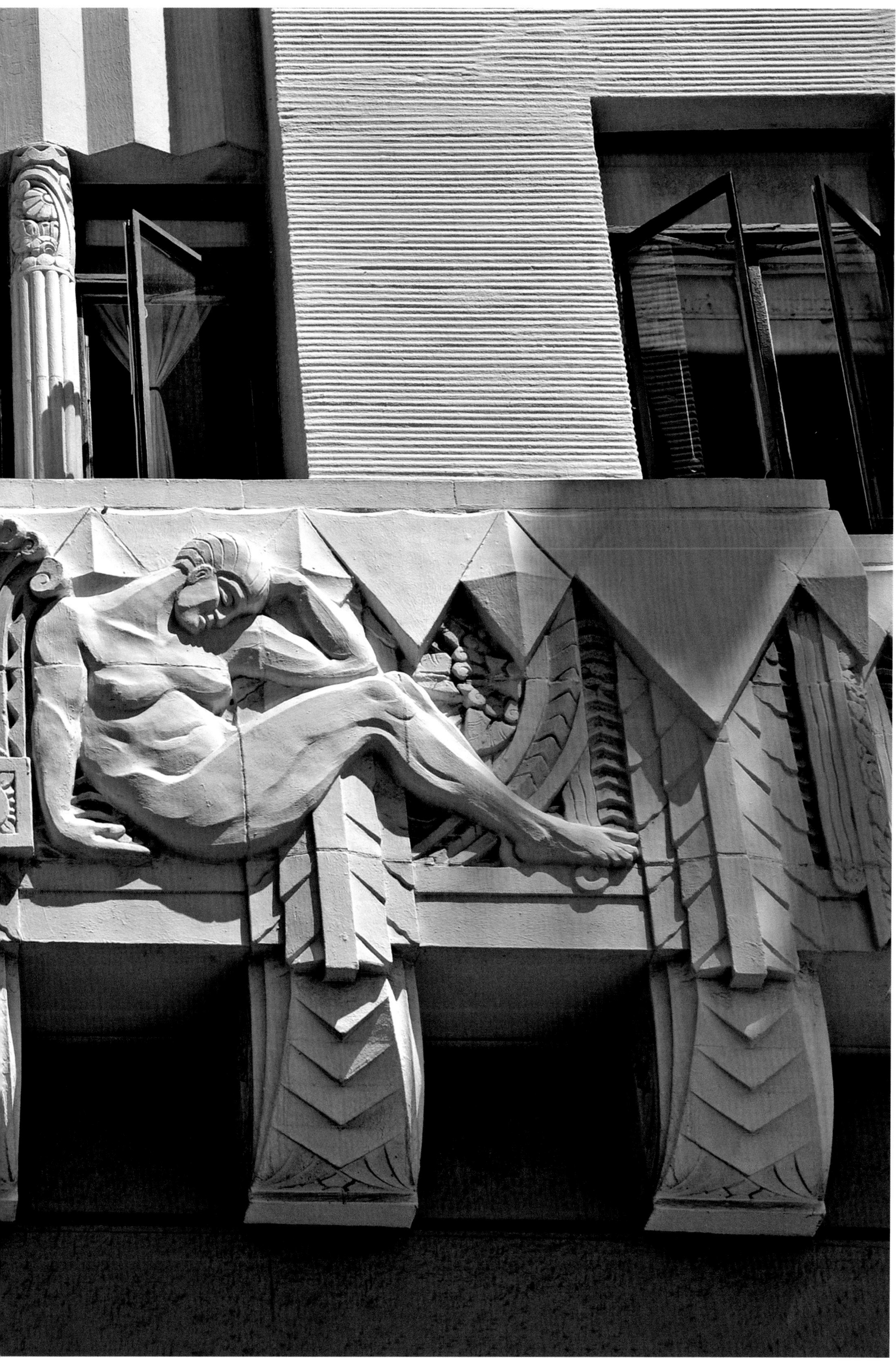

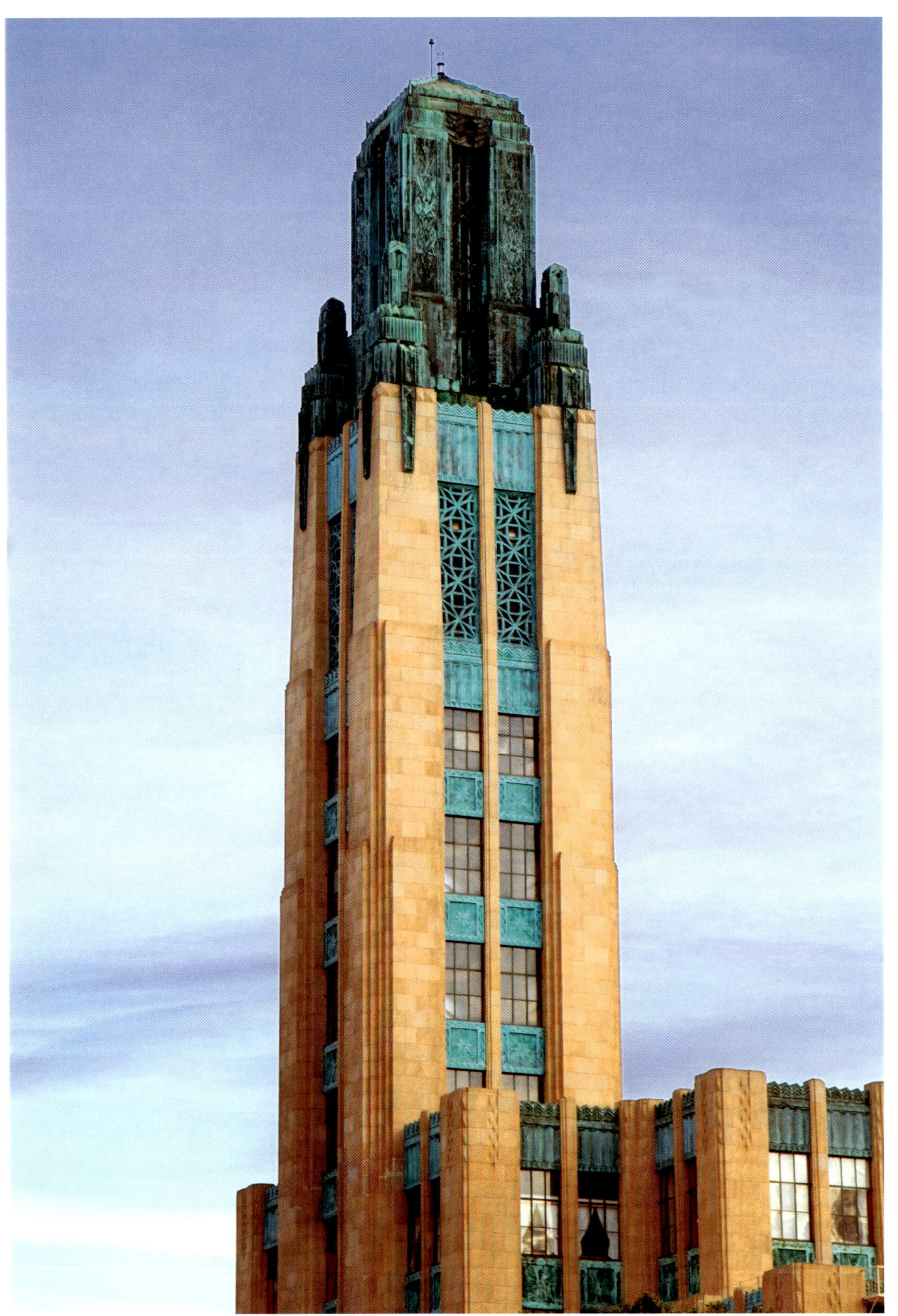

↑ *Bullock's Wilshire, now Southwestern Law School (John Parkinson and Donald B. Parkinson, 1929) 3050 Wilshire Blvd., photographed 2003.*

→ *Samuel-Novarro House (Lloyd Wright, 1928) 5609 Valley Oak Dr., photographed 2024.*

OVERLEAF: *Wiltern Theatre and Pellissier Building, ceiling detail (Morgan, Walls, and Clements, 1931) 3790 Wilshire Blvd., photographed 2010.*

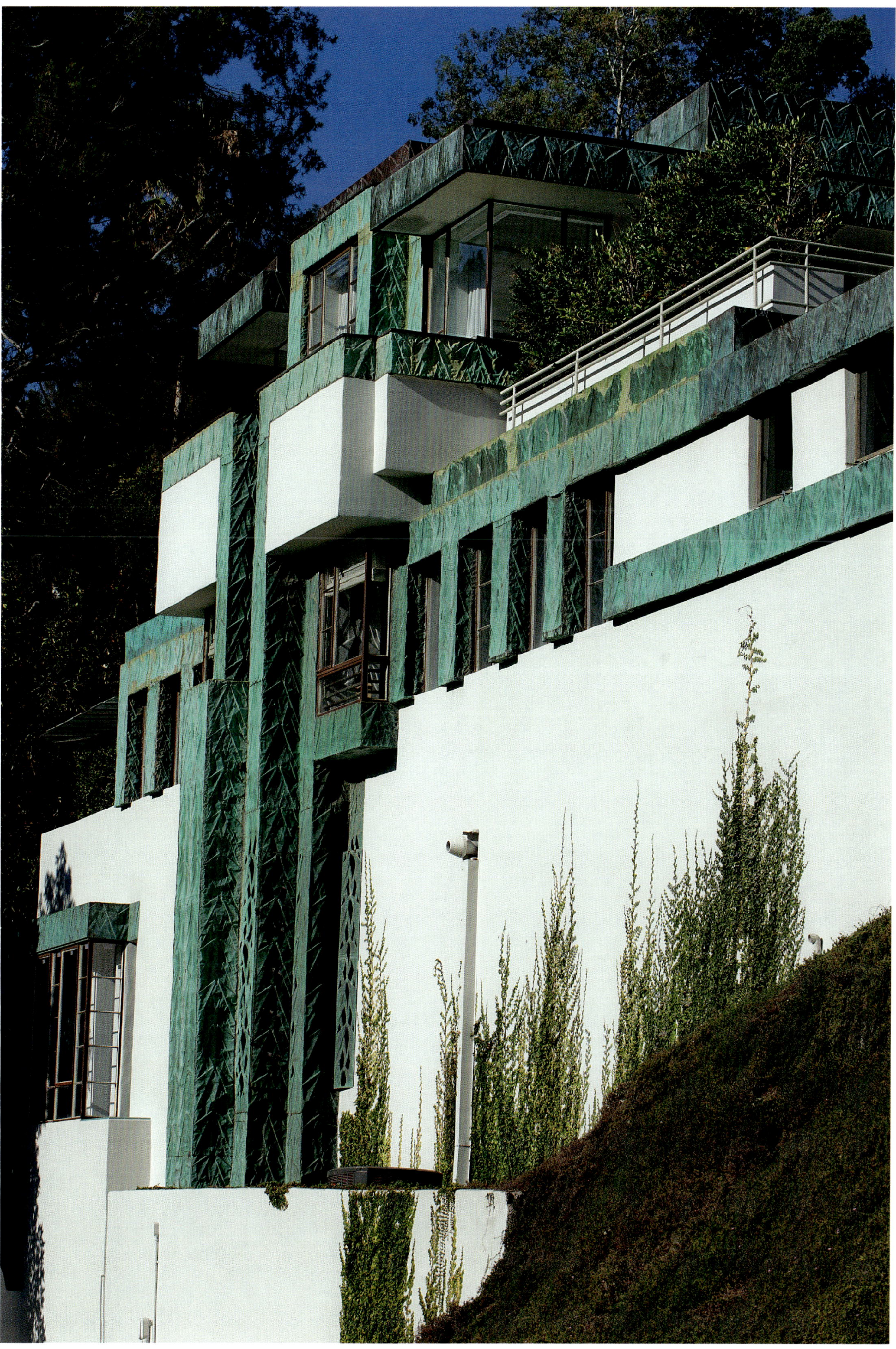

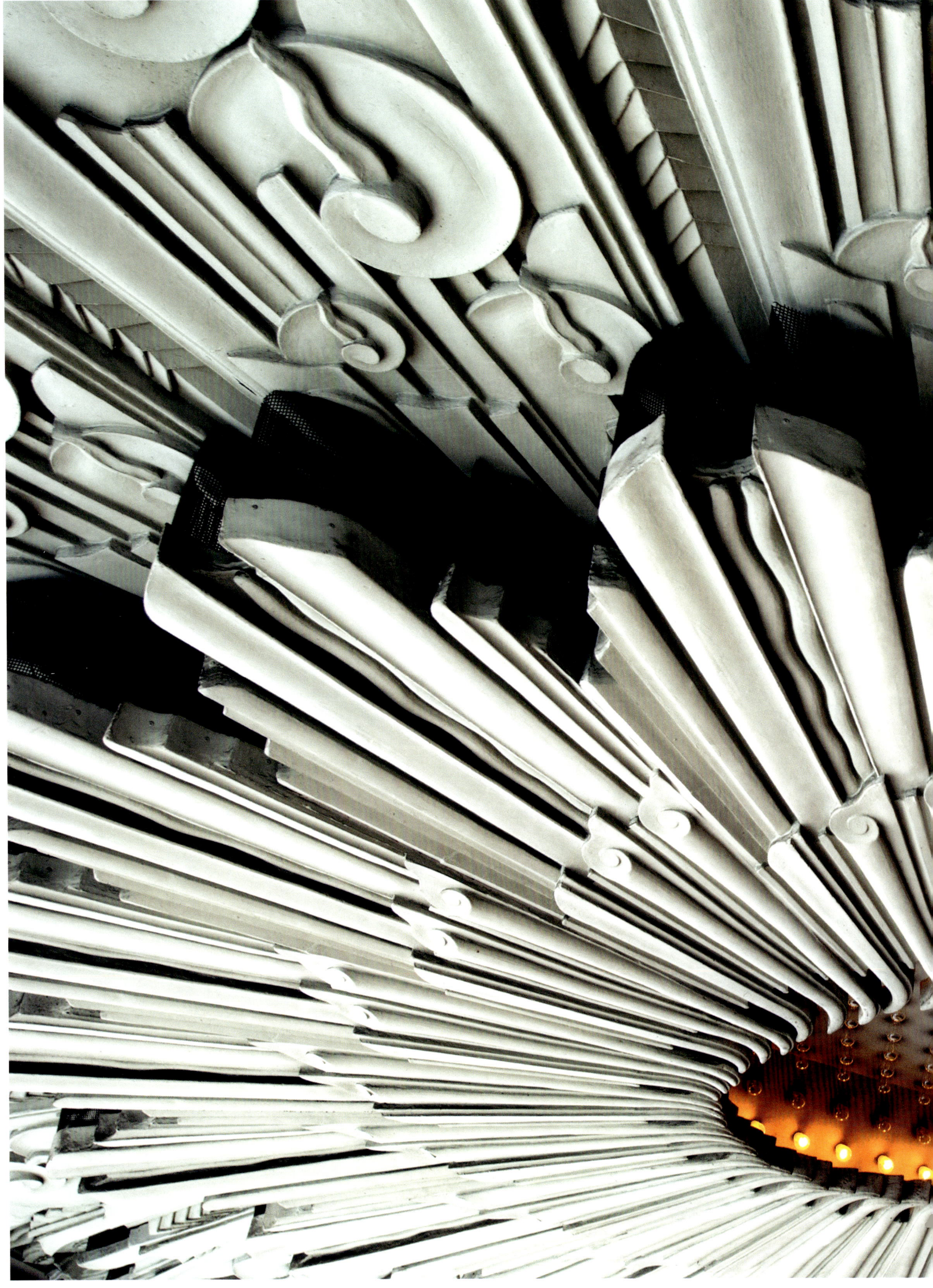

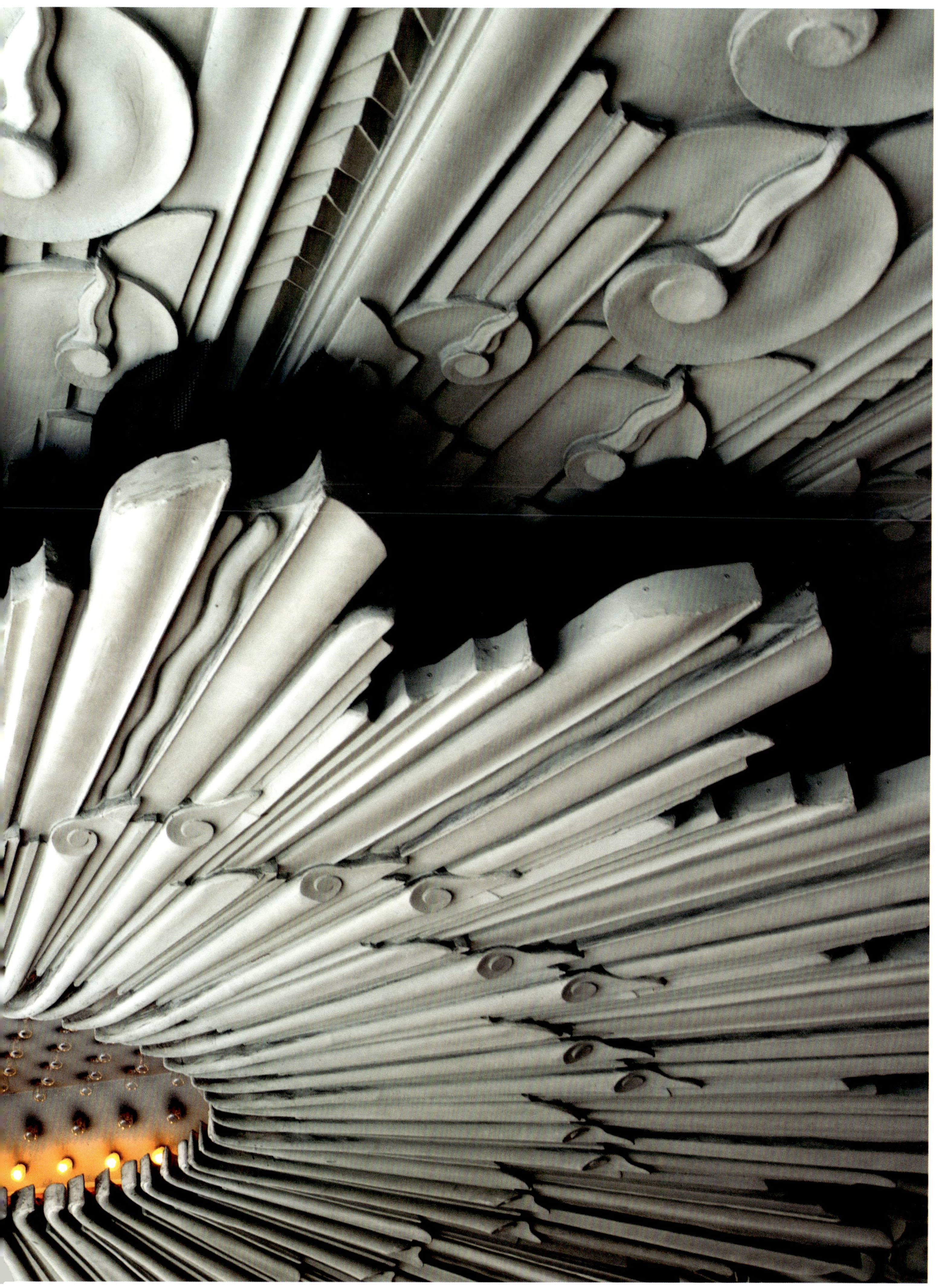

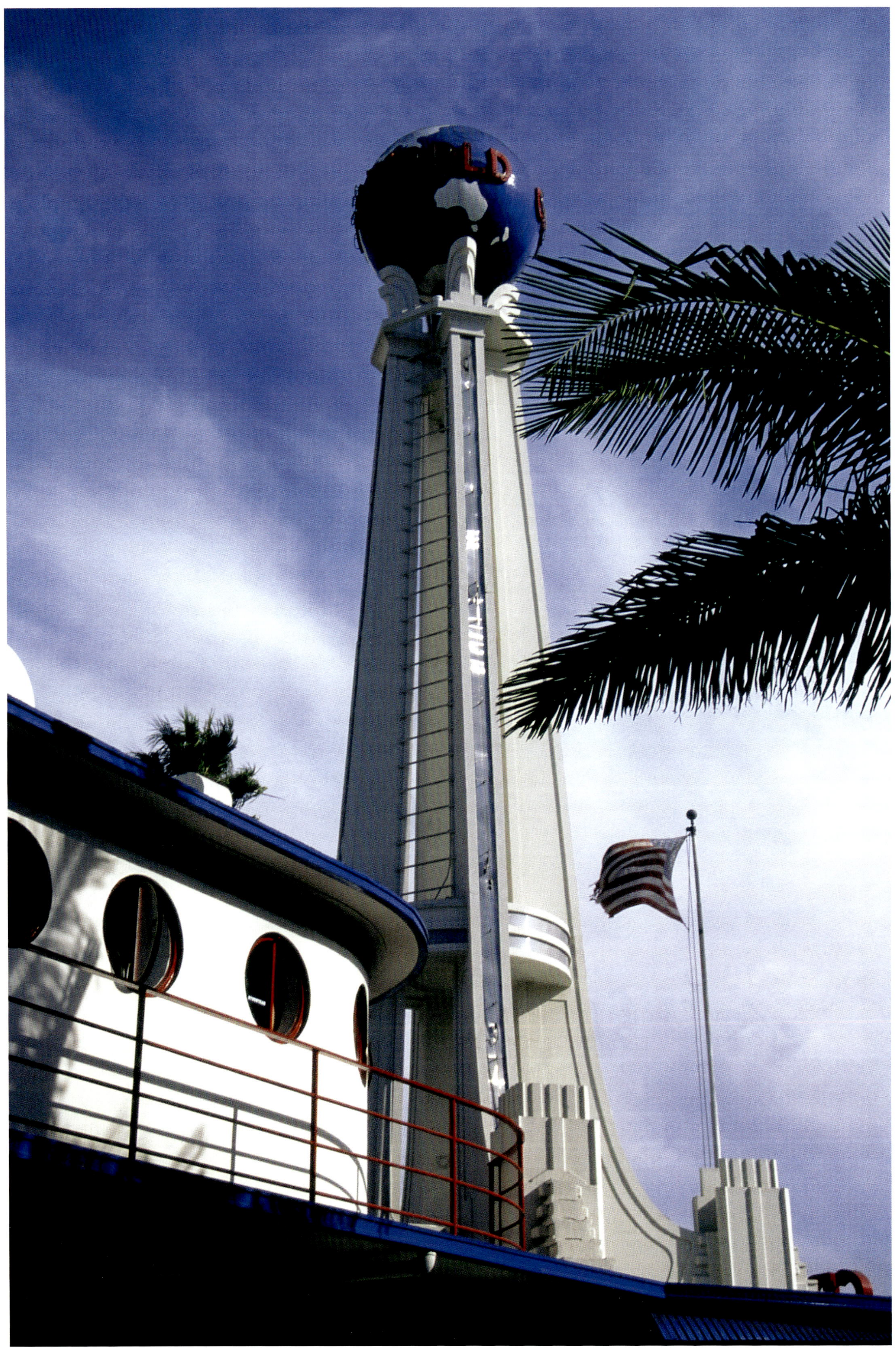

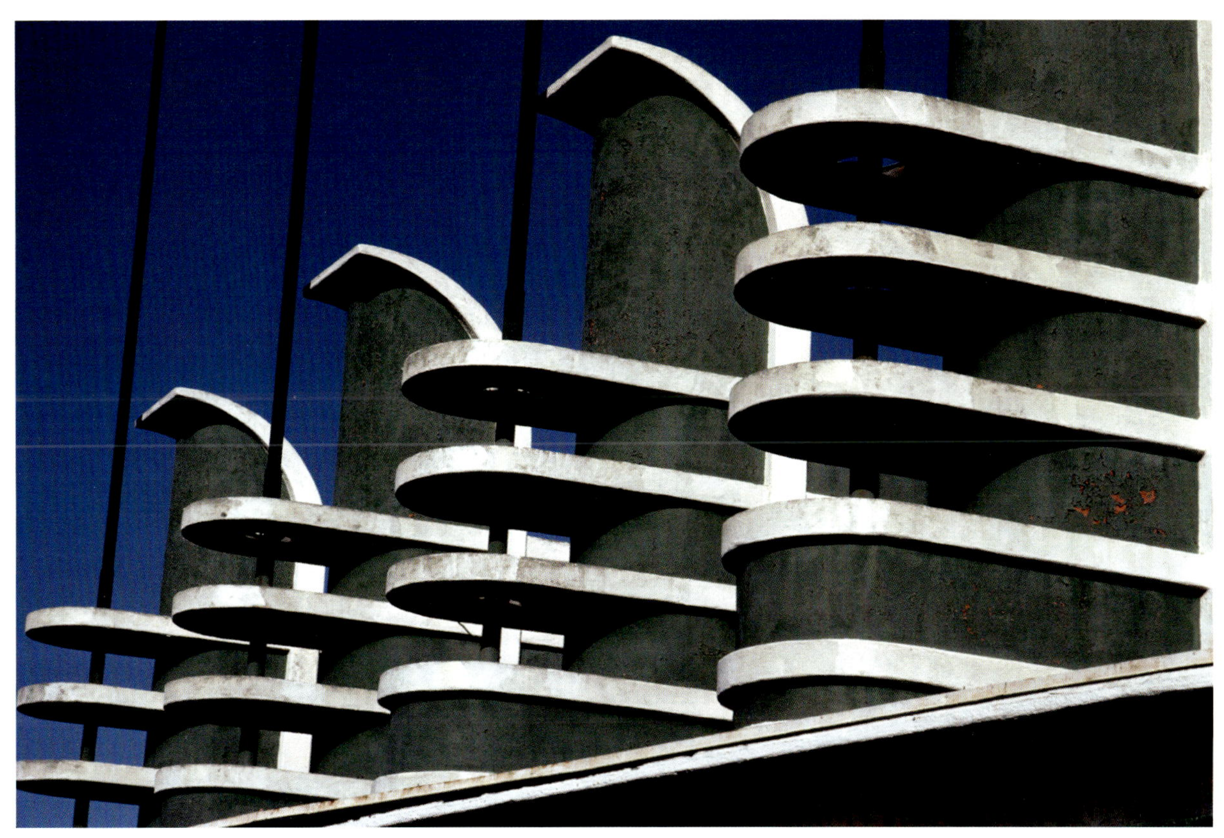

← *Crossroads of the World (Robert V. Derrah, 1936) 6671 Sunset Blvd., photographed 1989.*

↑ *Pan-Pacific Auditorium, exterior detail (Wurdeman & Becket, 1935) formerly at 7600 Beverly Blvd., photographed 1988.*

OVERLEAF: *Max Factor Building, now the Hollywood Museum (S. Charles Lee, 1931) 1660 N. Highland Ave., photographed 1995.*

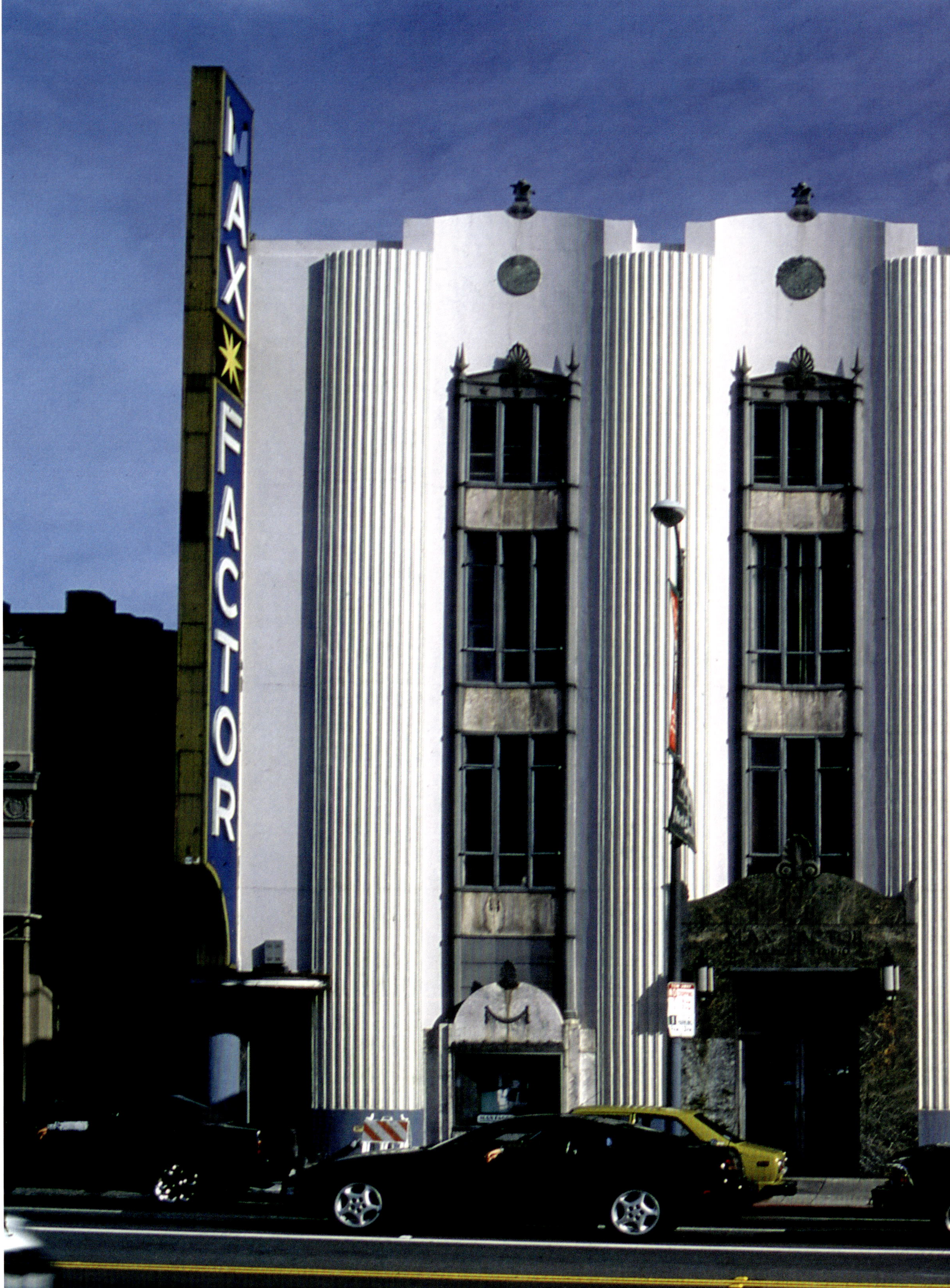
MAX FACTOR

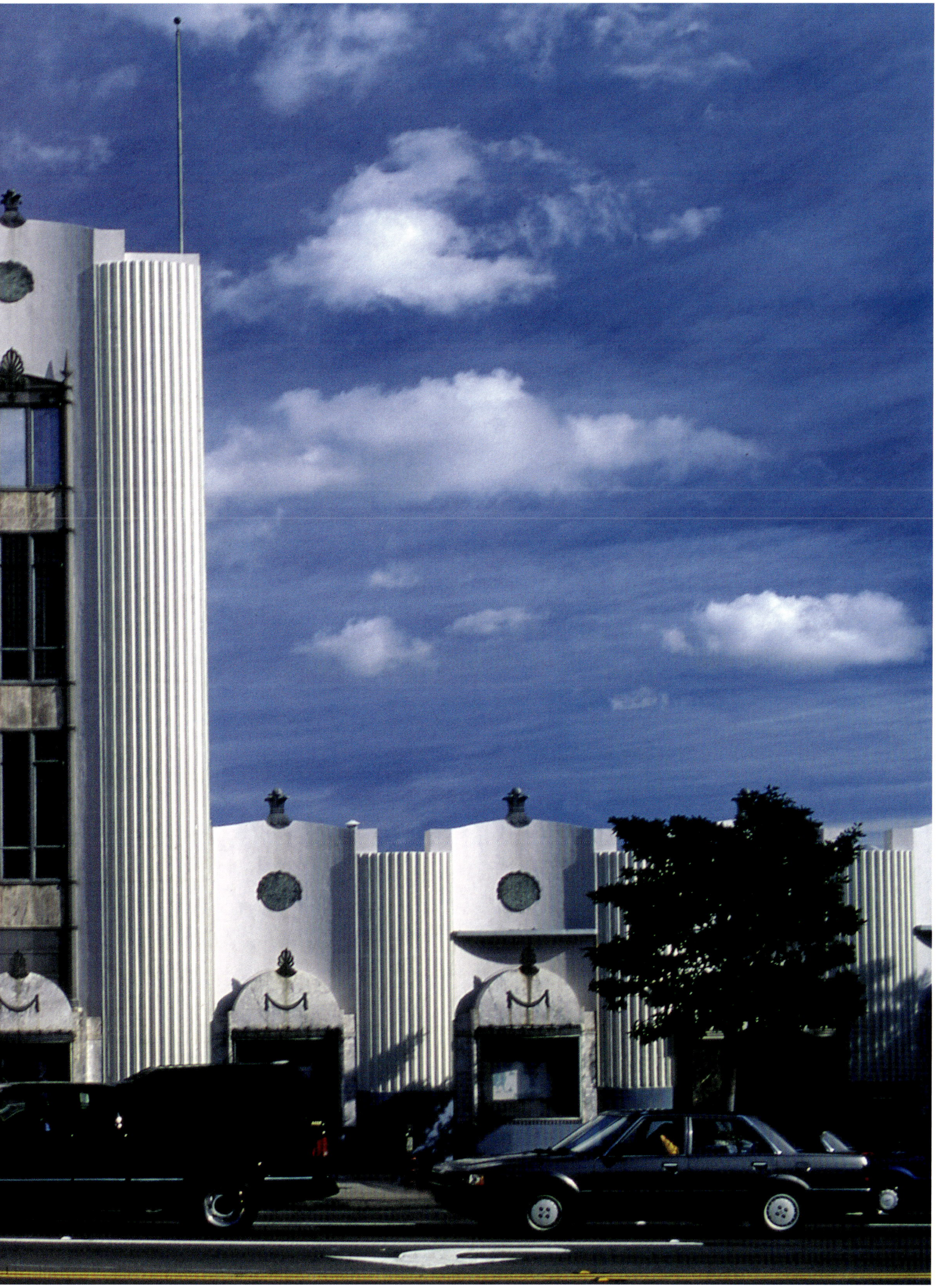

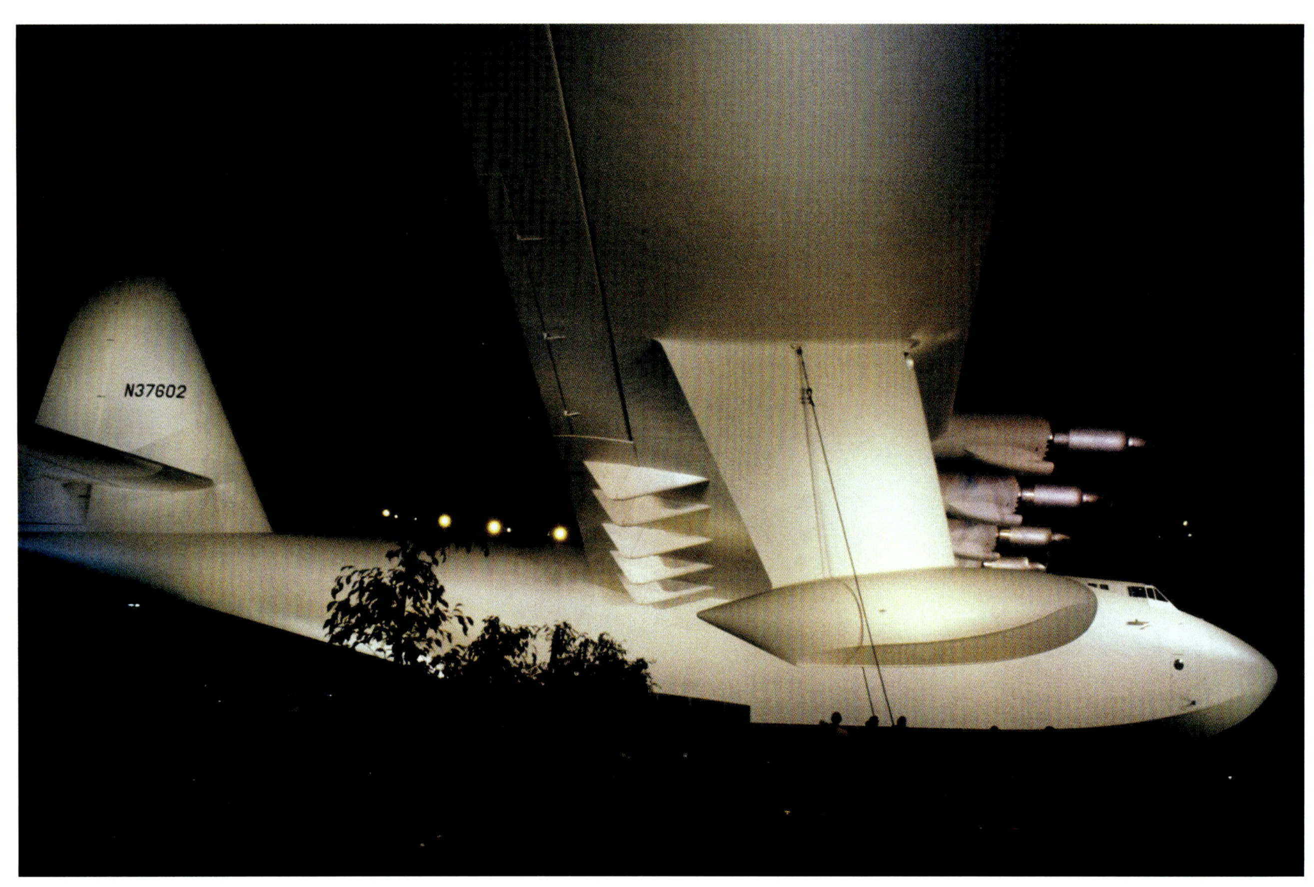

↑ Spruce Goose *(Howard Hughes, 1947) Formerly in Long Beach, now in McMinnville, Oregon. photographed 1982.*

→ *Burbank City Hall, interior stairwell detail (William Allen and George Lutzi, 1943) 275 E. Olive Ave., photographed, 2024.*

OVERLEAF: *High Tower Fourplex (Carl Kay, 1936) 2178 High Tower Dr., photographed 1985.*

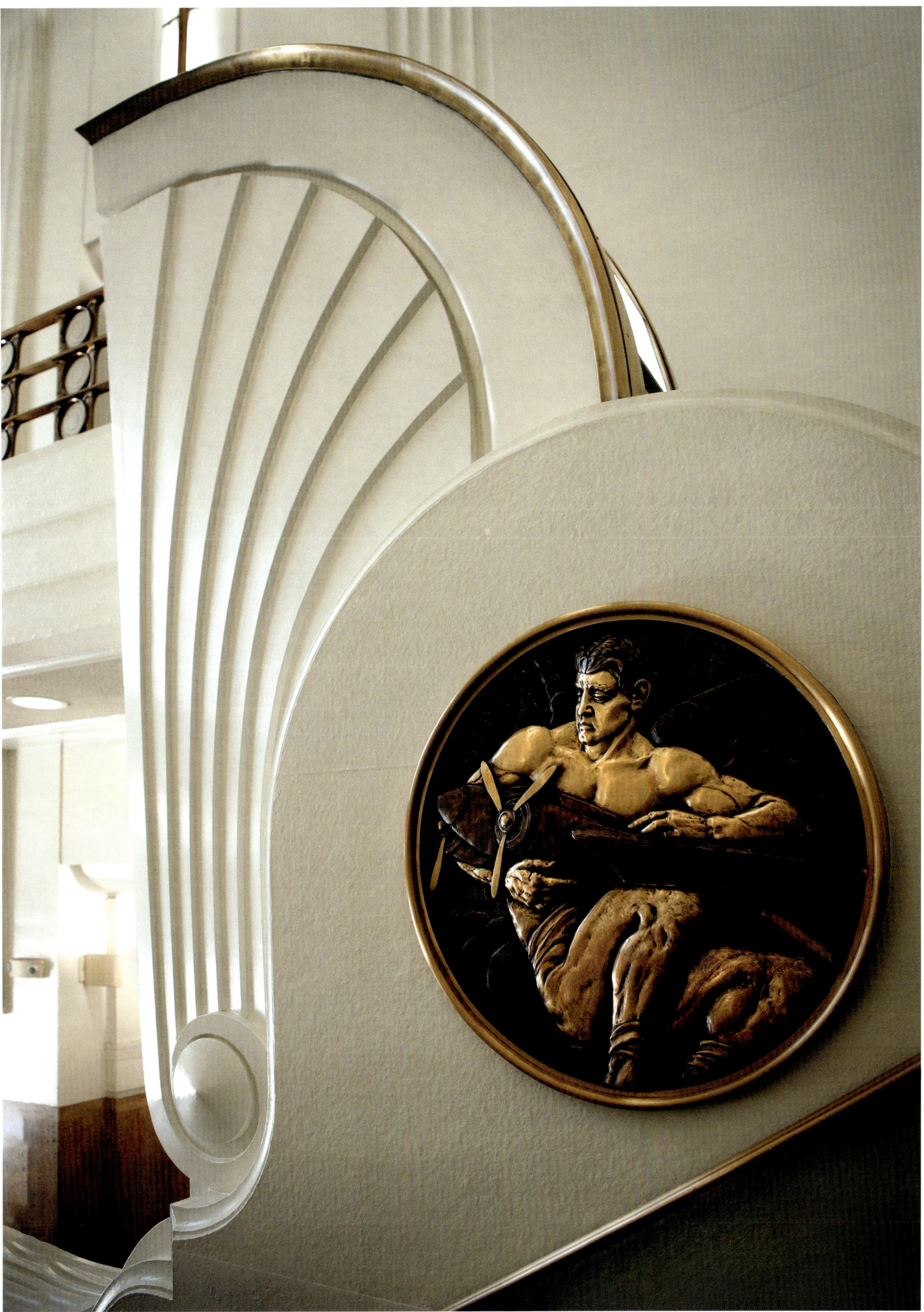

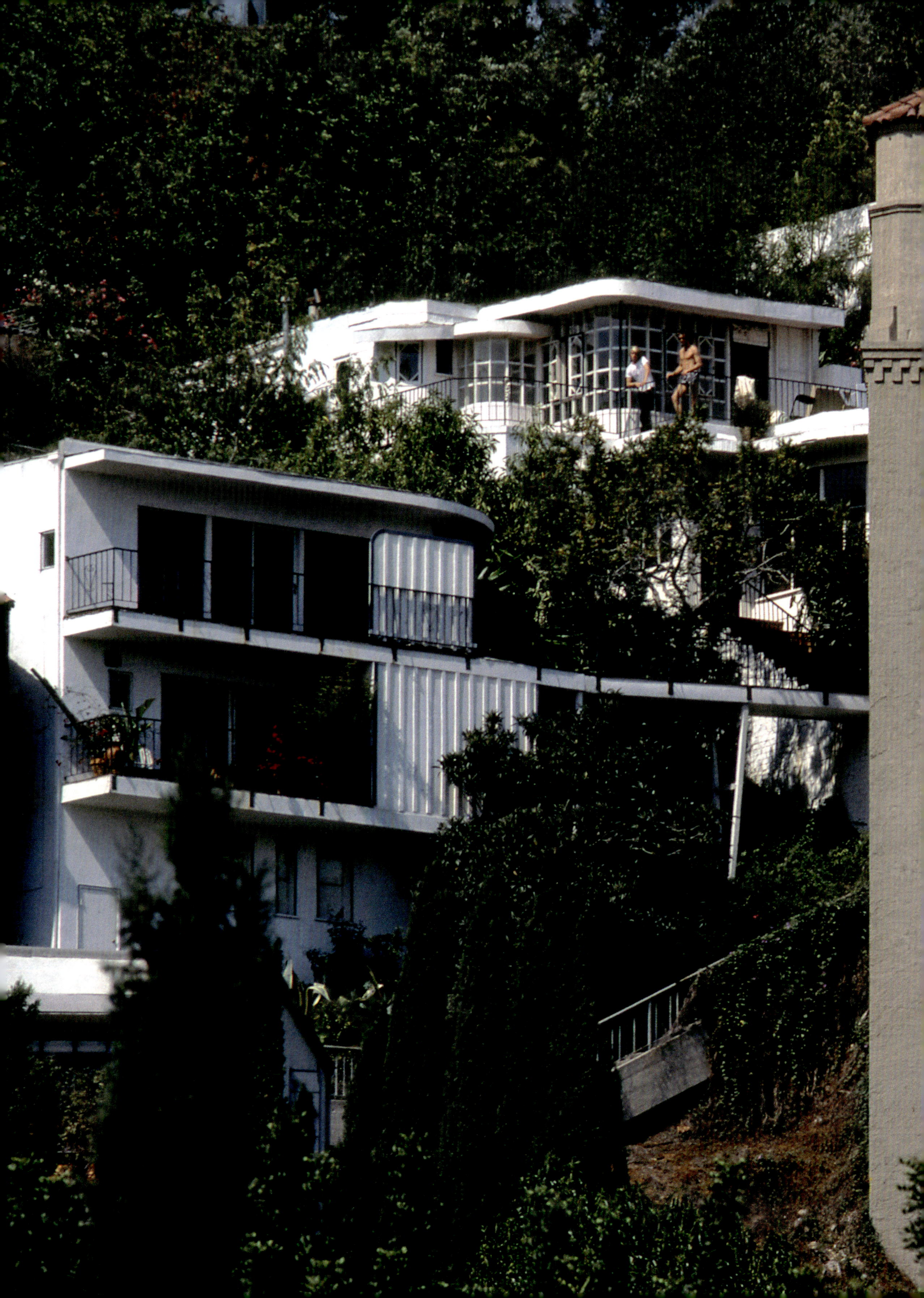

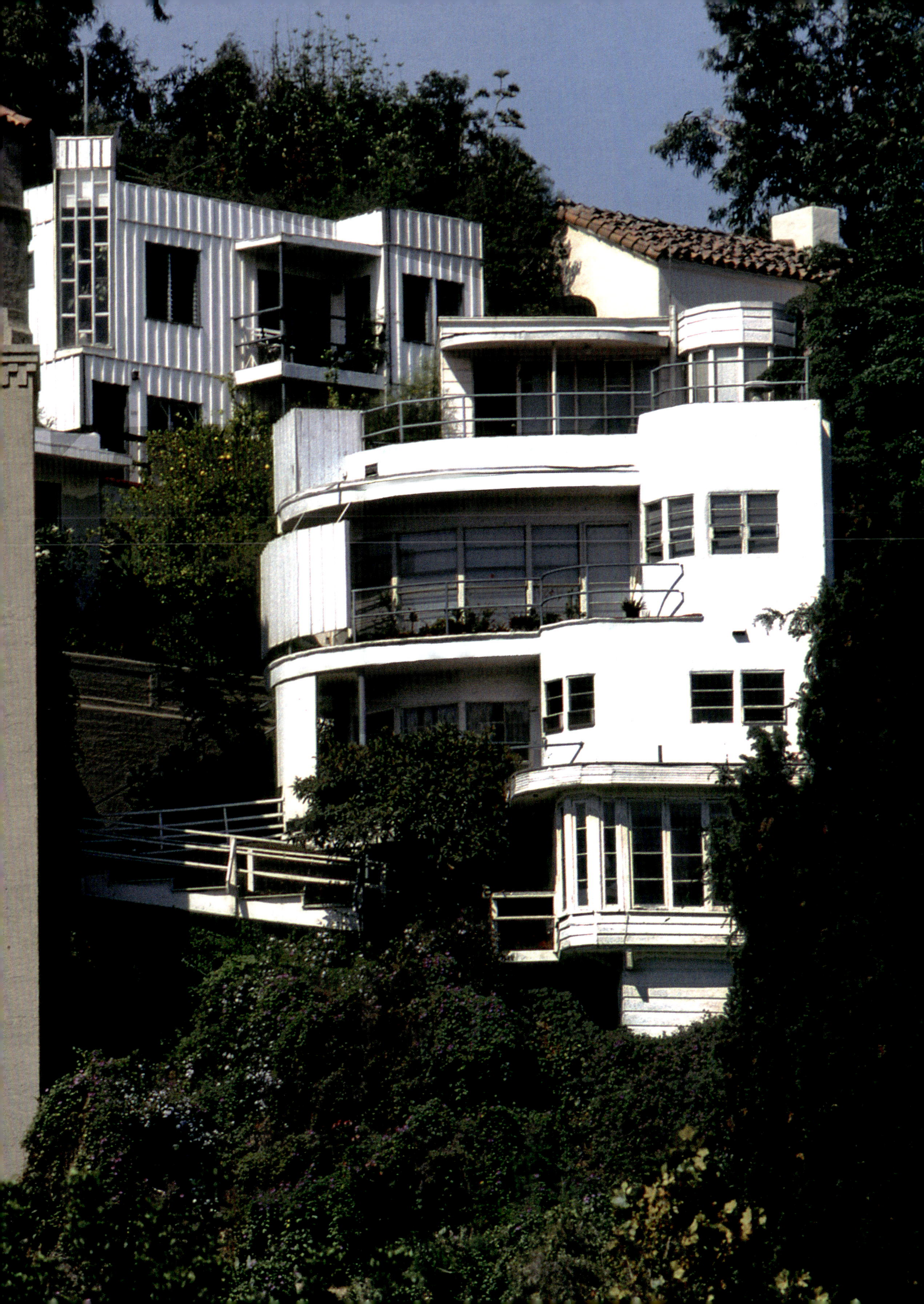

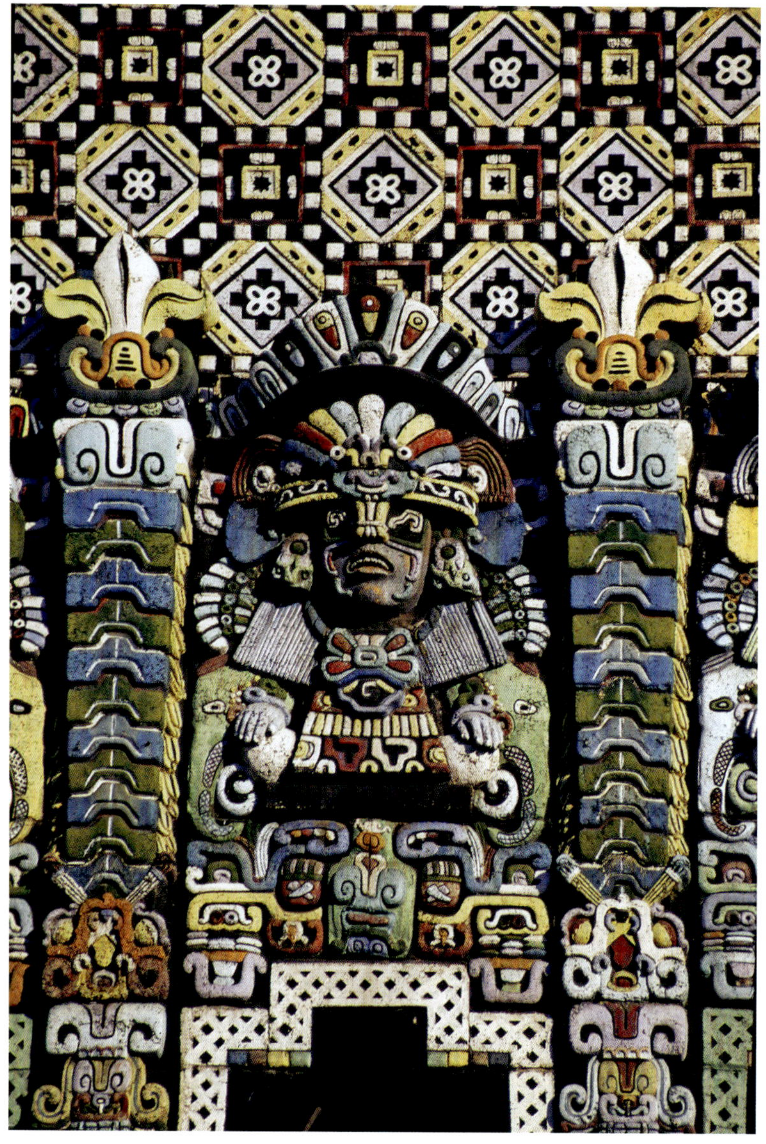

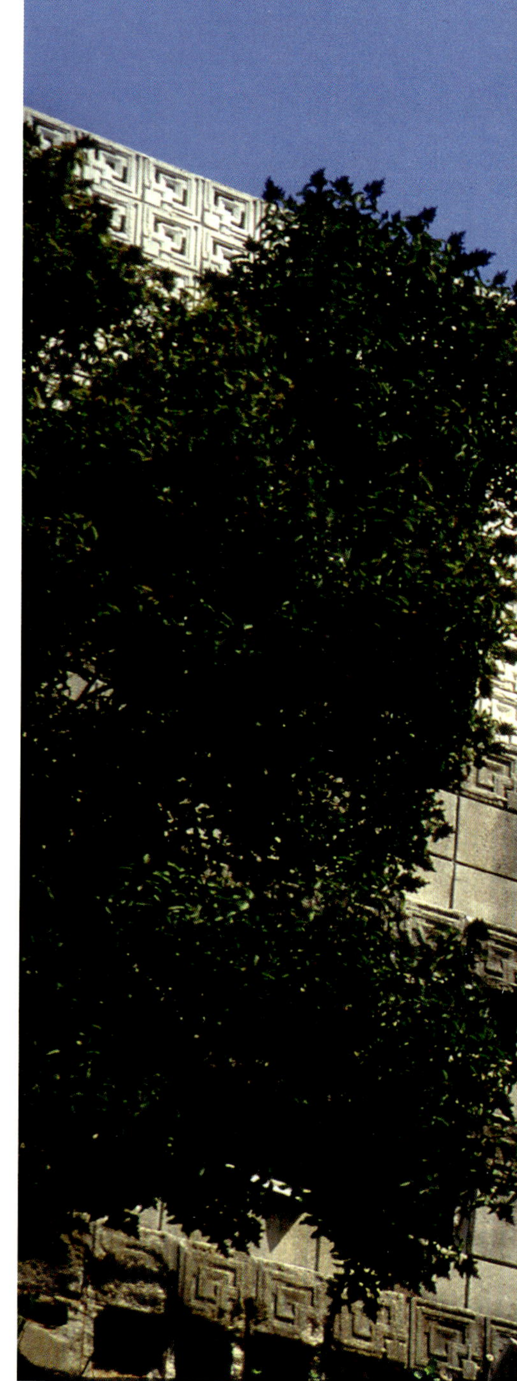

↑ *Mayan Theatre, exterior detail (Morgan, Walls, and Clements; façade by Francisco Cornejo, 1927) 1038 S. Hill St., photographed 2003.*

→ *Ennis House (Frank Lloyd Wright, 1924) 2607 Glendower Ave., photographed 2003.*

OVERLEAF: *Elks Lodge, now The MacArthur, exterior detail (Curlett and Beelman, 1924) 607 S. Park View St., photographed 2024.*

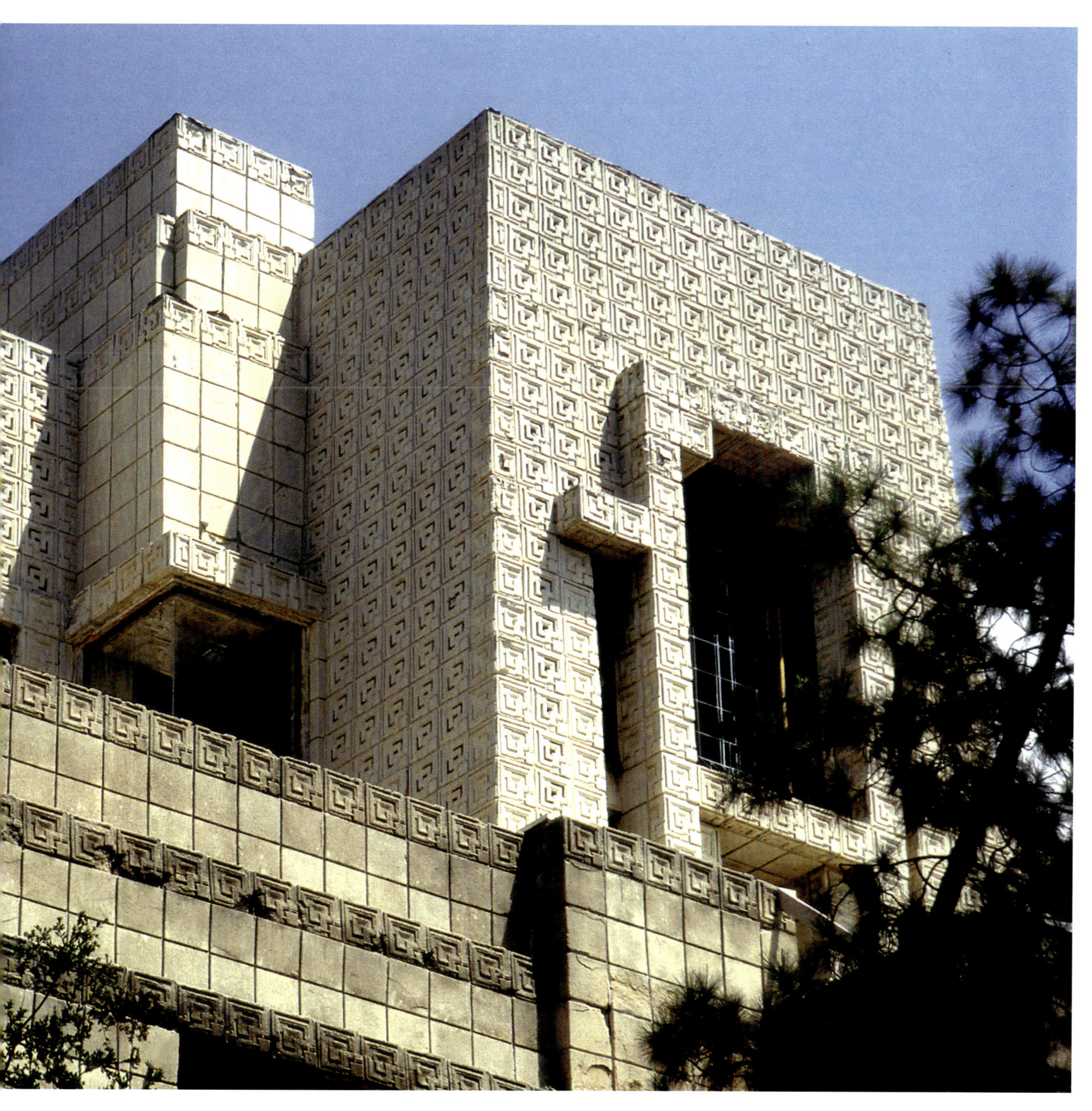

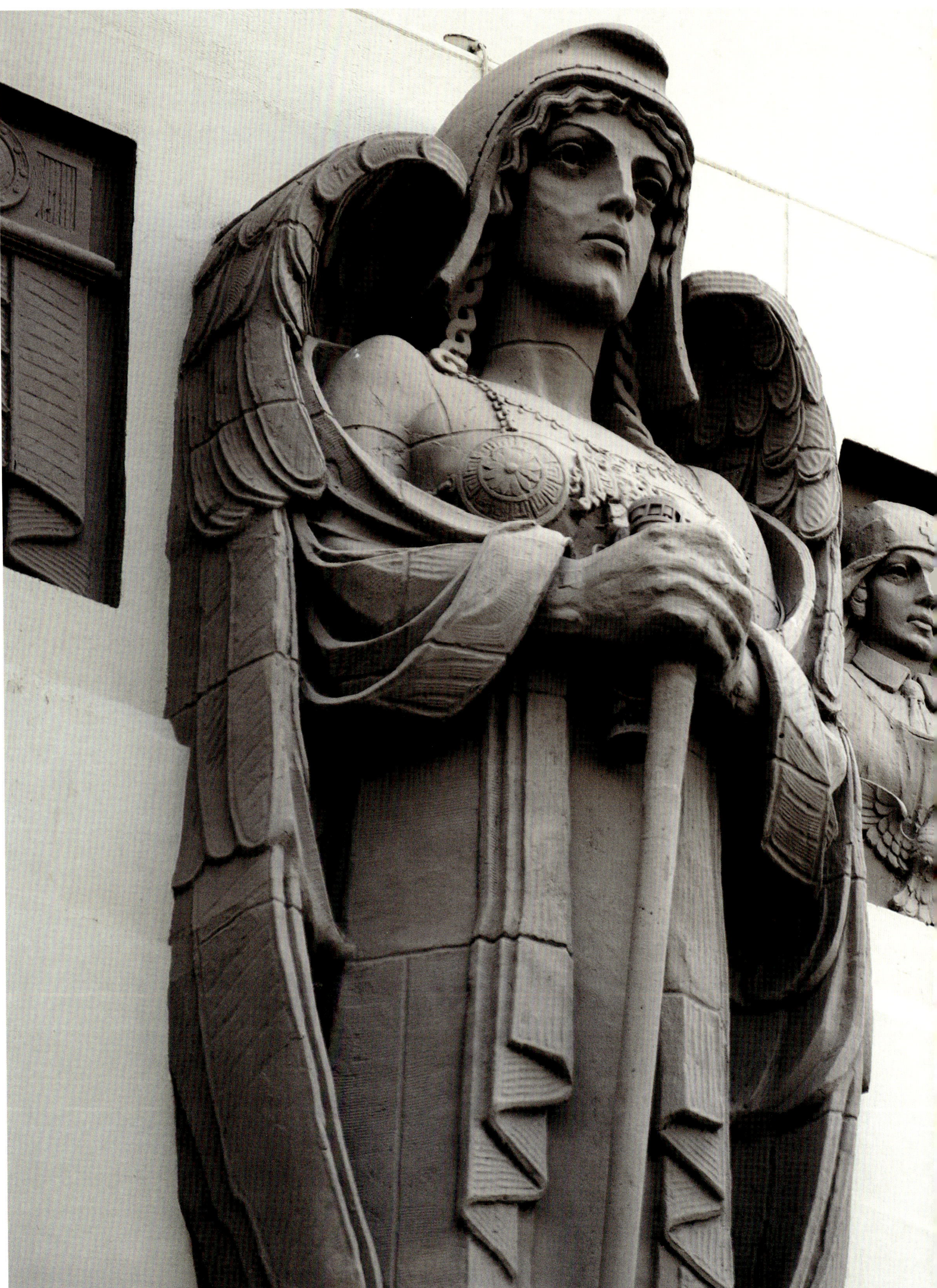

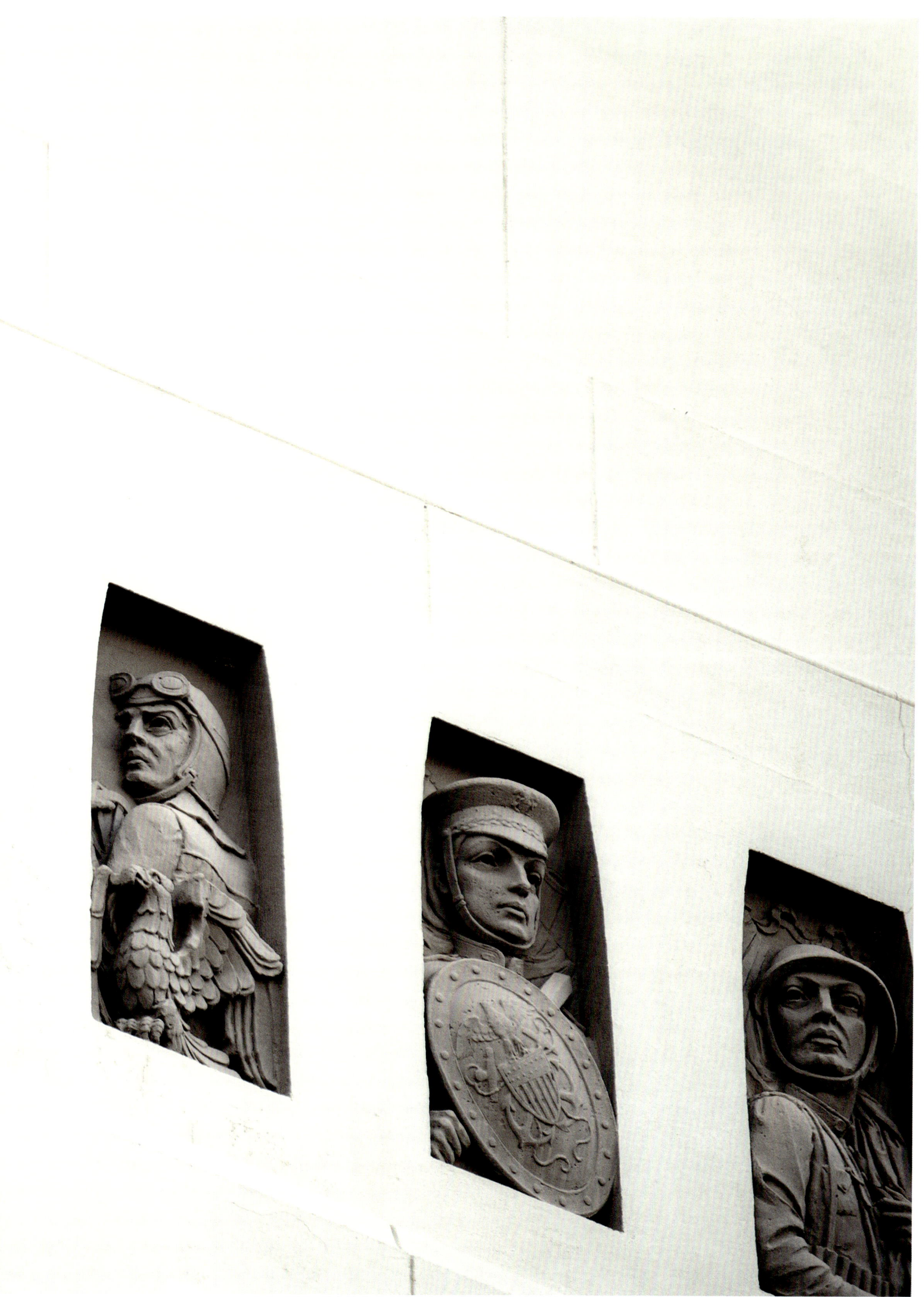

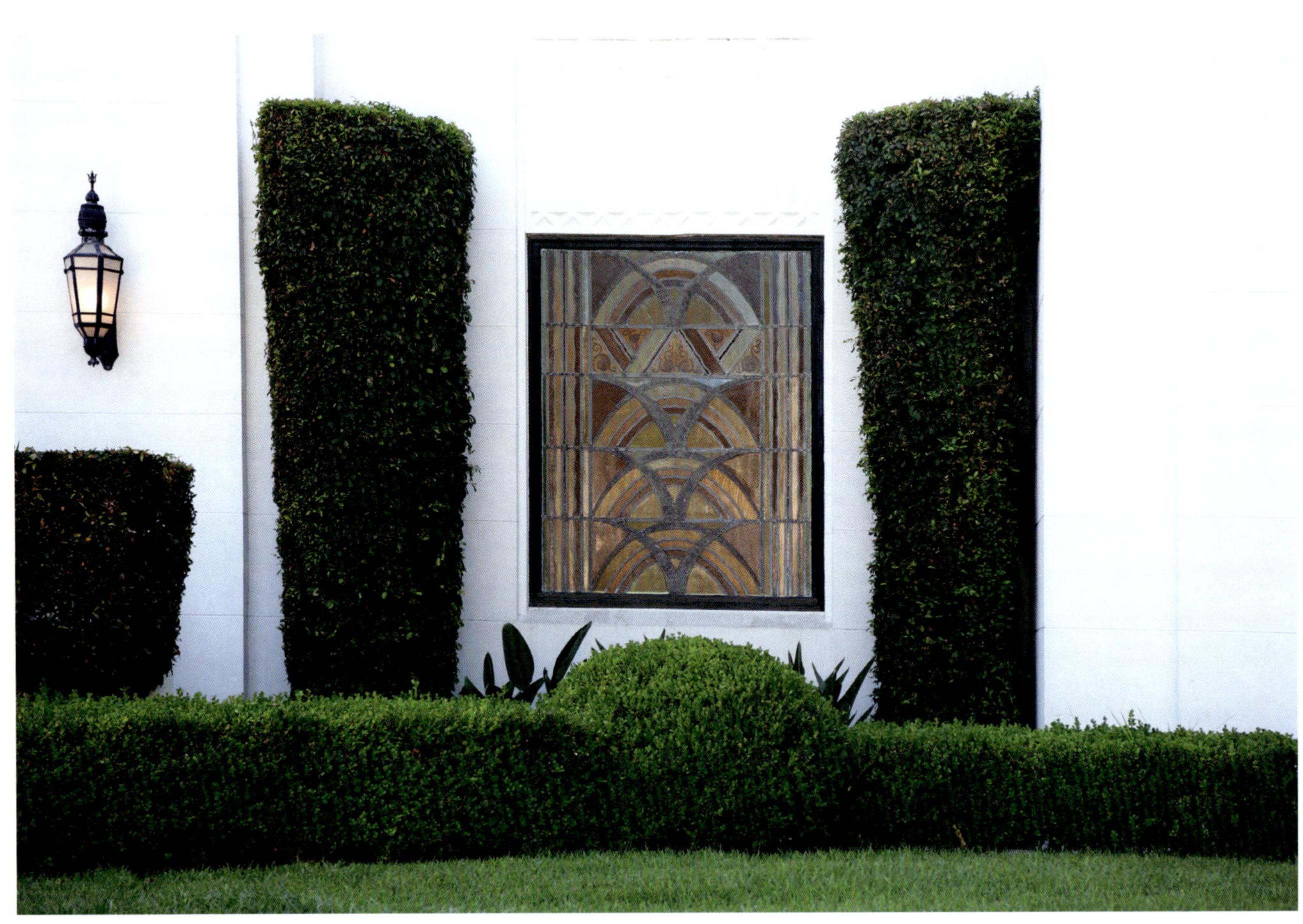

↑ *Smith House, window detail (Clarence J. Smale, 1930) 189 S. Hudson Ave., photographed 2024.*

→ *Sowden House, exterior detail (Lloyd Wright, 1926) 5121 Franklin Ave., photographed 2001.*

OVERLEAF: *Warner Building, façade detail (Marston and Maybury, 1927) 481 E. Colorado Blvd., photographed 2024.*

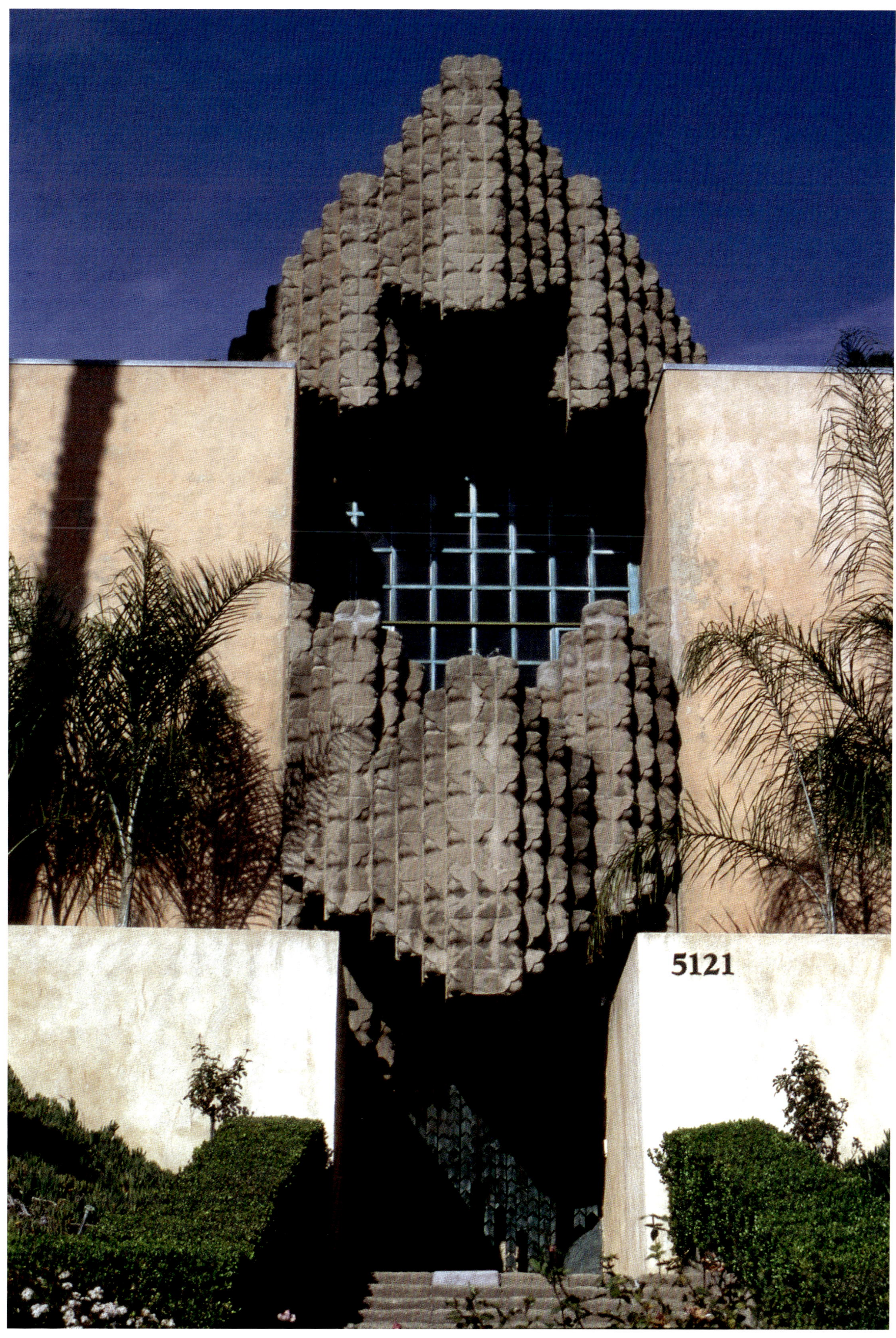
5121

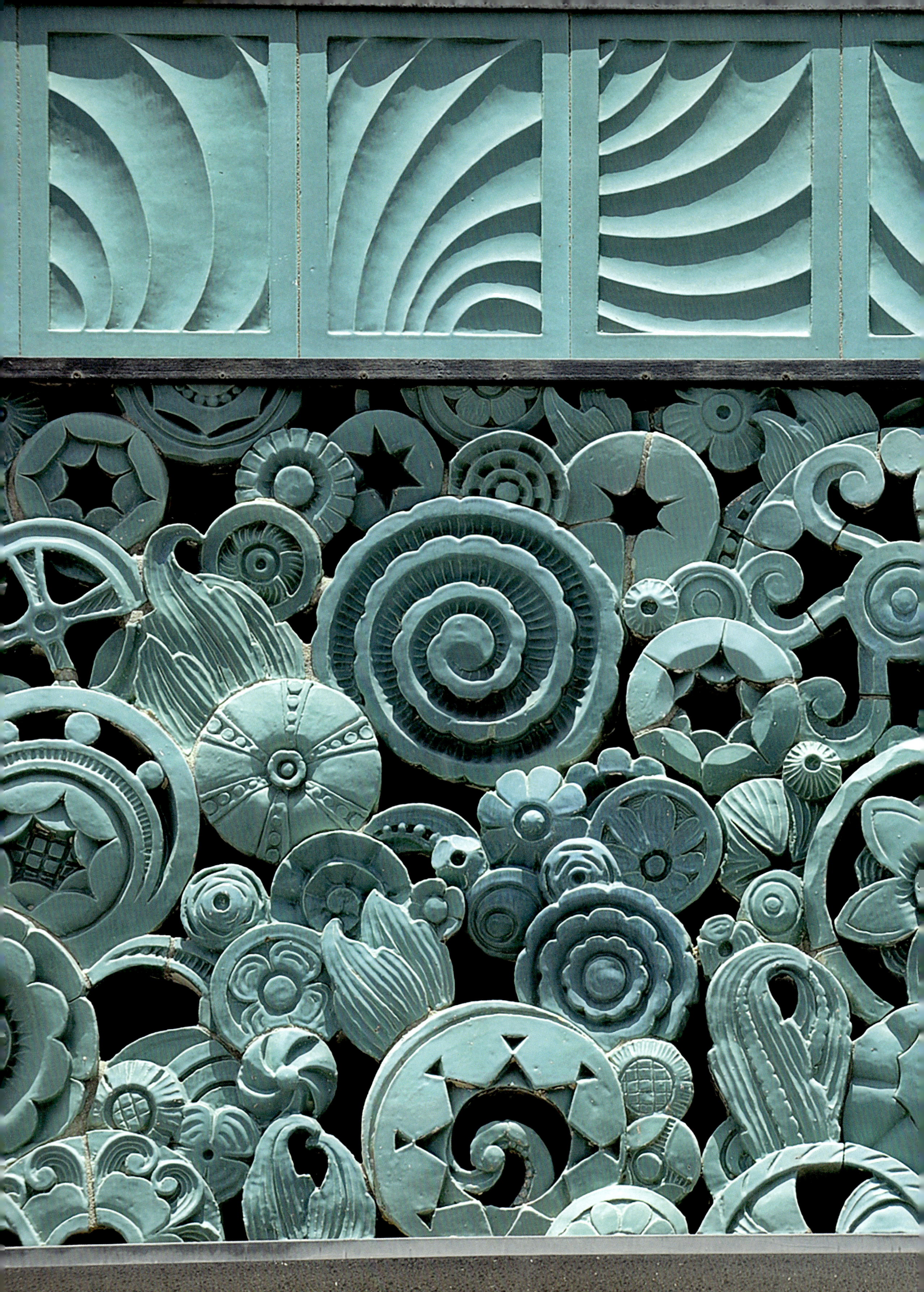

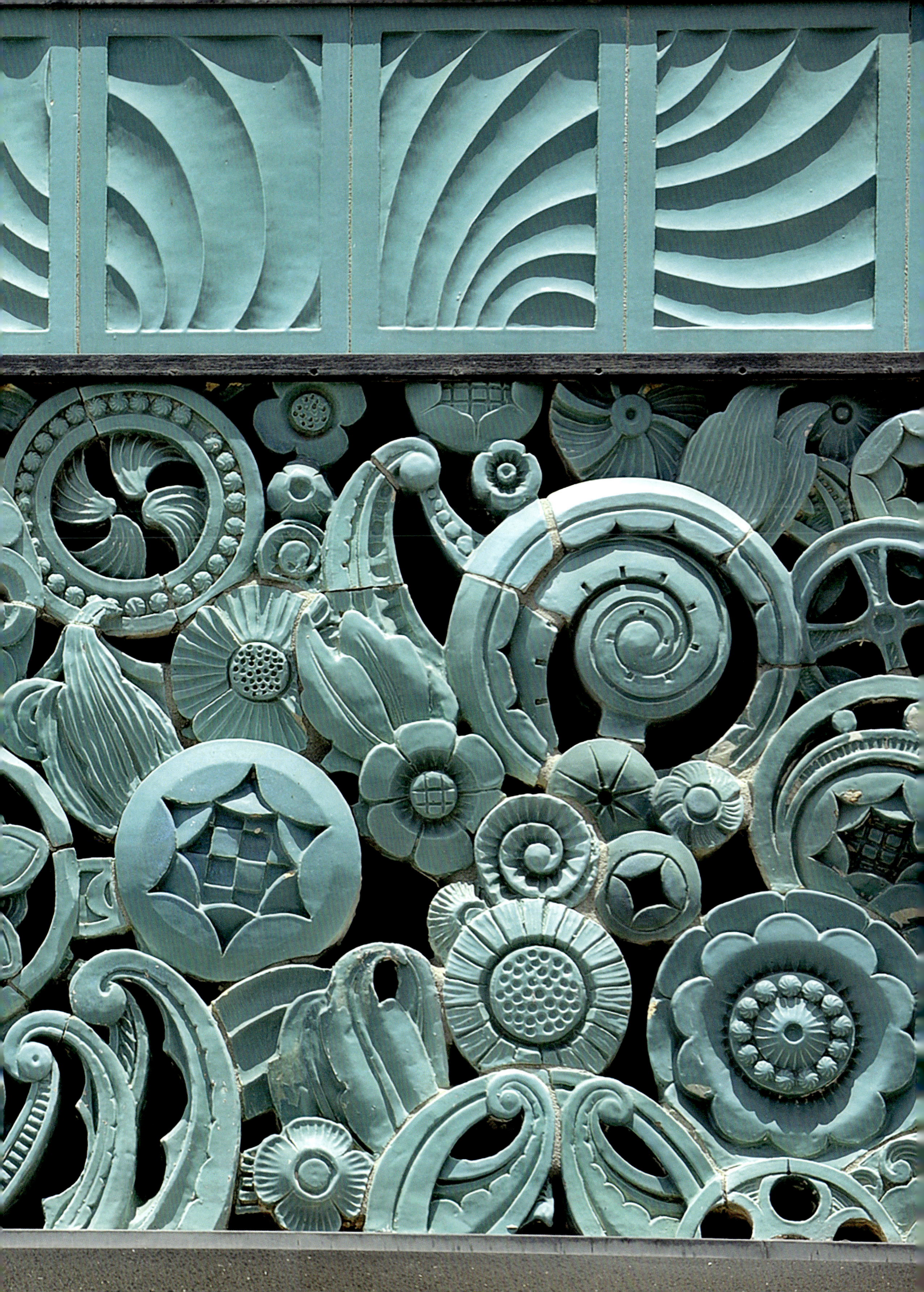

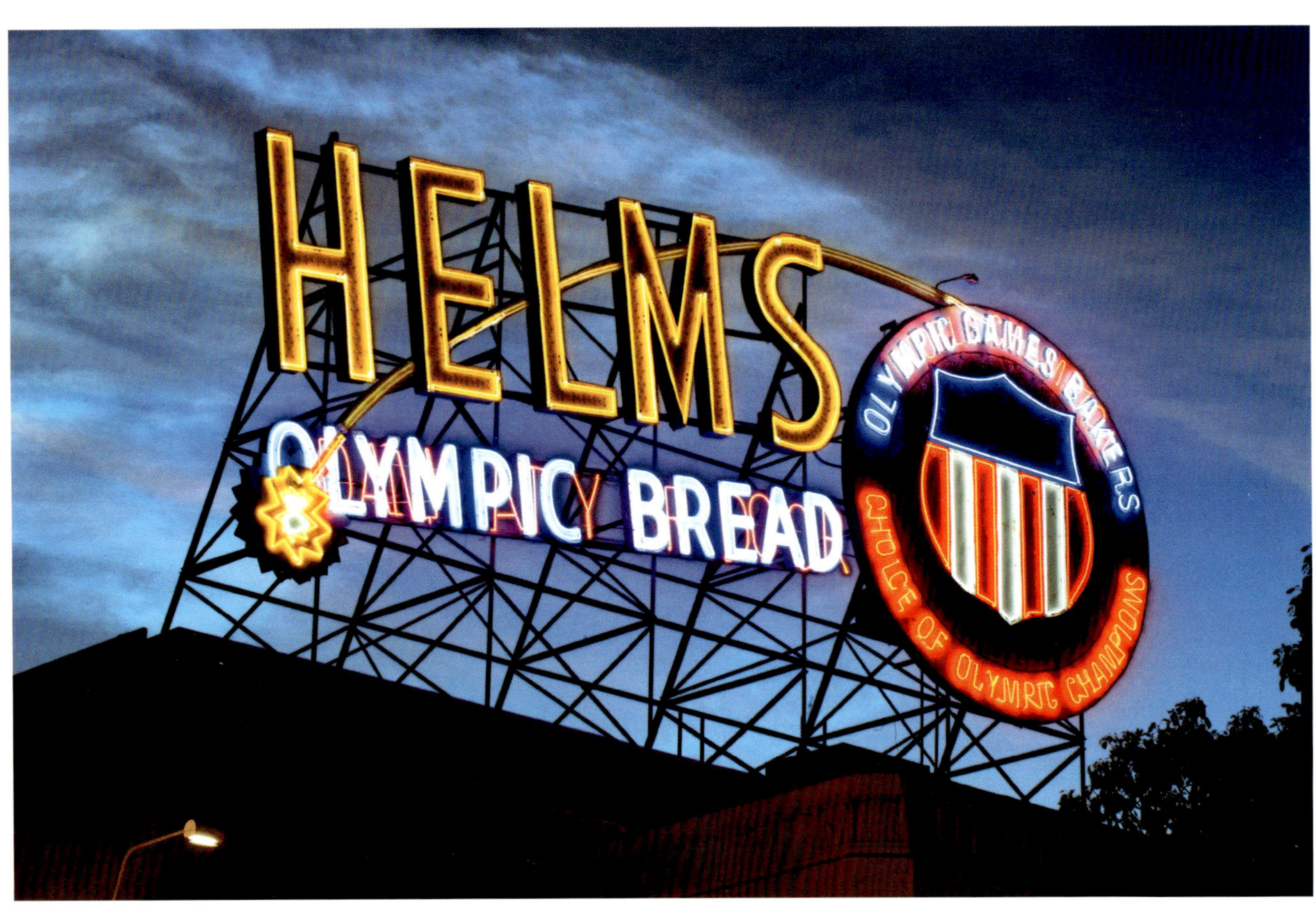

↑ *Helms Bakery, neon sign (E.L. Bruner, 1930) 8758 Venice Blvd., Culver City, photographed 2024.*

→ *Memorial Coliseum (John and Donald B. Parkinson, 1923) 3911 S. Figueroa St., photographed 1989.*

OVERLEAF: *Griffith Observatory, detail of mural (John C. Austin and Frederick M. Ashley, 1935, mural by Hugo Ballin, 1934) 2800 E. Observatory Rd., photographed 2024.*

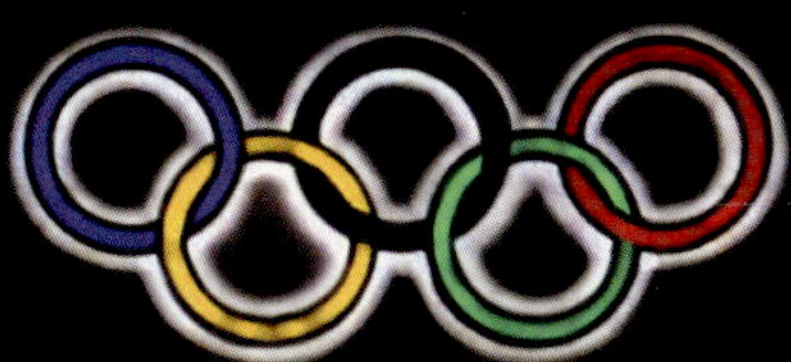
LOS ANGELES
MEMORIAL
COLISEUM

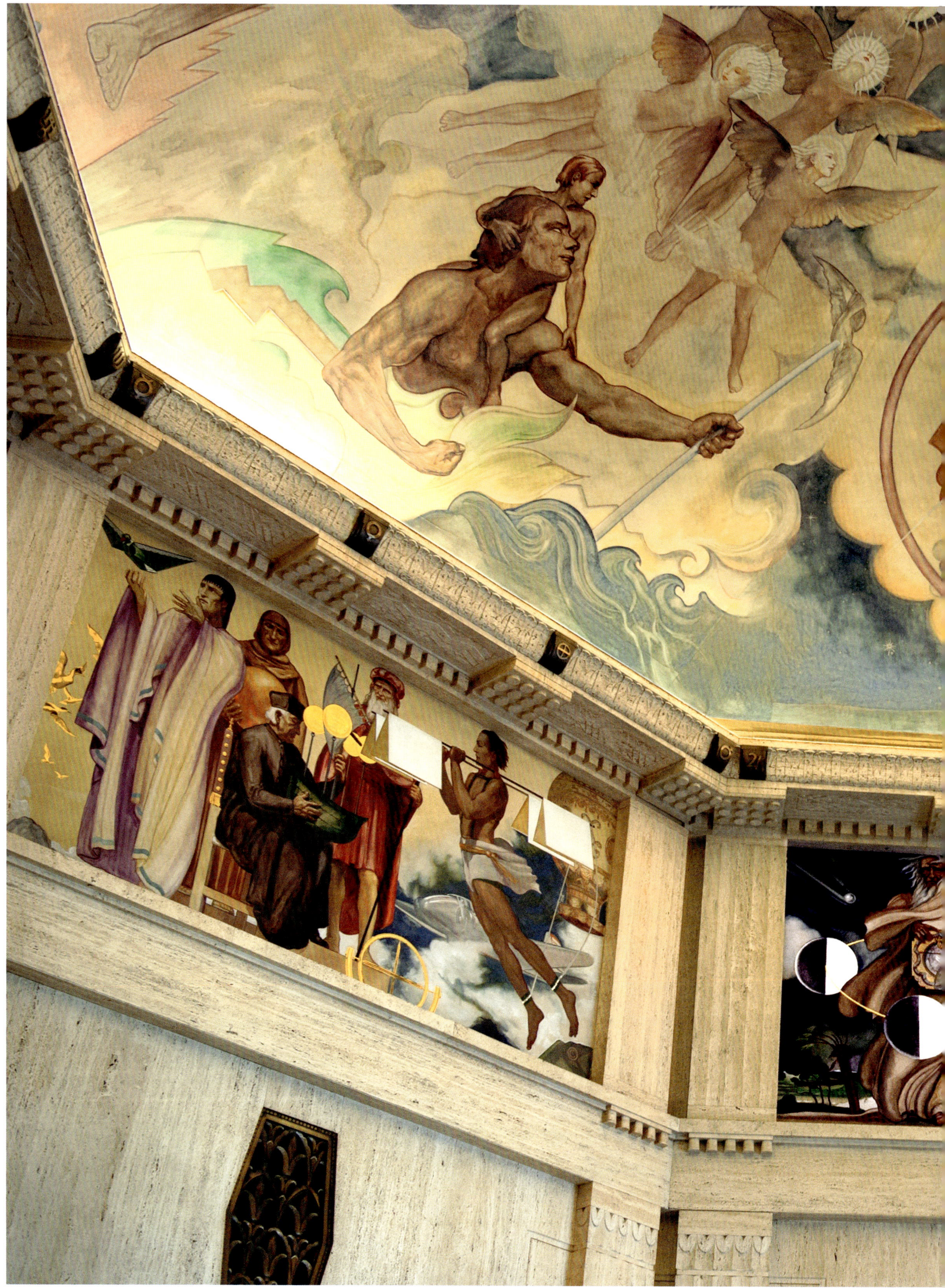

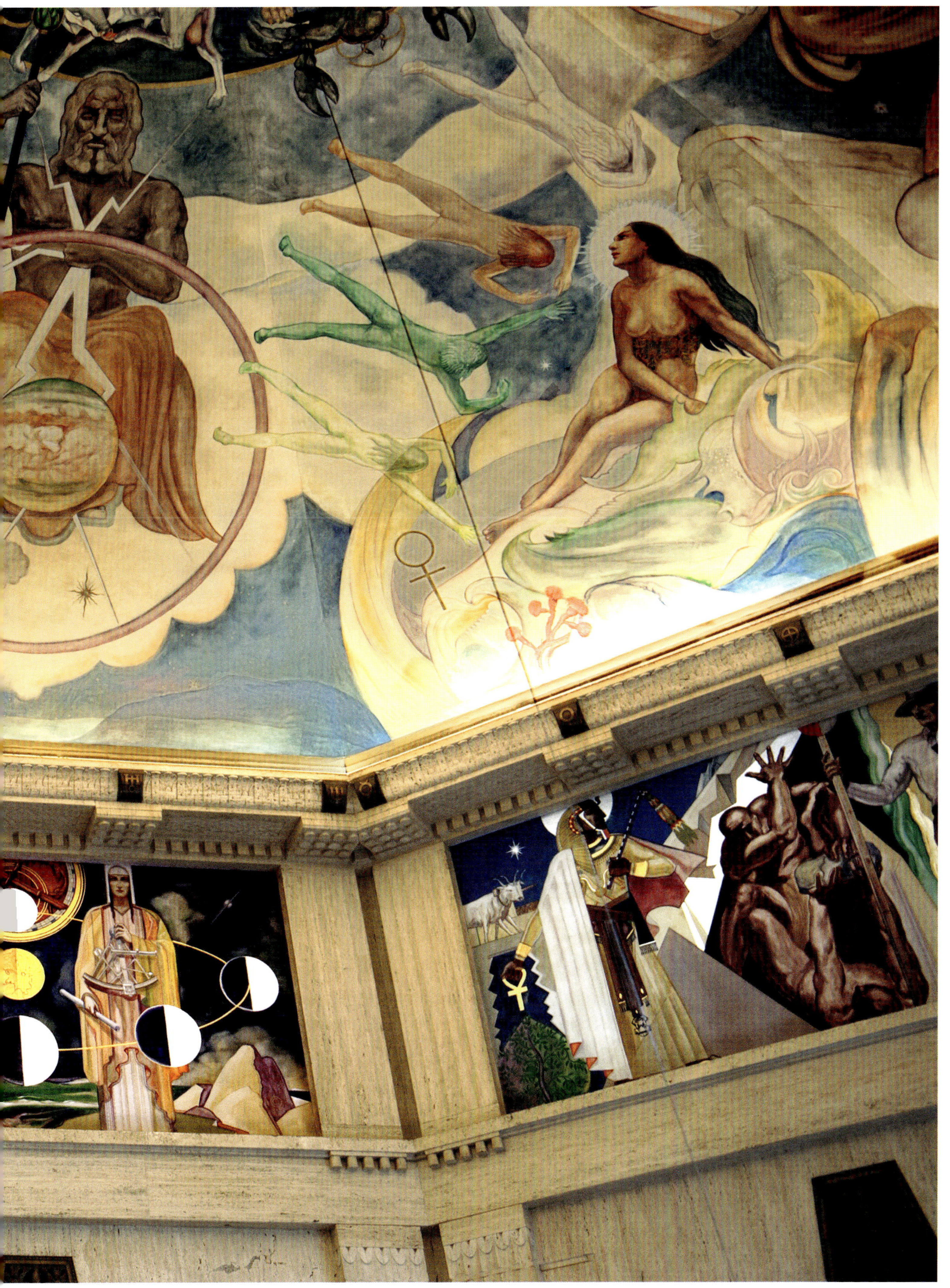

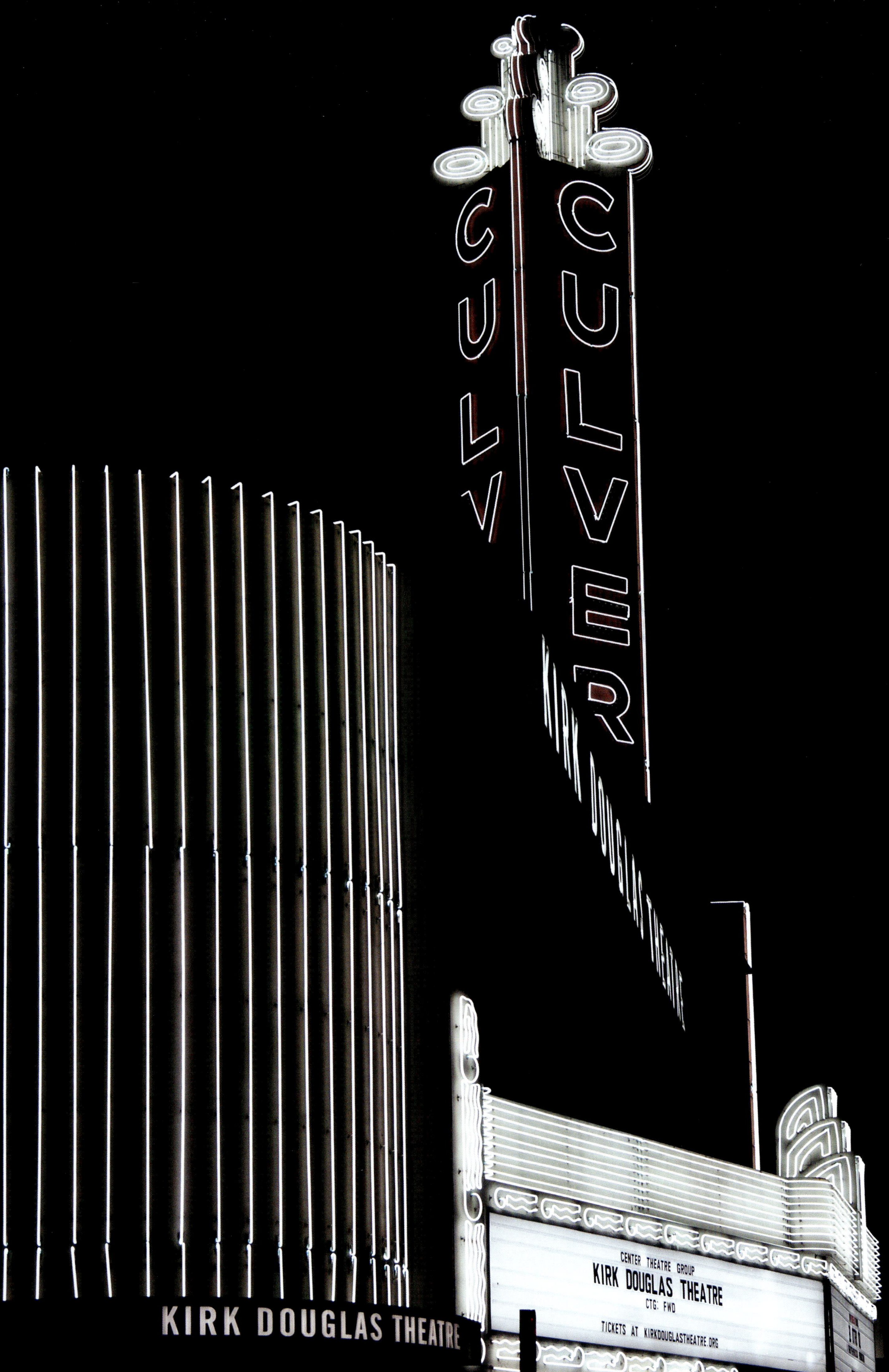
CULVER
KIRK DOUGLAS THEATRE
KIRK DOUGLAS THEATRE
CENTER THEATRE GROUP
KIRK DOUGLAS THEATRE
CTG: FWD
TICKETS AT KIRKDOUGLASTHEATRE.ORG

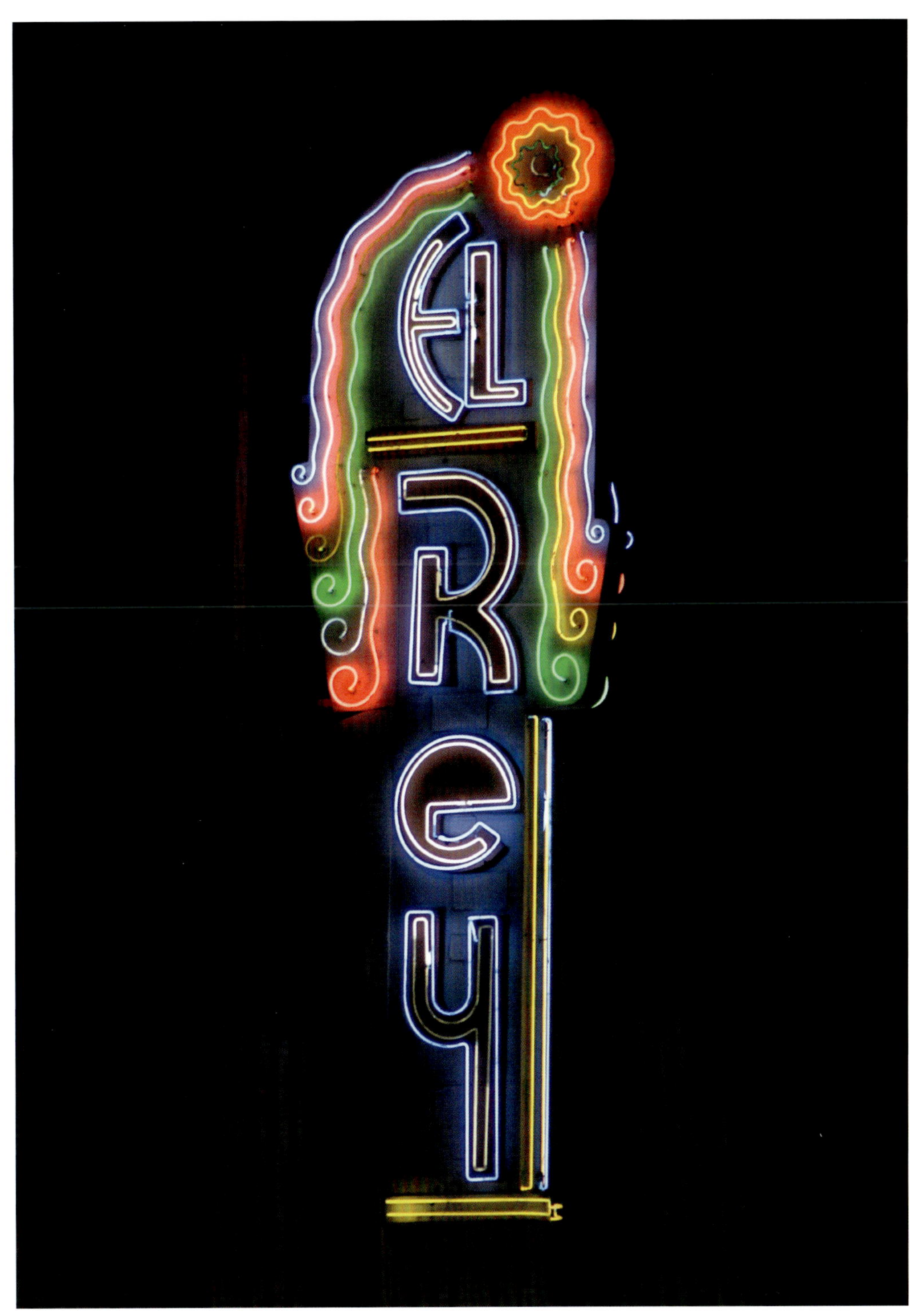

← *Culver Theater, now Kirk Douglas Theatre (Cark G. Moeller, 1946) 9820 W. Washington Blvd., Culver City, photographed 2024.*

↑ *El Rey Theatre, neon sign (Clifford A. Balch, 1936) 5515 Wilshire Blvd., photographed 2008.*

OVERLEAF: *Angelus Temple (A.F. Leict, 1925) 1100 Glendale Blvd., photographed 2024.*

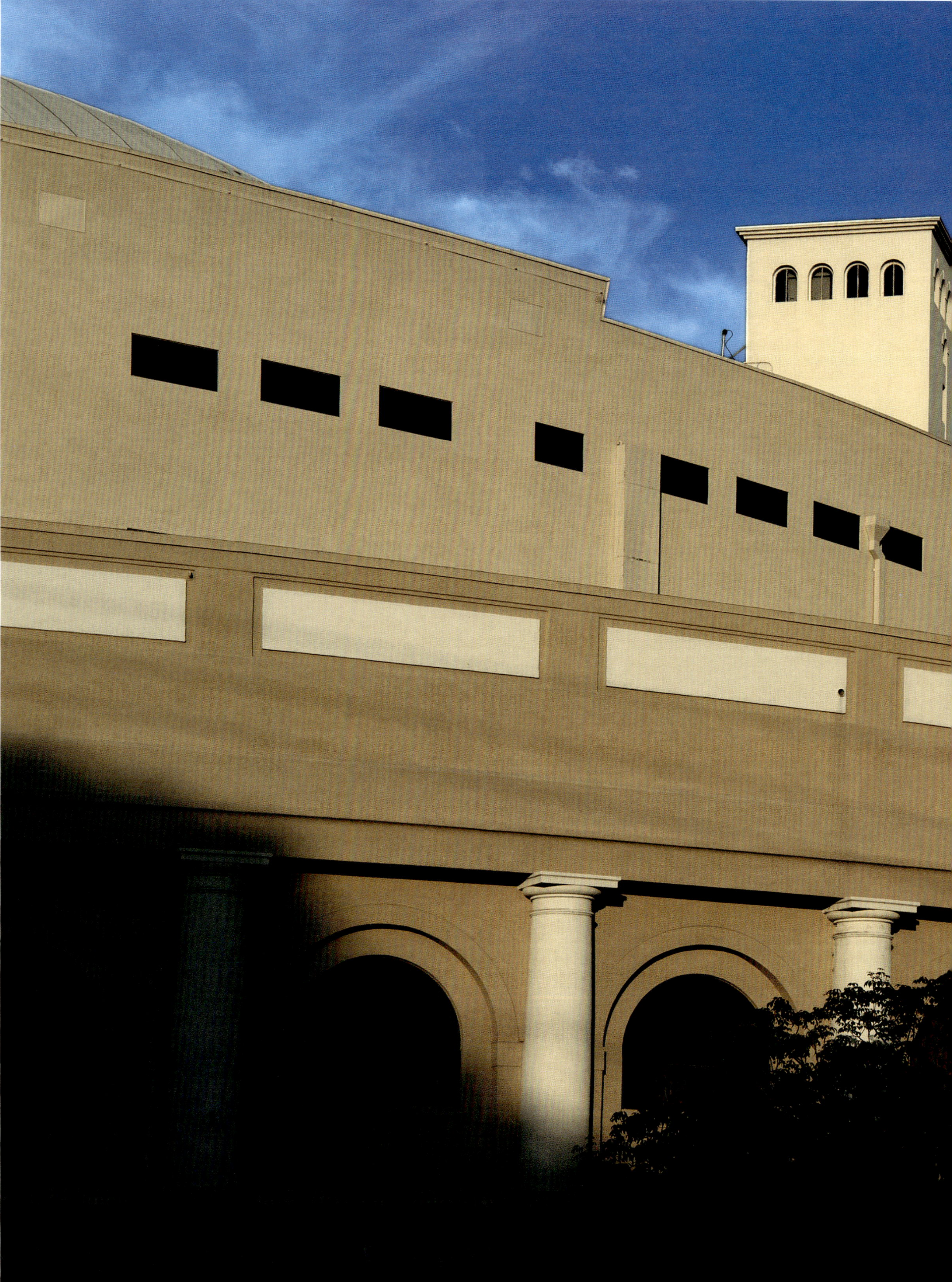

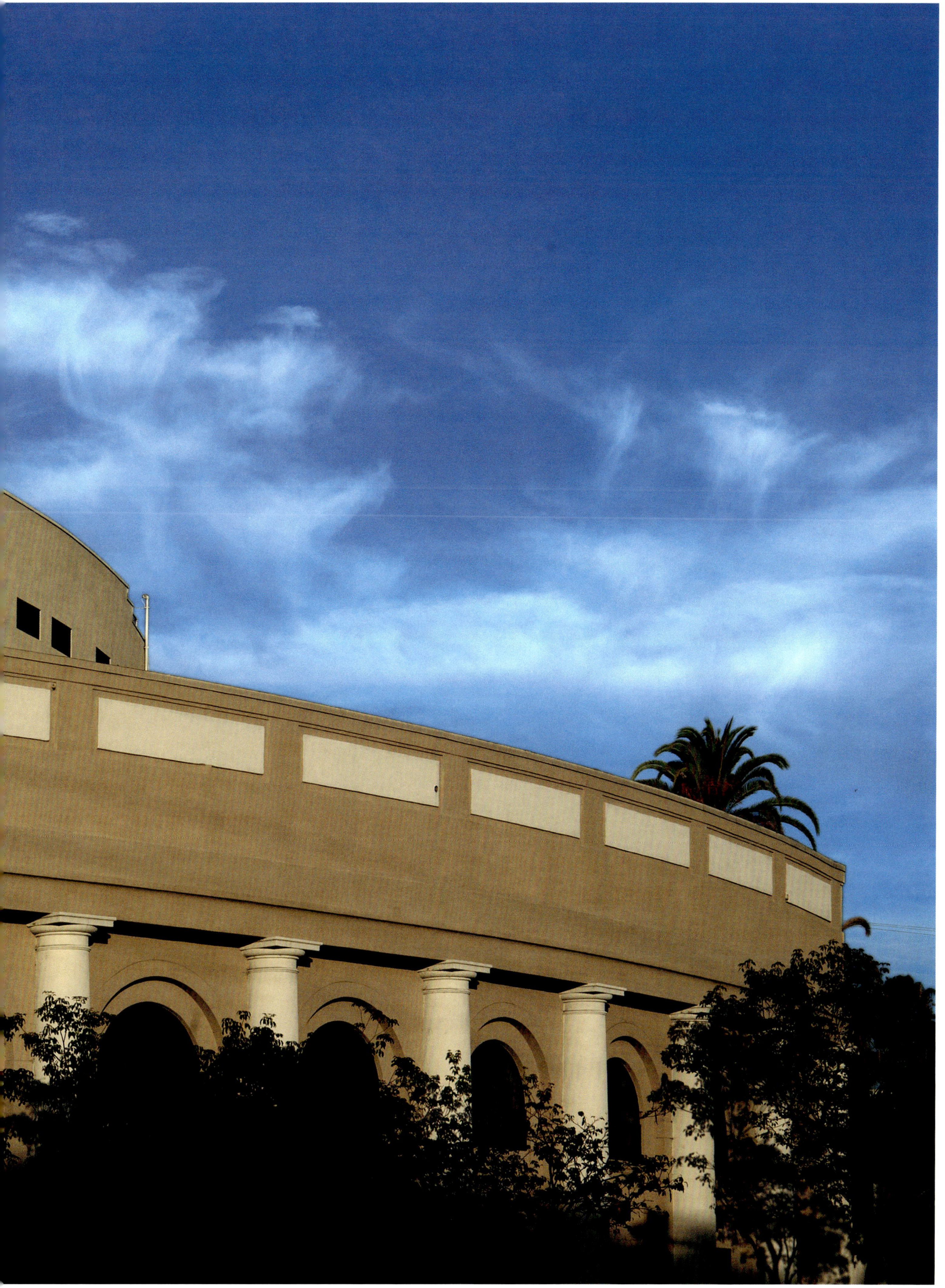

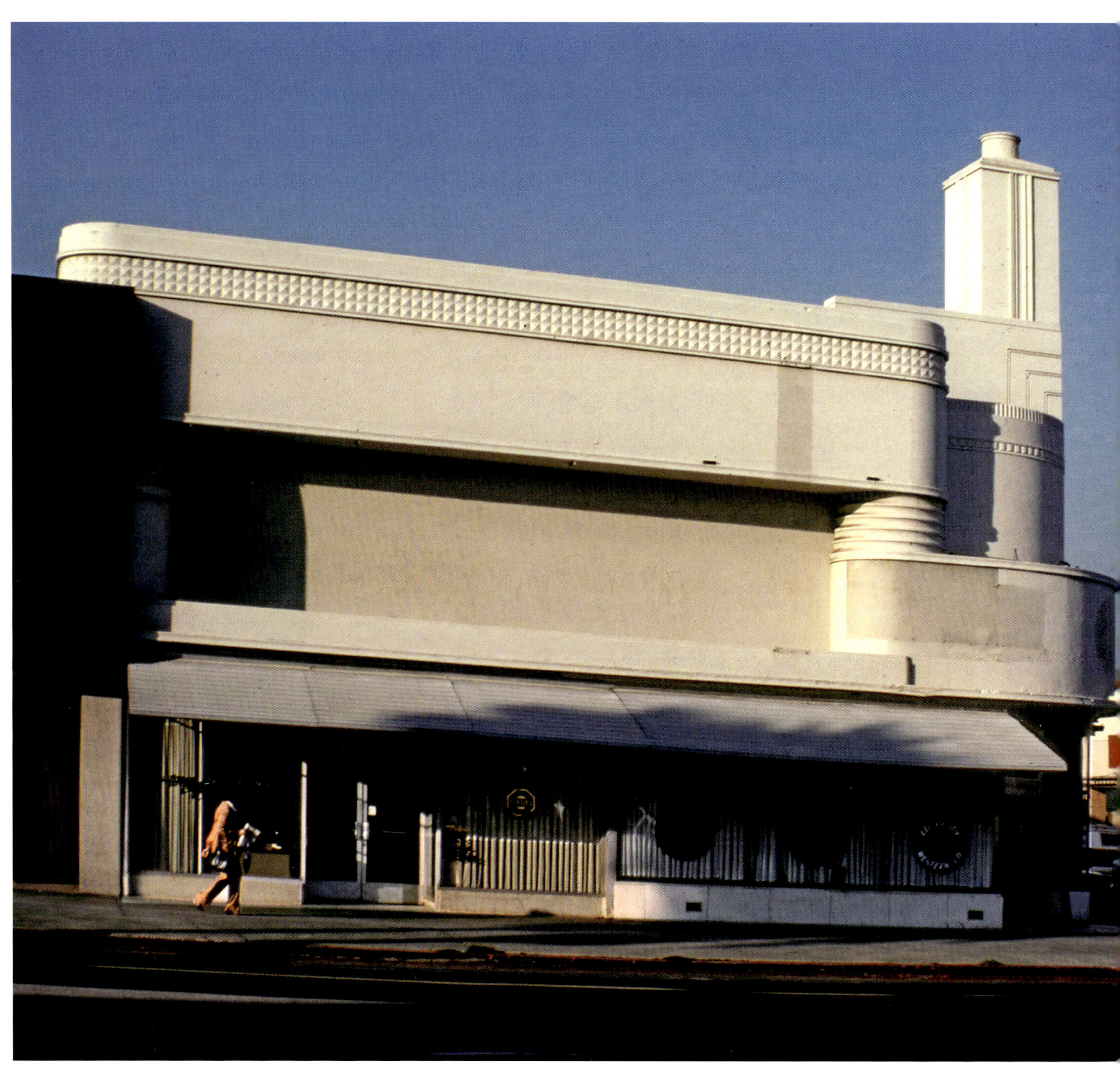

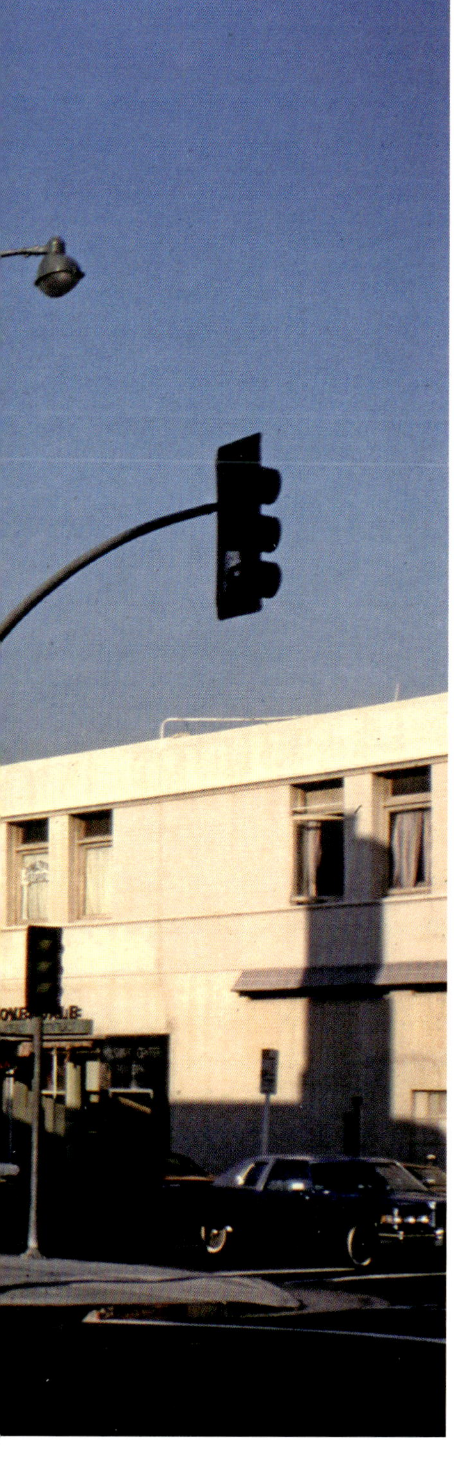

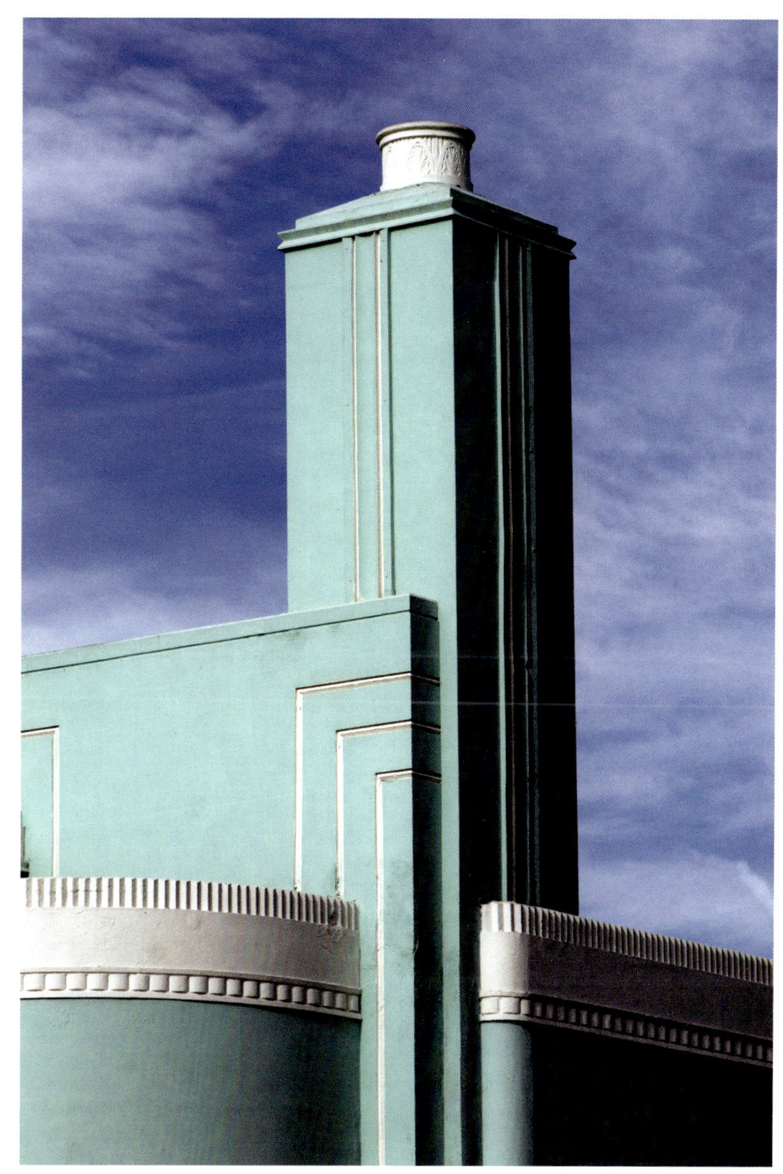

Sontag Building, exterior and tower detail (Norstom and Anderson, 1935) 5401 Wilshire Blvd., horizontal image photographed 1978, vertical image photographed 1994.

OVERLEAF: *Los Angeles Fire Department Fire Station 1 (P.K. Schabarum and Charles O. Brittain, 1940) 2260 Pasadena Ave., photographed 2024.*

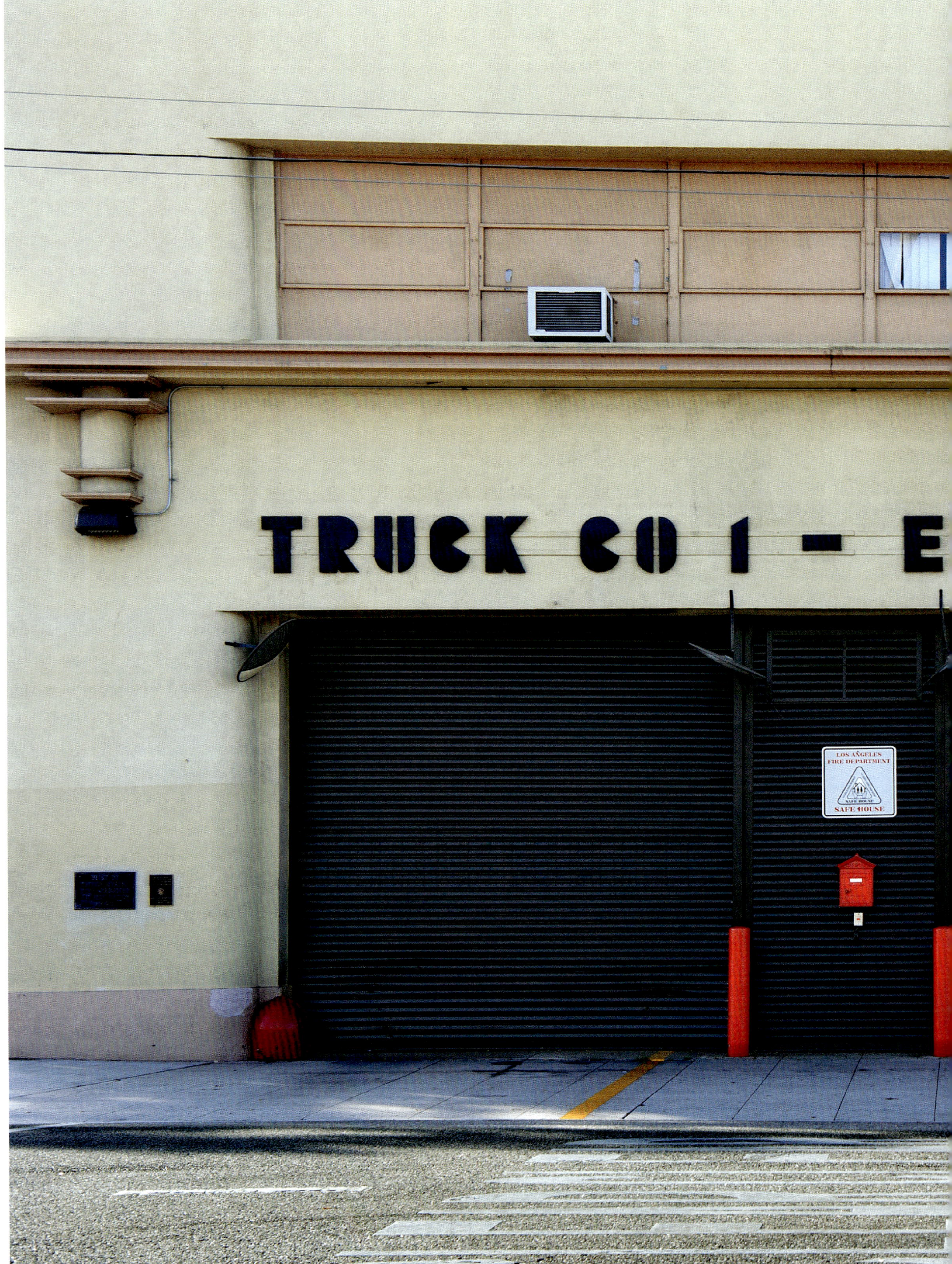
TRUCK CO 1 - E
LOS ANGELES
FIRE DEPARTMENT
SAFE HOUSE

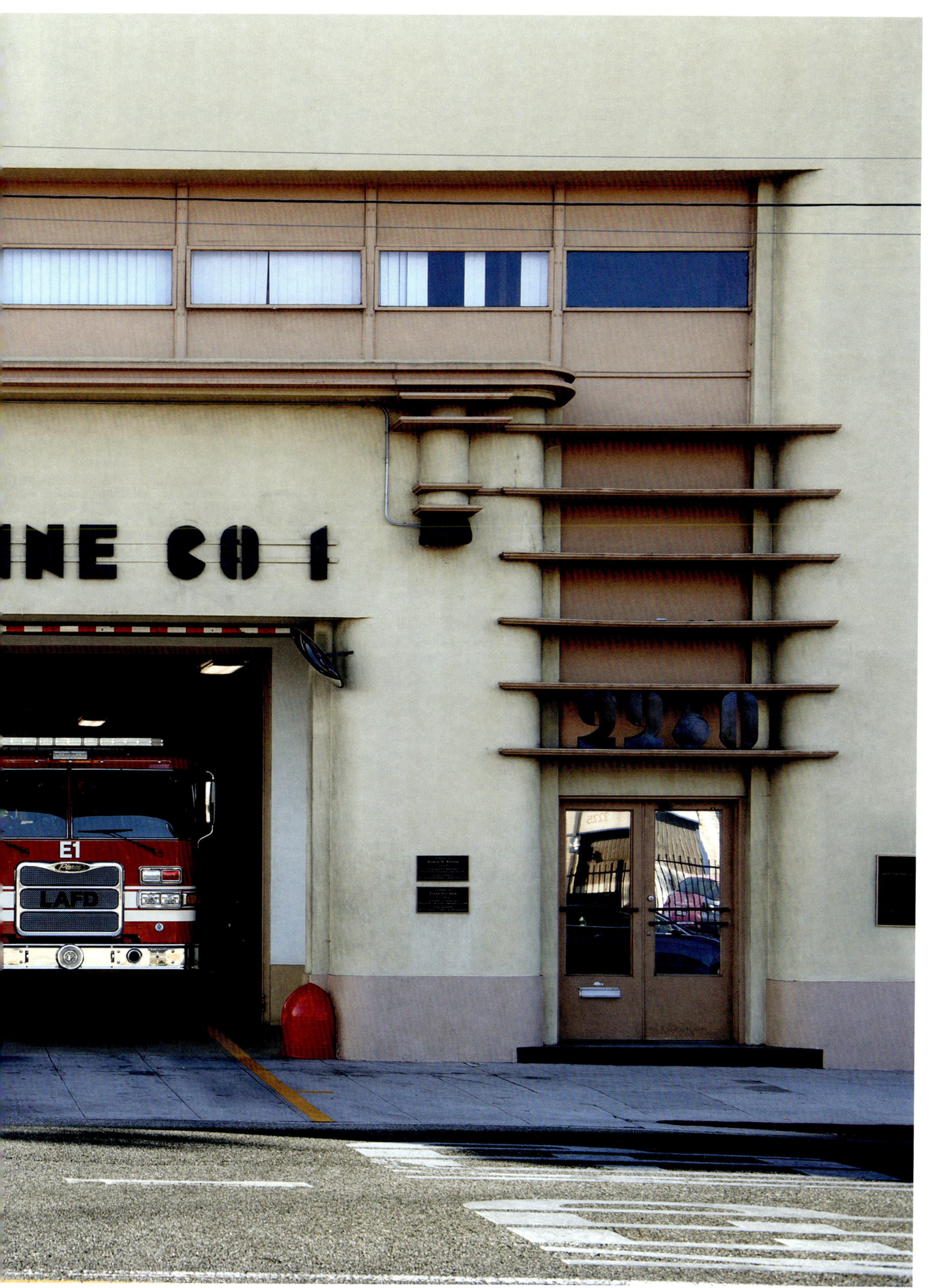
NE CO 1
E1
LAFD

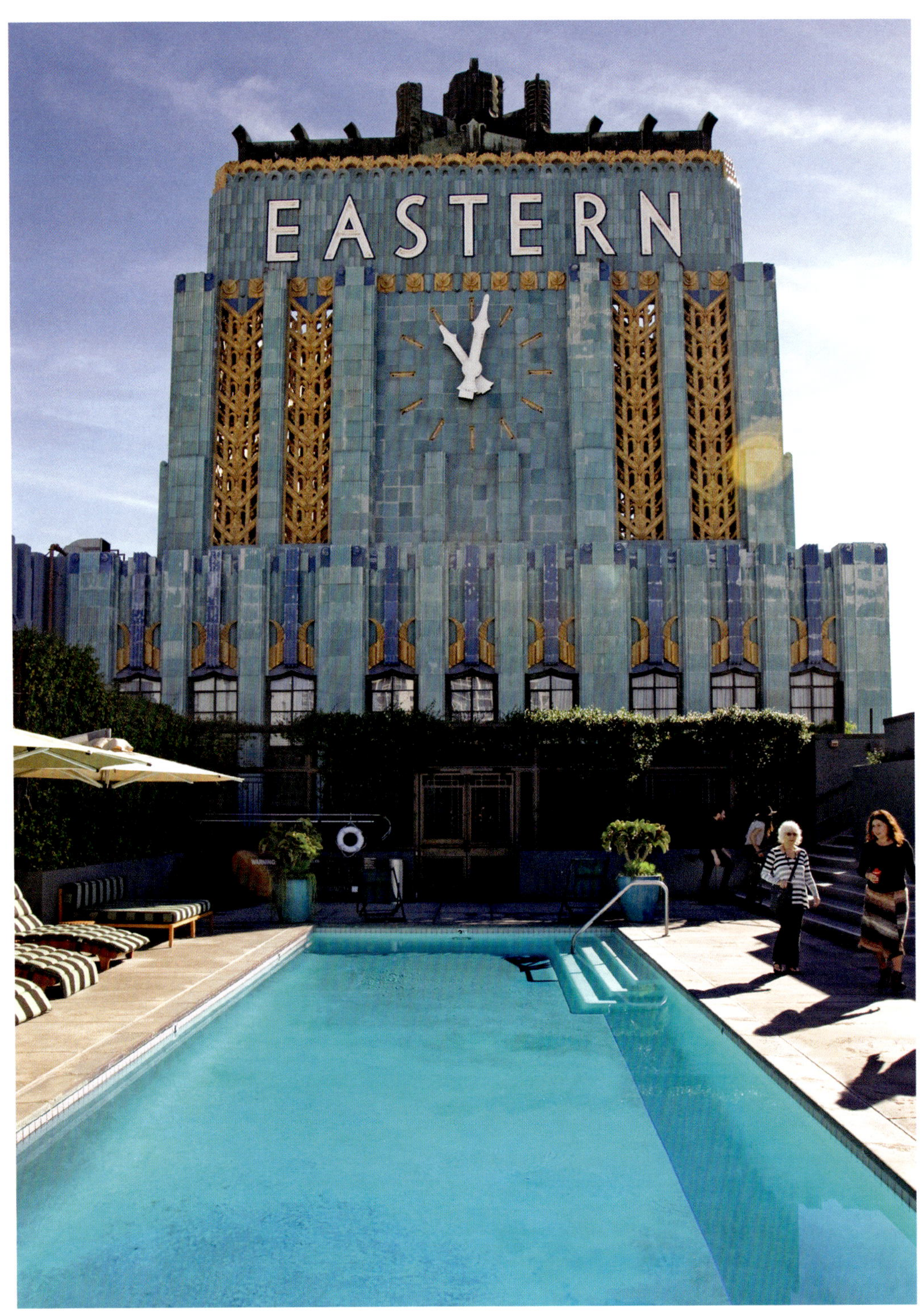

↑ *Eastern Columbia Building, now Eastern Columbia Lofts, clock tower and rooftop pool (Claud Beelman, 1929) 849 S. Broadway, photographed 2015.*

→ *Bay Cities Guaranty Building (Walker and Eisen, 1930) 221 Santa Monica Blvd., Santa Monica, photographed 2003.*

OVERLEAF: *Orpheum Theatre and Building (G. Albert Lansburgh, 1926) 842 S. Broadway, photographed 1984.*

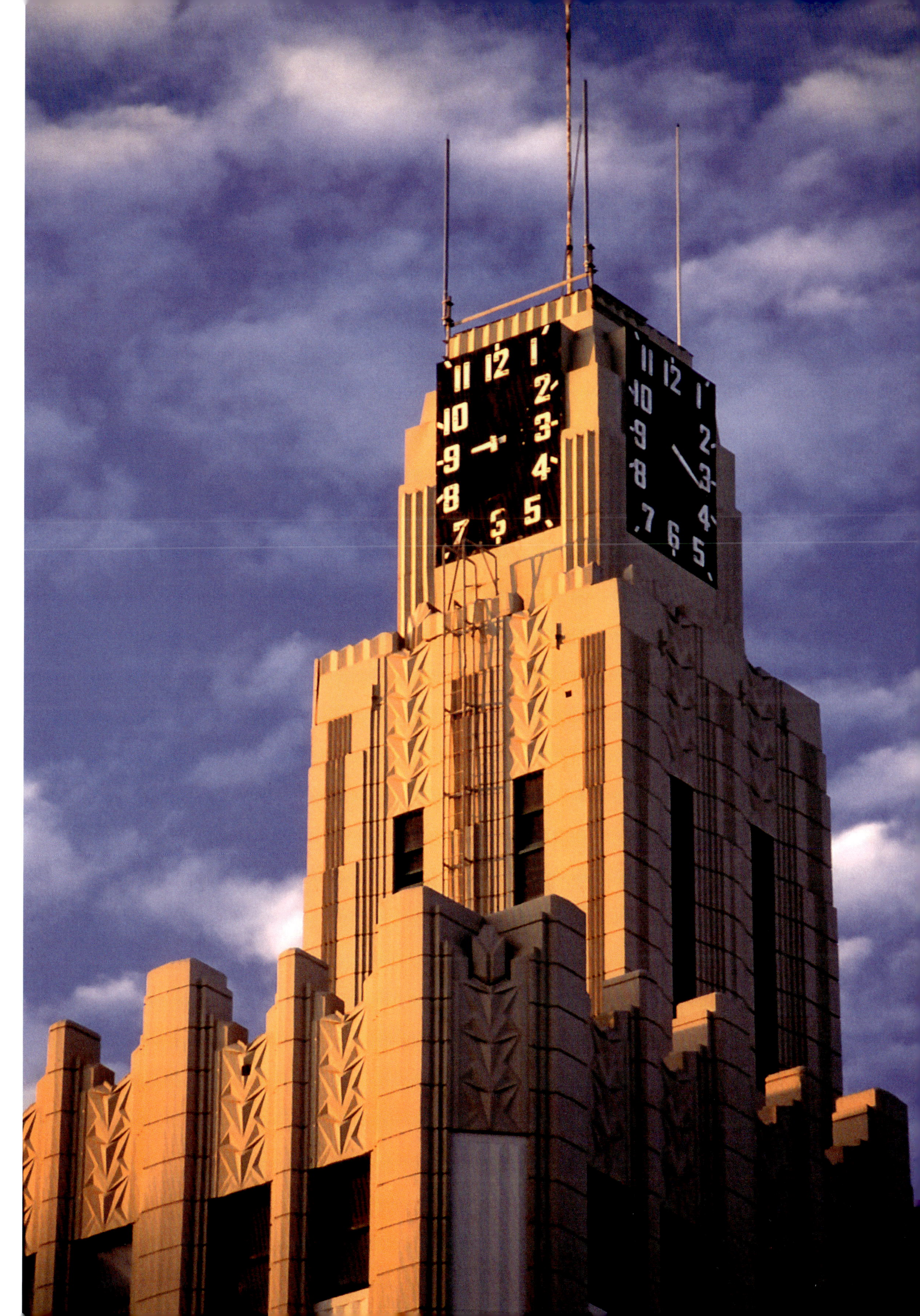

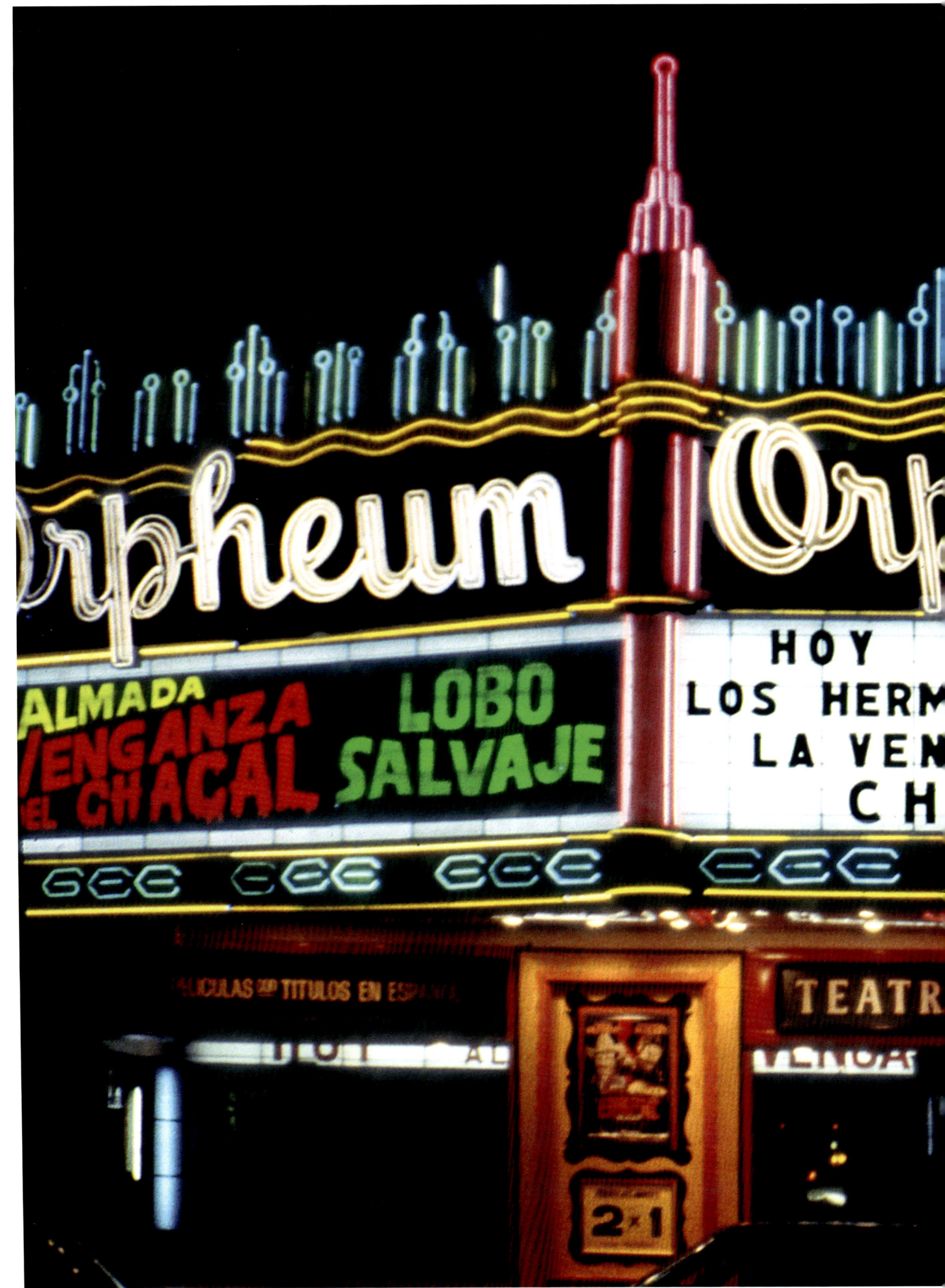

Orpheum
ALMADA
VENGANZA
CHACAL
LOBO
SALVAJE
HOY
LOS HERM
LA VEN
CH
TITULOS EN
TEATR
2x1

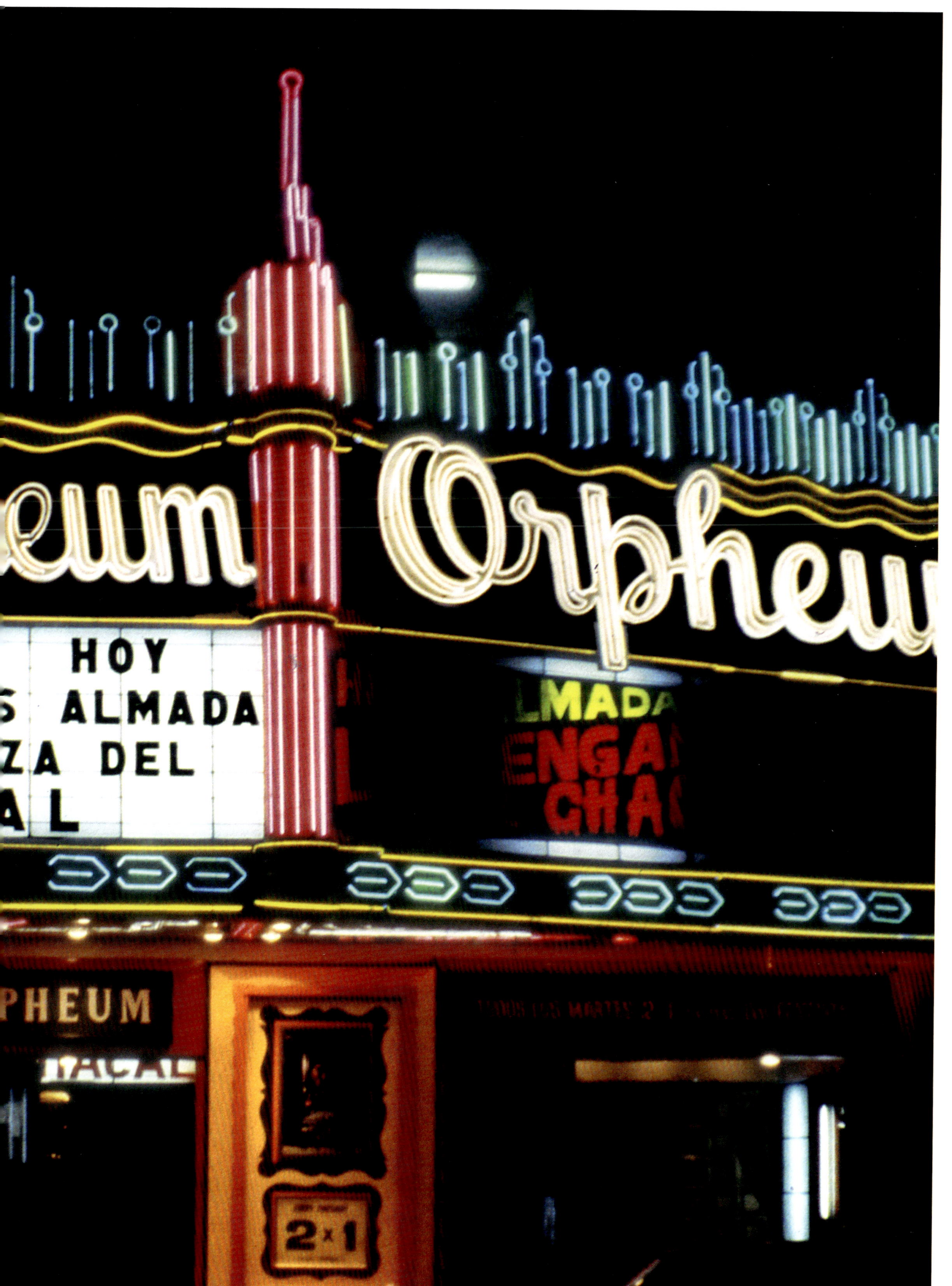

eum
Orpheu
HOY
S ALMADA
ZA DEL
AL
LMADA
ENGA
CHA
PHEUM
2 x 1

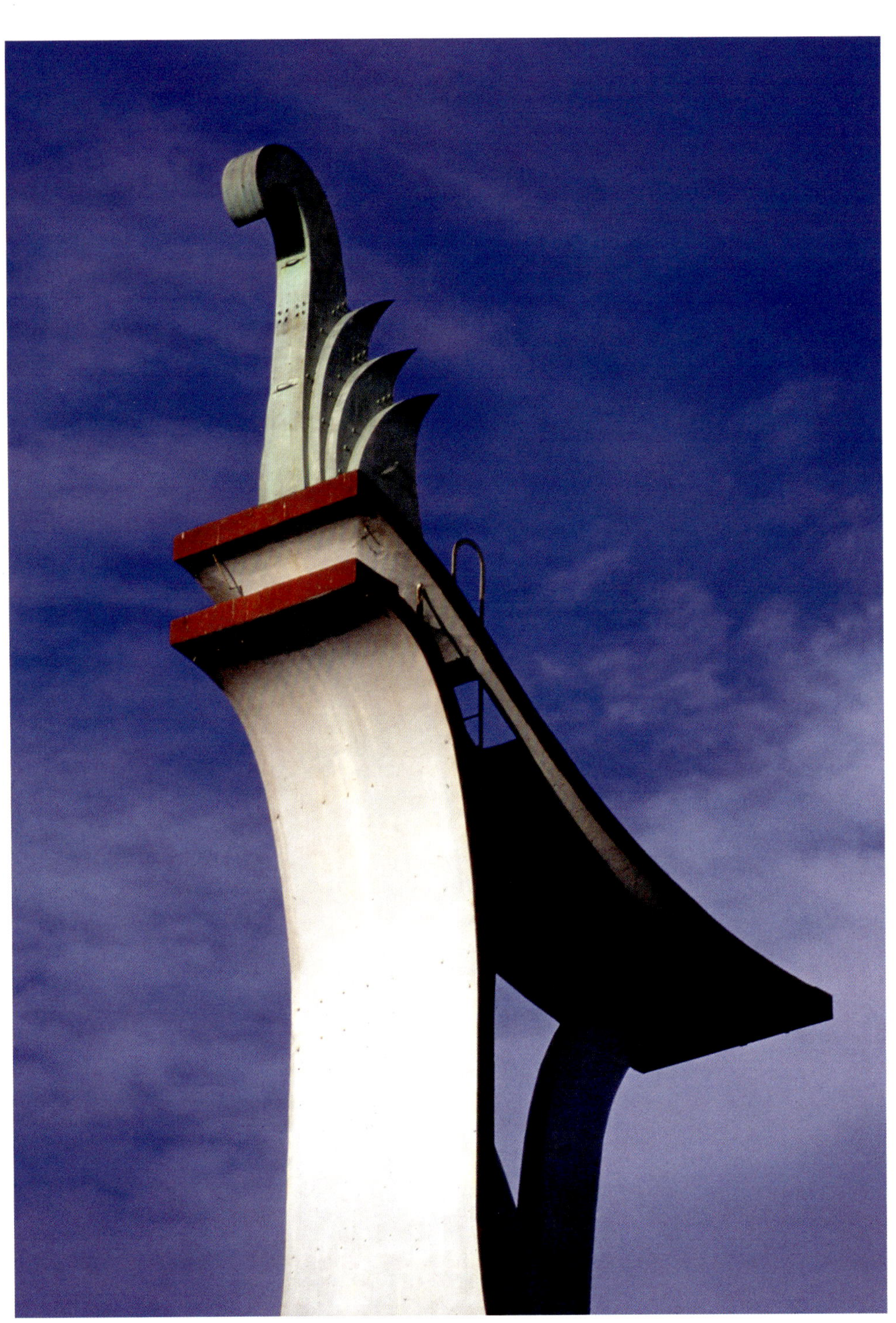

↑ *Loyola Theatre, exterior detail (Clarence Smale, 1946)*
8610 S. Sepulveda Blvd., photographed 1989.

→ *Alex Theatre, exterior detail (Lindley and Selkirk, 1925, façade remodeled by S. Charles Lee in 1940)*
216 N. Brand Blvd., Glendale, photographed 2009.

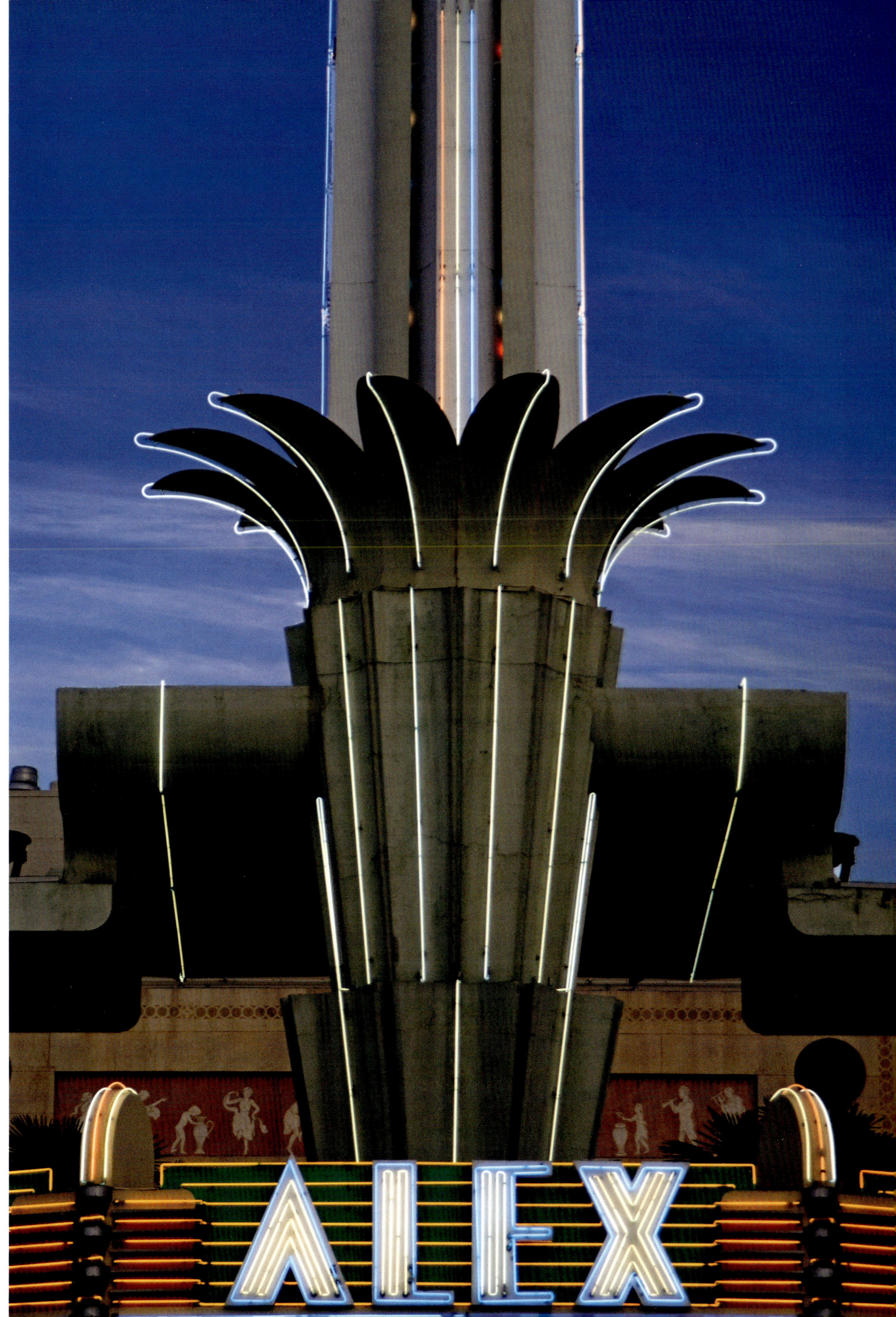
ALEX

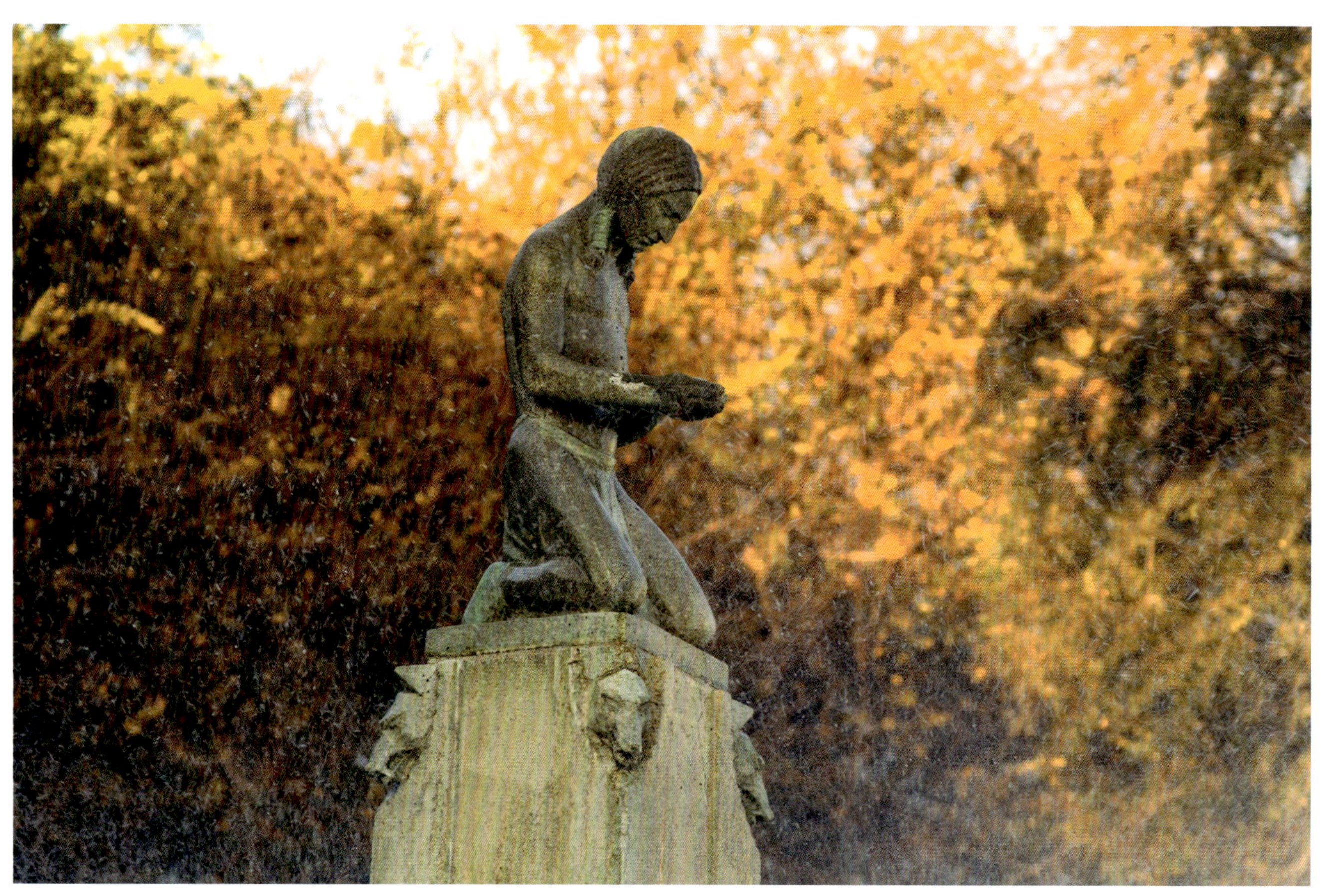

↑ *Electric Fountain, Beverly Gardens Park, detail of sculpture (sculpture by Robert Merrell Gage, 1931) 9439 Santa Monica Blvd., Beverly Hills, photographed 2008.*

→ *Sculpture of Saint Monica (Eugene Morahan, 1934) Wilshire Boulevard at Ocean Avenue, Santa Monica, photographed 2024.*

OVERLEAF: *Selig Clothing Store (Arthur E. Harvey, 1931) 265 S. Western Ave., photographed 2005.*

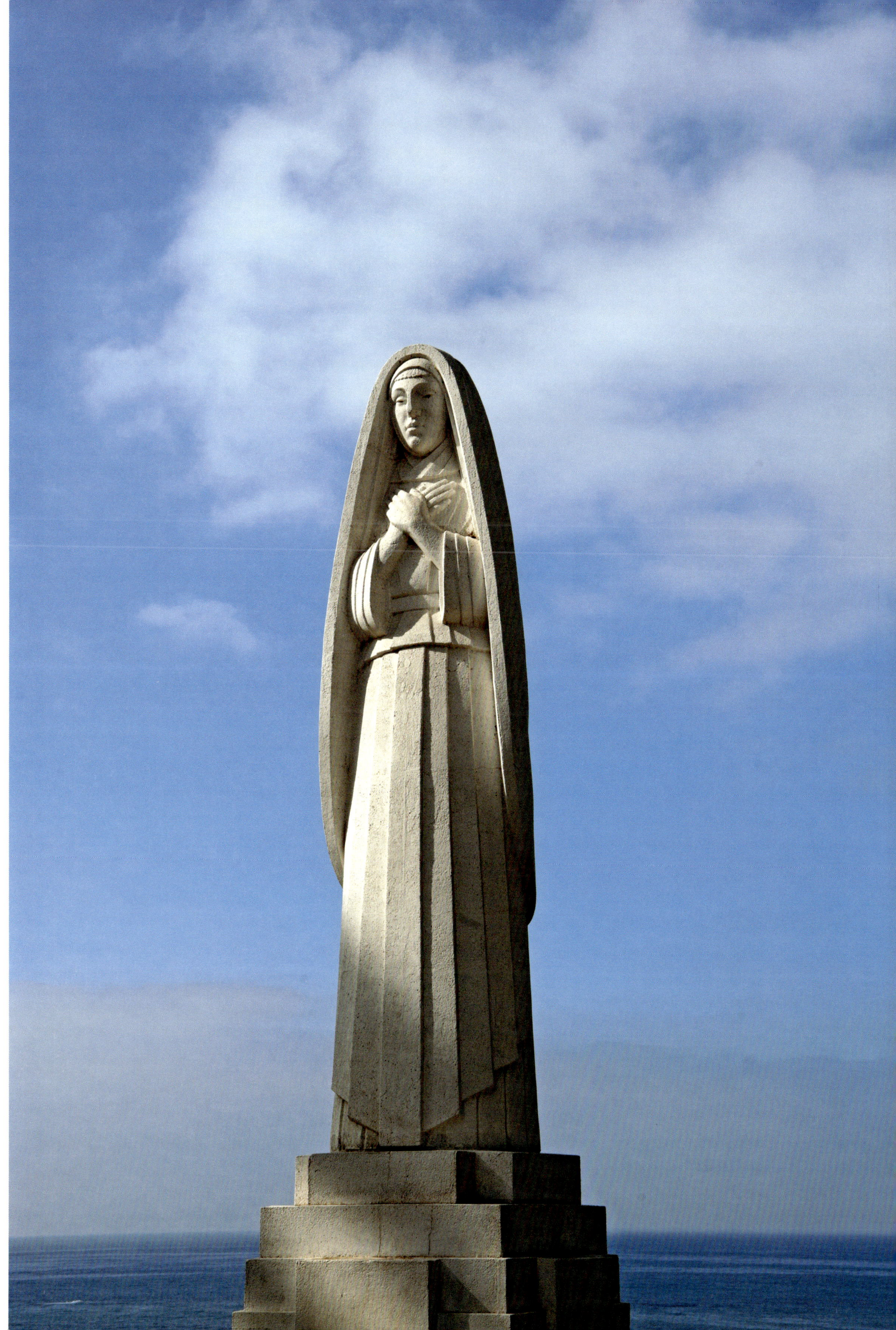

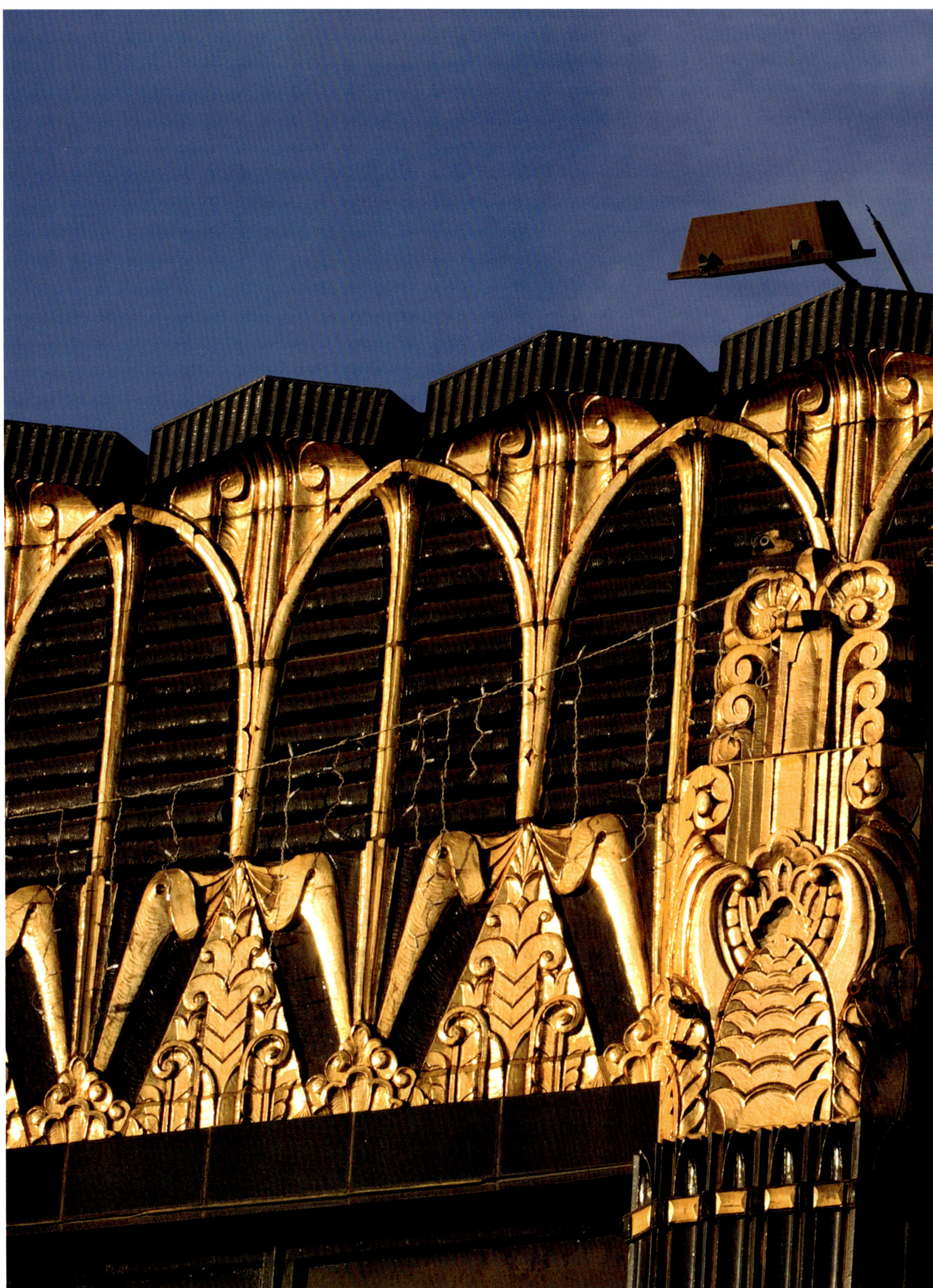

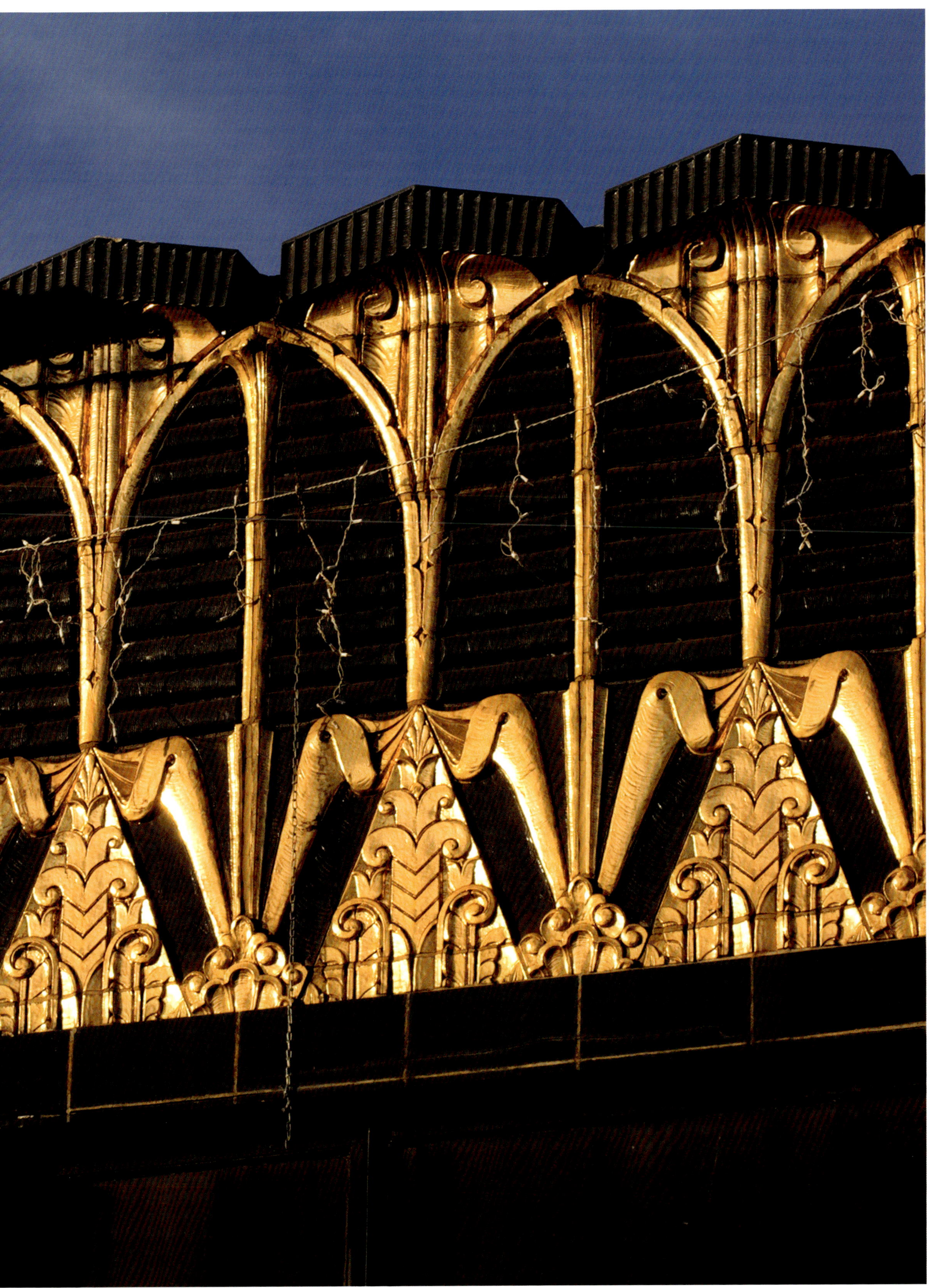

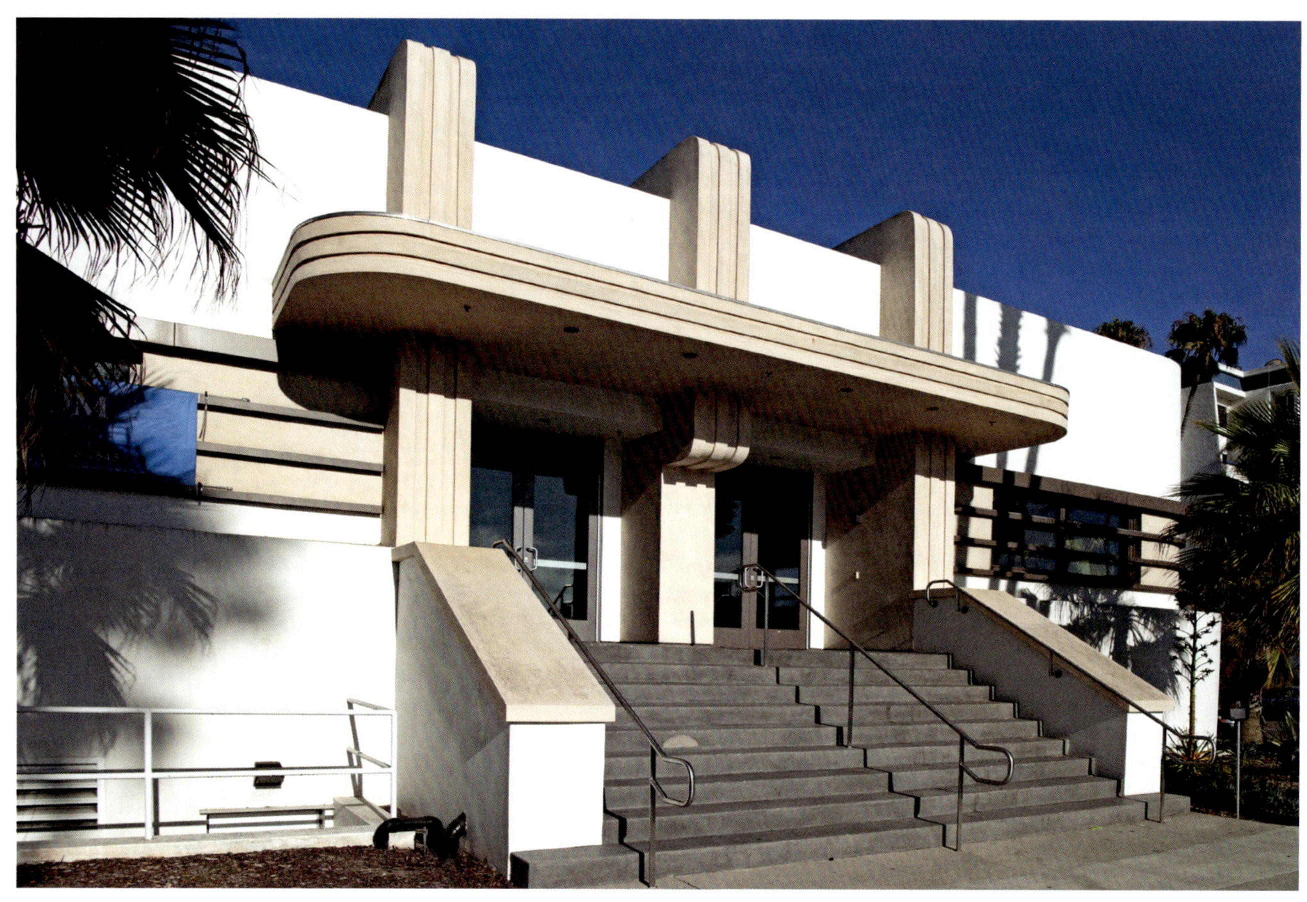

↑ *Eagles Building, now MA Center LA (Architect Unknown, 1949) 128 S. Catalina Ave., Redondo Beach, photographed 2024.*

→ *Maywood City Hall (Wilson, Merrill, Alexander, 1938) 4319 E. Slauson Ave., photographed 2024.*

OVERLEAF: *Oviatt Building, exterior detail (Walker and Eisen, 1928) 617 S. Olive St., photographed 2024*

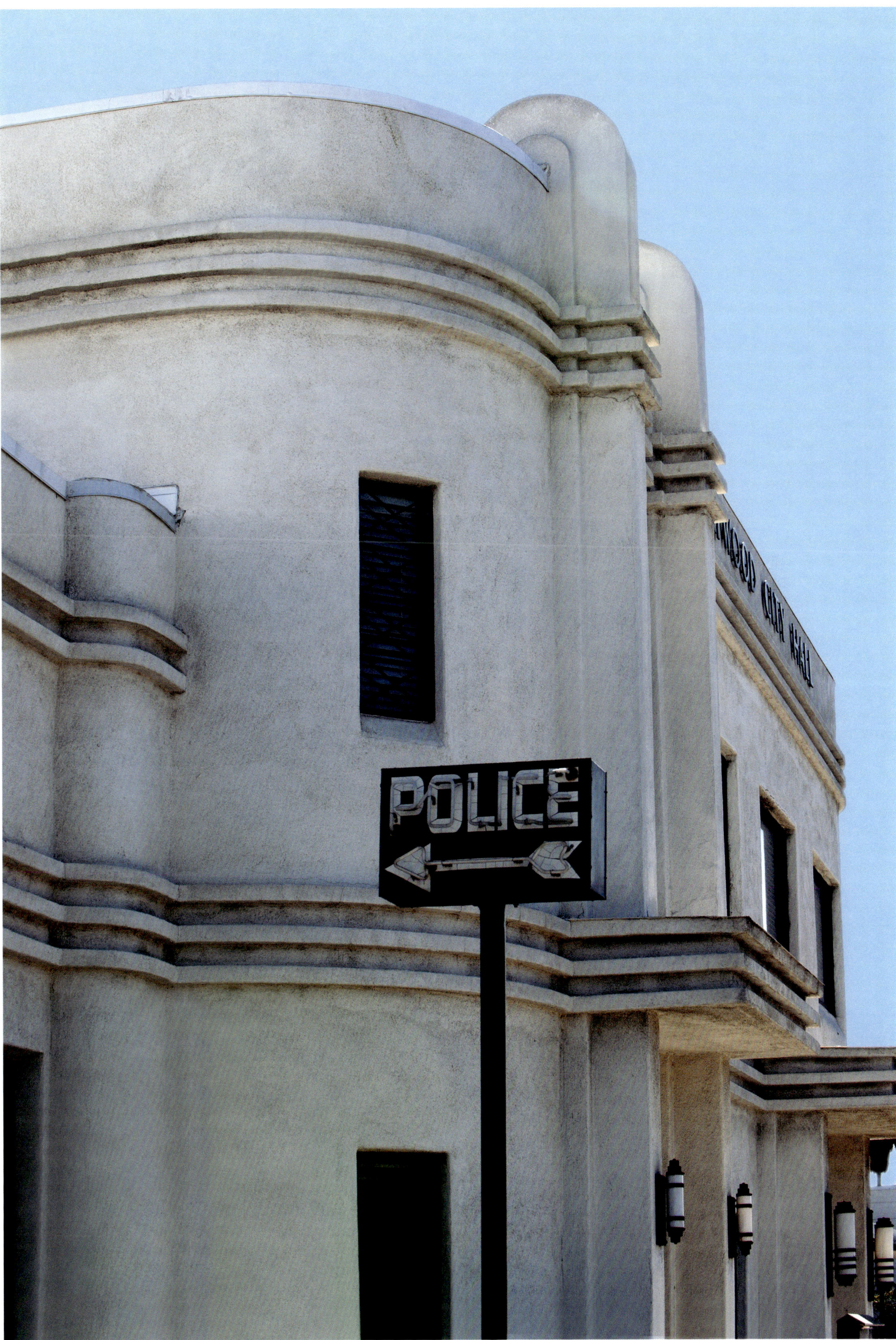
POLICE

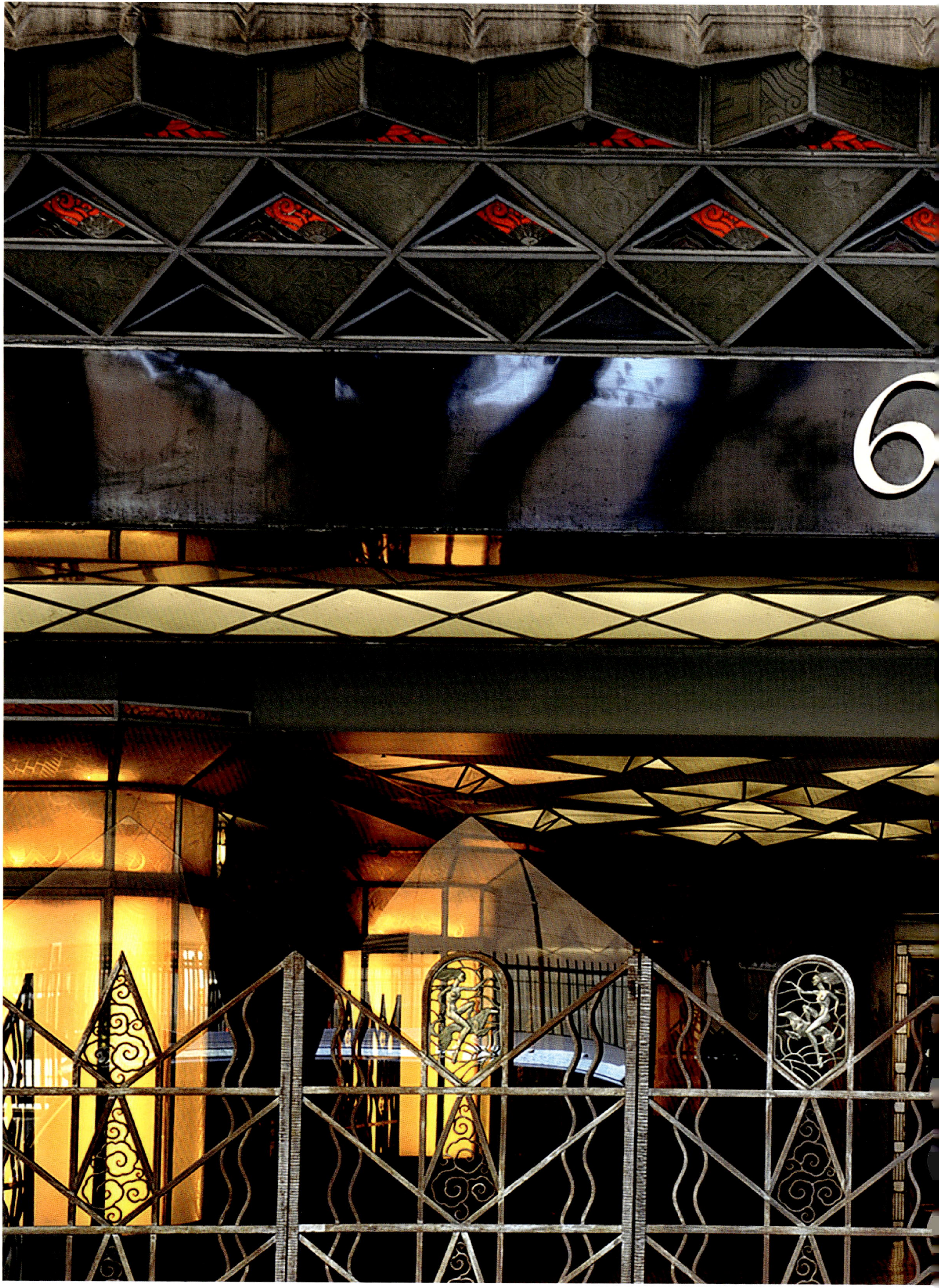

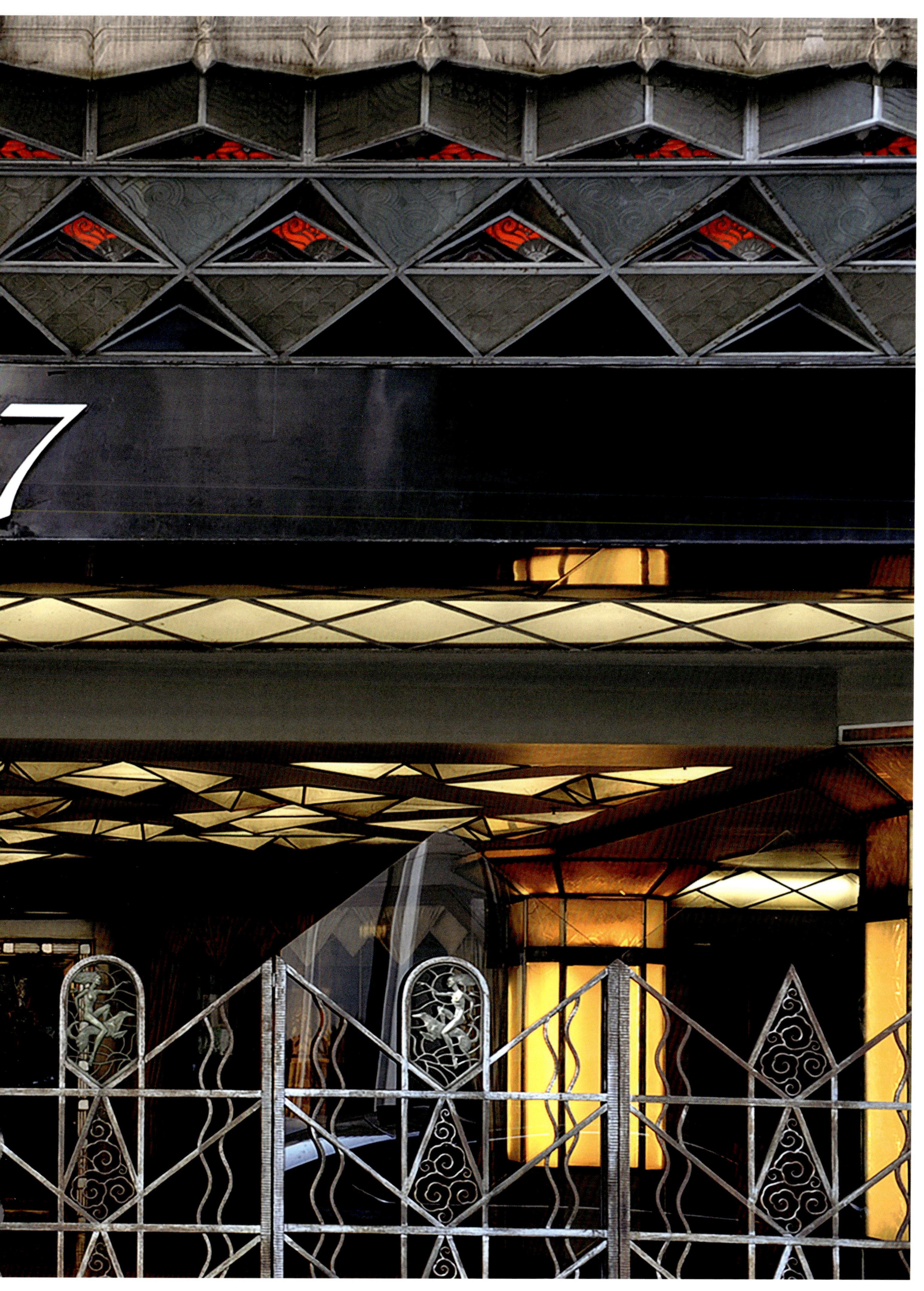

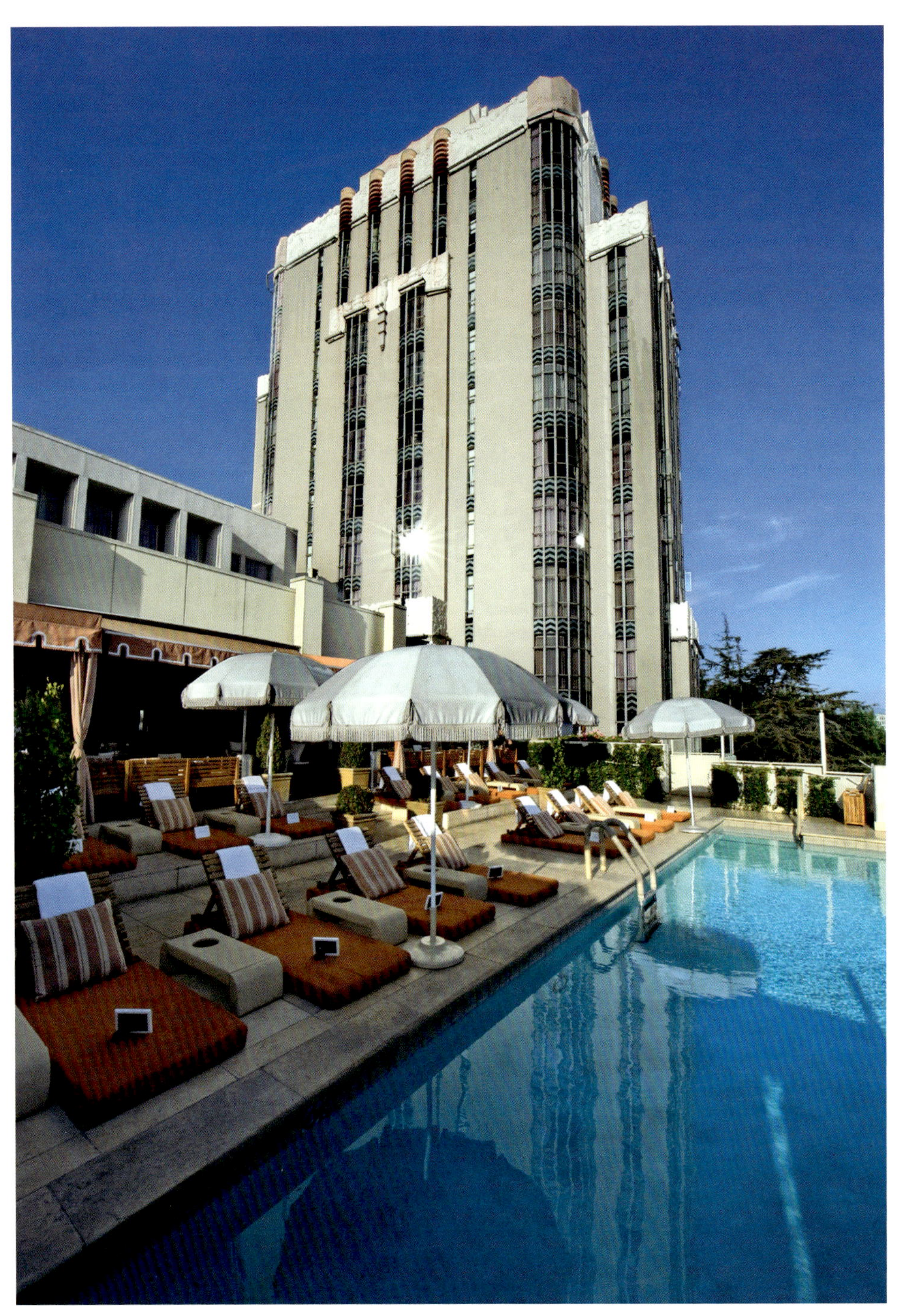

Sunset Tower Hotel (Leland A. Bryant, 1931)
8358 Sunset Blvd., West Hollywood, exterior and pool photographed 2015, exterior at night photographed 2016.

OVERLEAF: *Hollywood Theatre (S. Charles Lee, 1936)*
6764 Hollywood Blvd., photographed 1994.

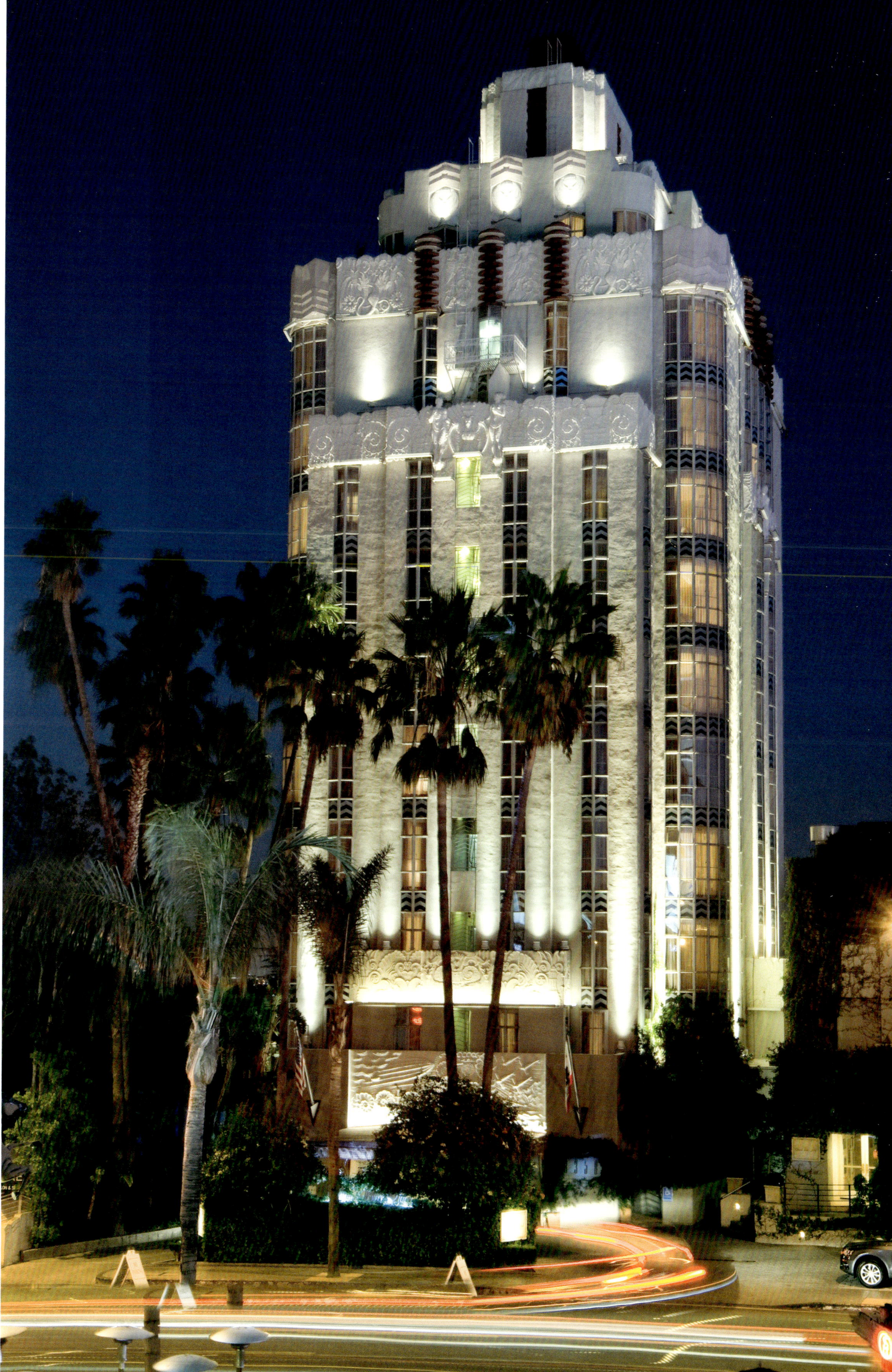

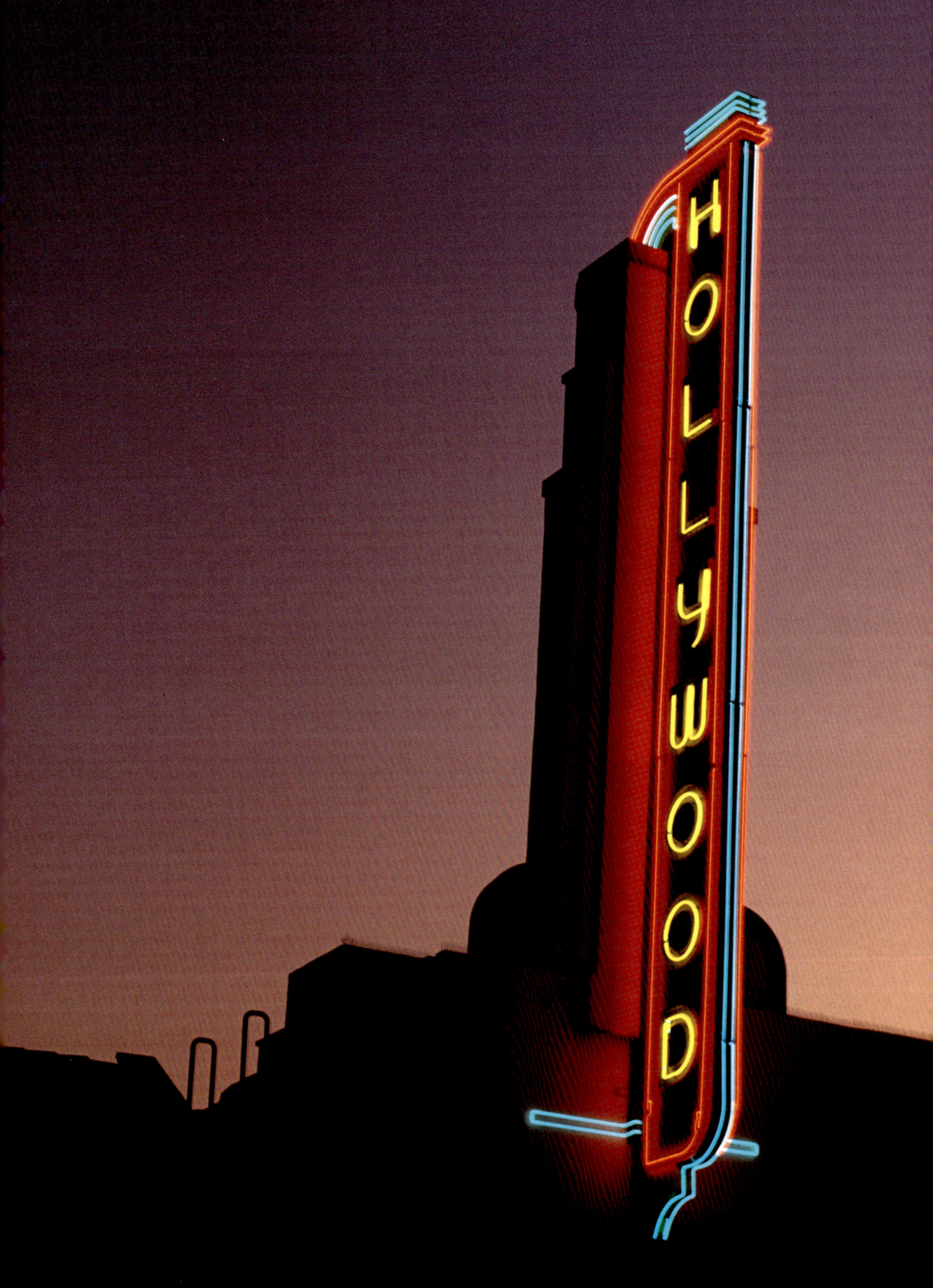
HOLLYWOOD

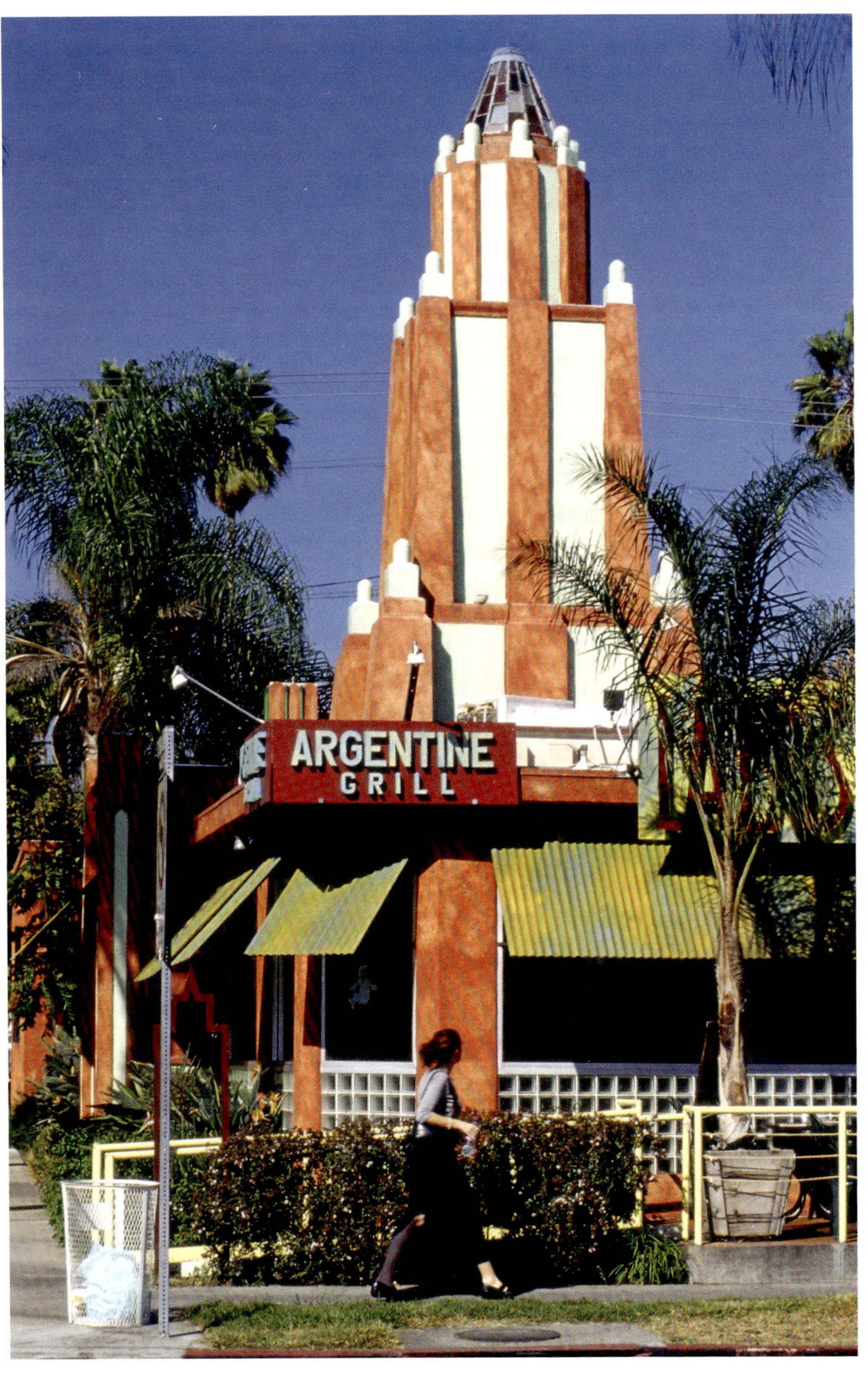
ARGENTINE
GRILL

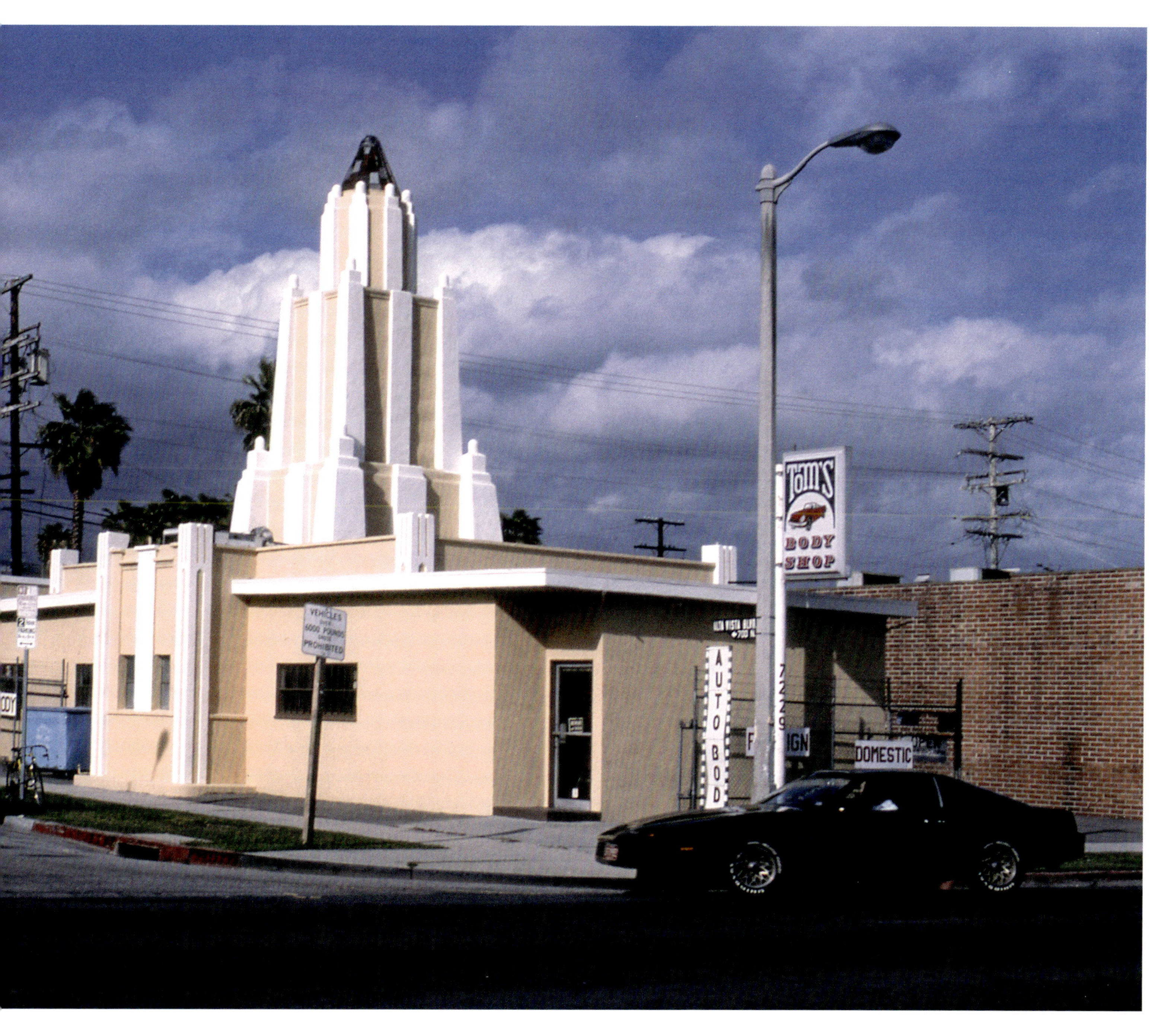

Argentine Grill, formerly Tom's Body Shop (architect unknown)
7229 Melrose Ave., Argentine Grill photographed, 1995,
Tom's Body Shop photographed 1977.

OVERLEAF: *Egyptian Theatre (Meyer and Holler, 1922)*
6712 Hollywood Blvd., photographed 2003.

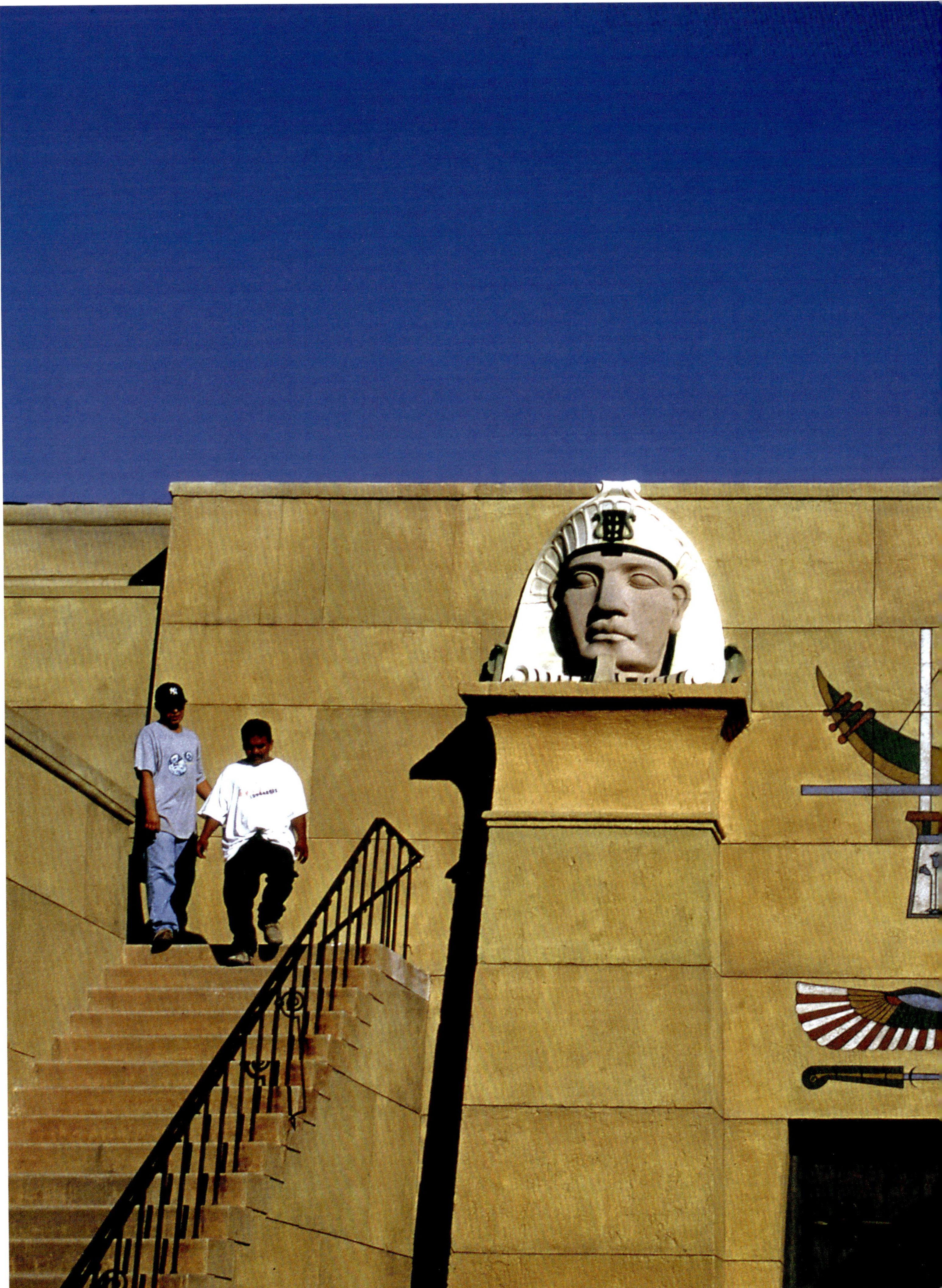

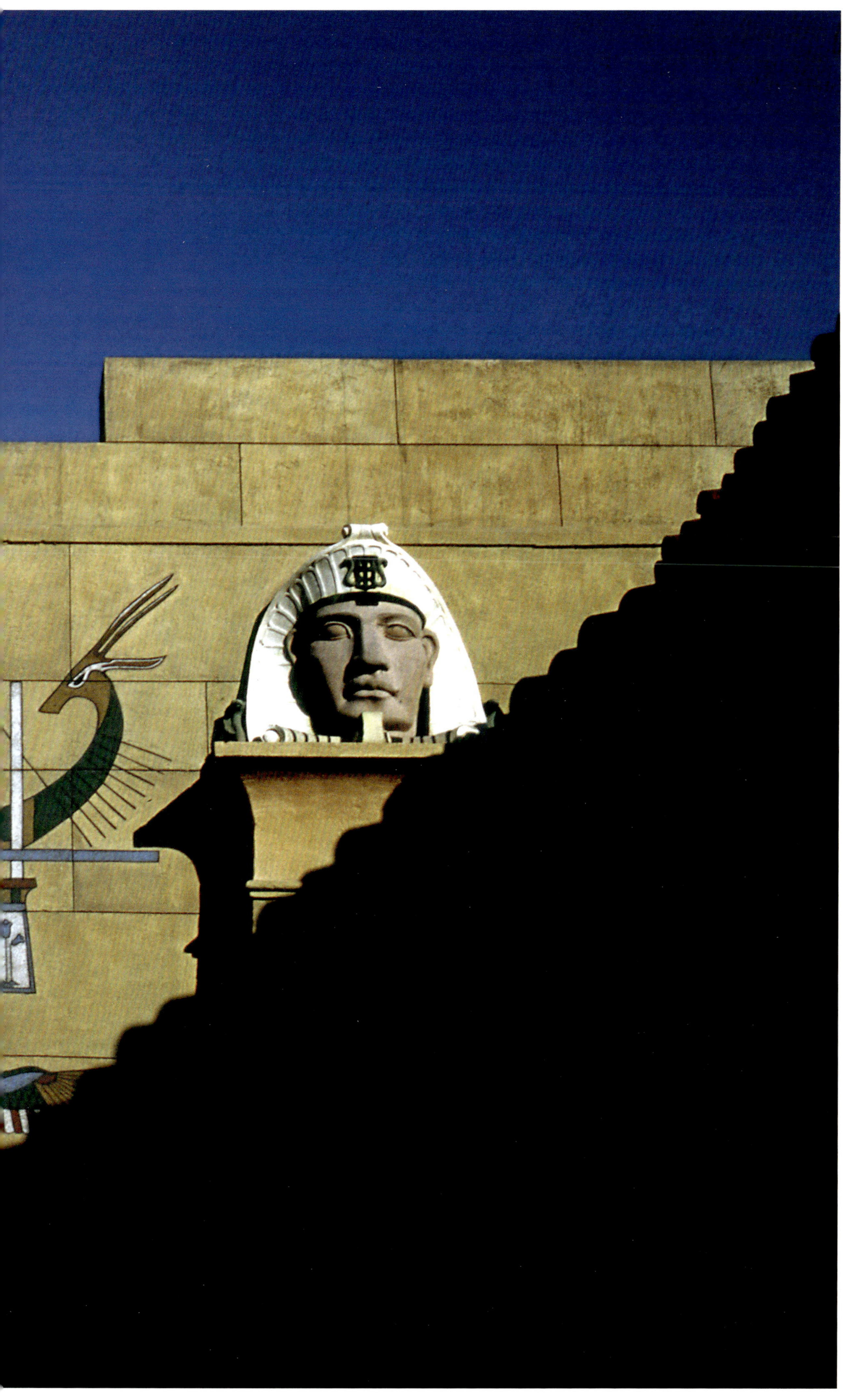

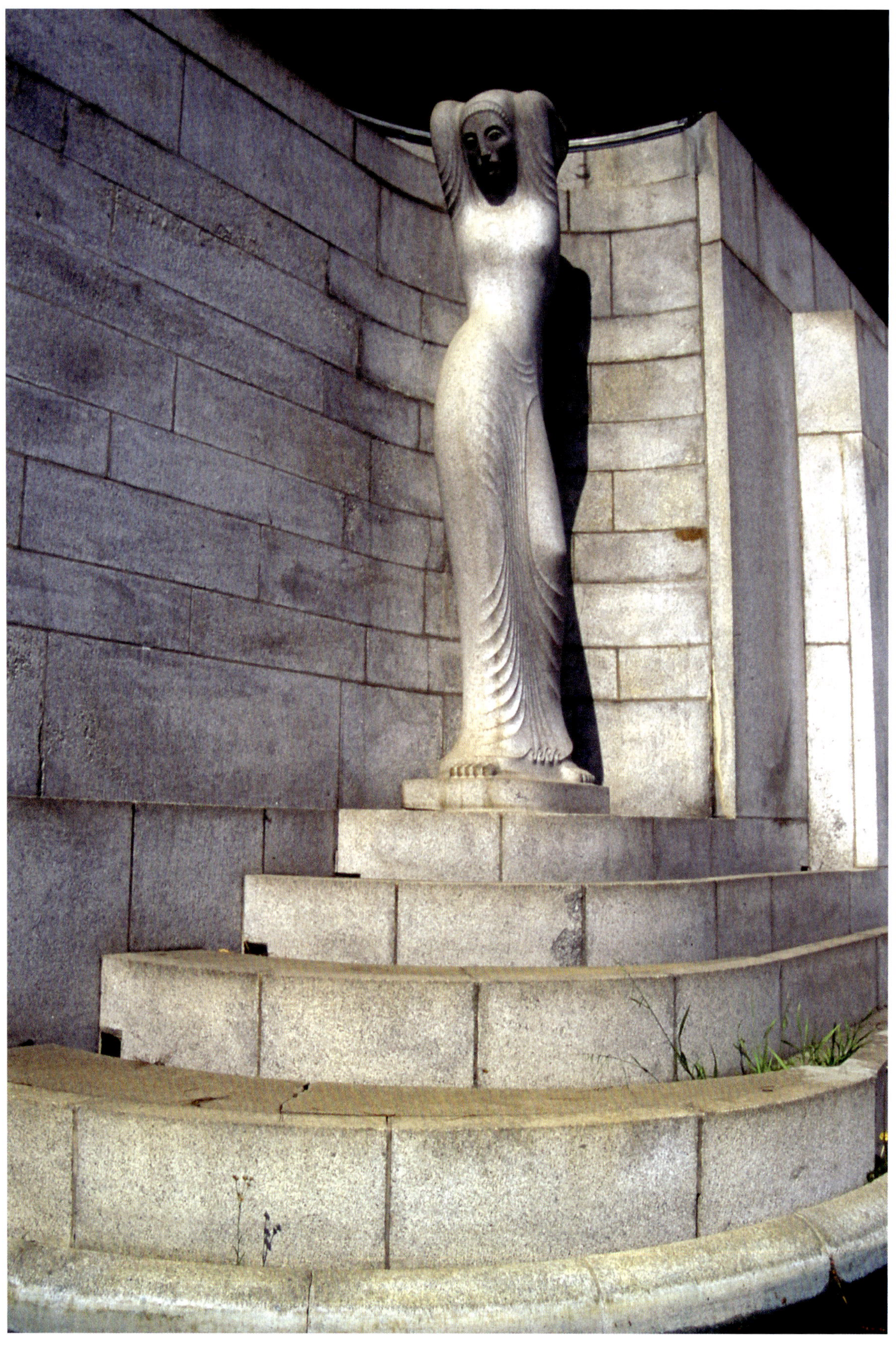

Muse of Music, Dance, Drama *at the Hollywood Bowl (sculpture by George Stanley, 1940) 2301 Highland Ave., photographed 1996.*

OVERLEAF: *Frolic Room, neon sign (sign designed by EPCO, 1958) 6245 Hollywood Blvd., photographed 2008.*

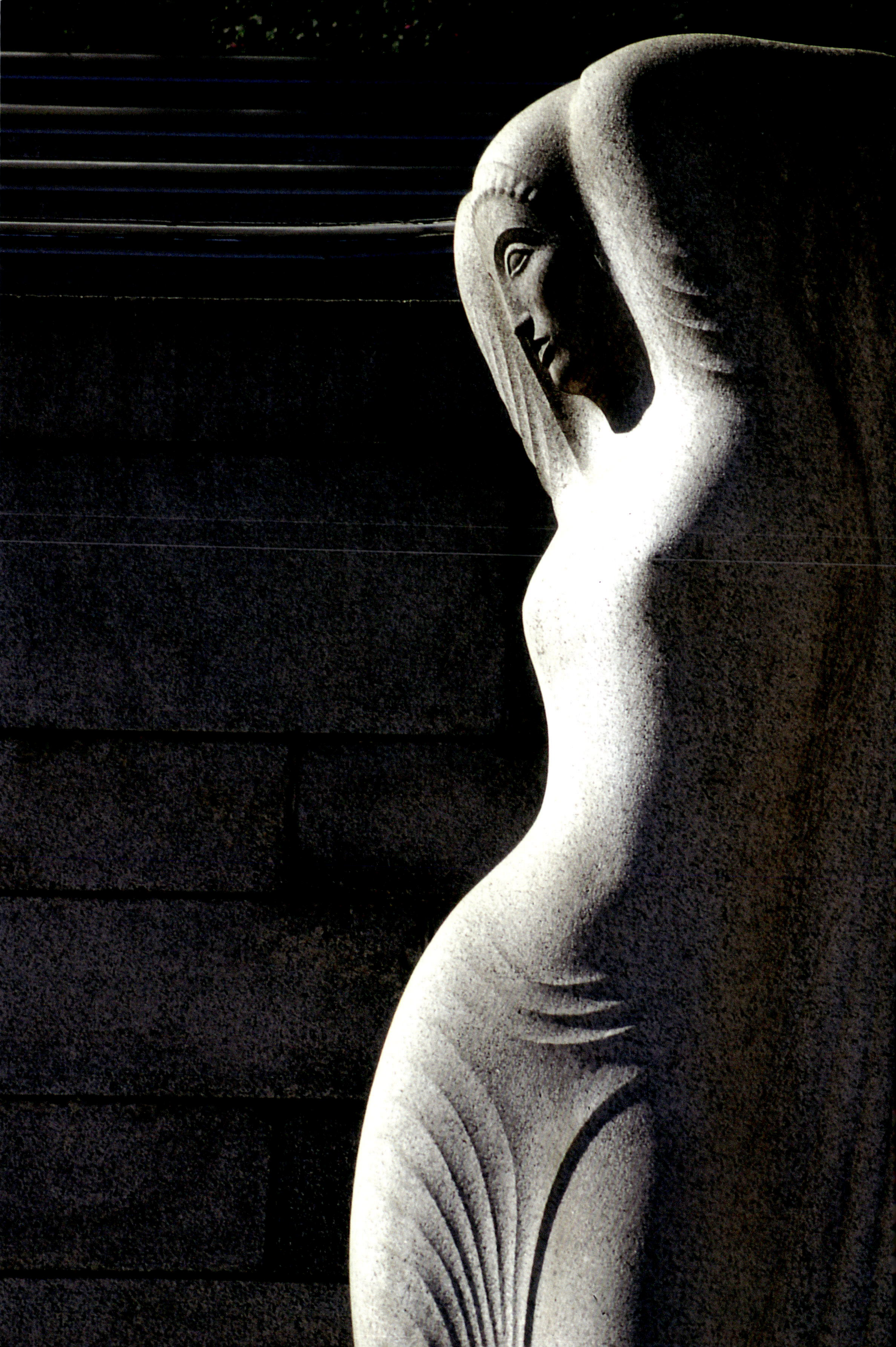

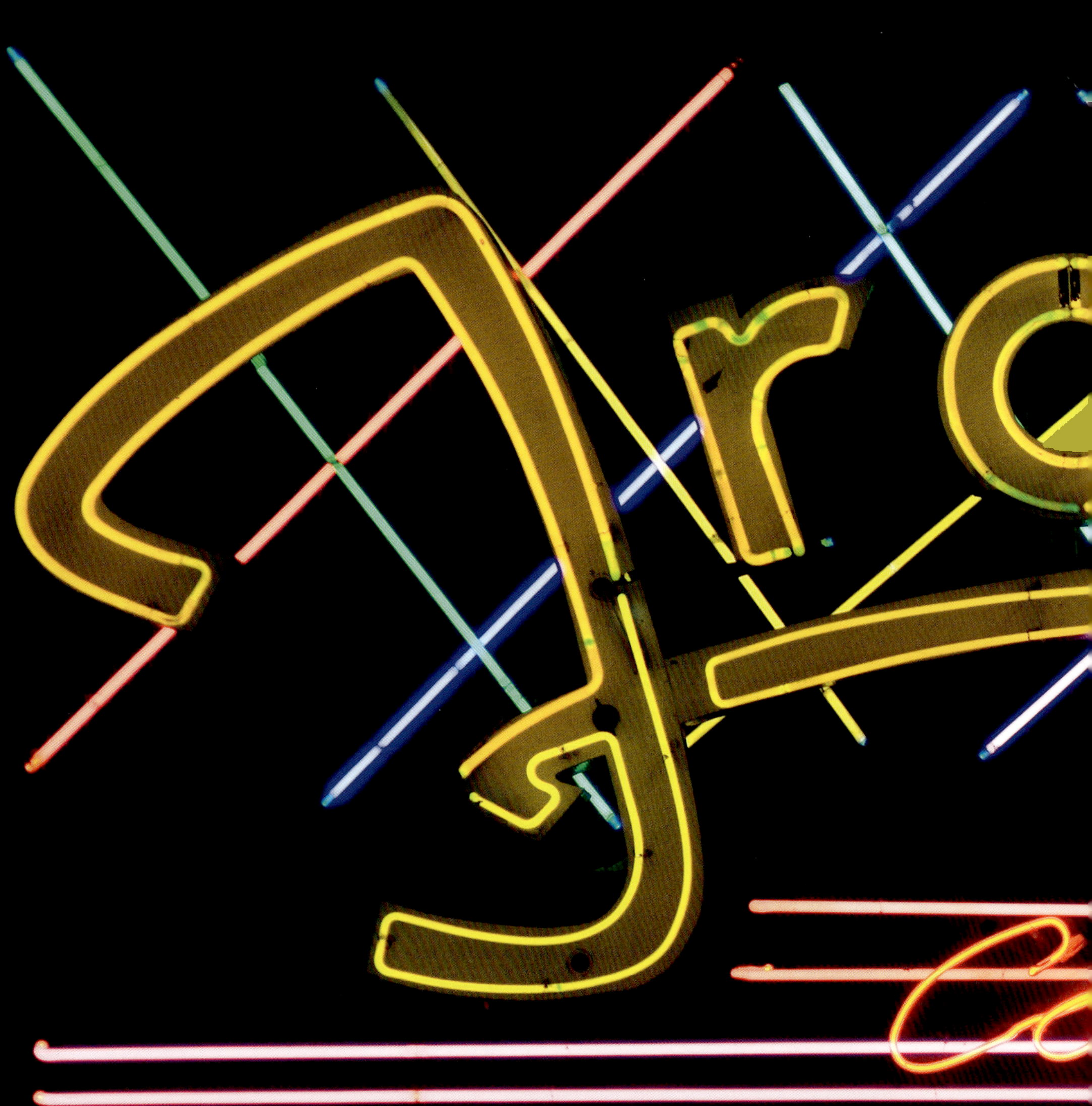

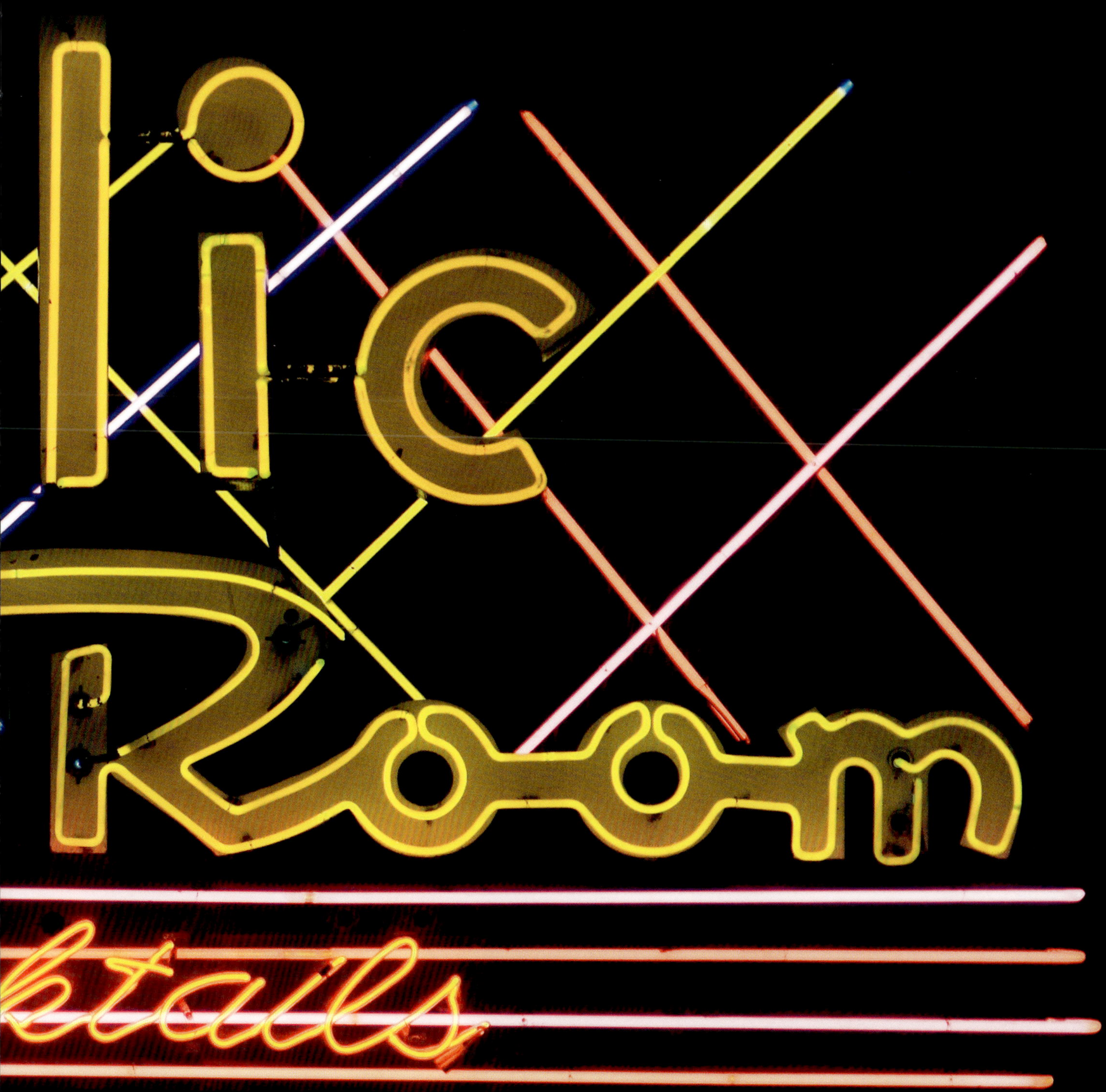
lic
Room
ktails

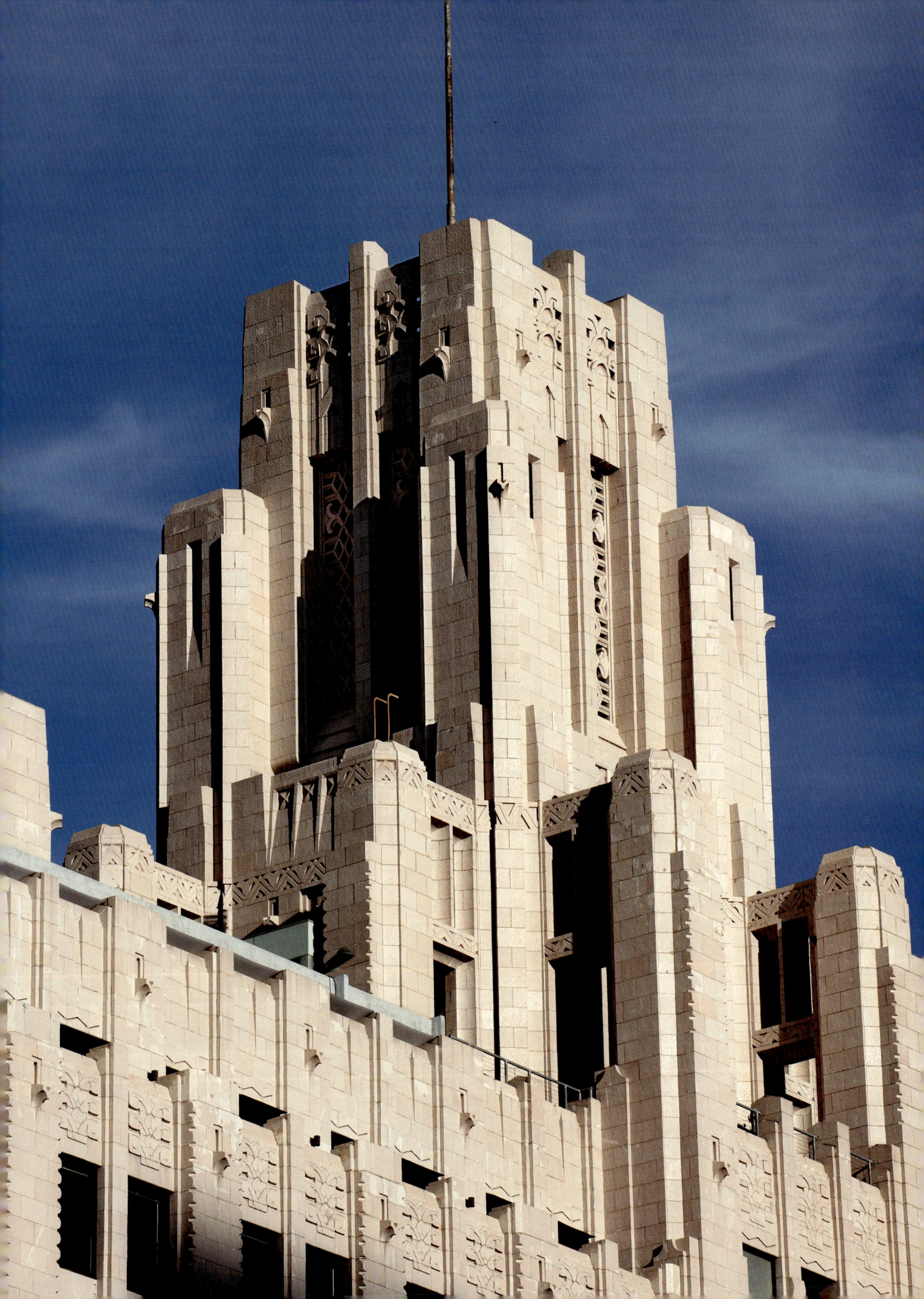

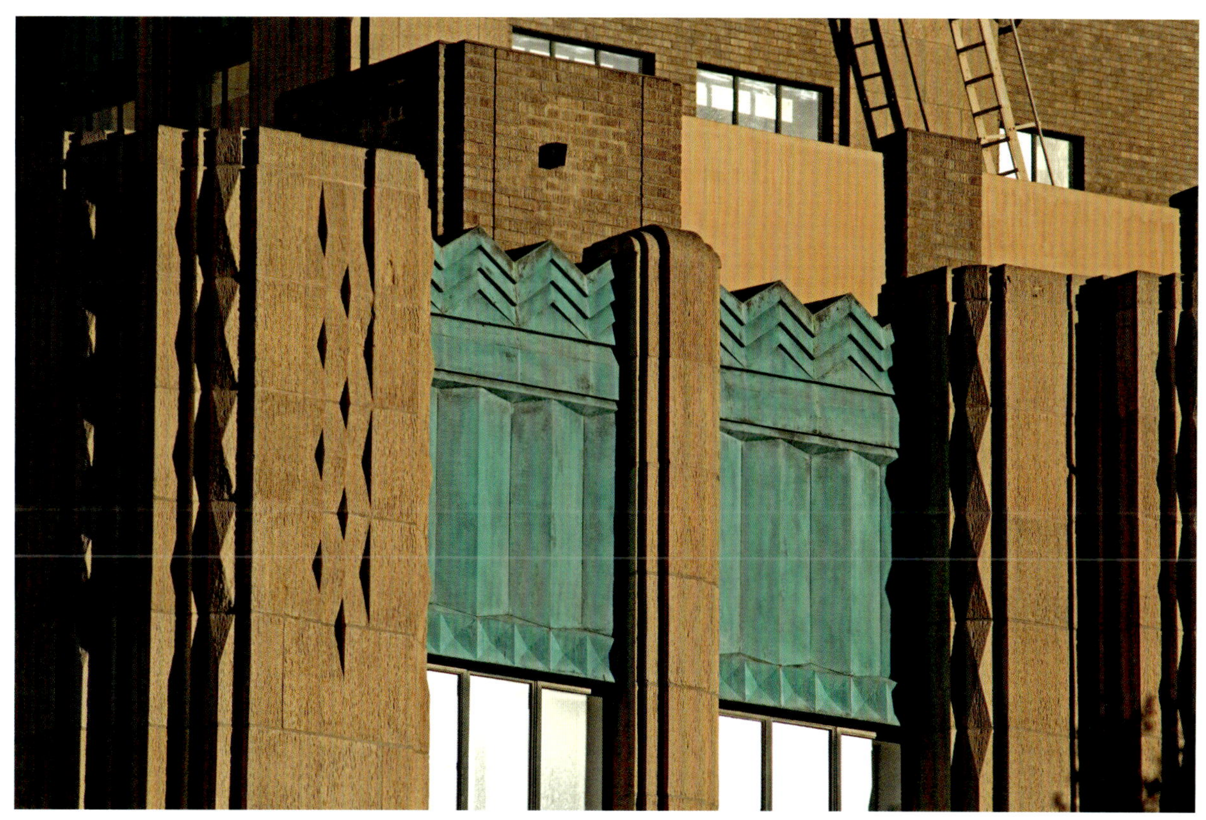

← *Title Guarantee and Trust Building, now Title Guarantee Building (John and Donald B. Parkinson, 1931) 411 W. 5th St., photographed 2024.*

↑ *Bullock's Wilshire, now Southwestern Law School, exterior detail (John Parkinson and Donald B. Parkinson, 1929) 3050 Wilshire Blvd., photographed 2003.*

OVERLEAF: *Burbank City Hall,* Four Freedoms *mural (William Allen and George Lutzi, mural by Hugo Ballin, 1943) 275 E. Olive Ave., photographed 2024.*

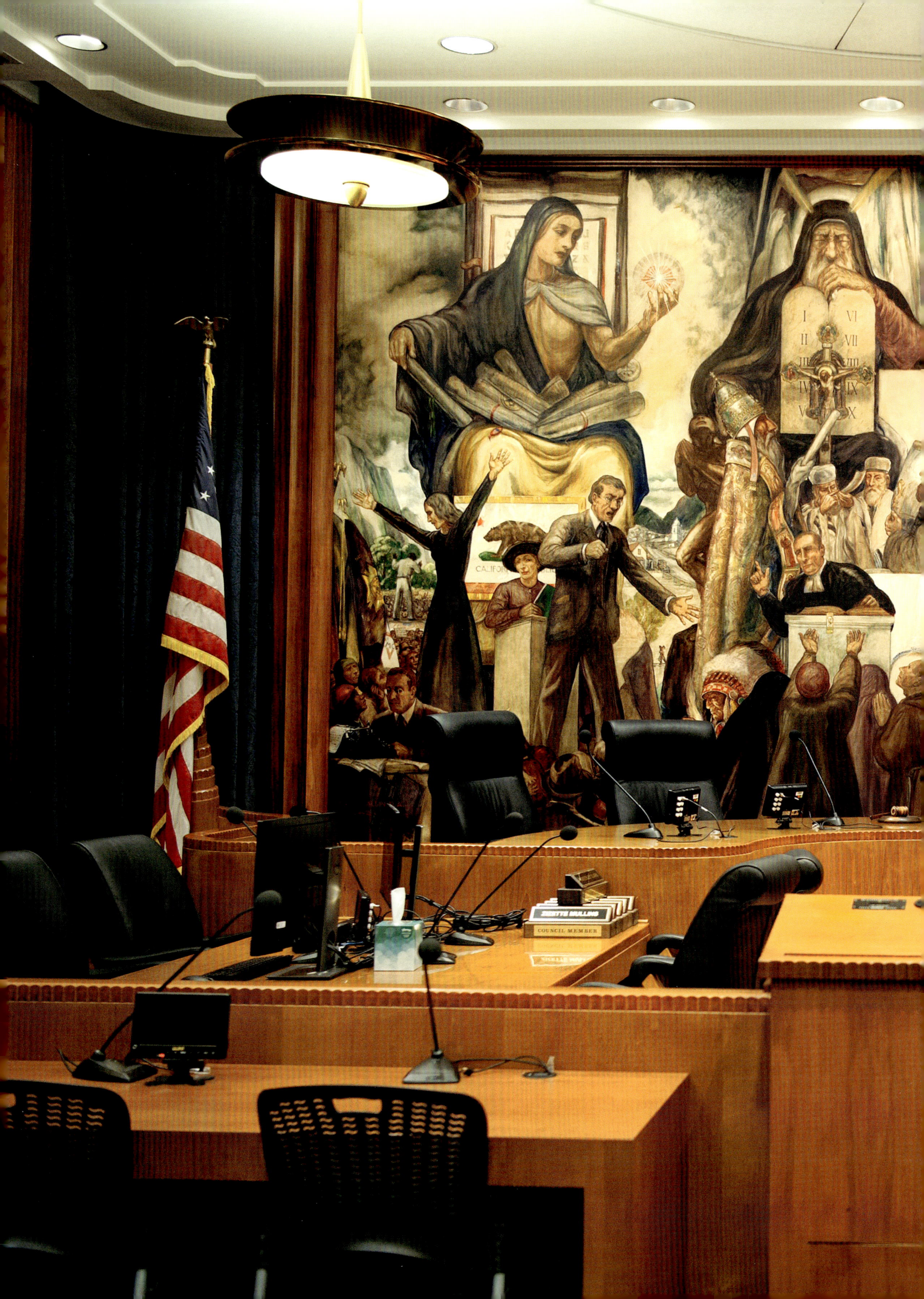
COUNCIL MEMBER

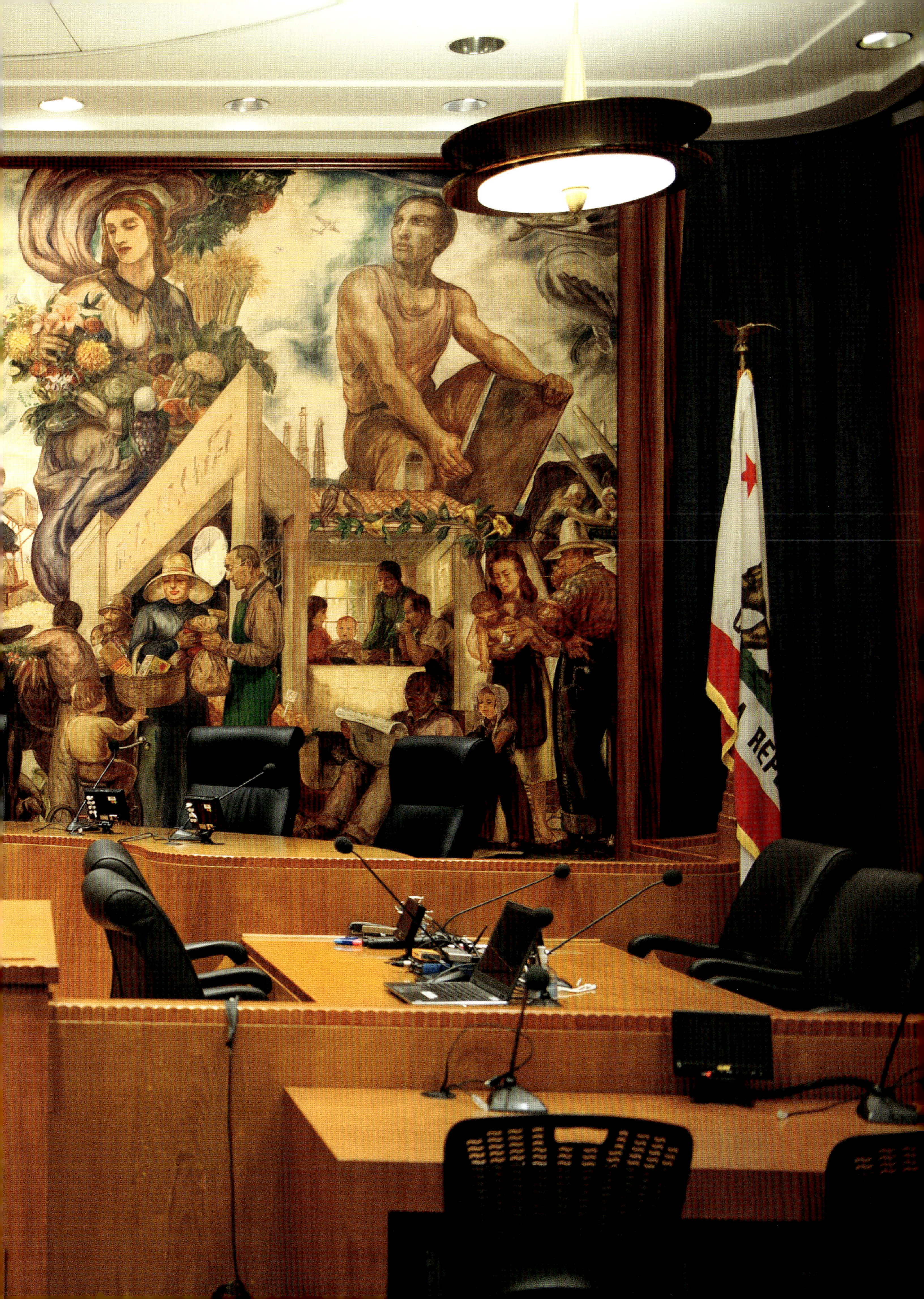

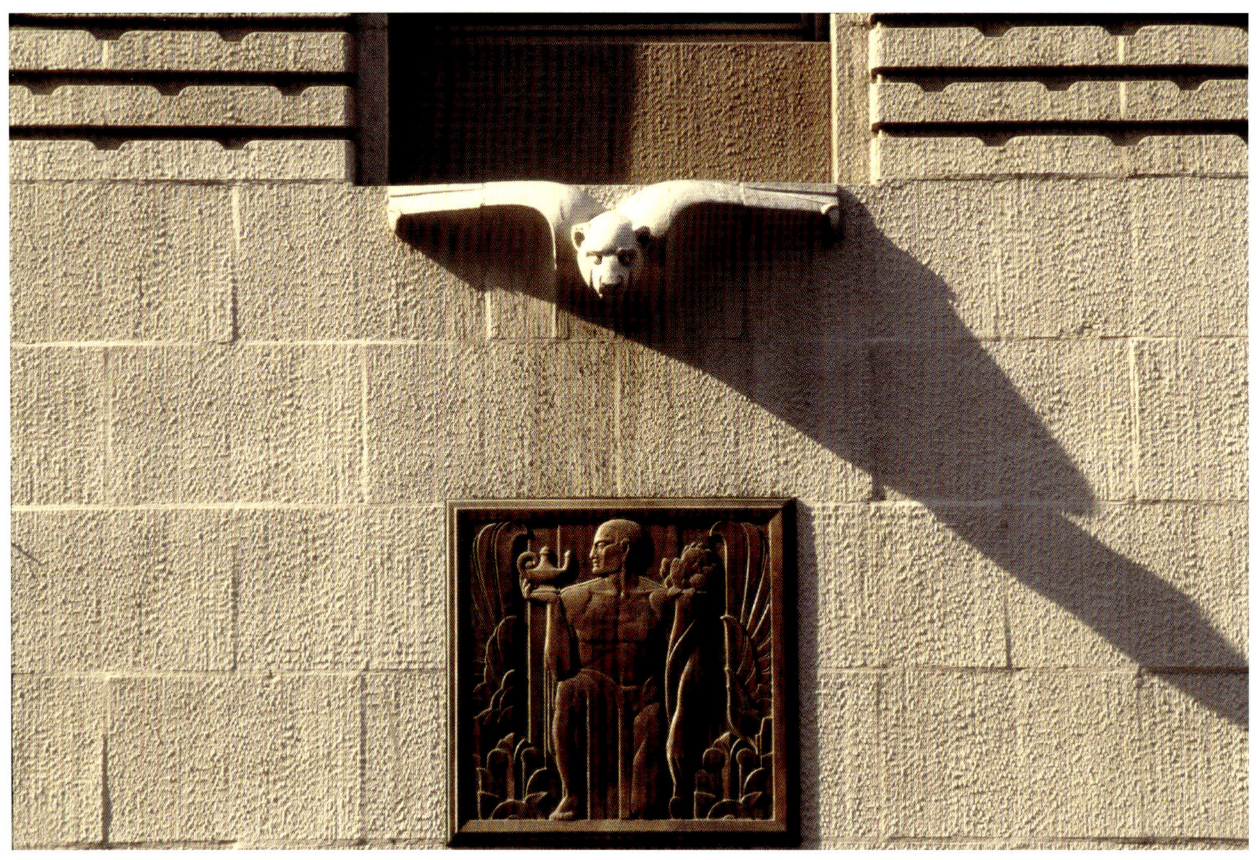

↑ *Bear Ornament (architect and year unknown) downtown Los Angeles, photographed 1989.*

→ *Elks Lodge, now The MacArthur, exterior detail (Curlett and Beelman, 1924) 607 S. Park View St., photographed 2024.*

OVERLEAF: *Sun Realty Building now Los Angeles Jewelry Center, exterior detail (Claud Beelman, 1931) 629 S. Hill St., photographed 2003.*

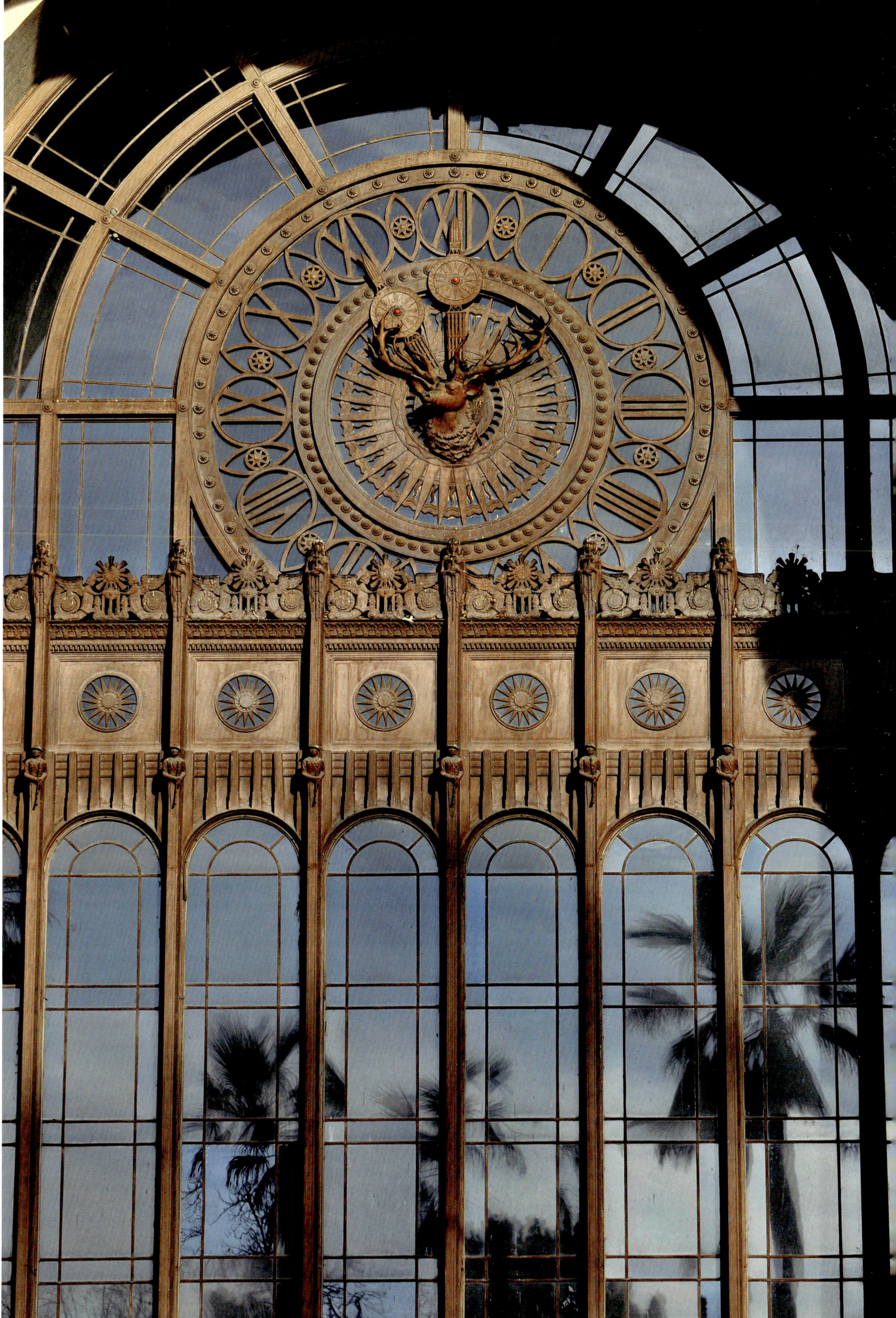

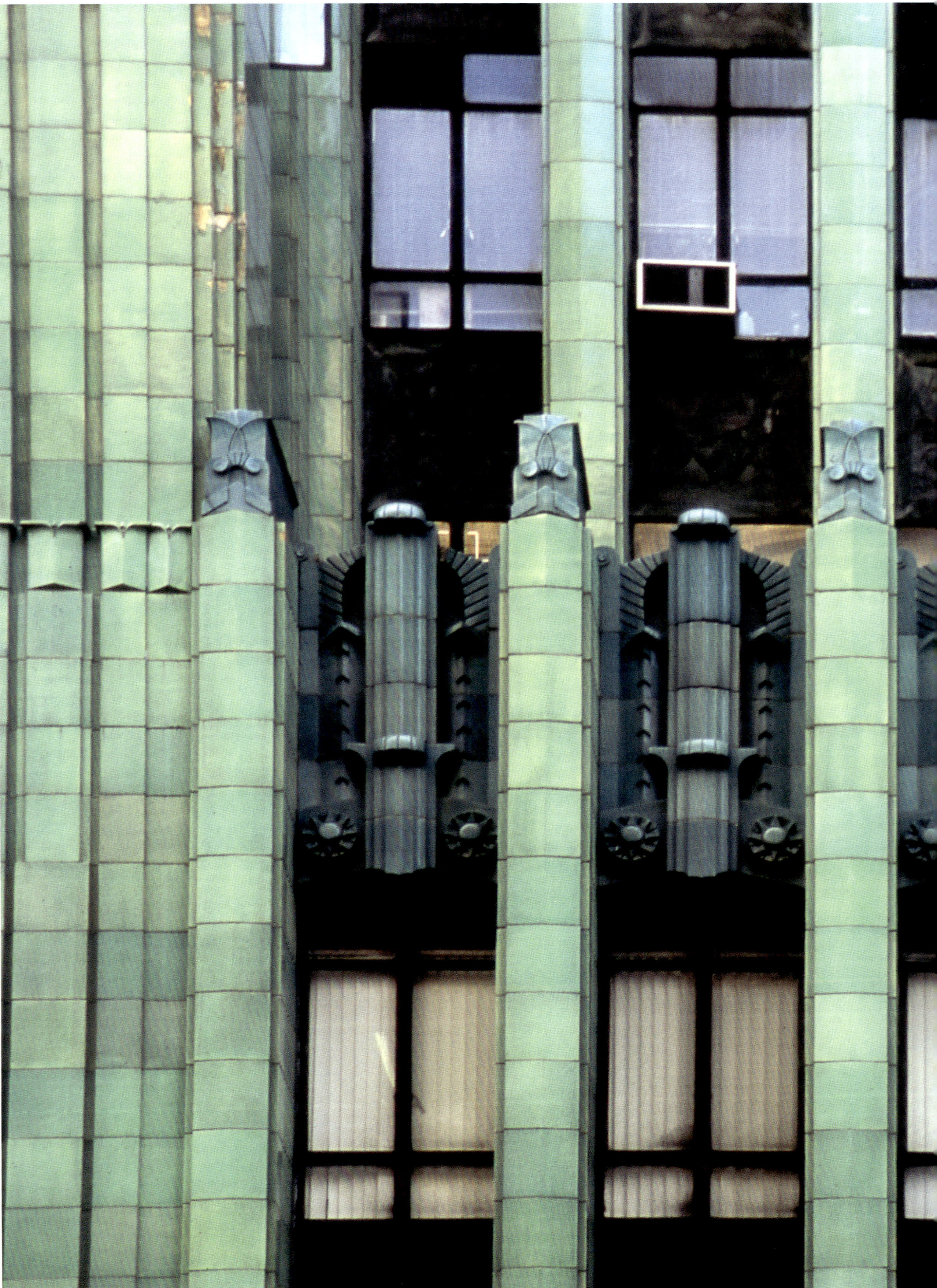

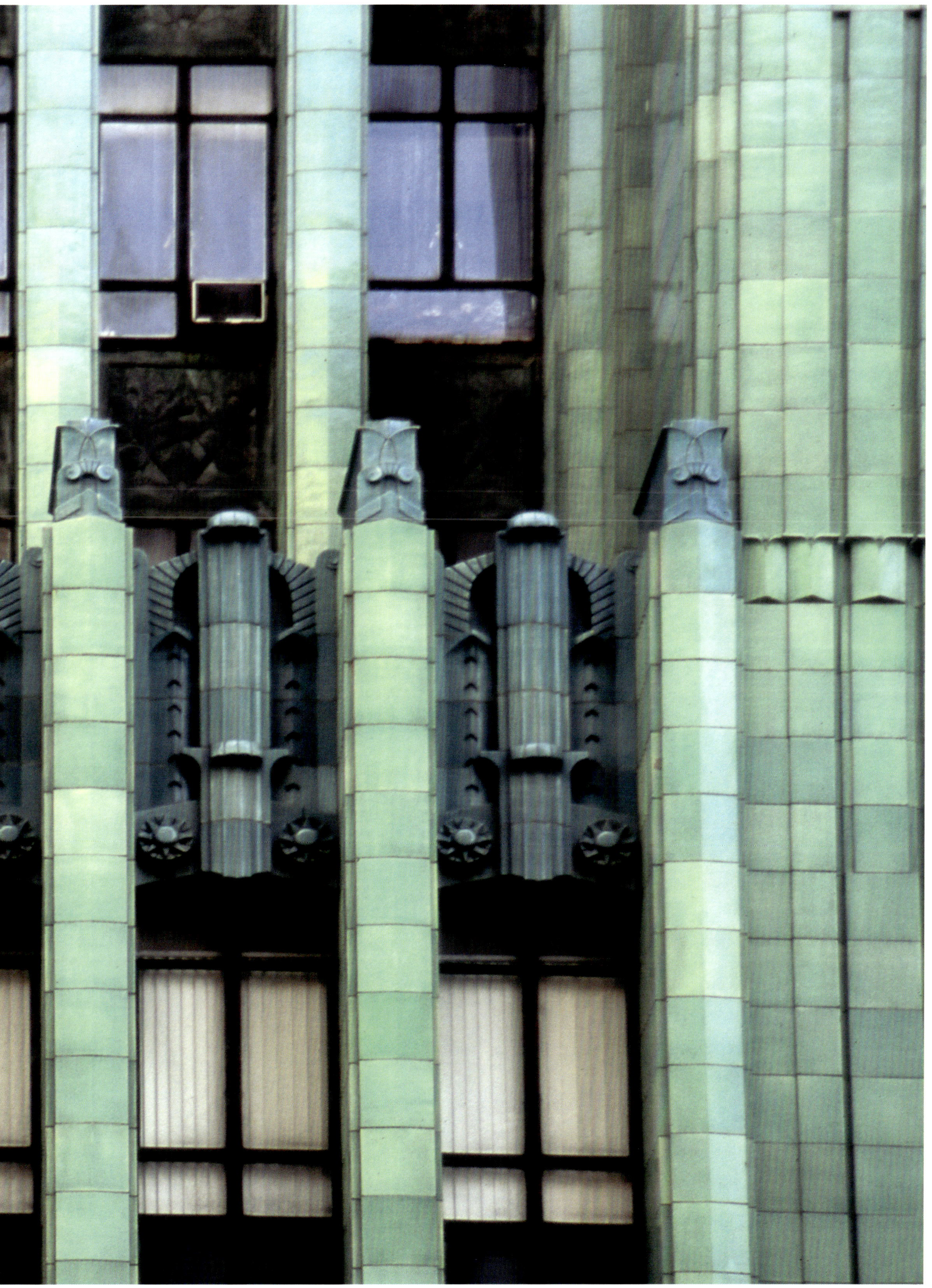

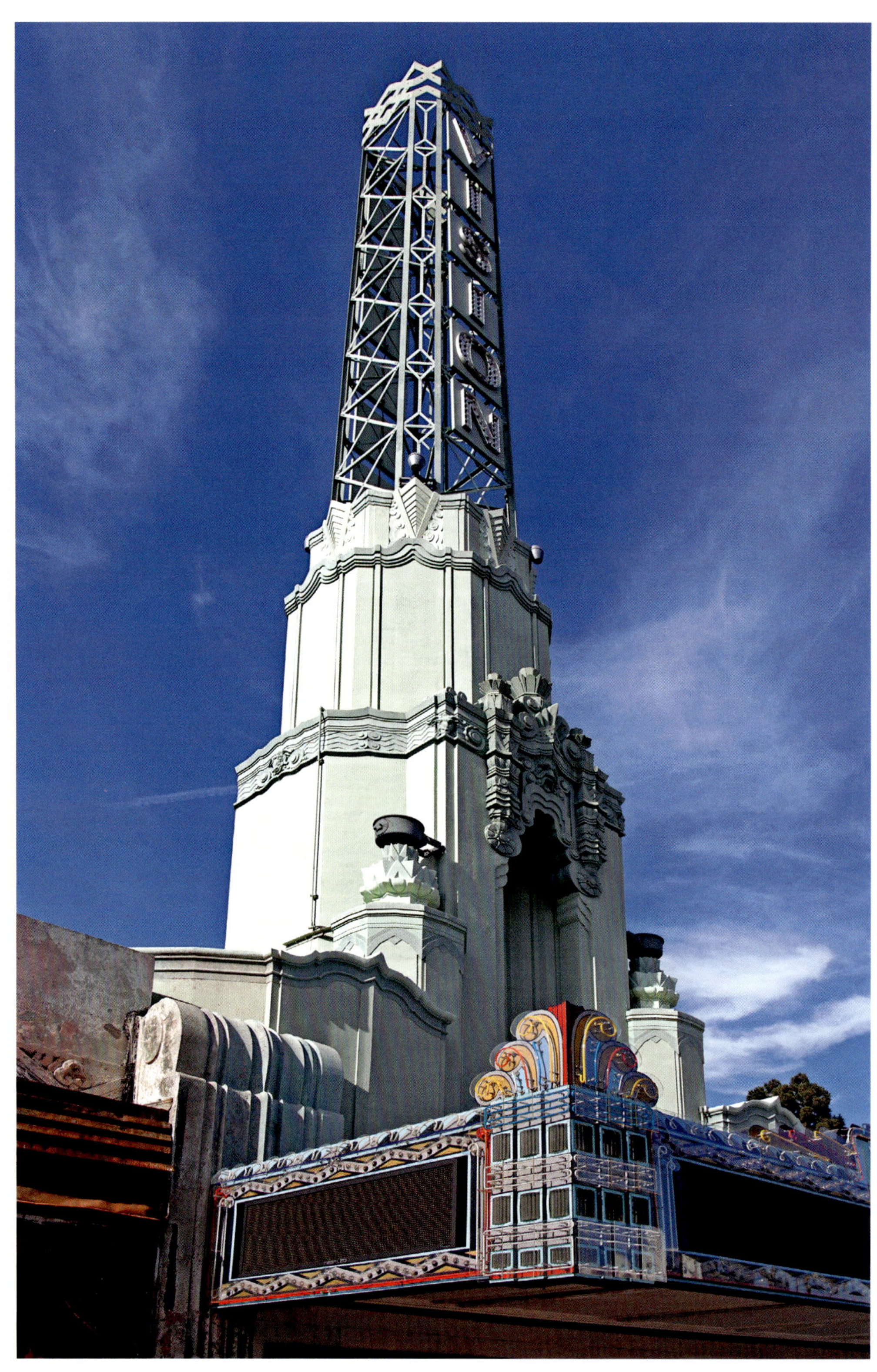

↑ *Leimert Theater, now Vision Theater (Morgan, Walls, and Clements, 1932) 3341 W. 43rd Pl., photographed 2024.*

→ *Pantages Theatre sign (B. Marcus Priteca, 1930) 6233 Hollywood Blvd., photographed 2010.*

OVERLEAF: *Citizen News Building, exterior detail (Francis D. Rutherford, 1931) 1545 Wilcox Ave., photographed 2024.*

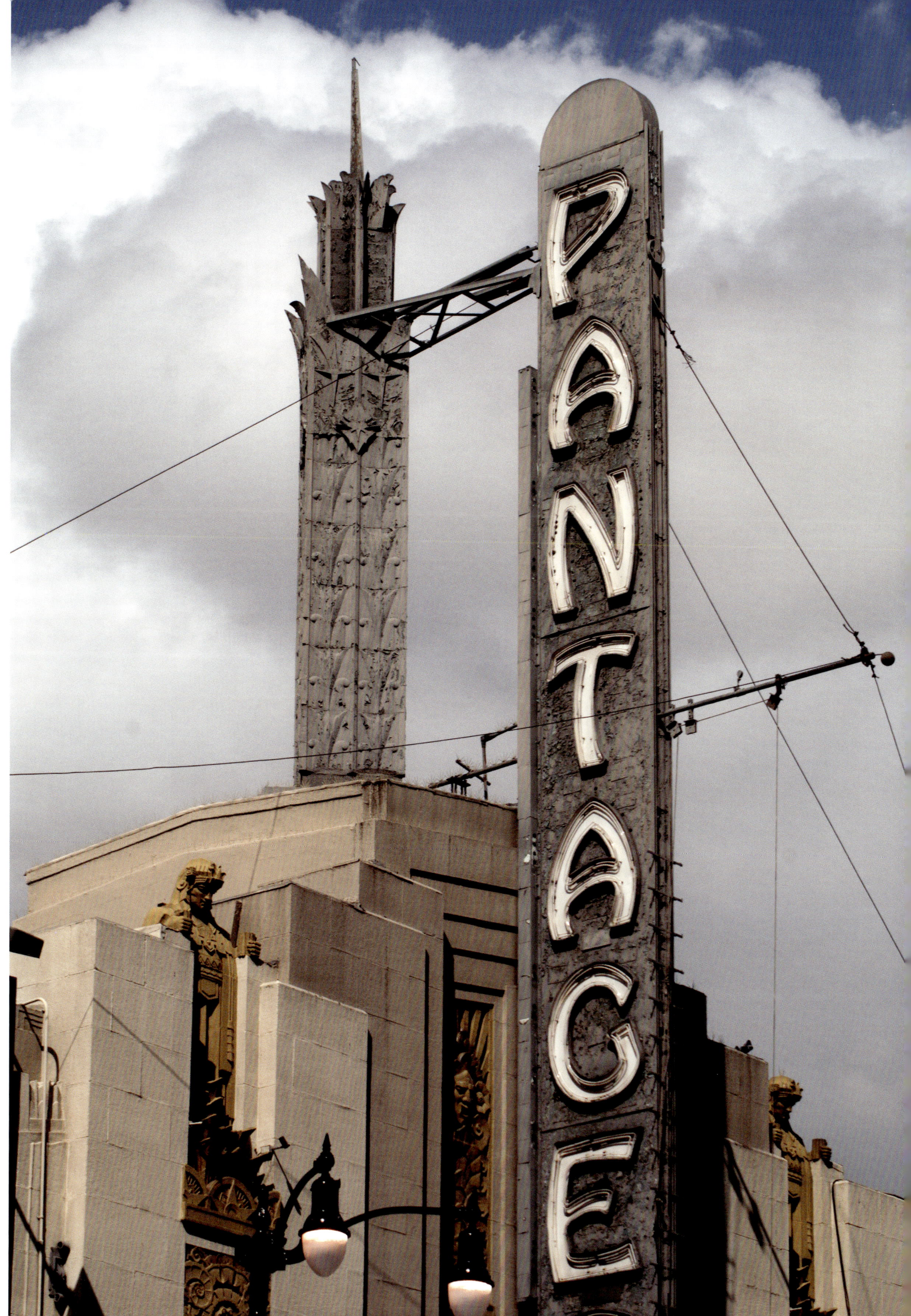
PANTAGE

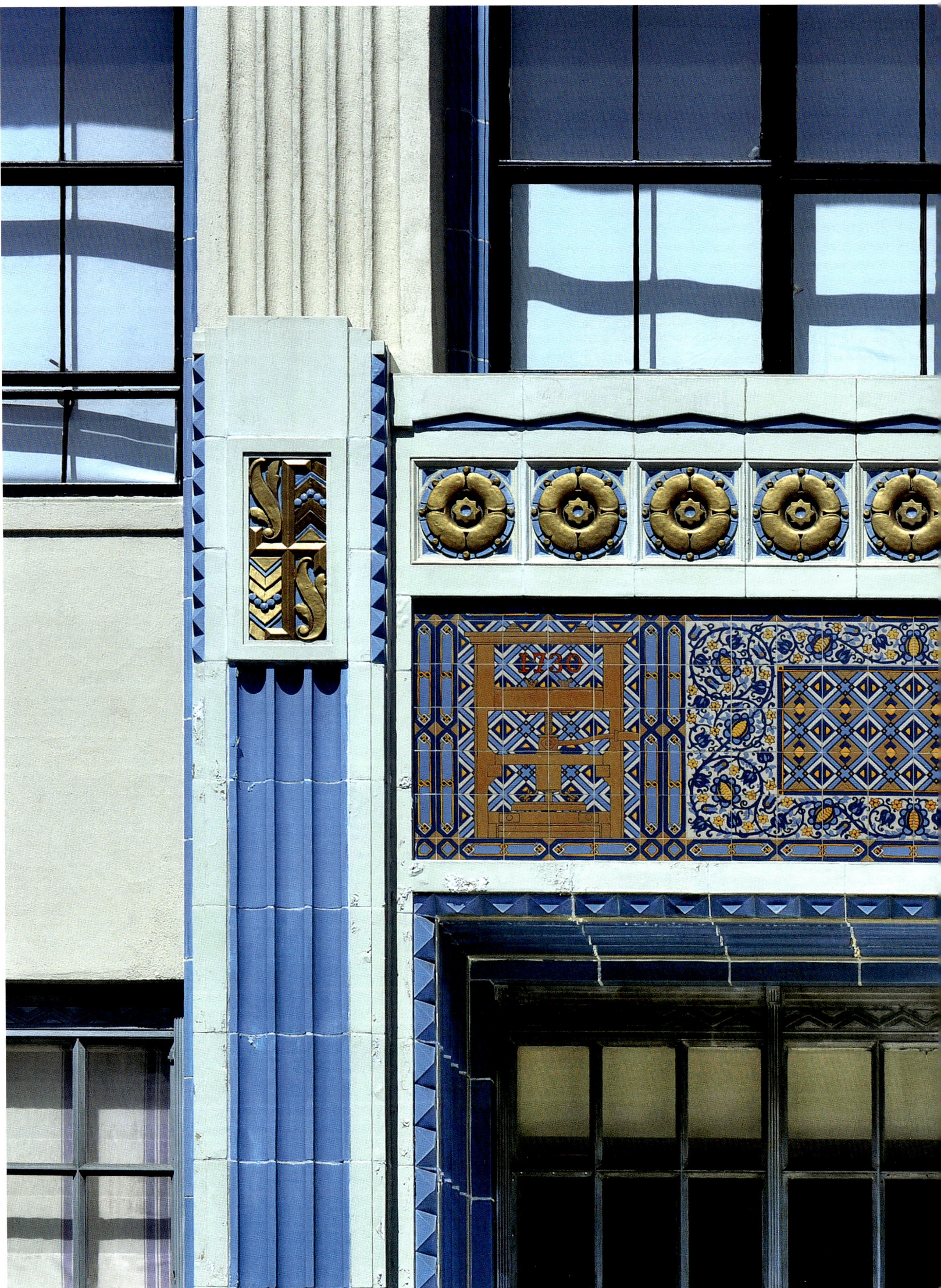
1730

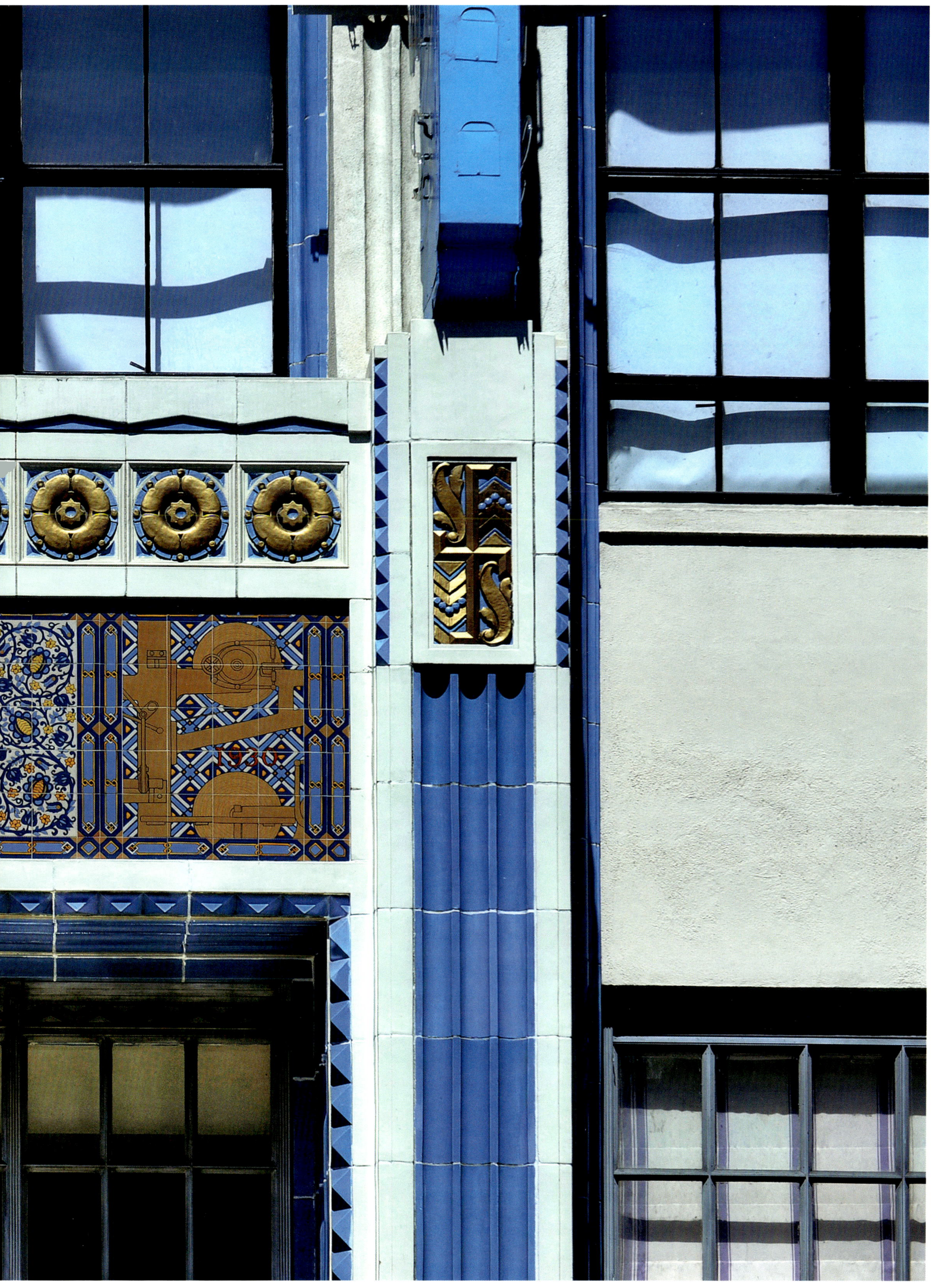
1930

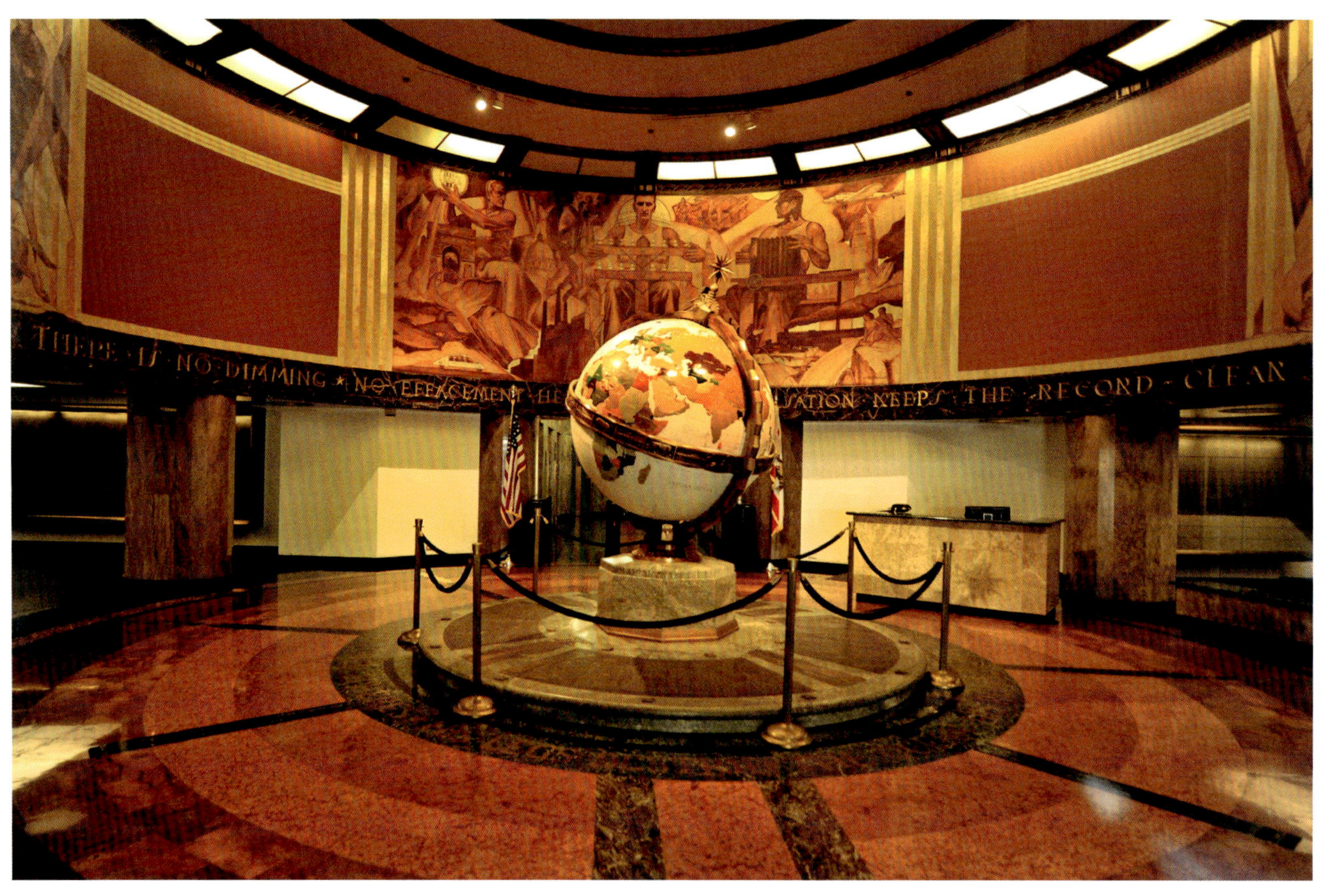

↑ Los Angeles Times *Building, interior with mural (Gordon B. Kaufmann, mural by Hugo Ballin, 1935) 202 W. 1st St., photographed 2024.*

→ *Los Angeles Central Library, rotunda ceiling (Bertram G. Goodhue and Carleton Winslow, 1926) 630 W. 5th St., photographed 2024.*

OVERLEAF: *Hollywood Bowl, Orchestra Shell (Hodgetts and Fung with Gruen Associates, 2004) 2301 Highland Ave., photographed 2004*

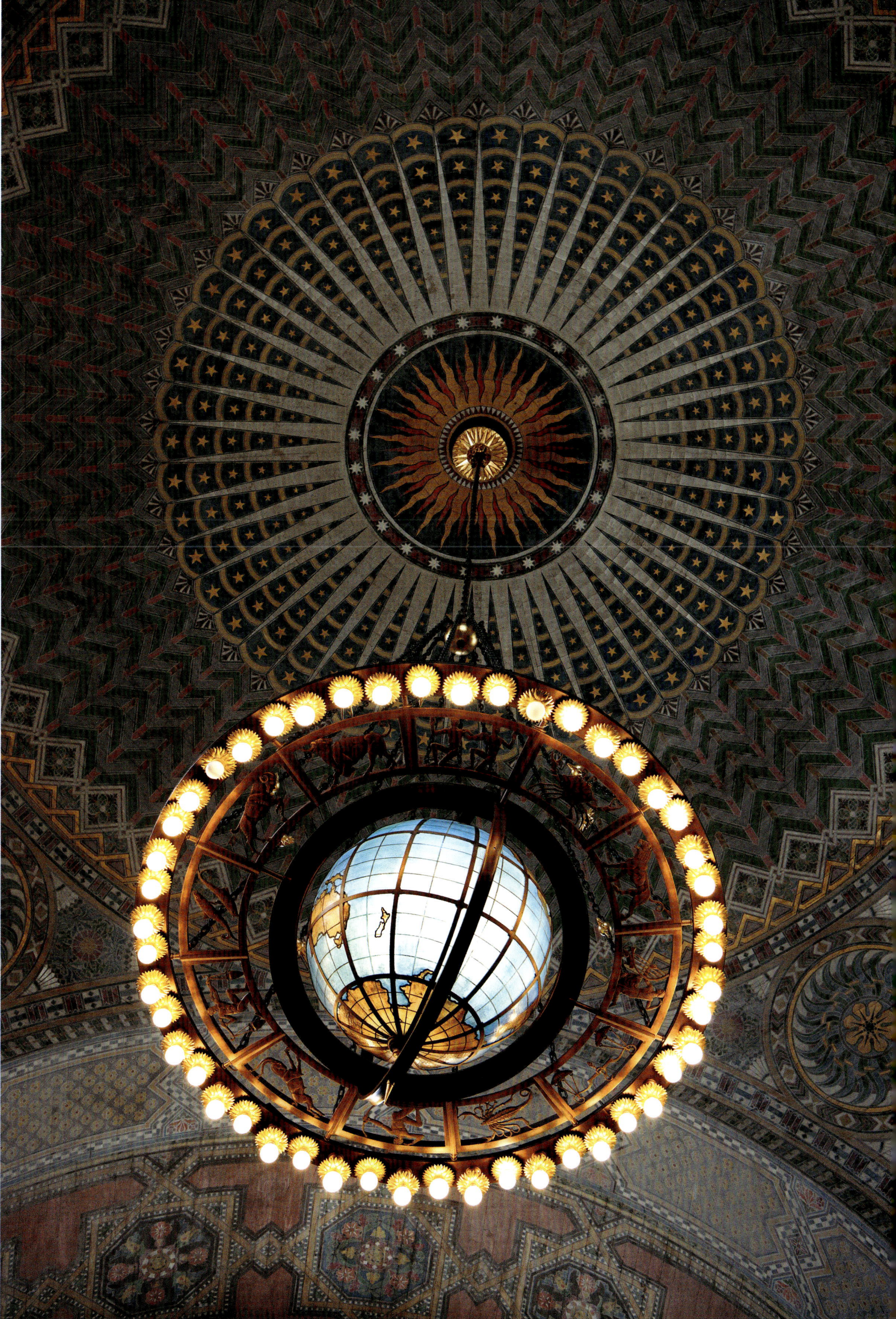

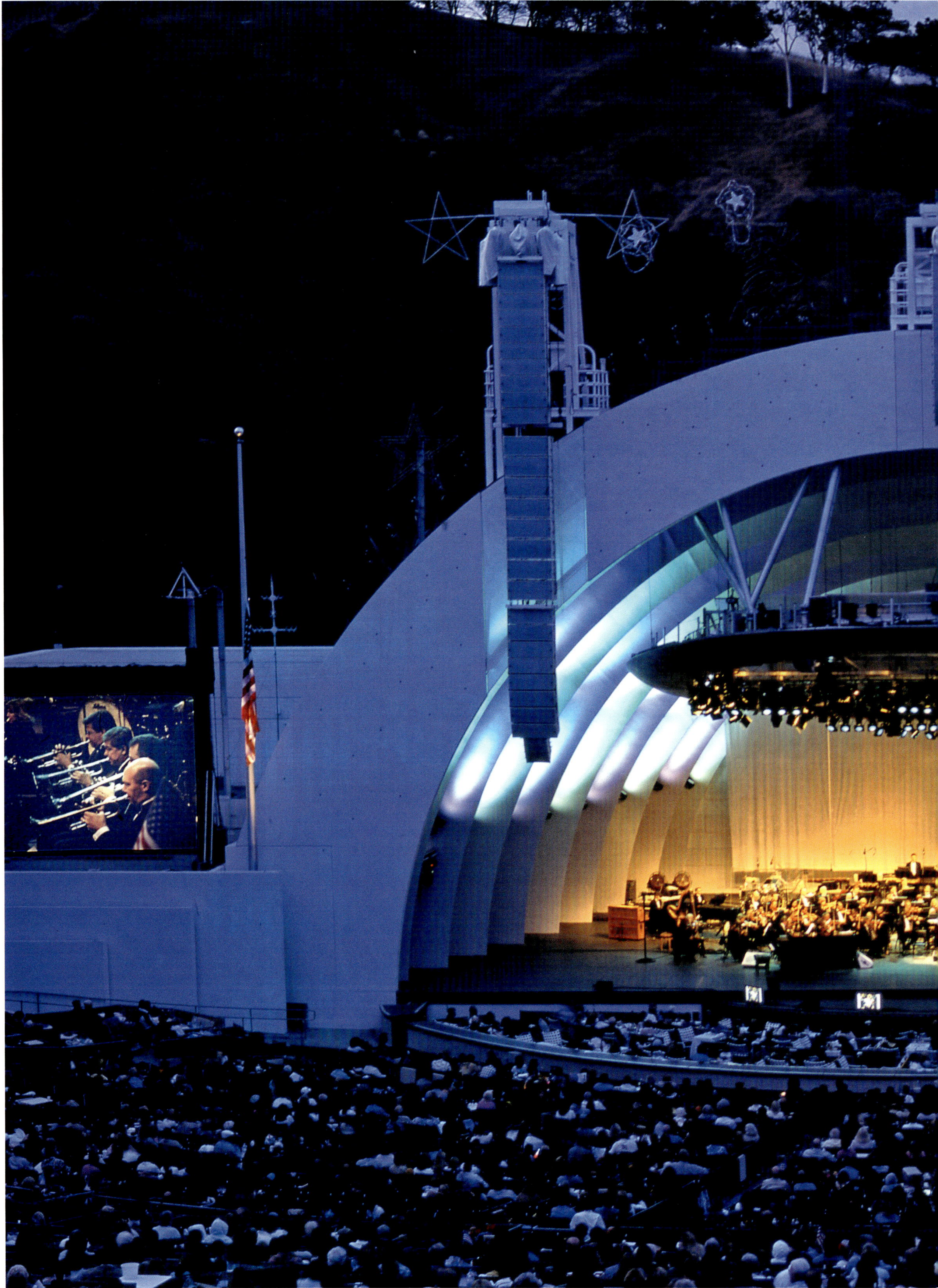

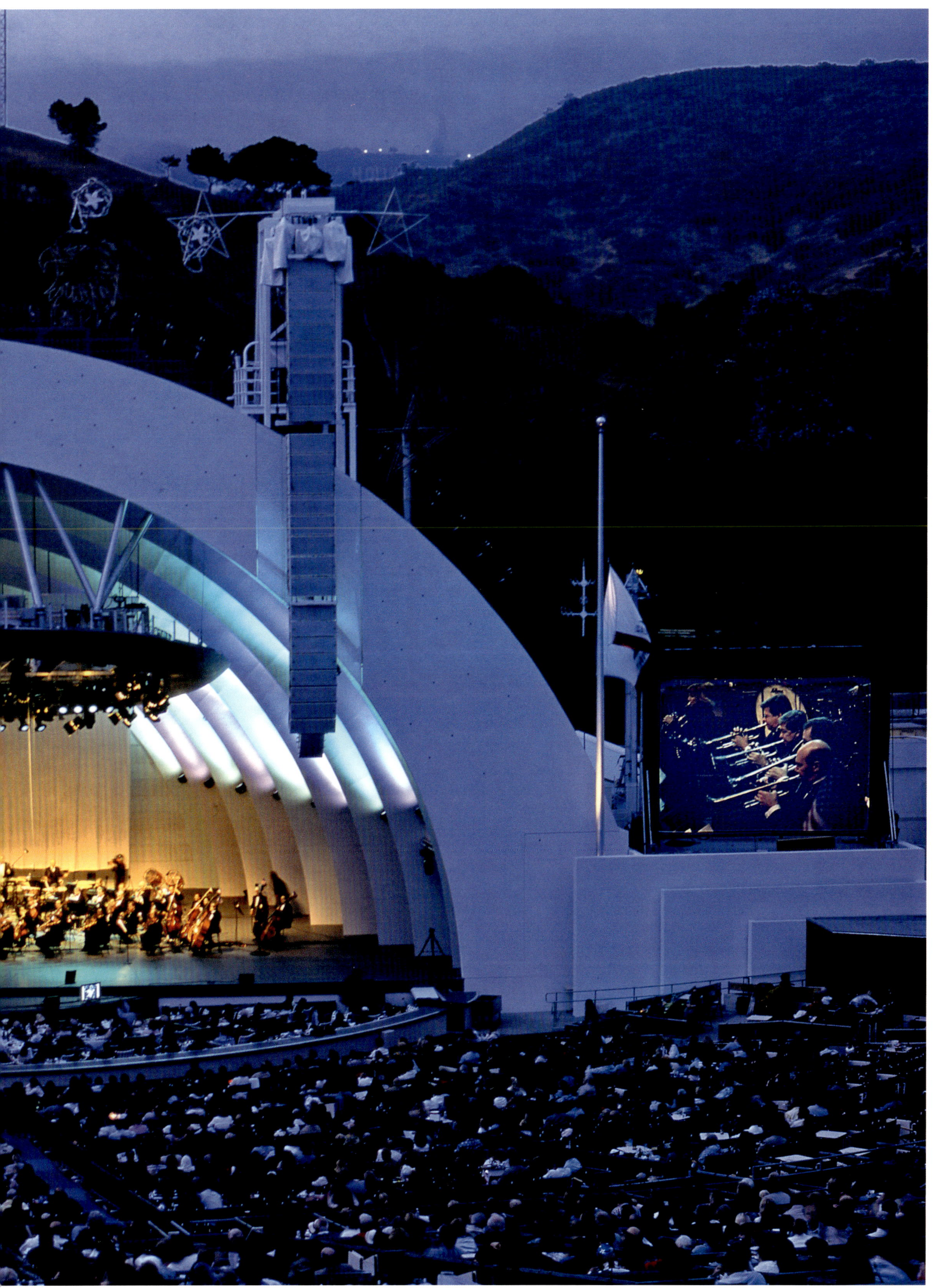

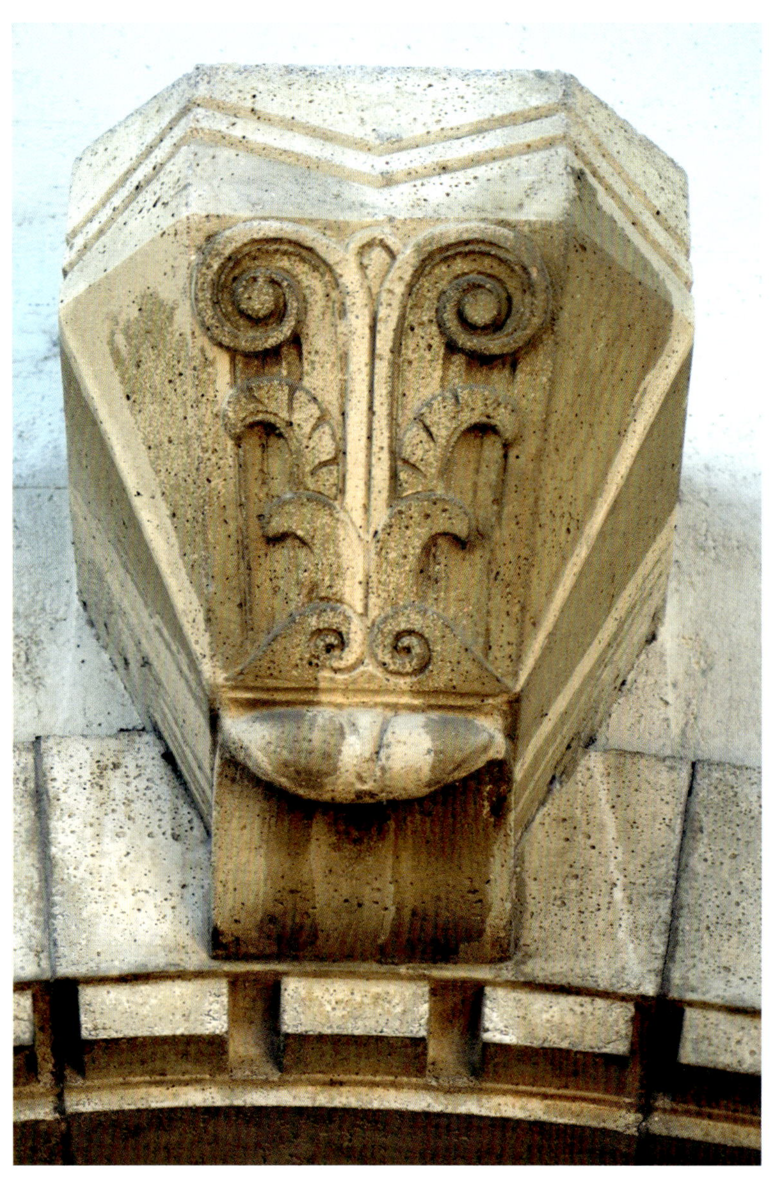

Catalina Casino, exterior detail and archway (David Malcom Renton, 1929) Avalon, Catalina Island, photographed 2008.

OVERLEAF: *Samson Tyre and Rubber Company, now Citadel Outlets (Morgan, Walls, and Clements, 1929) 5675 Telegraph Rd., Commerce, photographed 2024.*

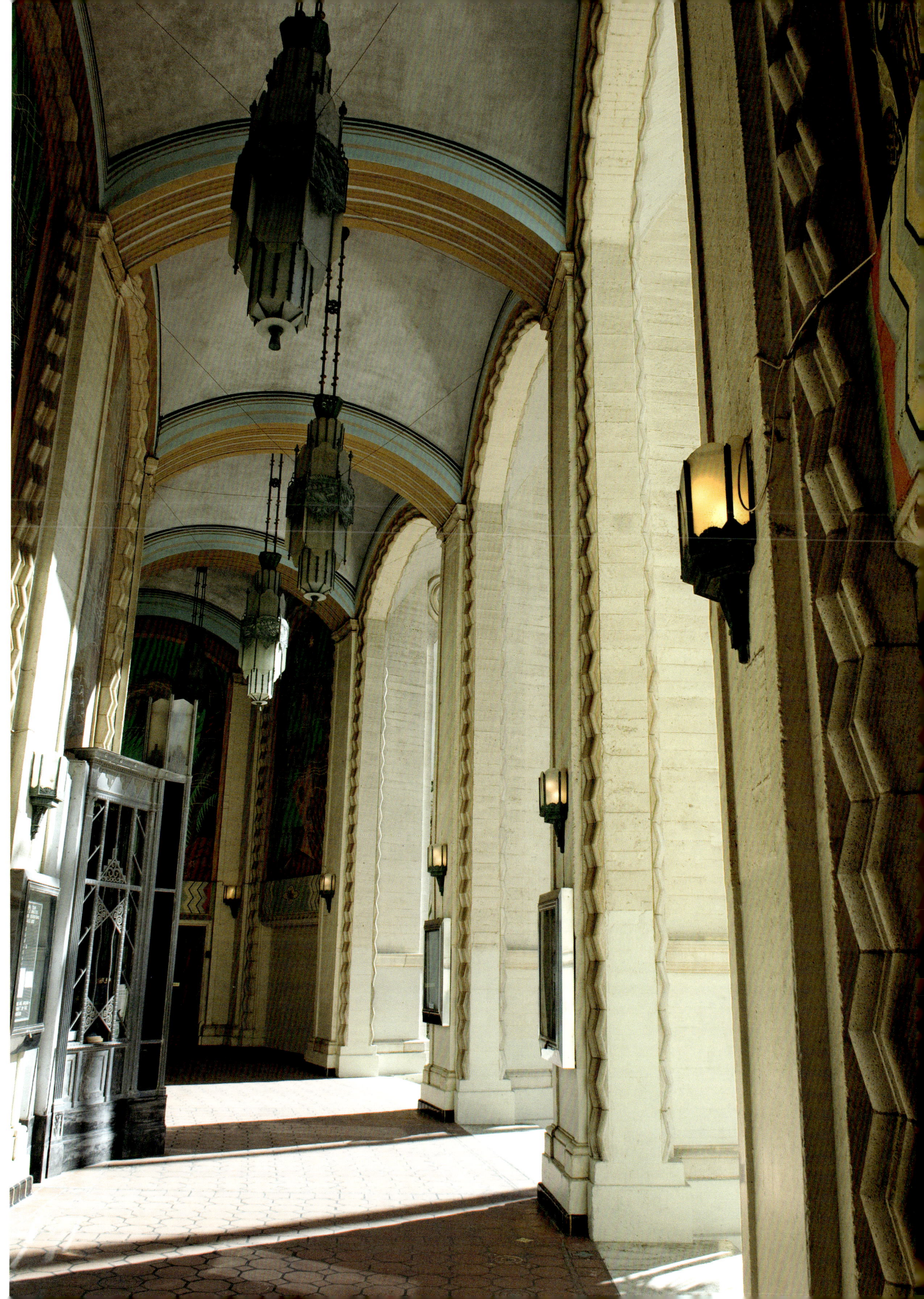

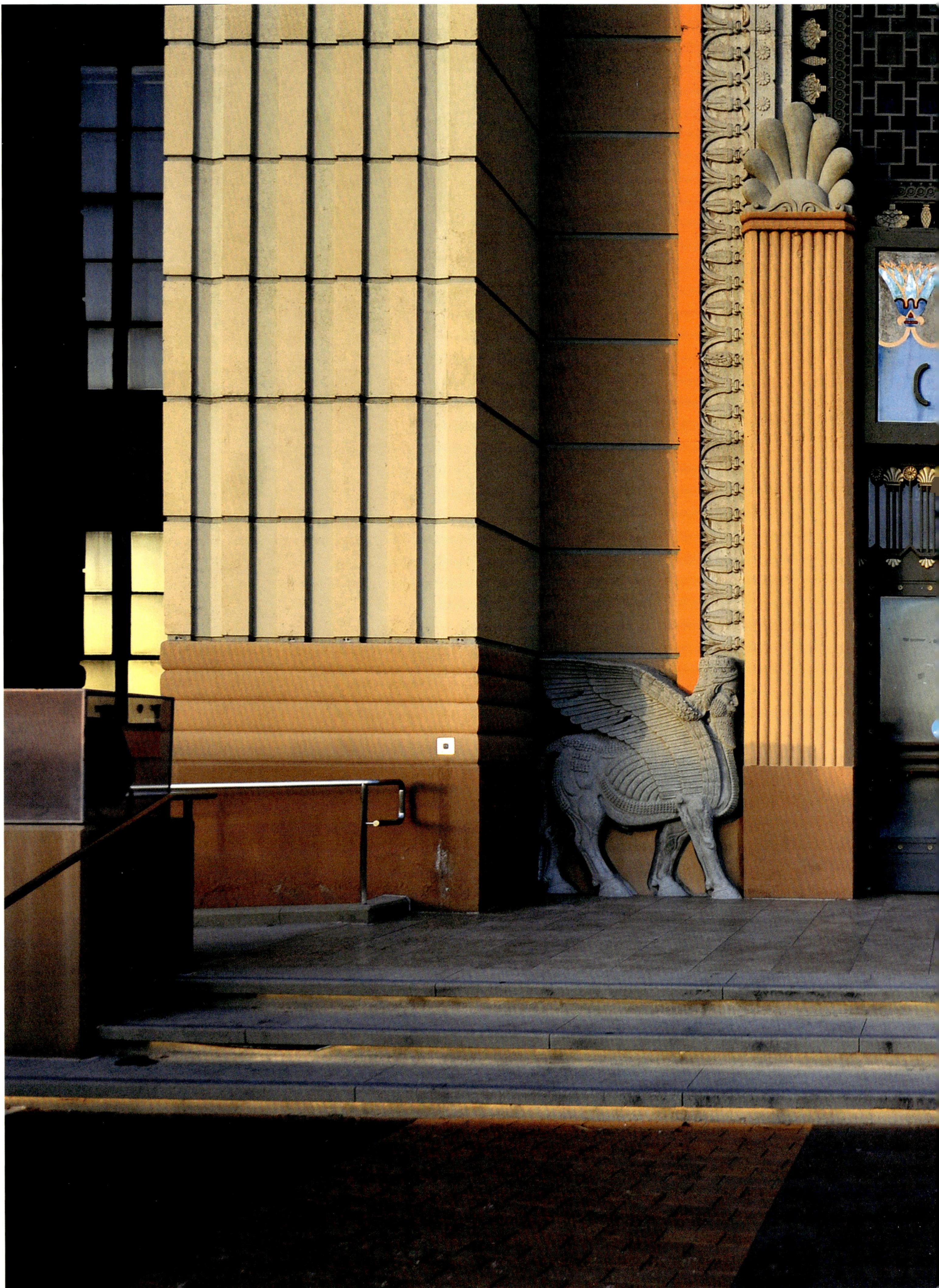

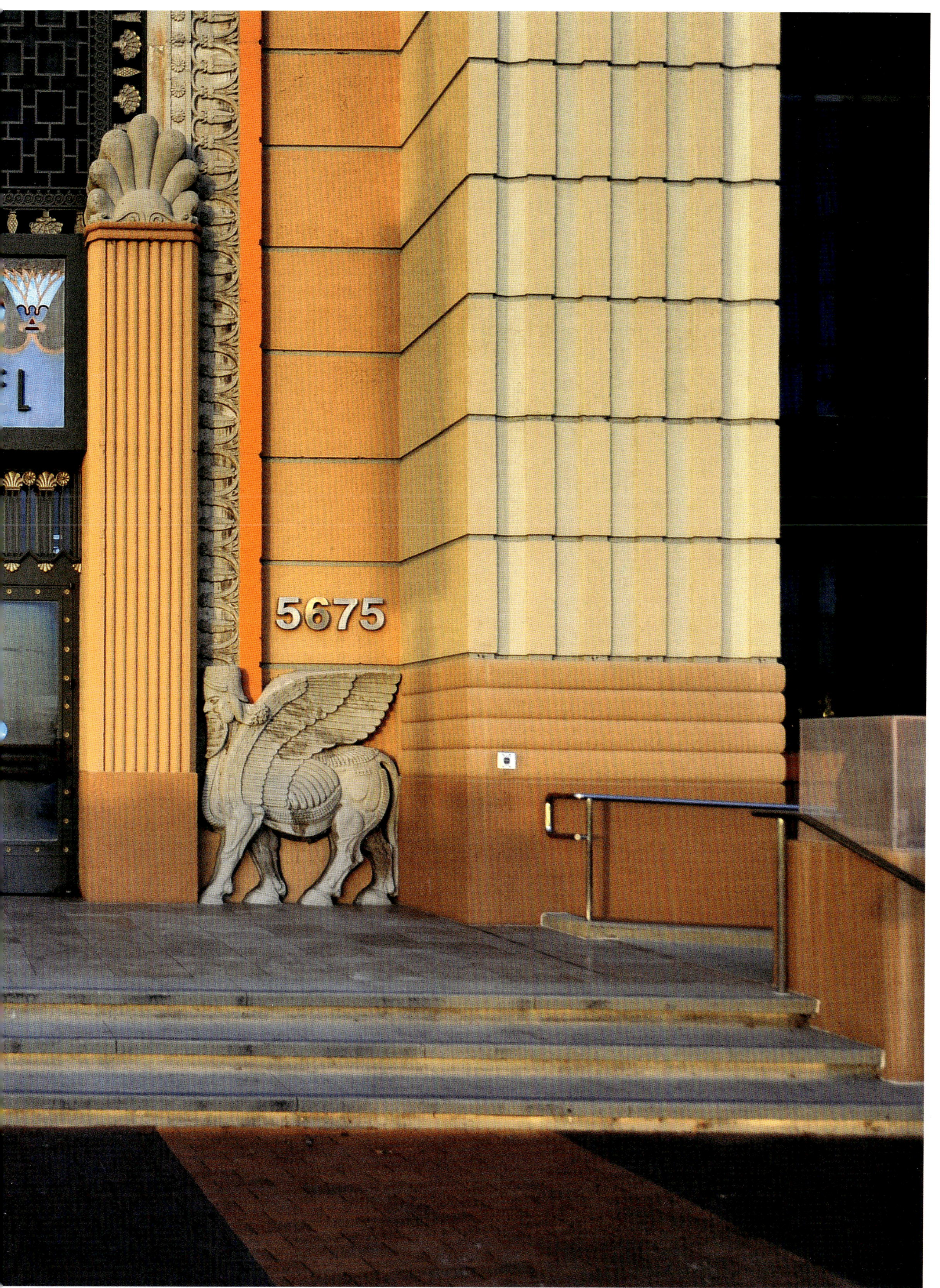
5675

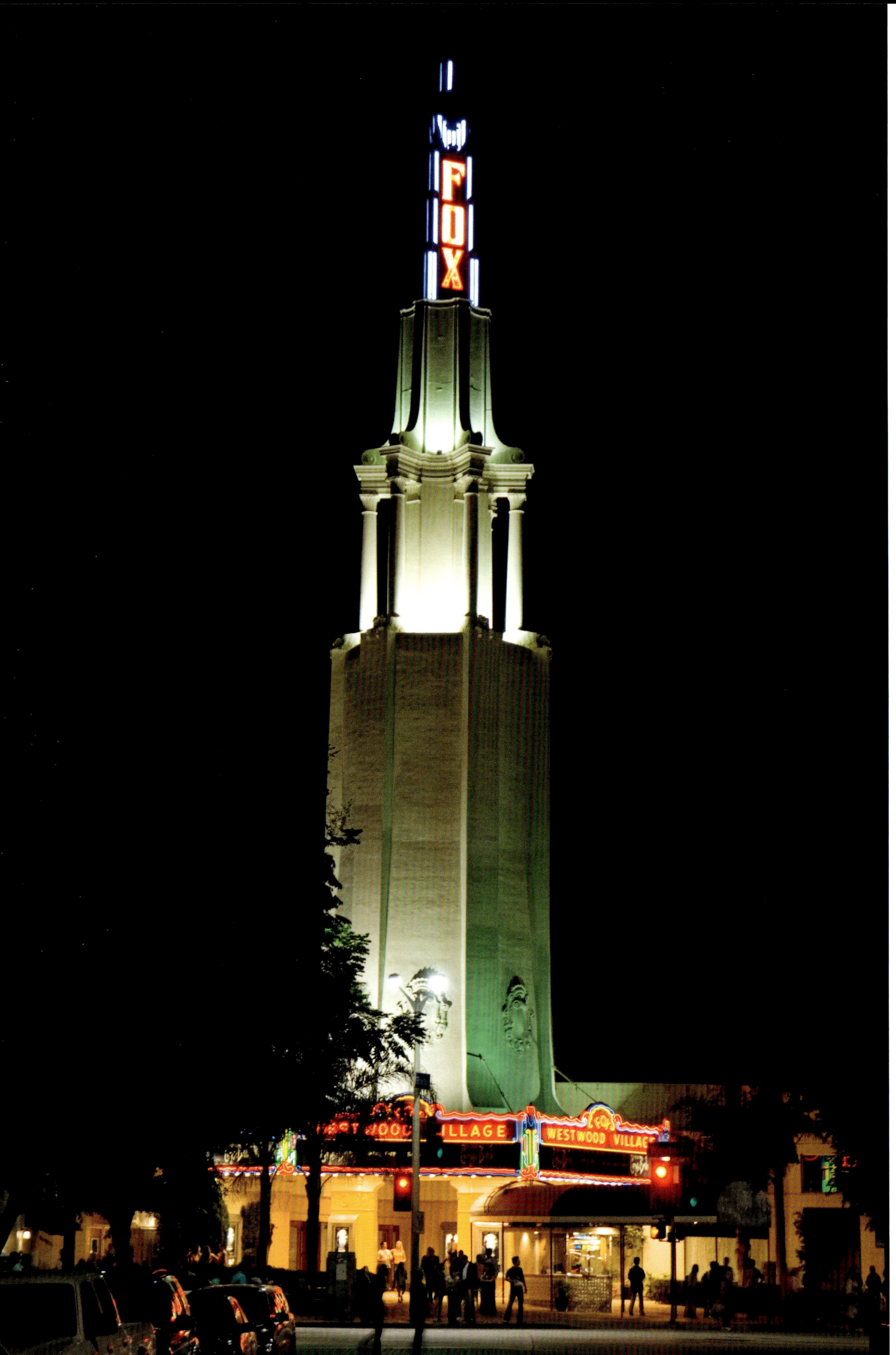
FOX
WESTWOOD VILLAGE

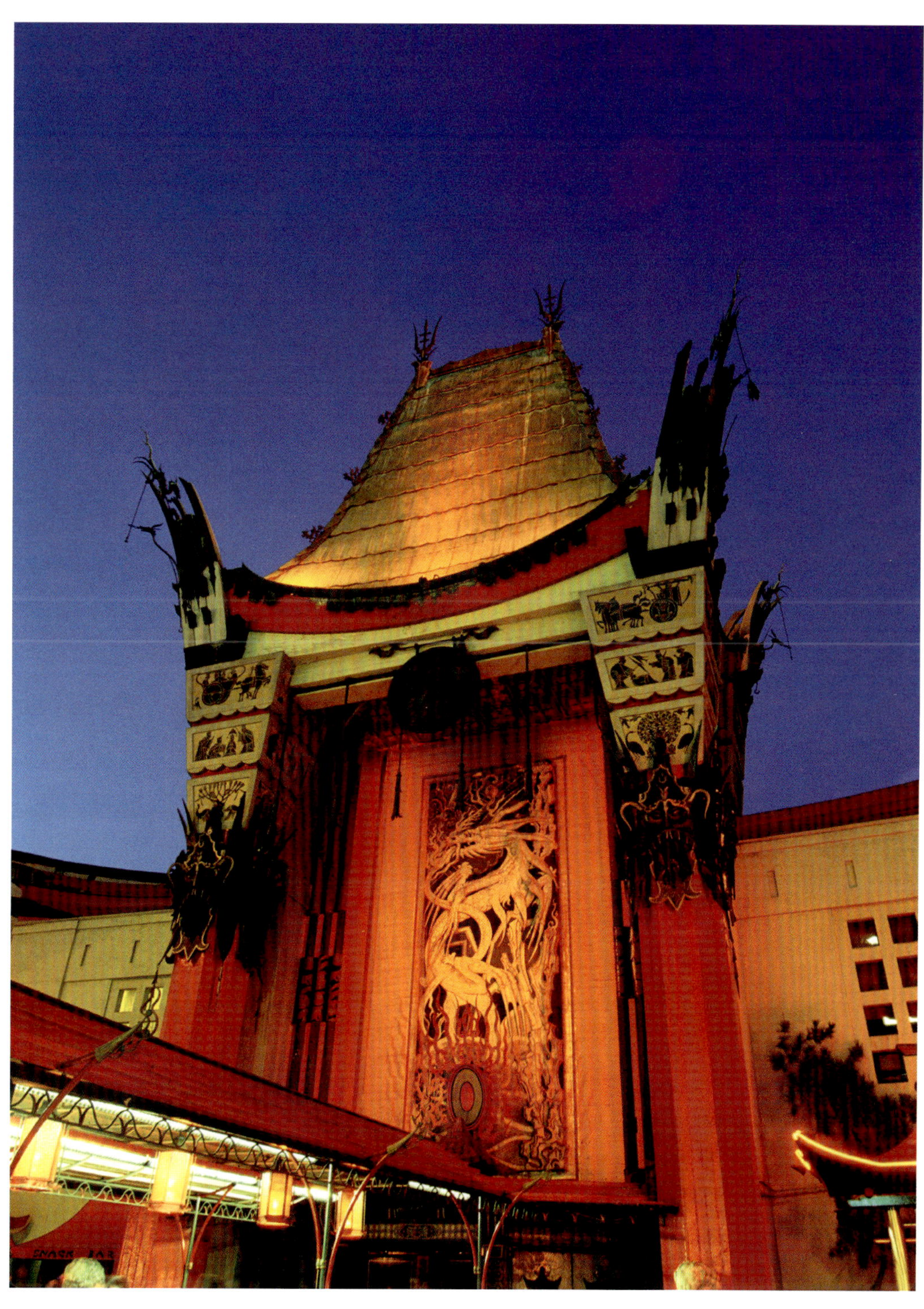

← *Fox Village Theatre (Percy Parke Lewis, 1931) 959 Broxton Ave., photographed 2005.*

↑ *Grauman's Chinese Theater, now TCL Chinese Theater (Meyer and Holler, 1927) 6925 Hollywood Blvd., photographed 1994.*

OVERLEAF: *Los Angeles Central Library (Bertram G. Goodhue and Carleton Winslow, 1926) 630 W. 5th St., photographed 2008.*

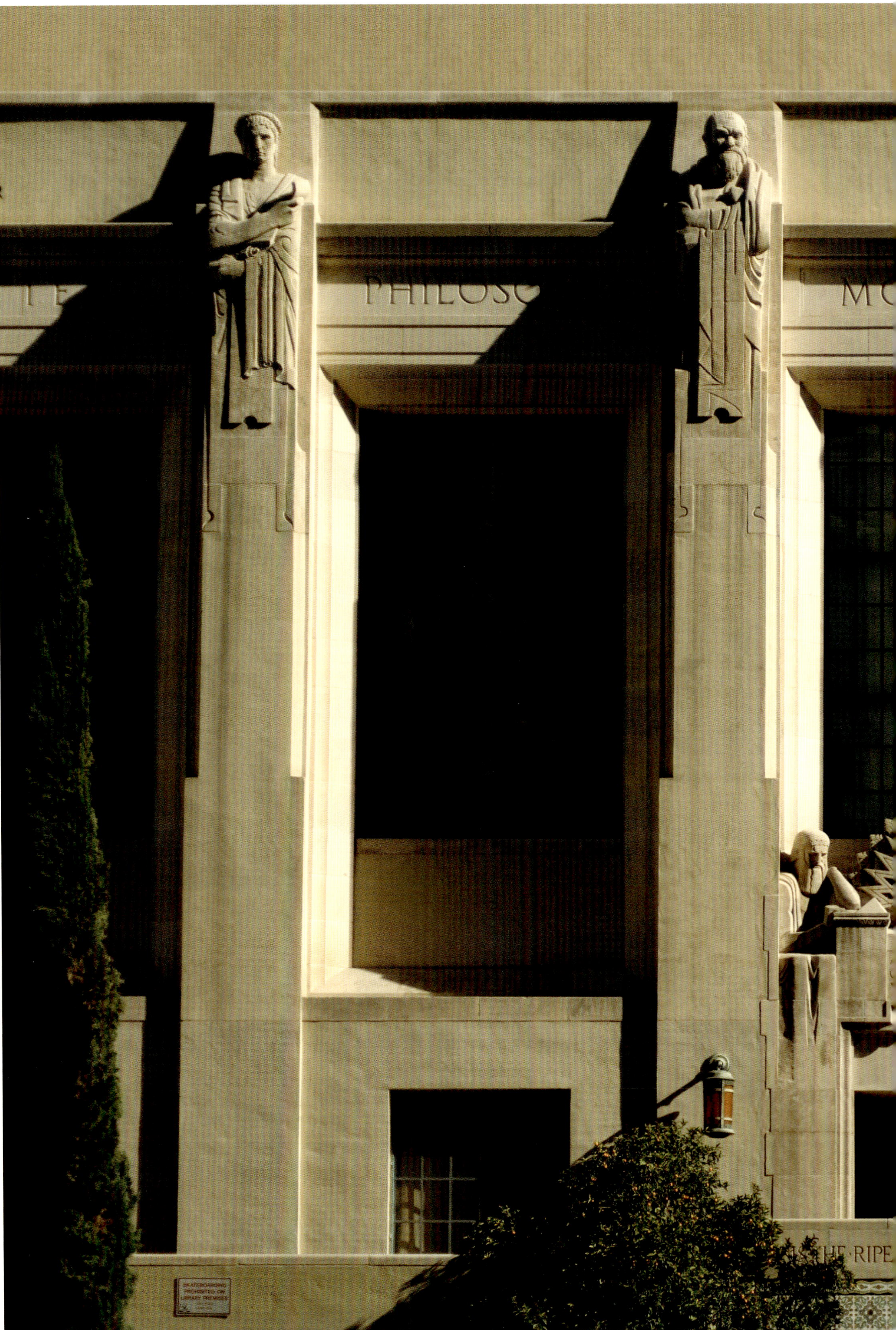
SKATEBOARDING
PROHIBITED ON
LIBRARY PREMISES

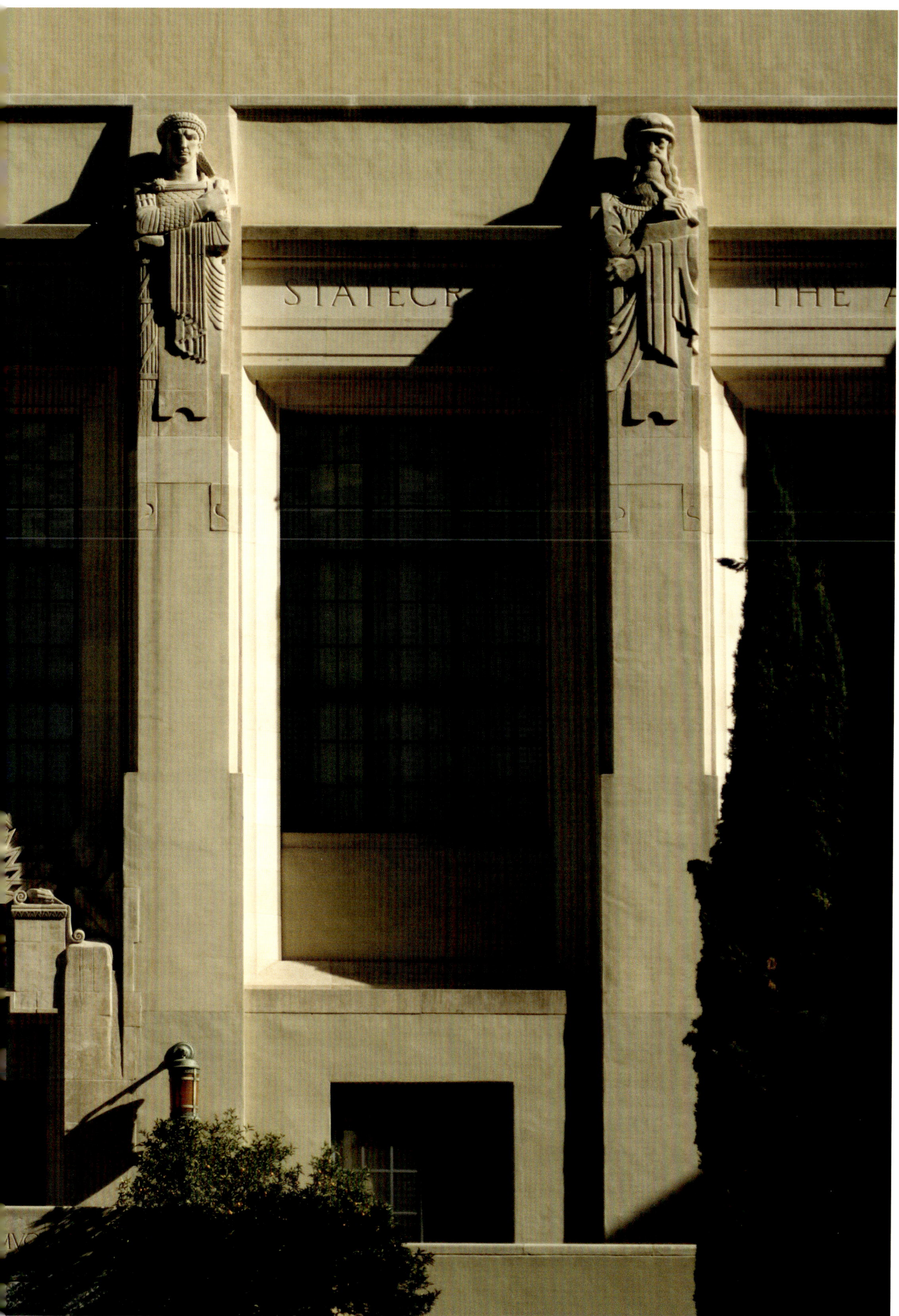
STATECR
THE A

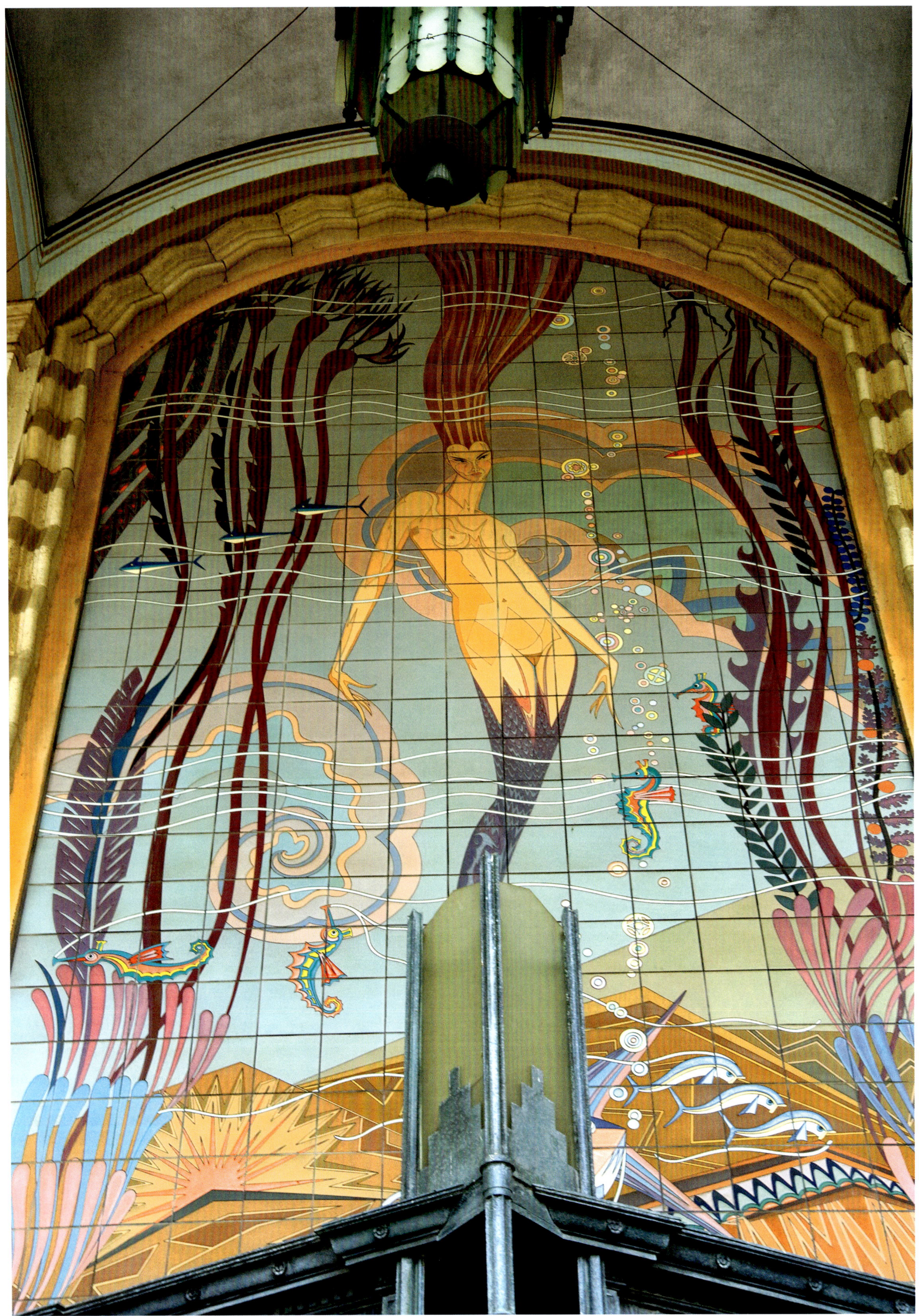

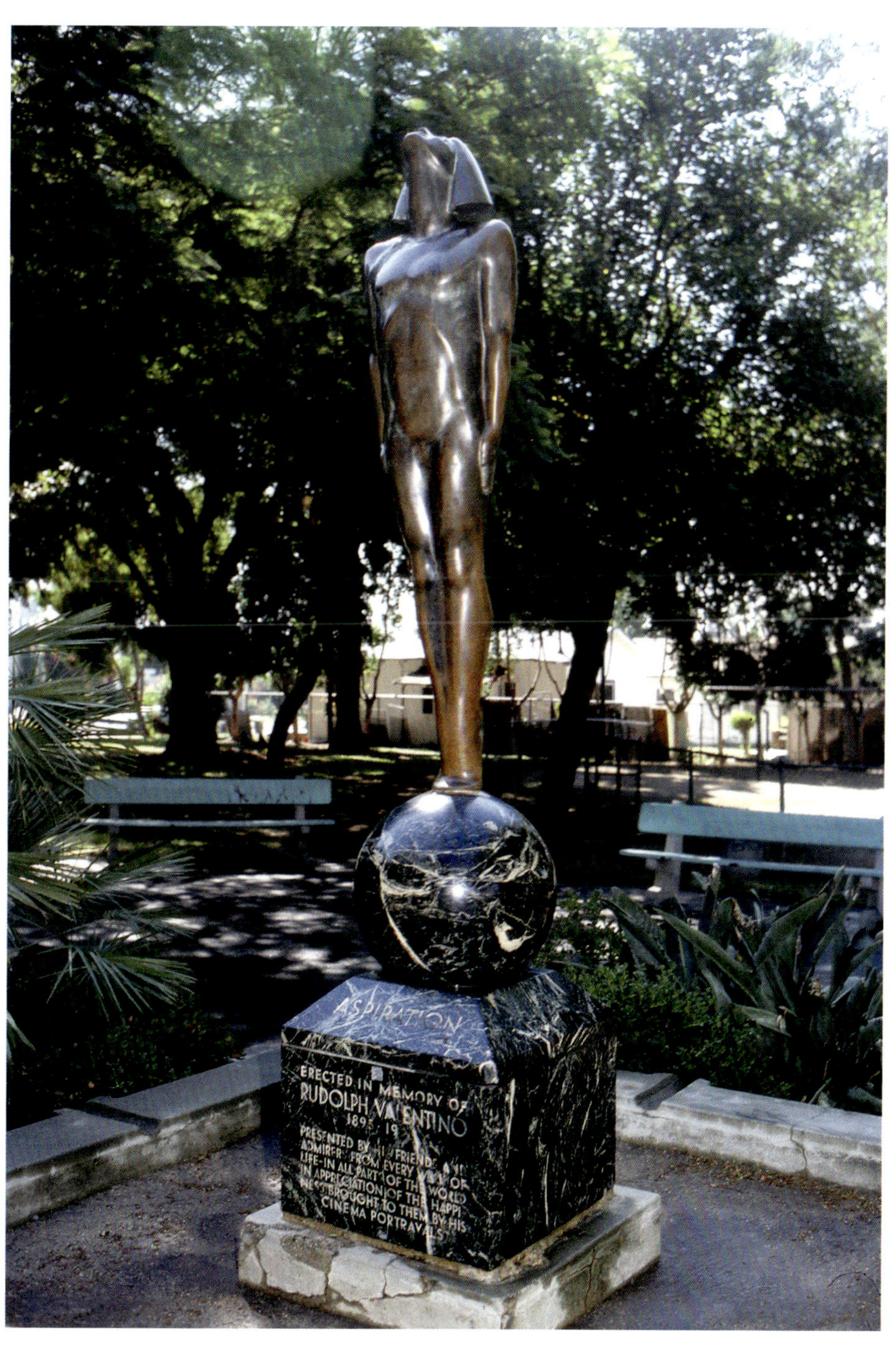

← *Catalina Casino, tile mural (David Malcom Renton, mural by John Gabriel Beckman, 1929) Avalon, Catalina Island, photographed 2016.*

↑ Aspiration *(Roger Noble Burnham, 1930) De Longpre Park, 1350 N. Cherokee Ave., memorial to Rudolph Valentino, photographed 1989.*

OVERLEAF: *Santa Anita Park, grandstand (Gordon B. Kaufmann, 1934) 285 W. Huntington Dr., Arcadia, photographed 2024.*

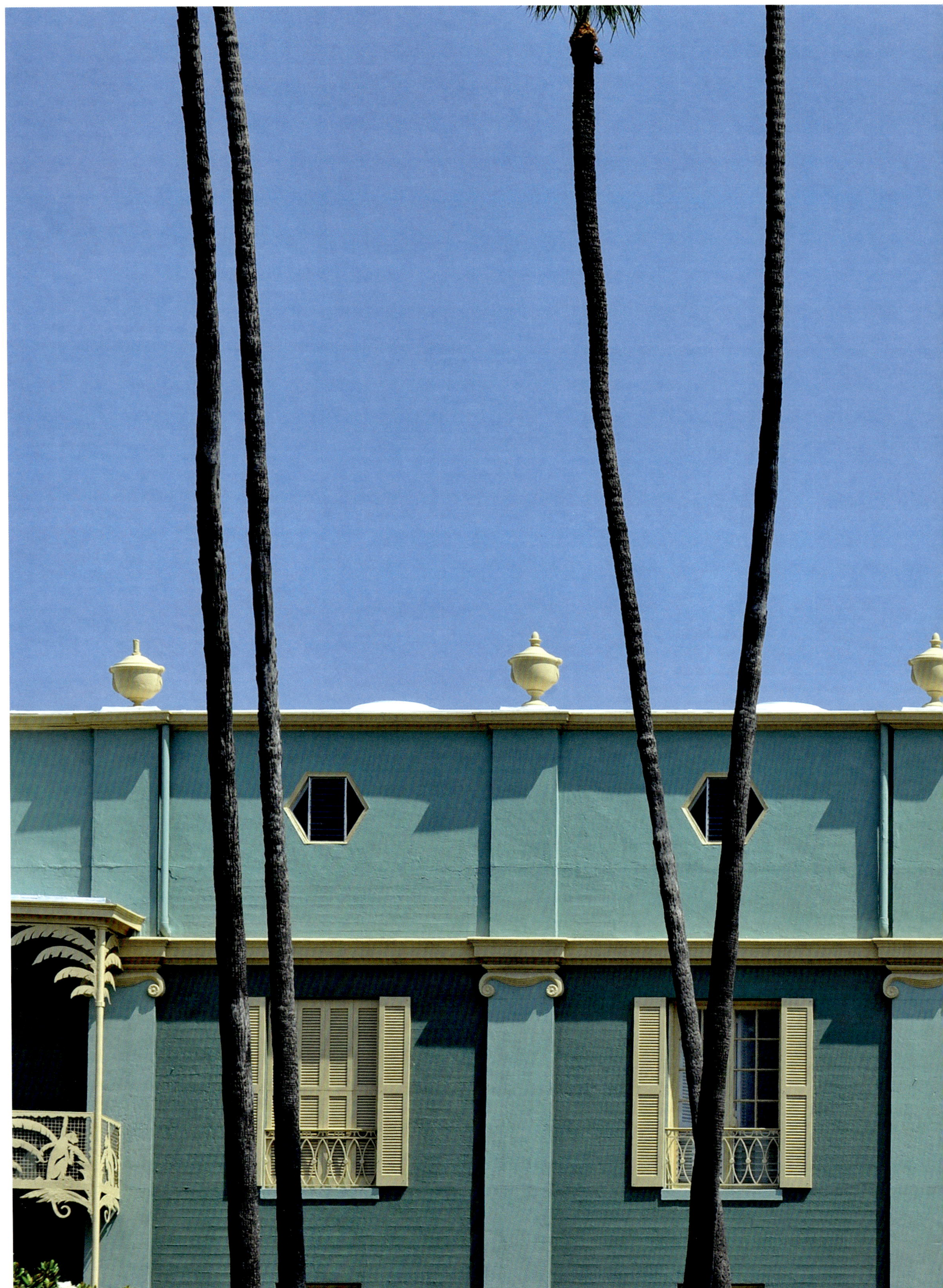

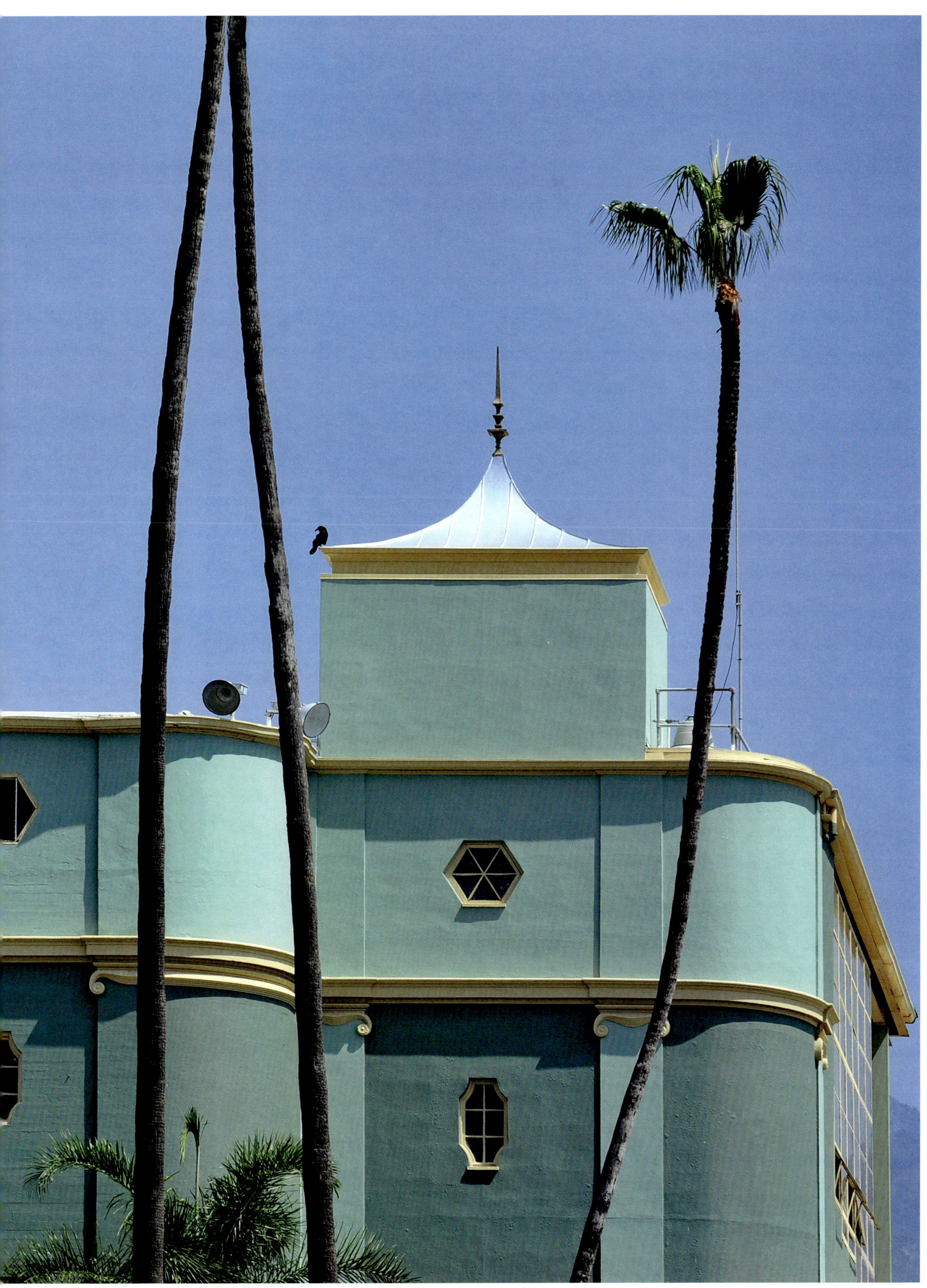

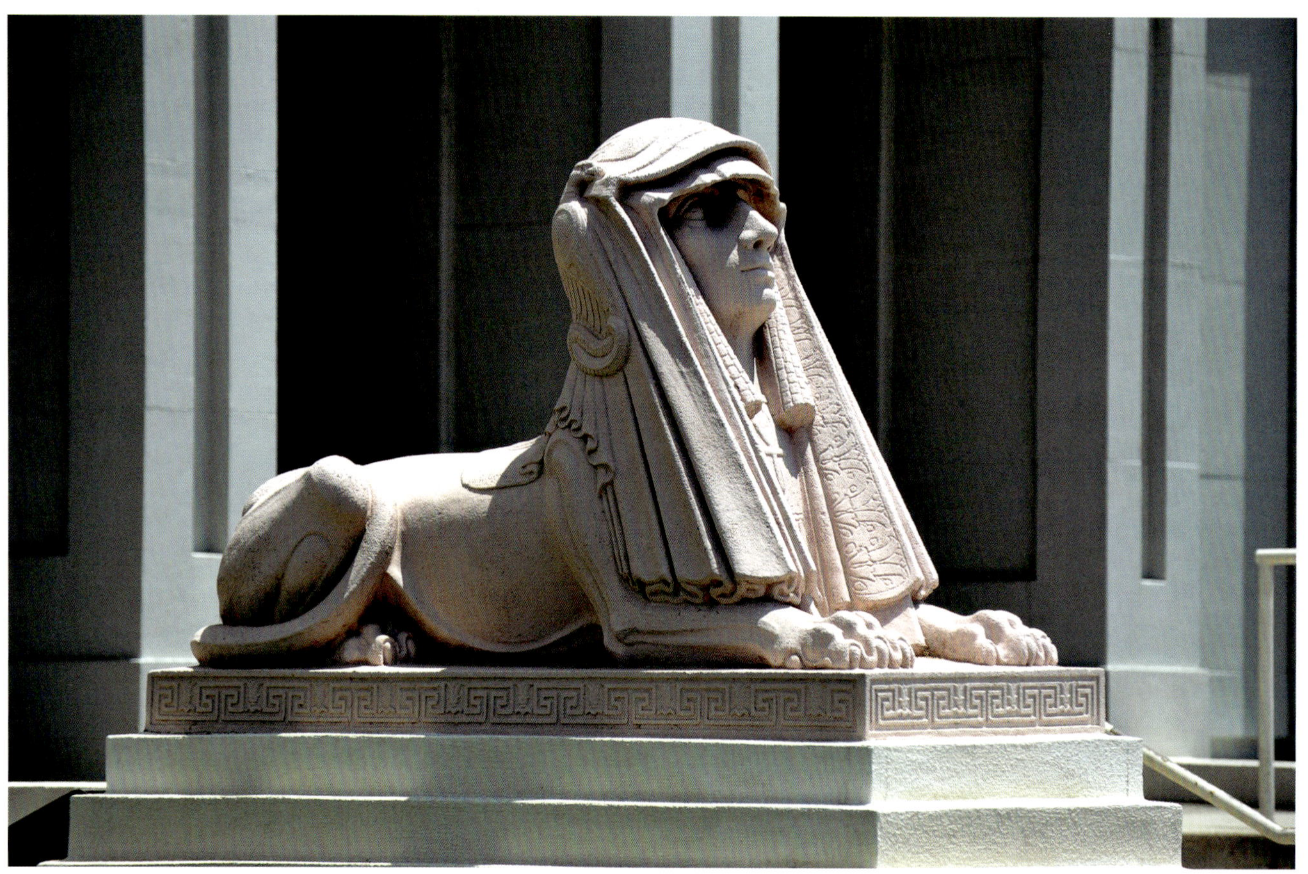

↑ *Pasadena Scottish Rite statue (Joseph J. Blick, statue by D. Manuelli, 1925) 150 N. Madison Ave., Pasadena, photographed 2024.*

→ *Moxley's Dog and Cat Hospital (Paul W. Nelson, 1930) 940 N. Highland Ave., photographed 1989.*

OVERLEAF: *Catalina Casino (David Malcom Renton, 1929) Avalon, Catalina Island, photographed 2016.*

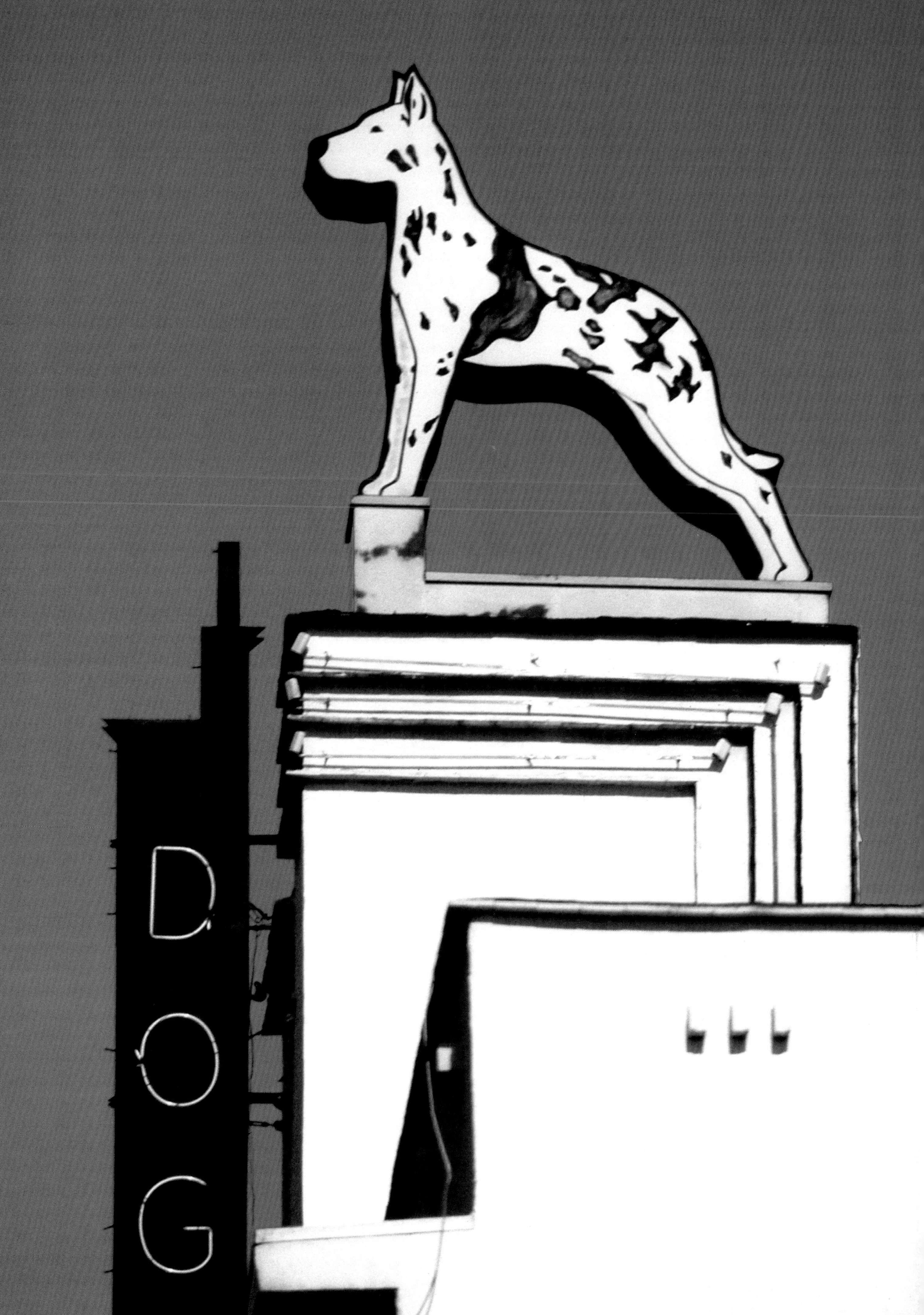
DOG

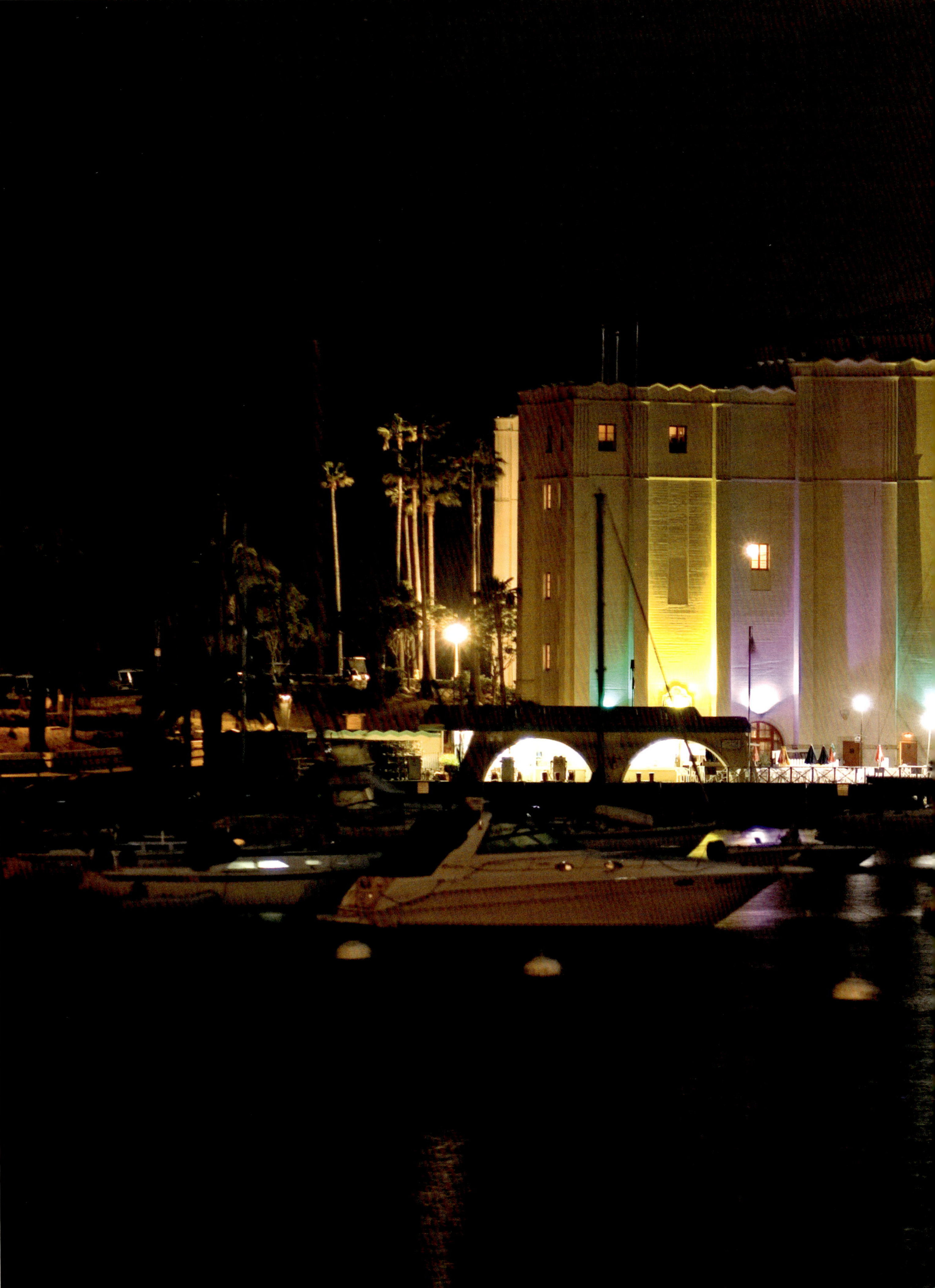

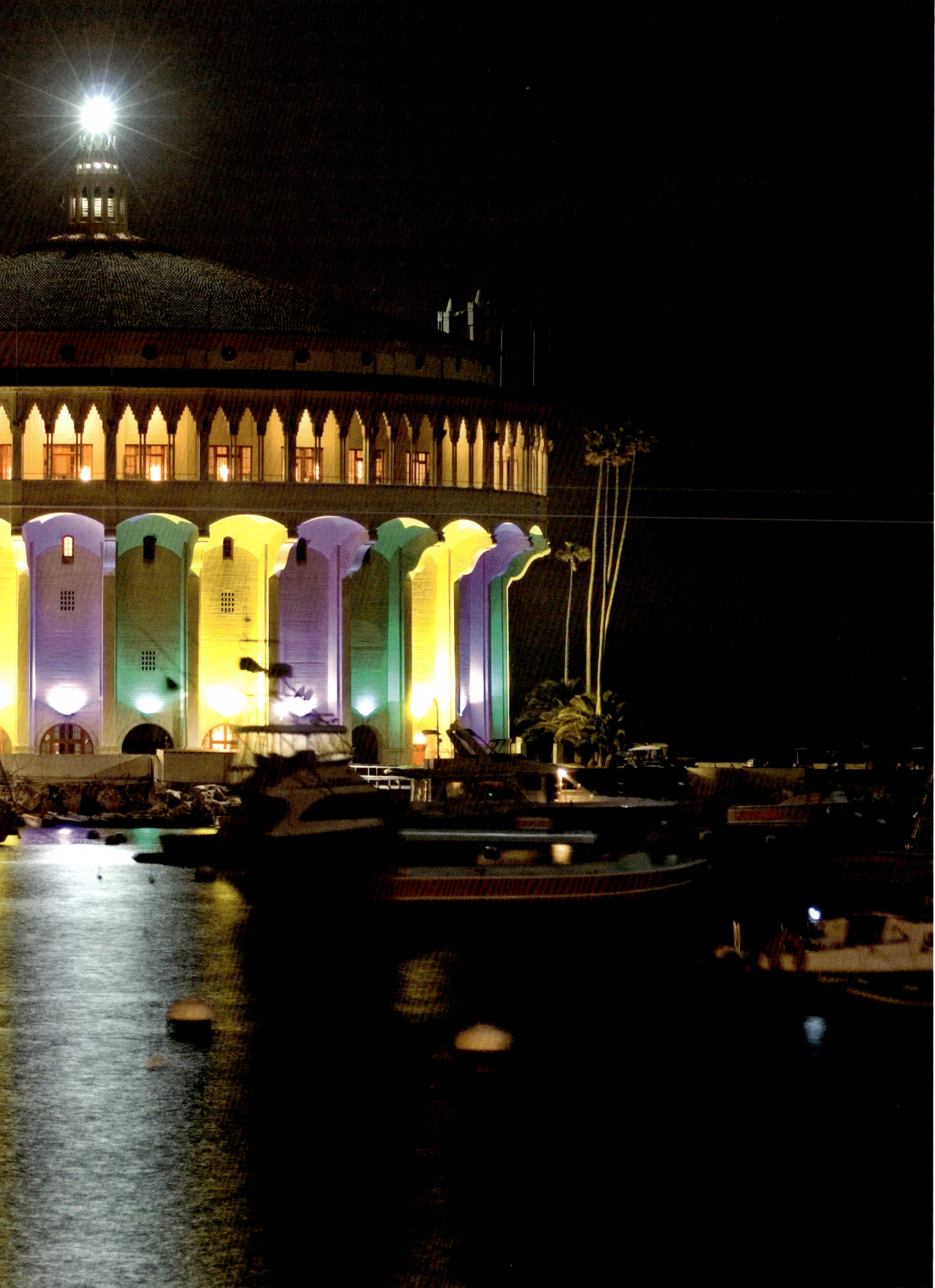

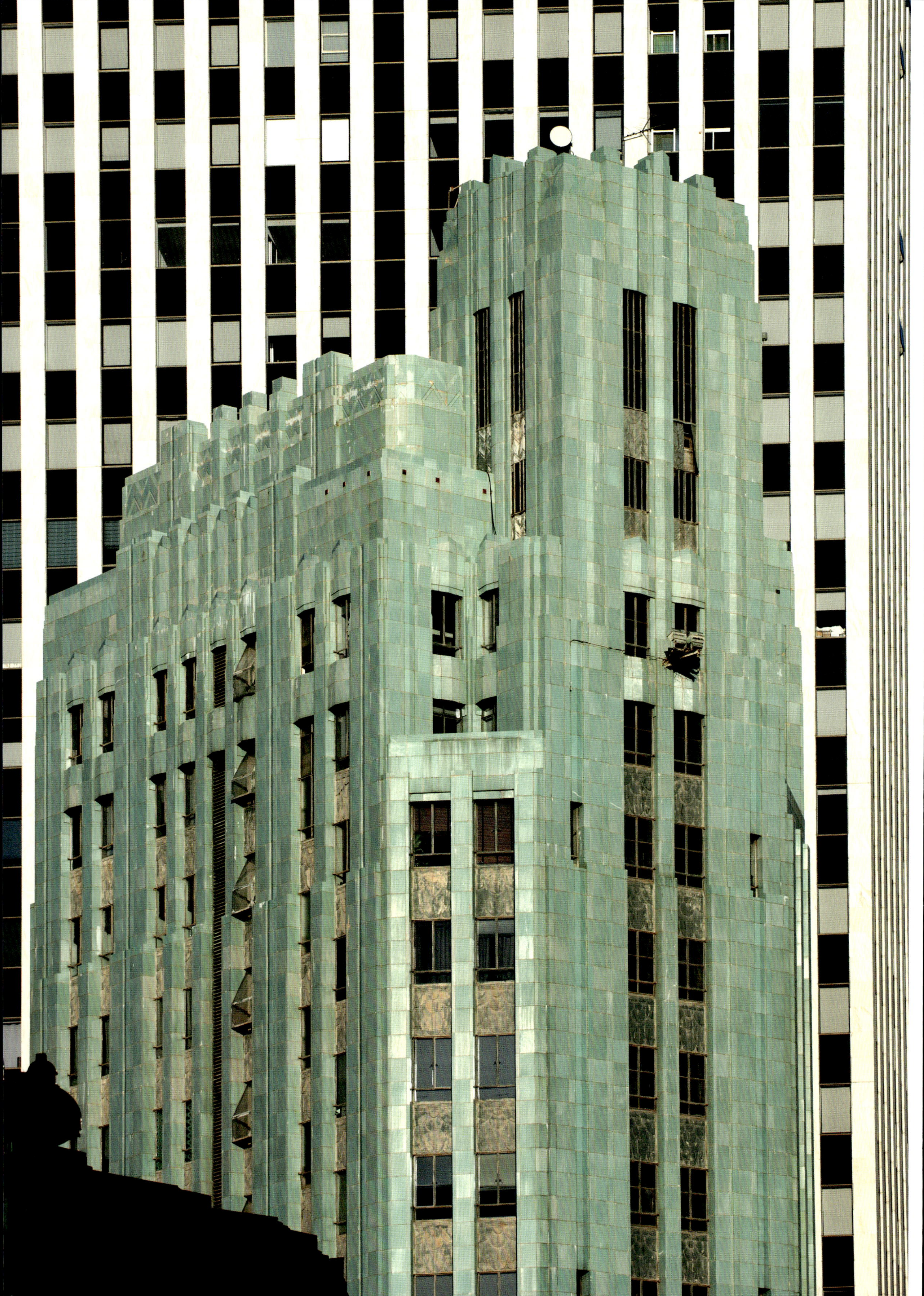

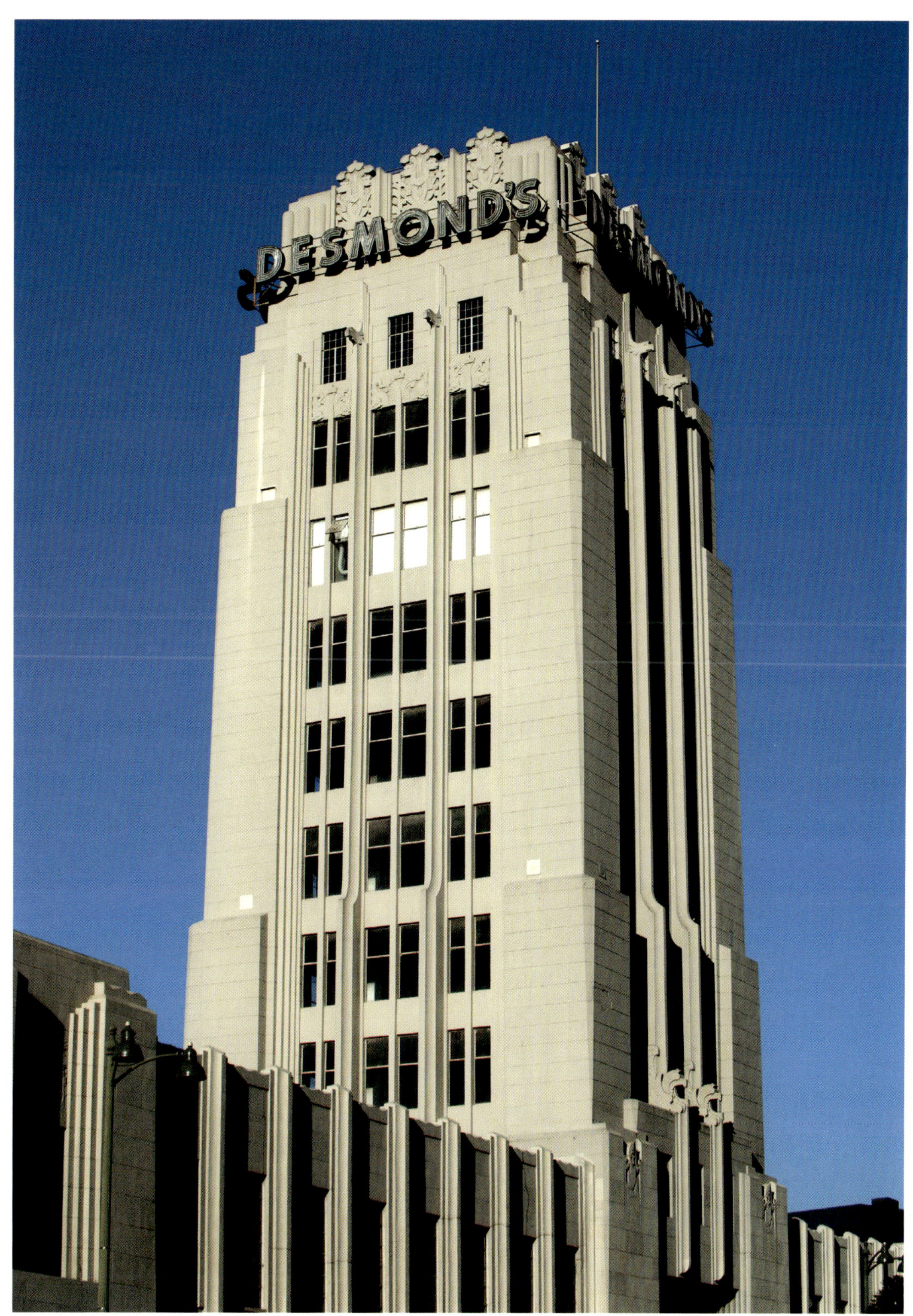

← *Wiltern Theatre and Pellissier Building (Morgan, Walls, and Clements, 1931) 3790 Wilshire Blvd., photographed 2010.*

↑ *Desmond's Department Store exterior detail, (Gilbert Stanley Underwood, 1928) 5514 Wilshire Blvd., photographed 2024.*

OVERLEAF: *Richardson Apartments (H. Guthrie Thursby, 1940) 3919 W. 8th St., photographed 2024.*

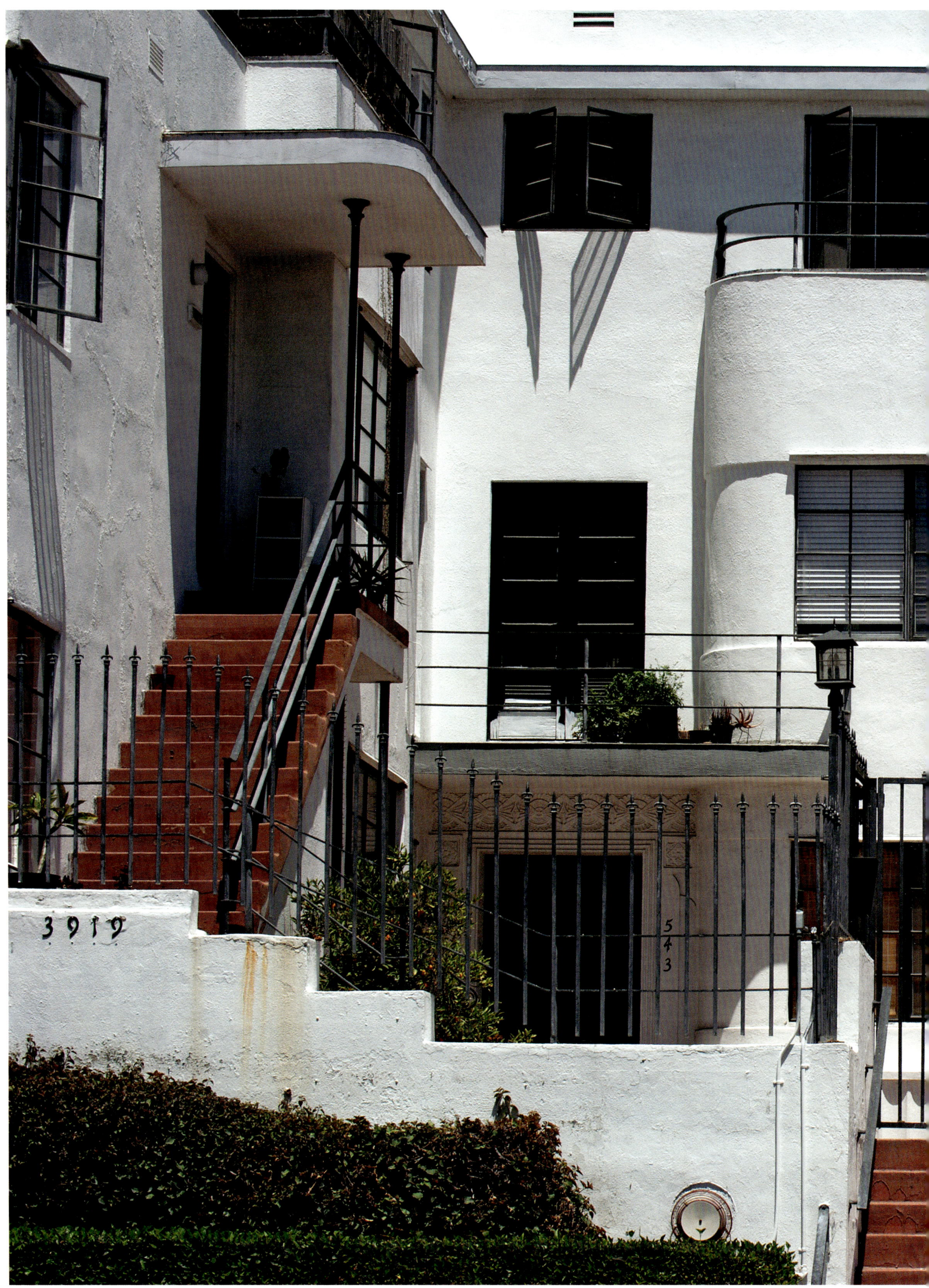
3919
543

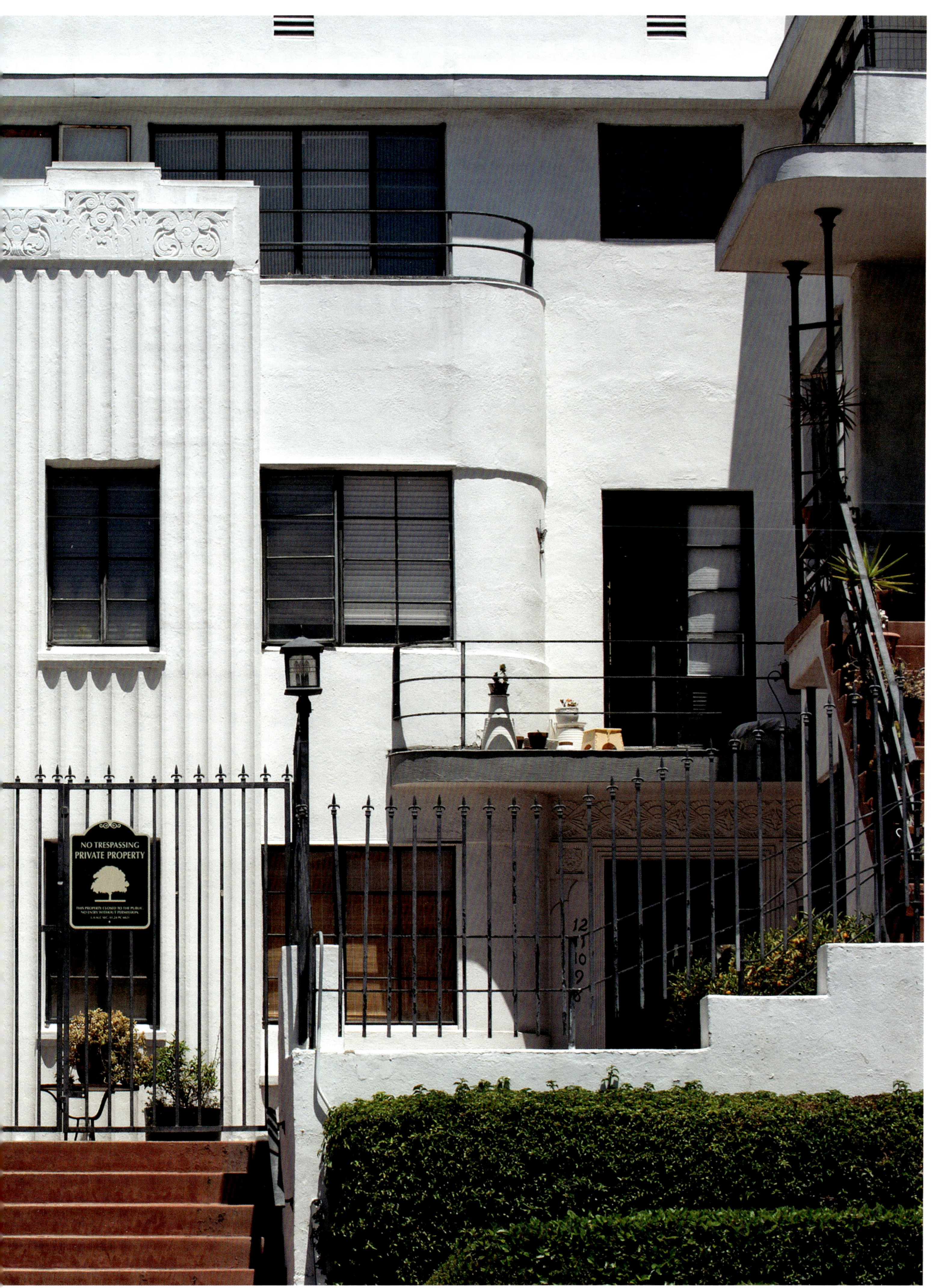
NO TRESPASSING
PRIVATE PROPERTY
THIS PROPERTY CLOSED TO THE PUBLIC.
NO ENTRY WITHOUT PERMISSION.

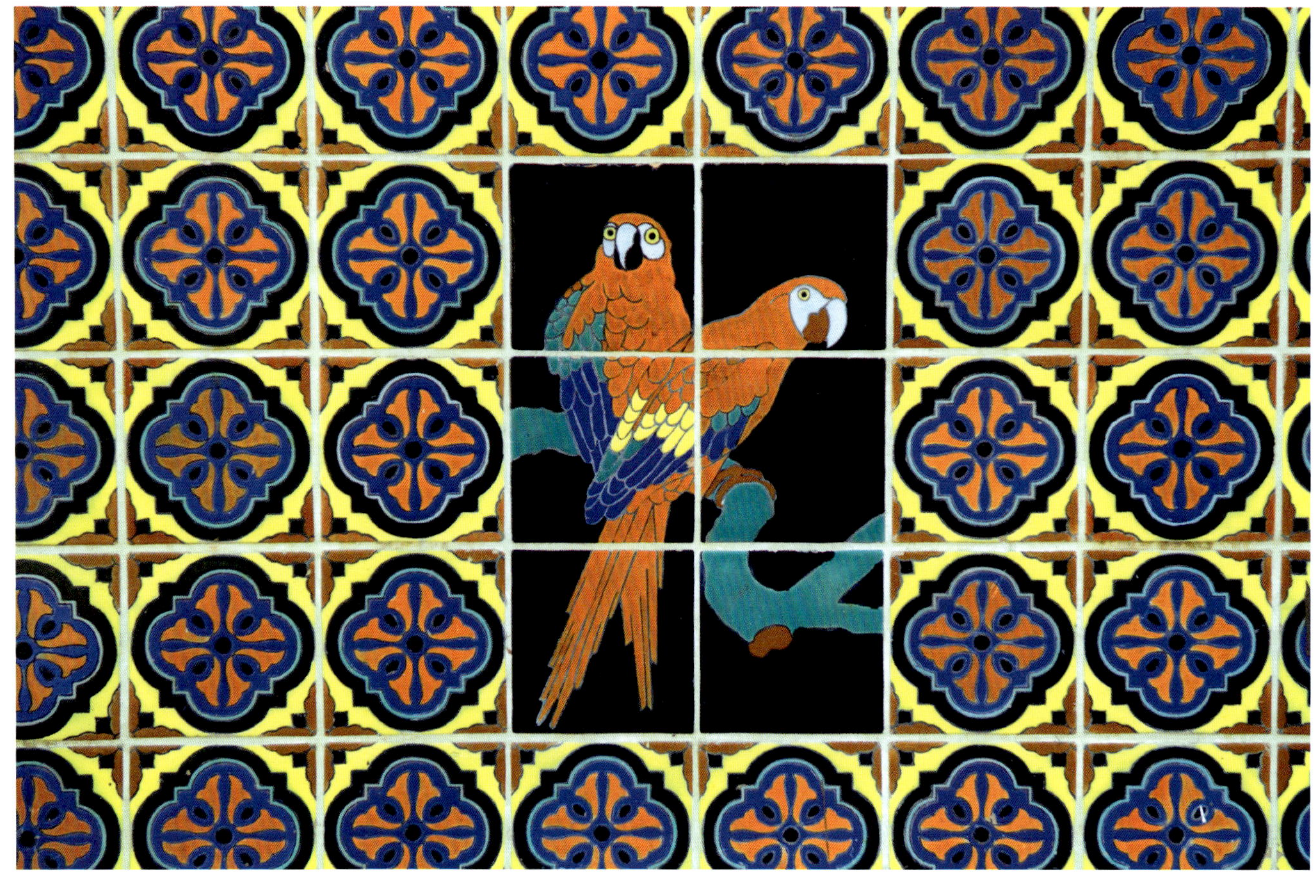

↑ *The Bird Park, Wrigley Memorial (Pennet, Parsons, and Frost, 1924) 1400 Avalon Canyon Rd., Avalon, photographed 2008.*

→ *Indian Room, neon sign (designer and year unknown) 952 S. Pacific Ave., San Pedro, photographed 2010.*

OVERLEAF: *Commercial Building (architect and year unknown) 862 N. Atlantic Ave., Long Beach, photographed 2024.*

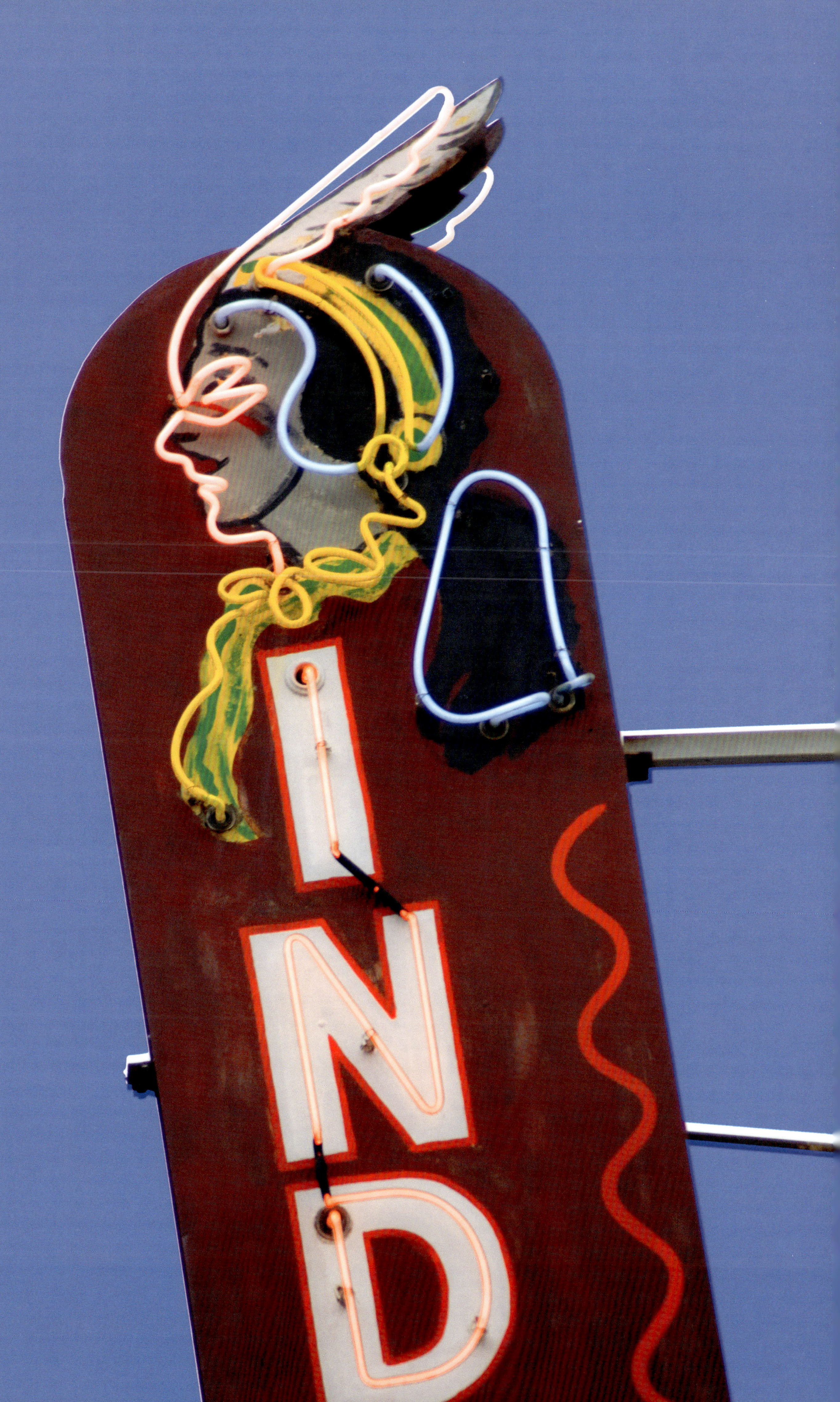
IND

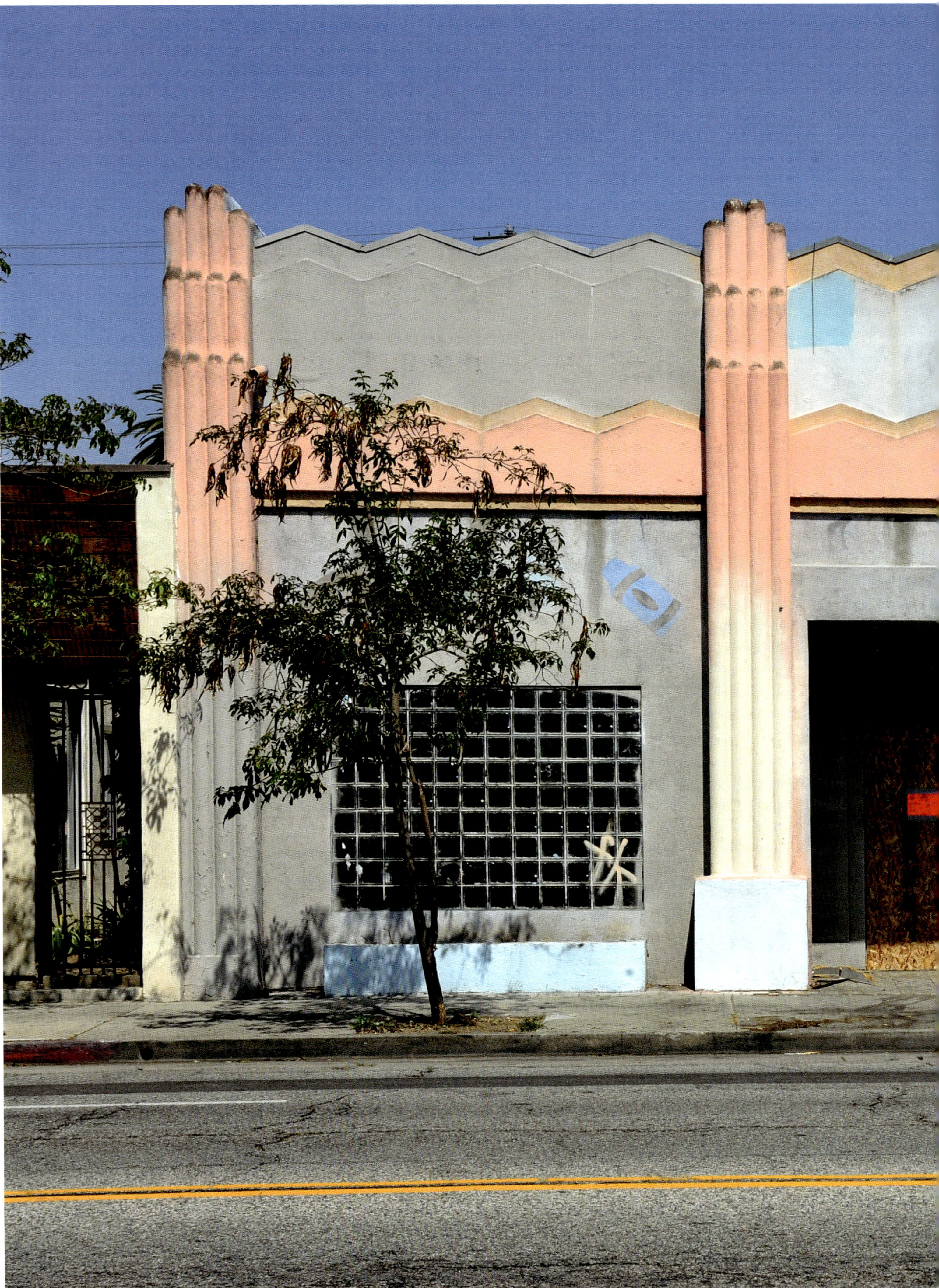

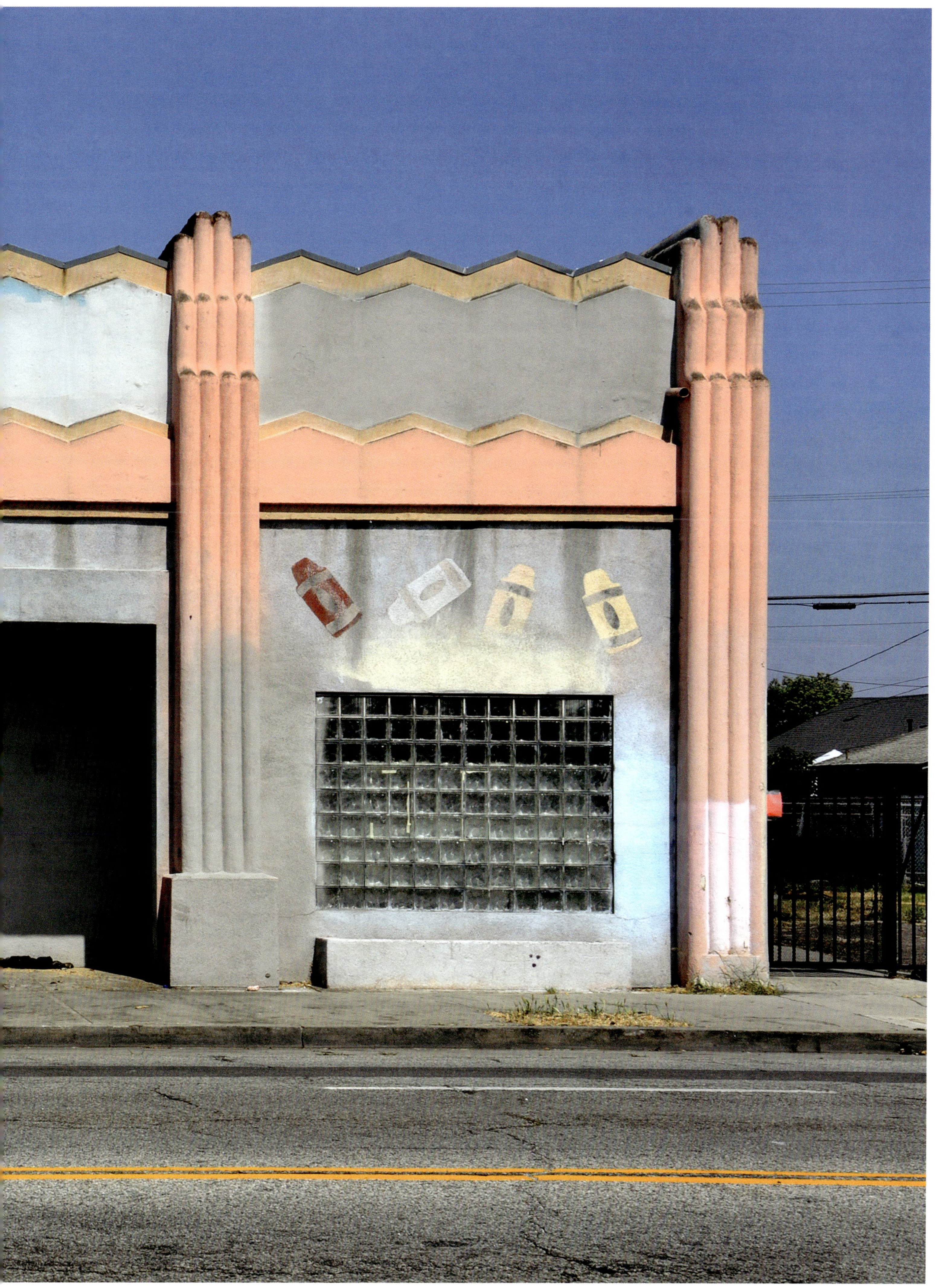

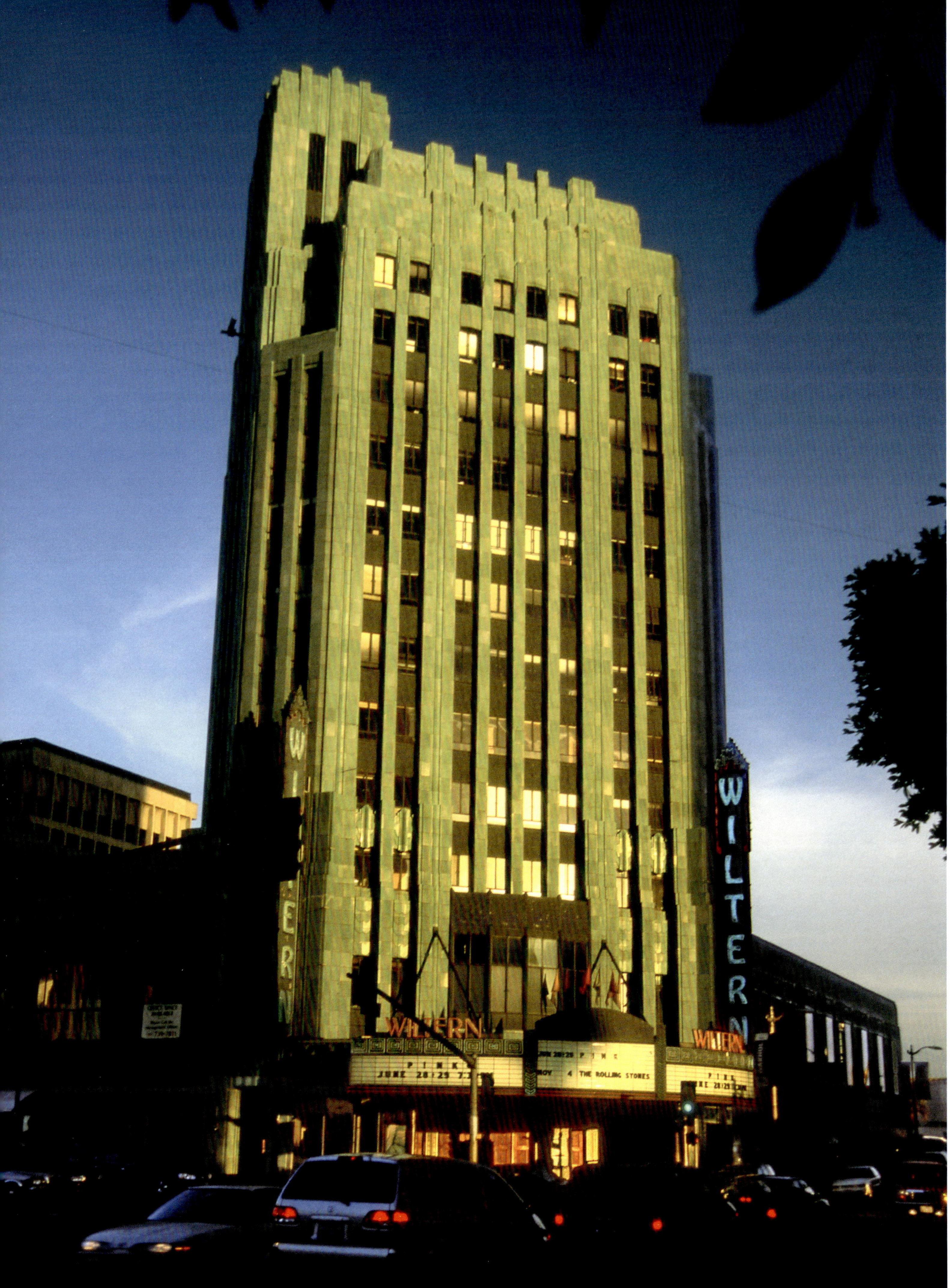
WILTERN
WILTERN
P I N K
THE ROLLING STONES
WILTERN

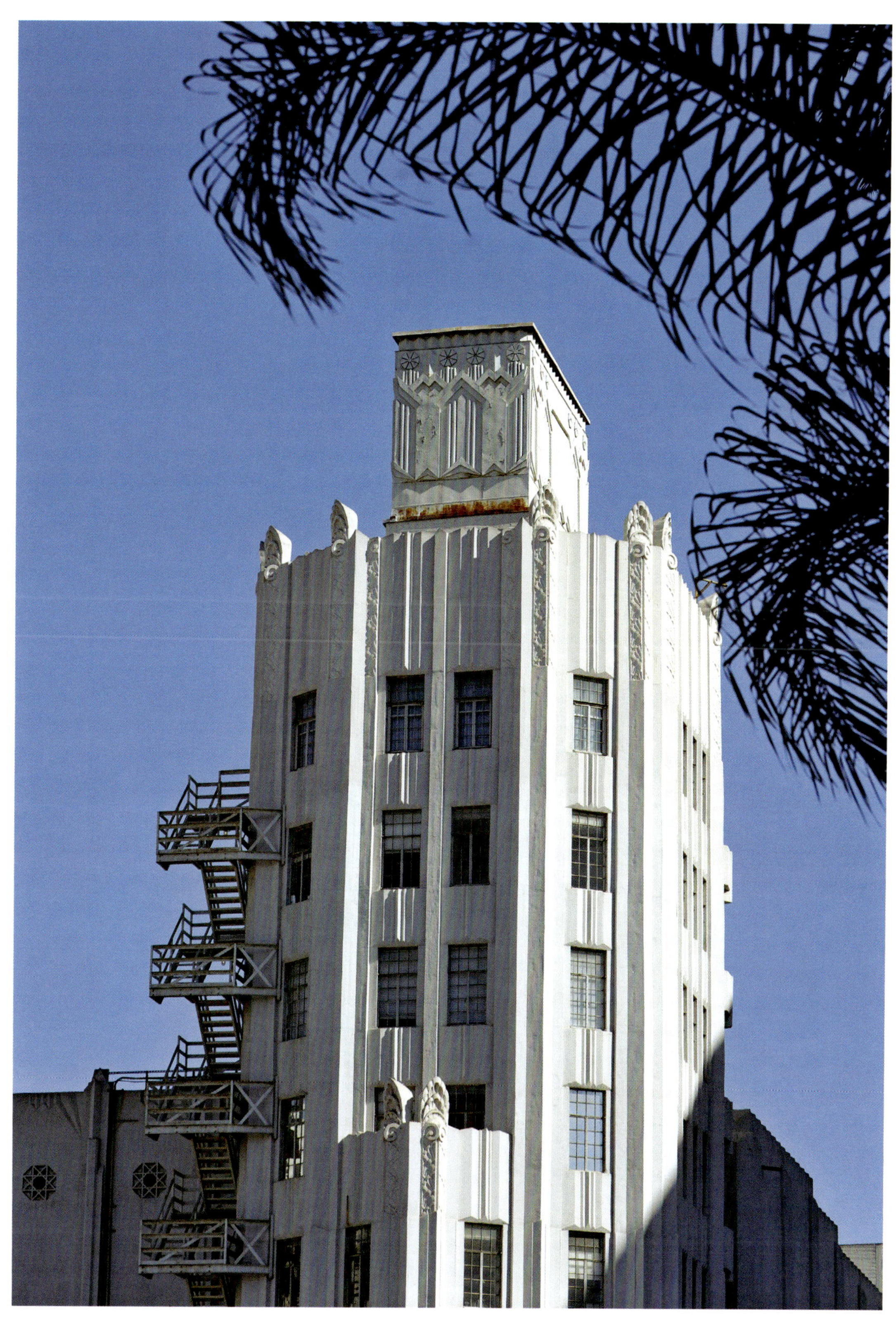

← *Wiltern Theatre and Pellissier Building (Morgan, Walls, and Clements, 1931) 3790 Wilshire Blvd., photographed 2002.*

↑ *Fox Wilshire Theatre, now Saban Theater (S. Charles Lee, 1930) 8440 Wilshire Blvd., Beverly Hills, photographed 2024.*

OVERLEAF: *Electric Fountain, Beverly Gardens Park, detail of sculpture (sculpture by Robert Merrell Gage, 1931) 9439 Santa Monica Blvd., Beverly Hills, photographed 1988.*

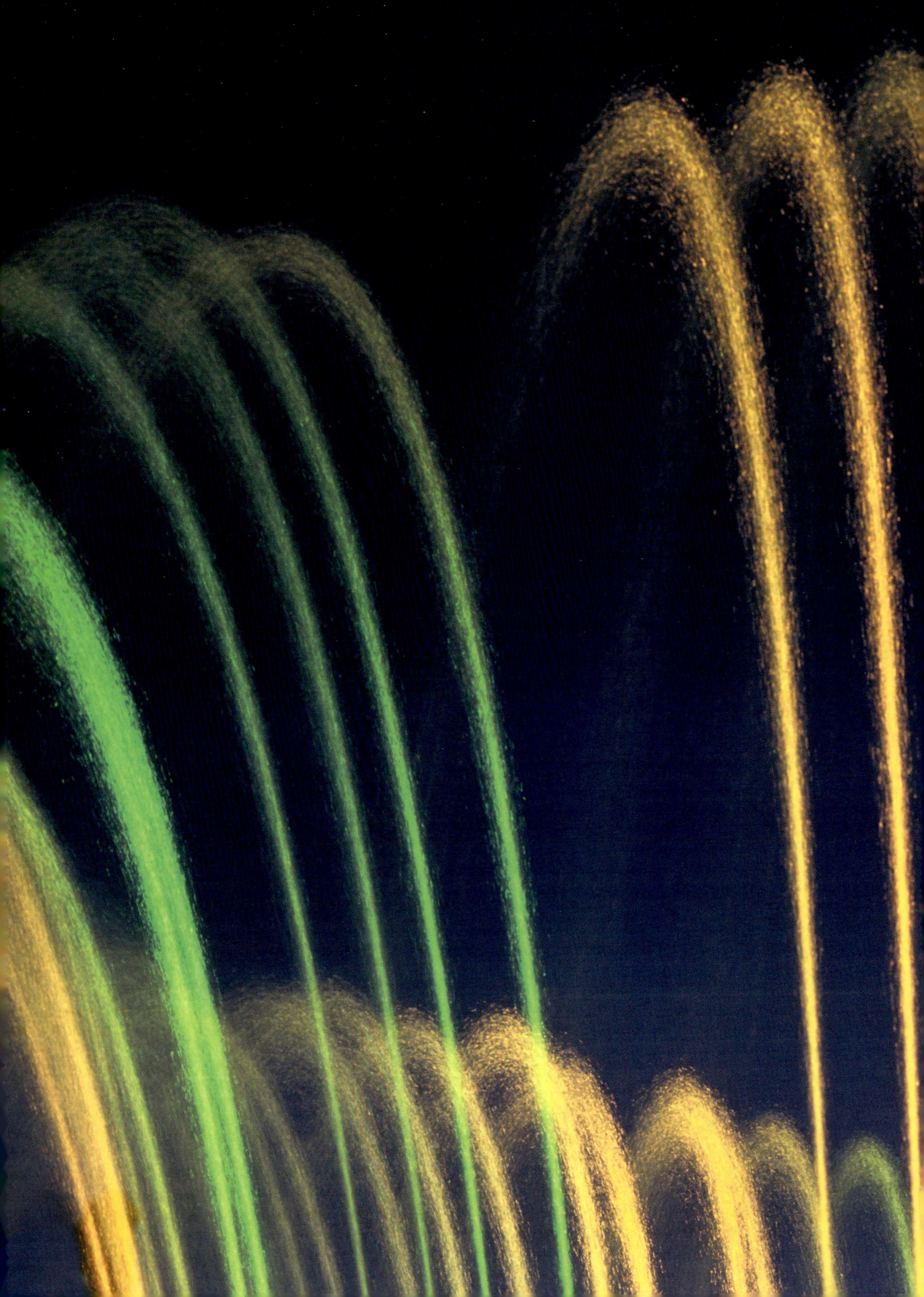

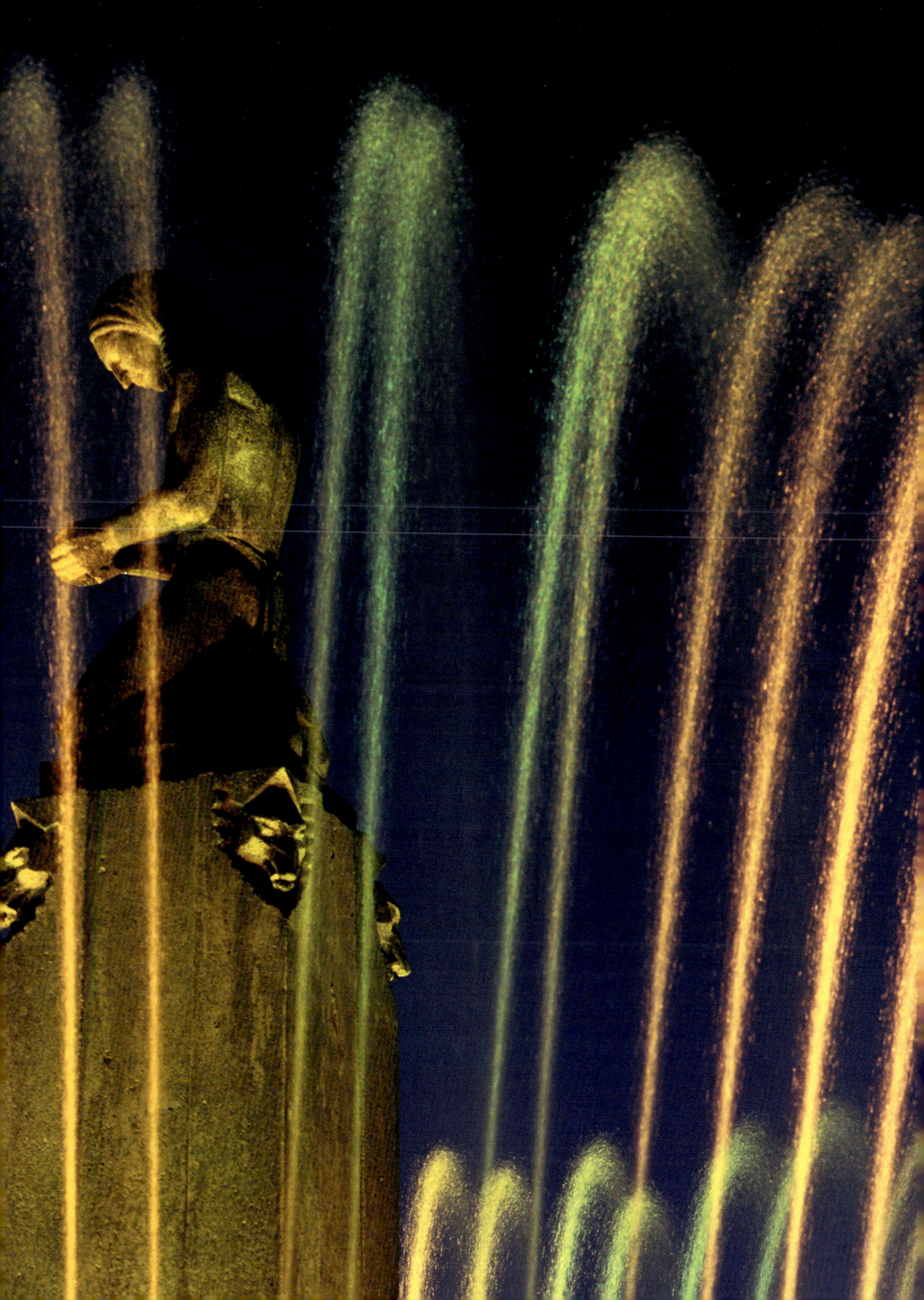

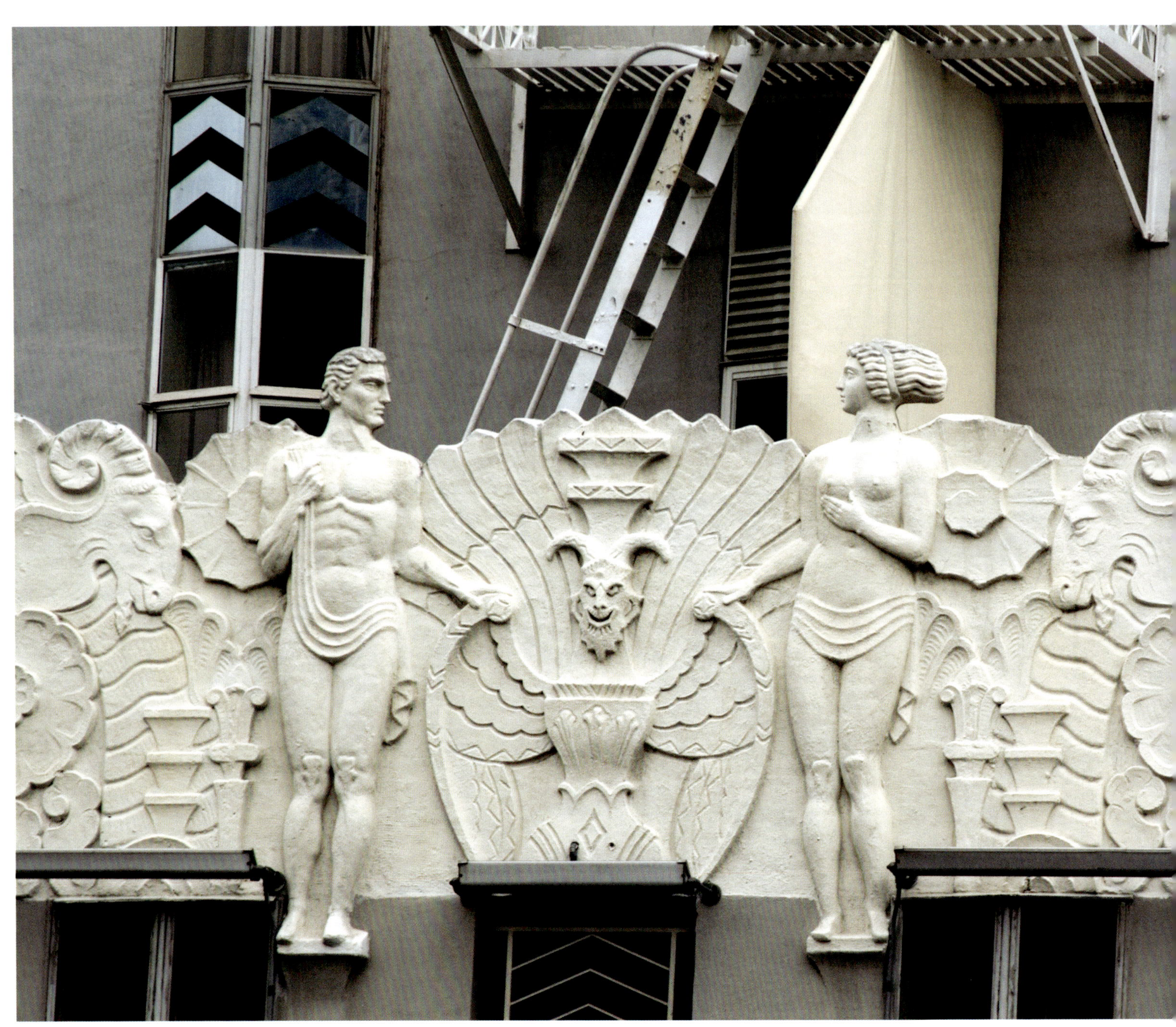

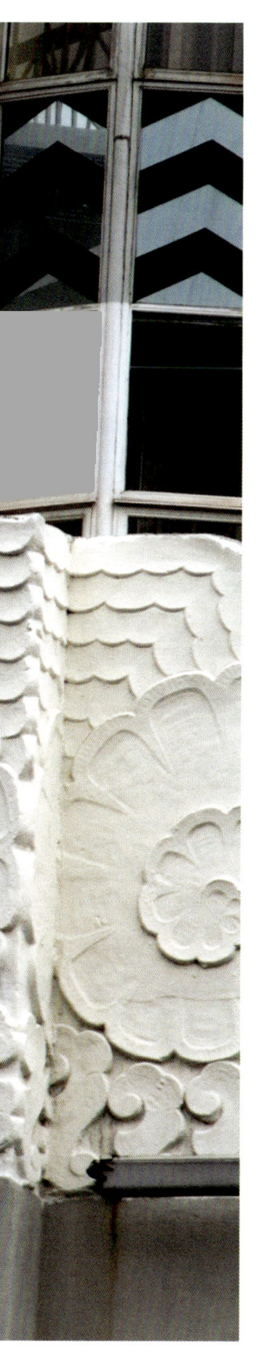

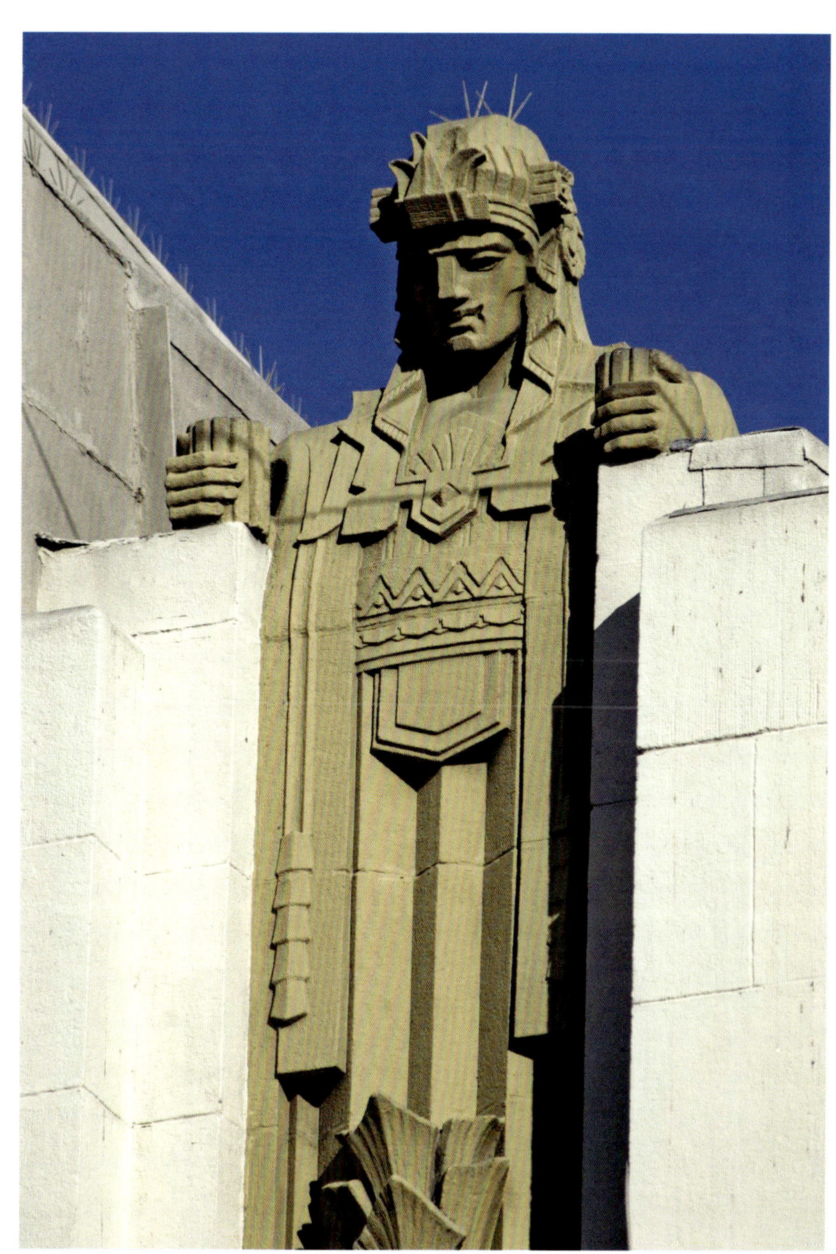

← *Sunset Tower Hotel, exterior detail (Leland A. Bryant, 1931)*
8358 Sunset Blvd., West Hollywood, photographed 1985.

↑ *Pantages Theatre, exterior detail (B. Marcus Priteca, 1930)*
6233 Hollywood Blvd., photographed 2010.

OVERLEAF: *Vogue Theater (William Glenn Blach, 1949)*
246 6th Street, Oxnard, photographed 1977.

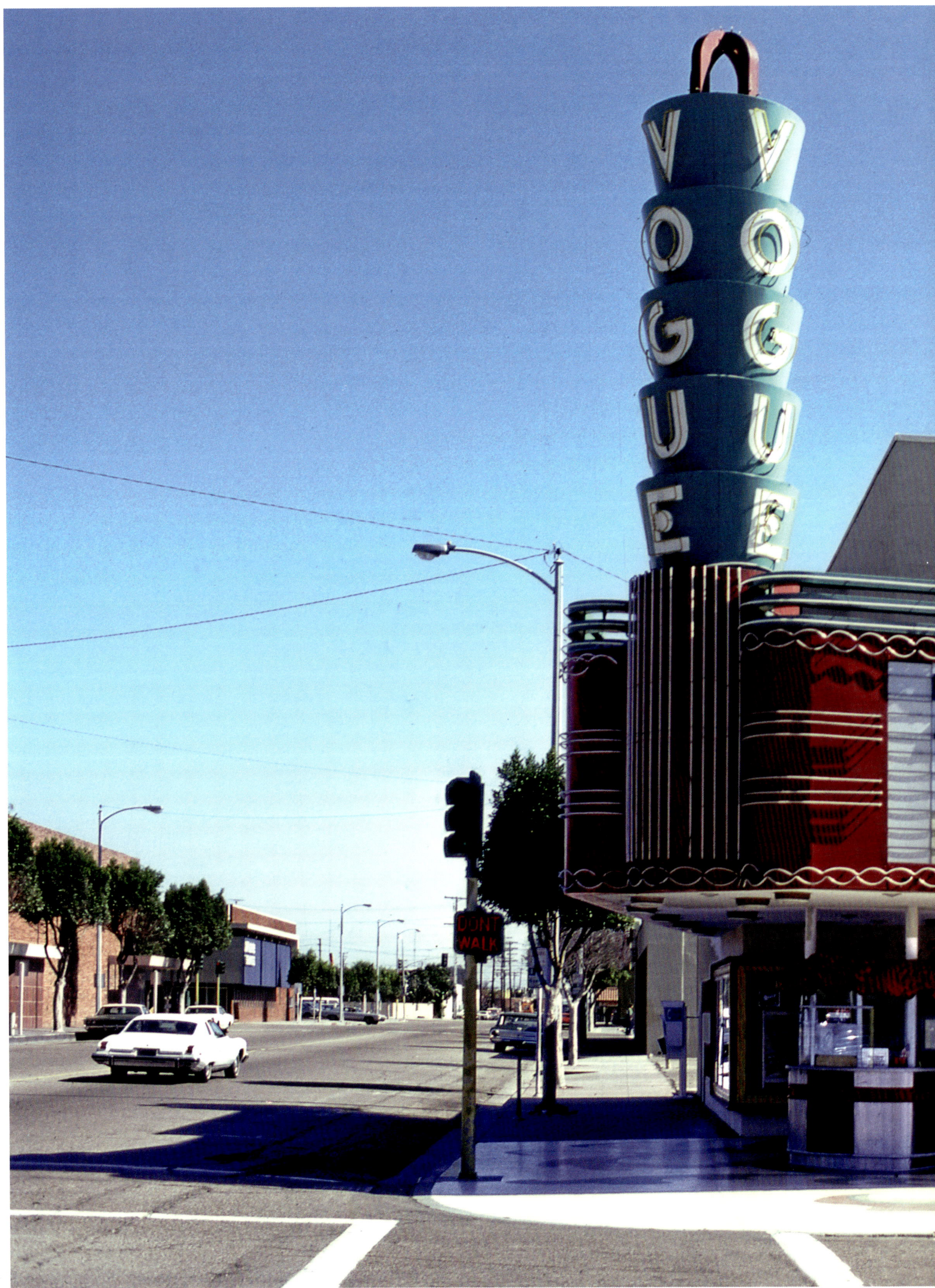
VOGUE
VOGUE
DONT
WALK

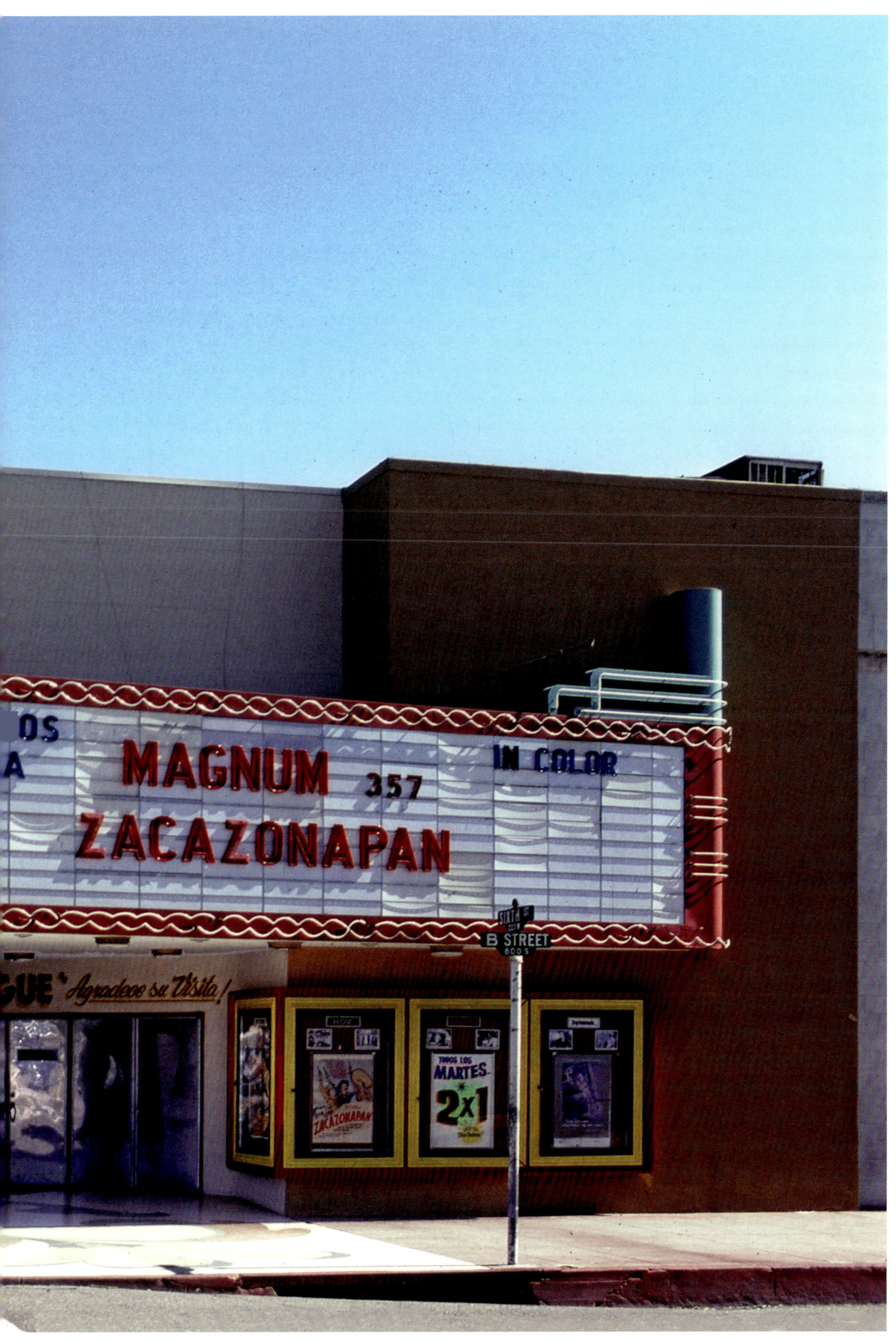

MAGNUM 357
ZACAZONAPAN
IN COLOR
SIXTH ST
B STREET
600 S
Agradece su Visita!
HOY
TODOS LOS MARTES
2x1
ZACAZONAPAN

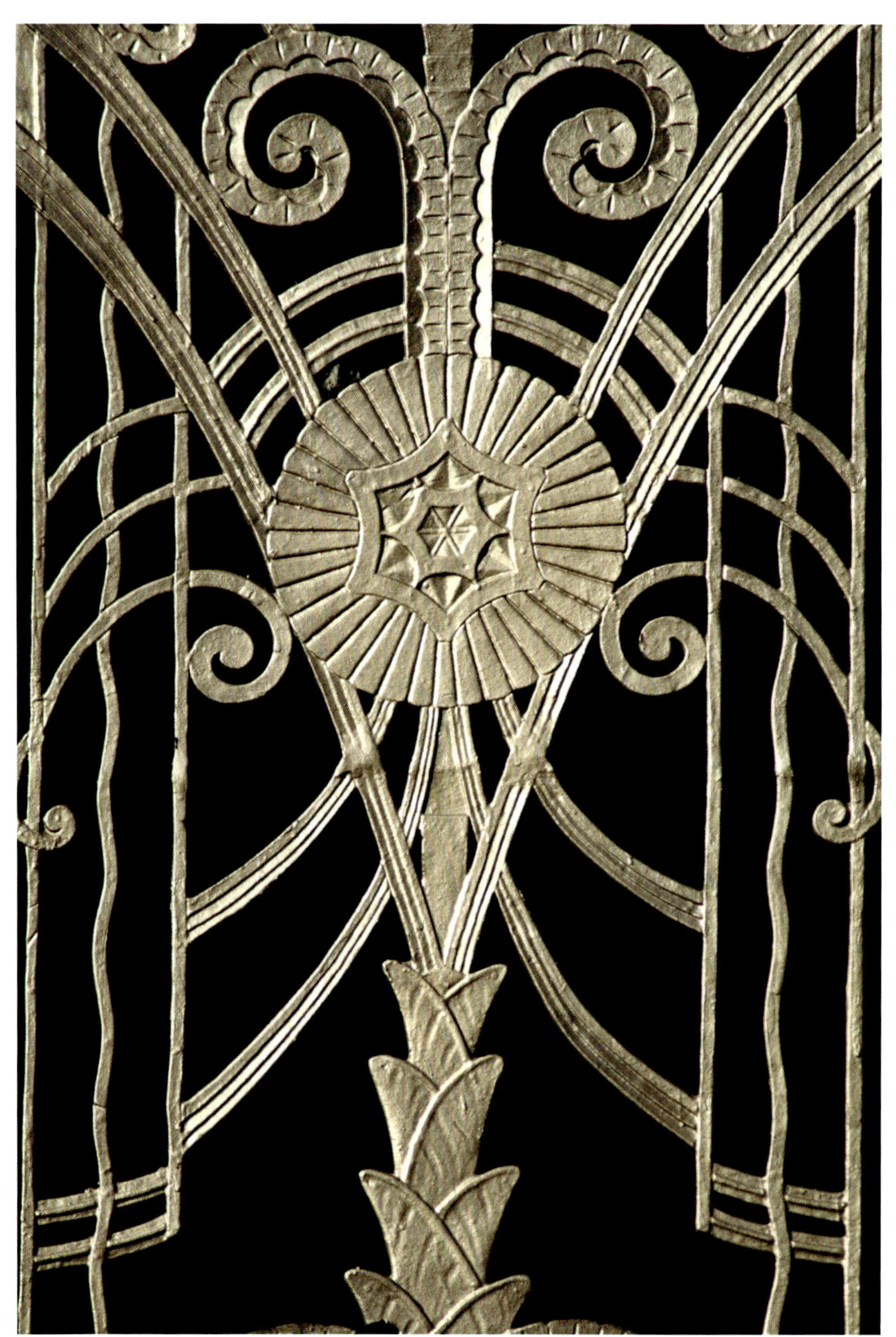

↑ *Shane Building, detail (S. Norton and F. Wallis, 1930) 6650 Hollywood Blvd., photographed 2008.*

→ *Commercial Building (J.R. Harris, 1931) 7290 Beverly Blvd., photographed 2003.*

OVERLEAF: *Georgian Hotel (M. Eugene Durfee, 1931) 1415 Ocean Ave., Santa Monica, photographed 1992.*

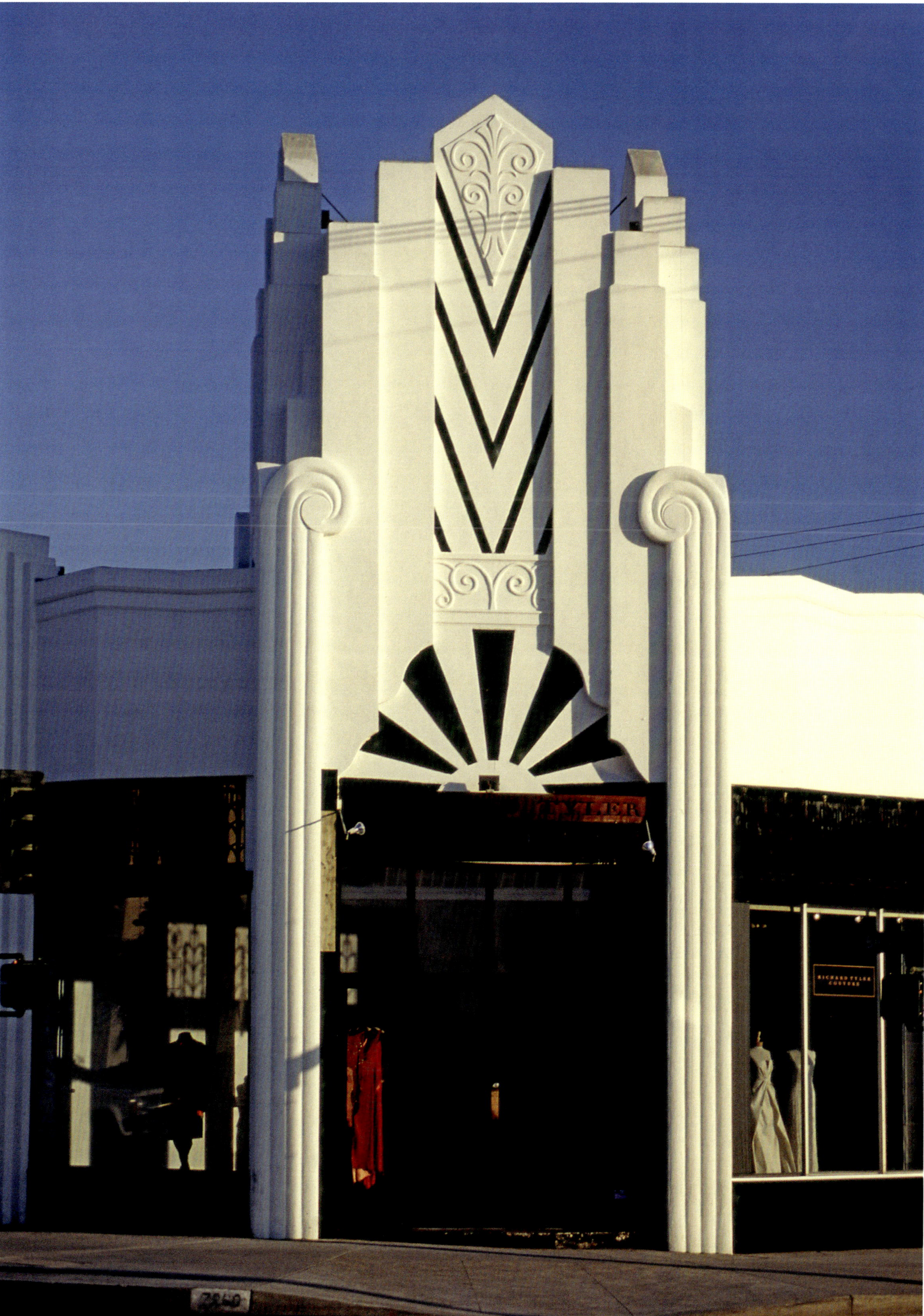

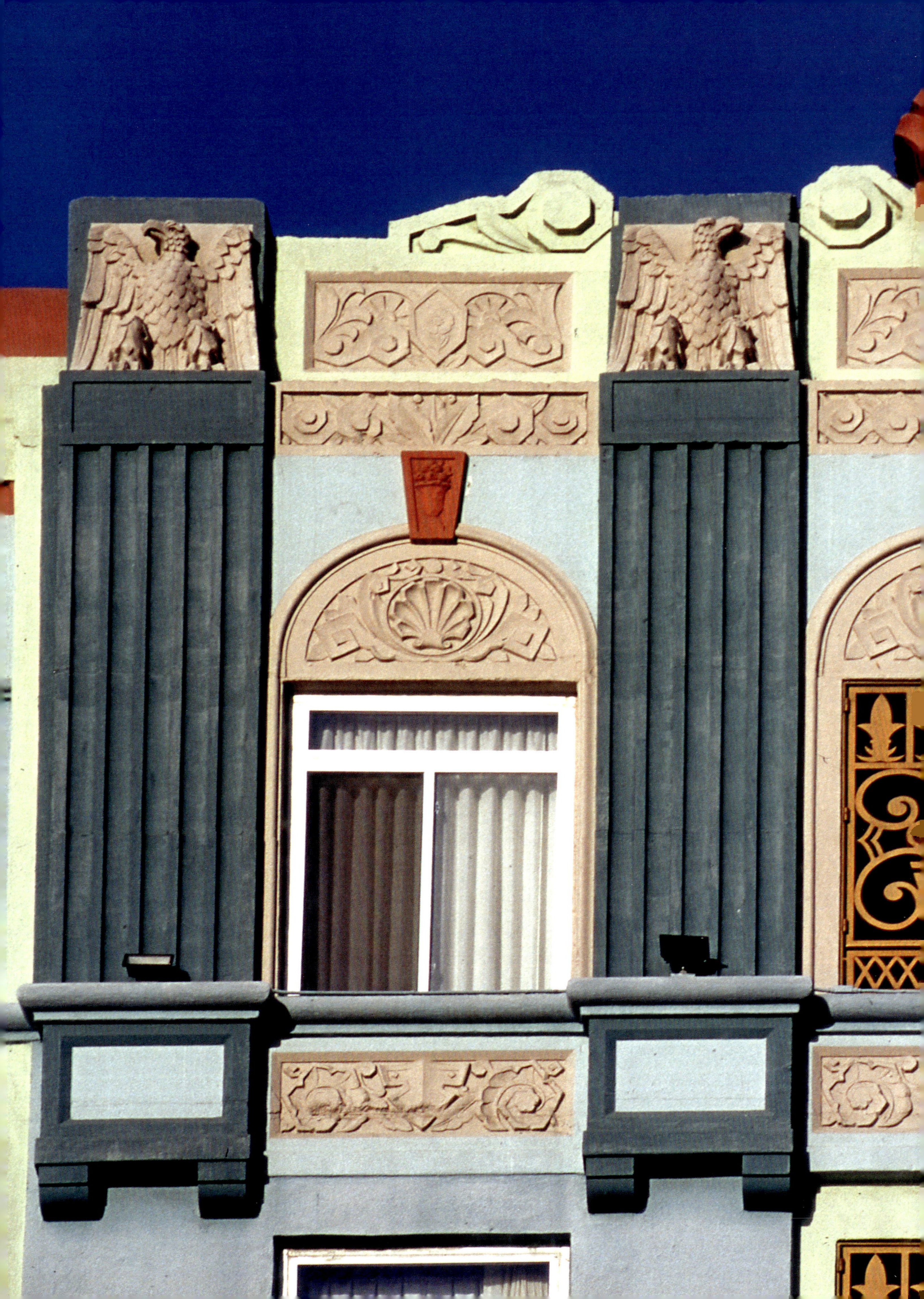

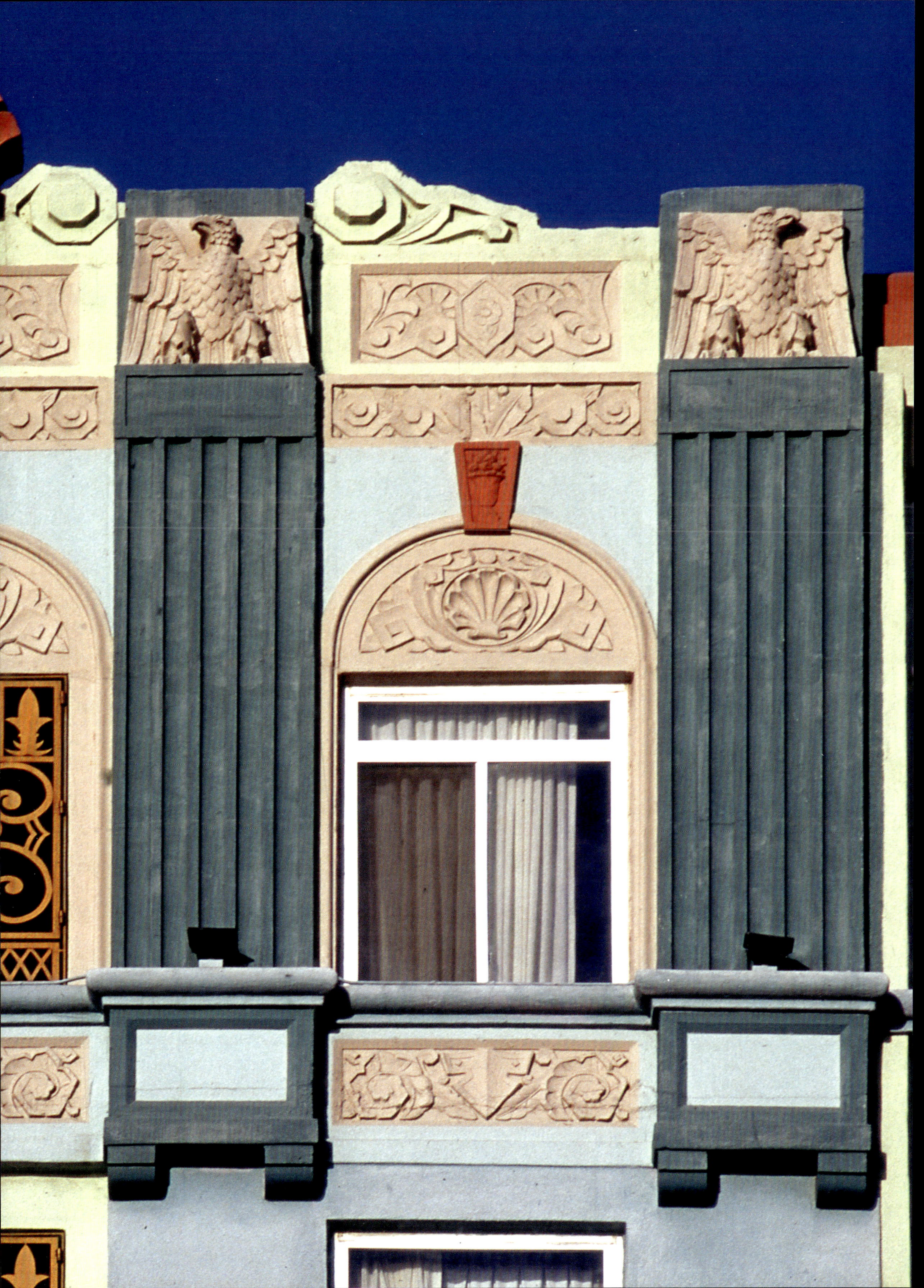

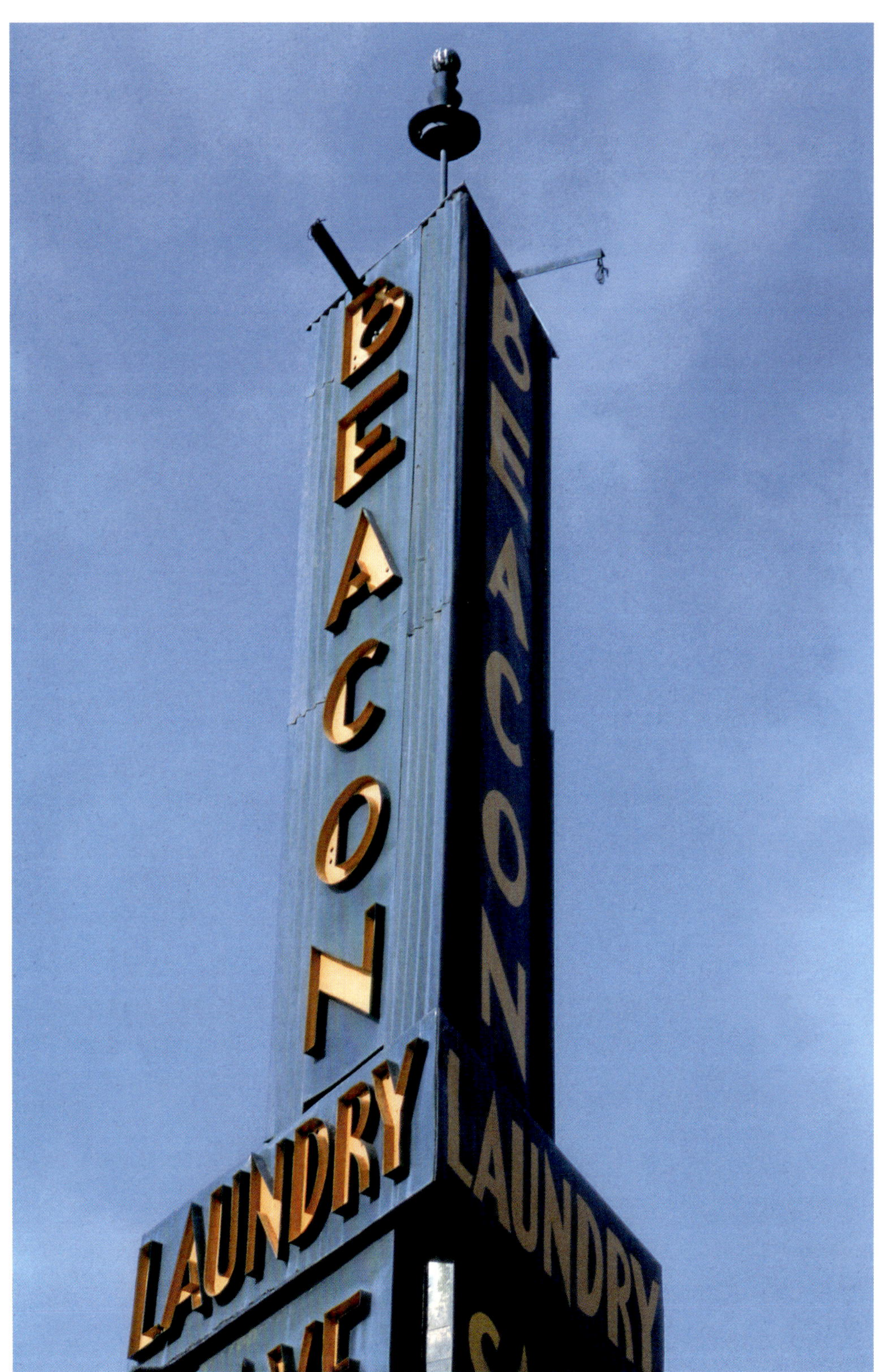

↑ *Beacon Laundry sign (architect unknown, 1931) 8695 Washington Blvd., Culver City, photographed 1988.*

→ *Academy Theatre, now Academy Cathedral (S. Charles Lee, 1939) 3100 W. Manchester Blvd., Inglewood, photographed 2024.*

OVERLEAF: *Nuart Theatre, neon detail (architect unknown, 1929) 11272 Santa Monica Blvd., photographed 1988.*

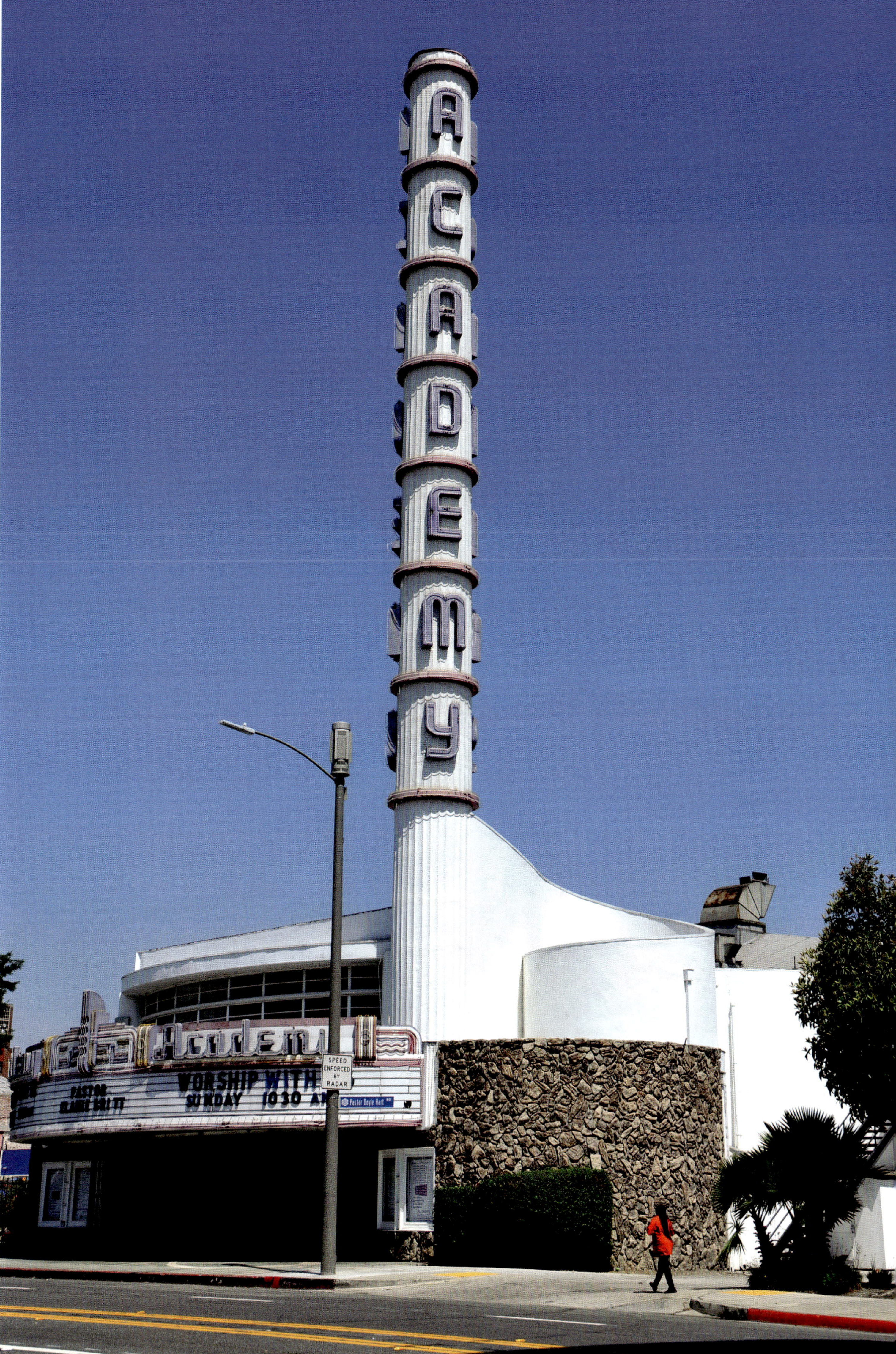
ACADEMY
PASTOR
VORSHIP WITH
SUNDAY 1030
SPEED ENFORCED BY RADAR
Pastor Doyle Hart

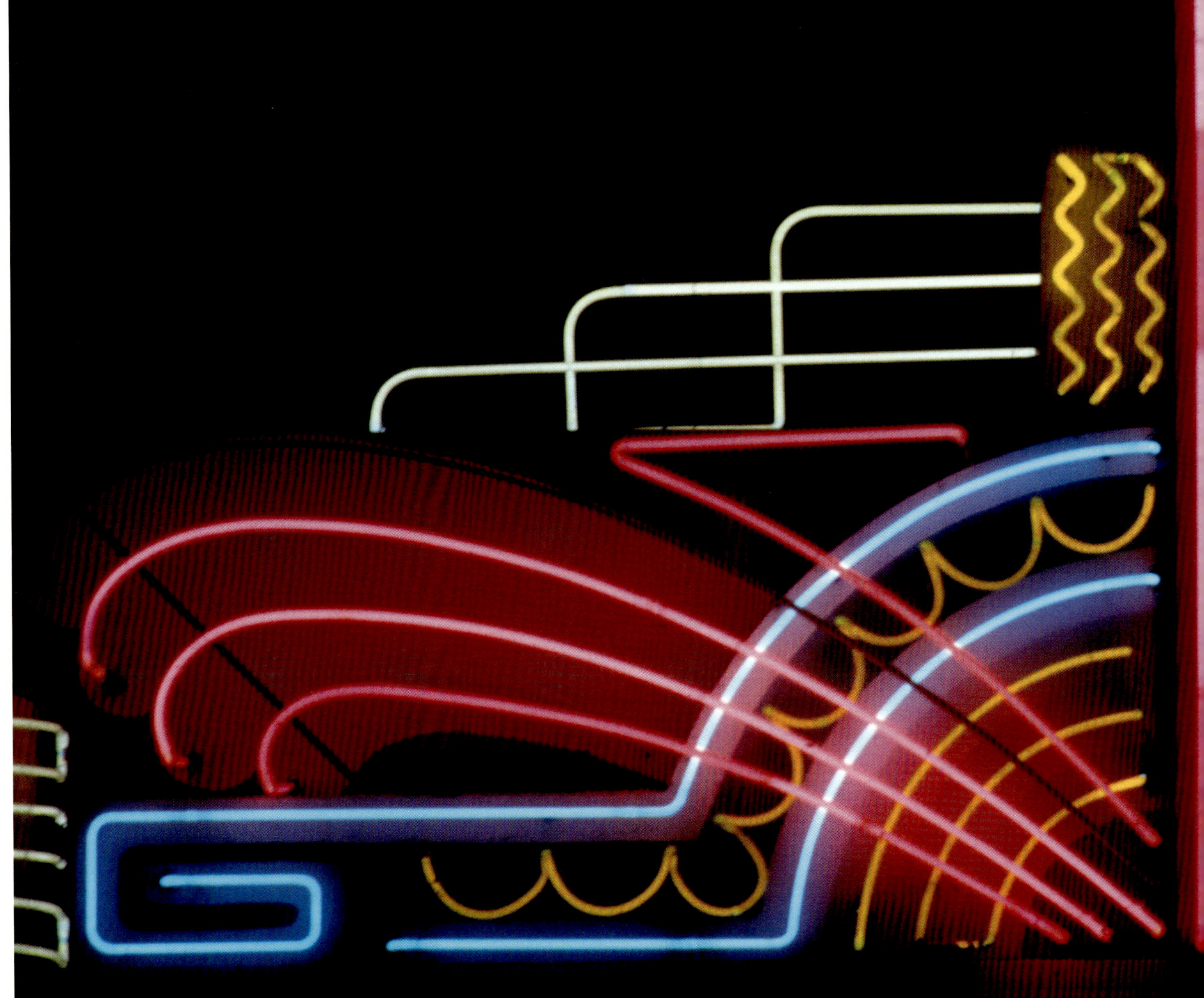

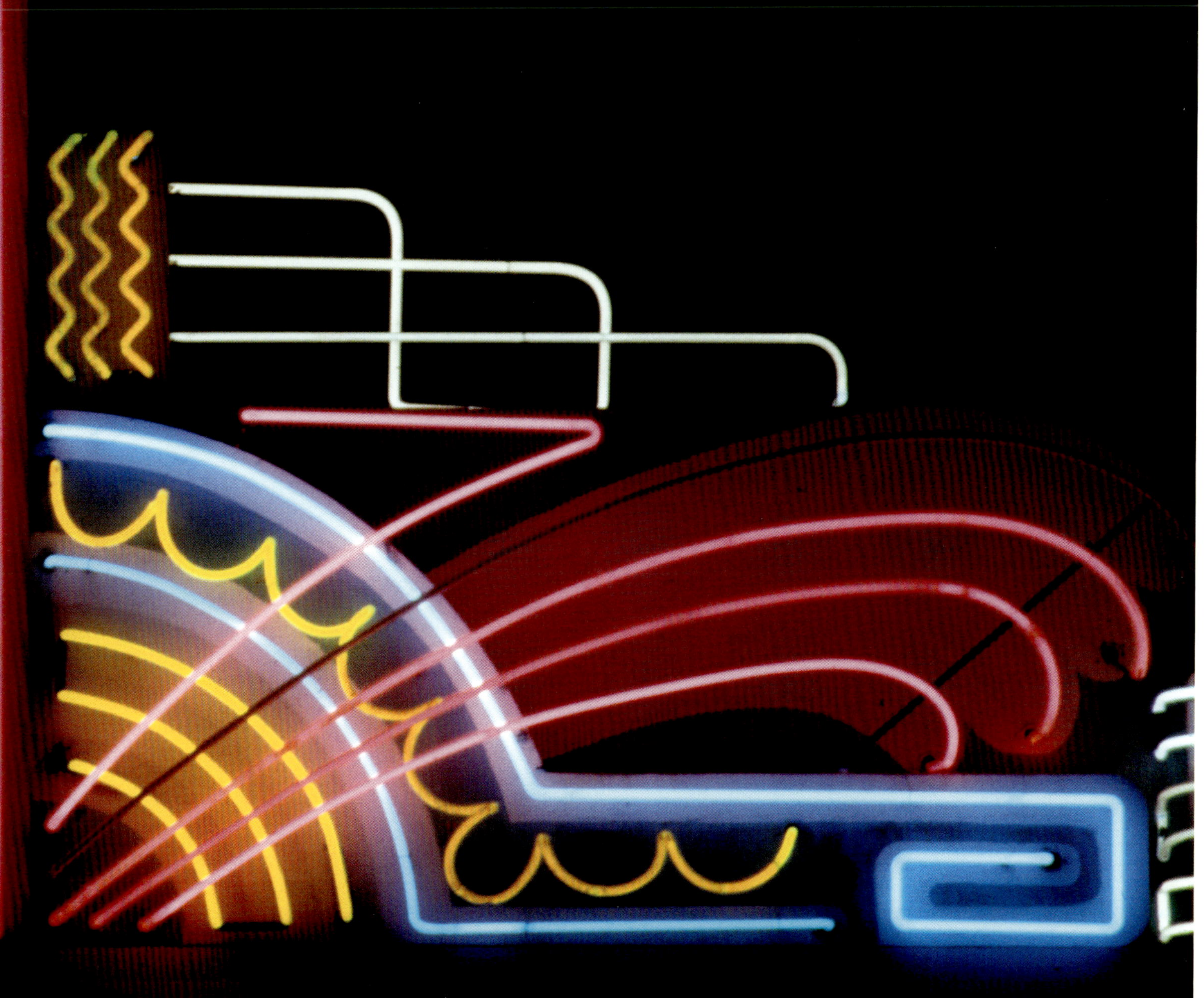

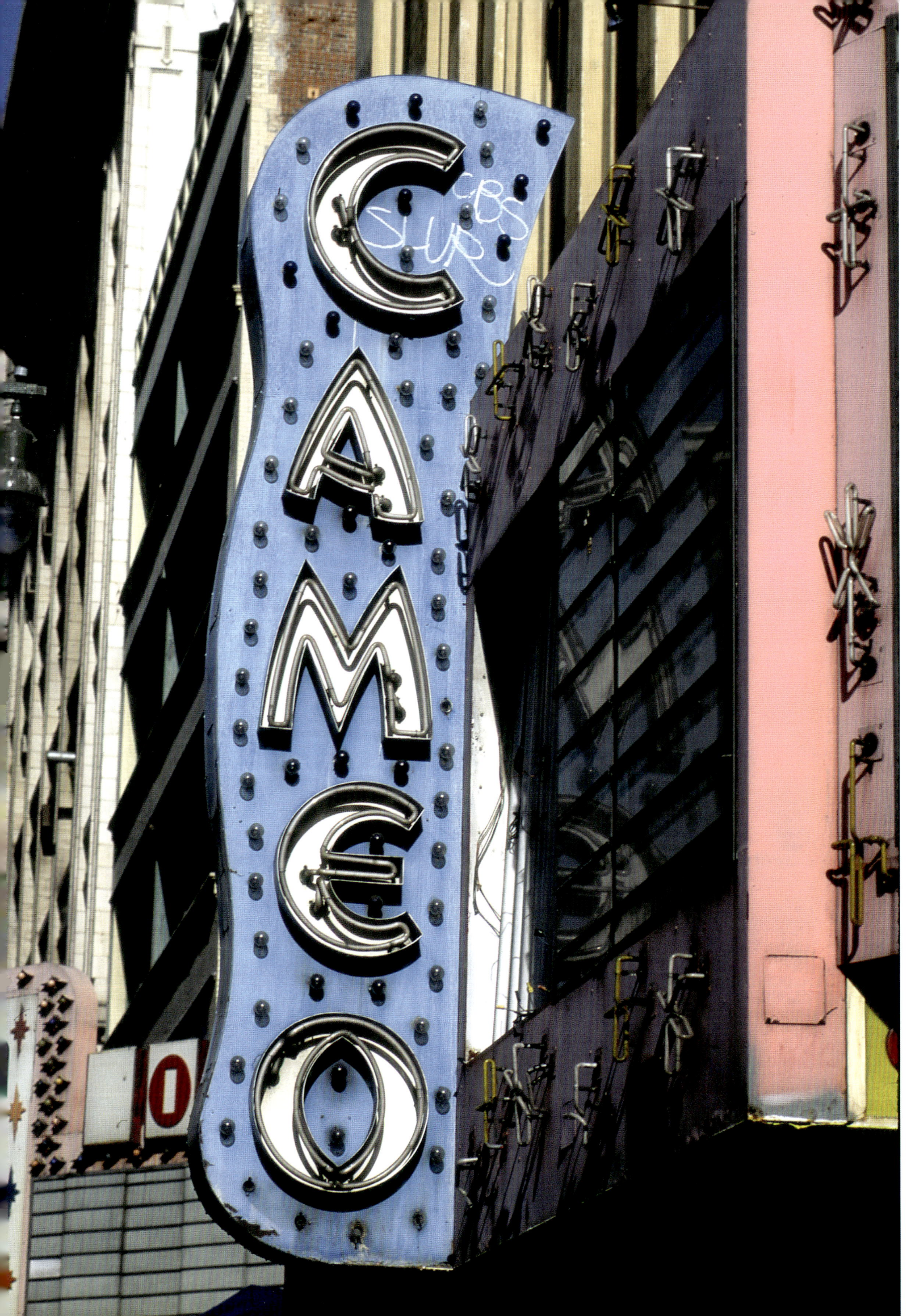
CAMEO

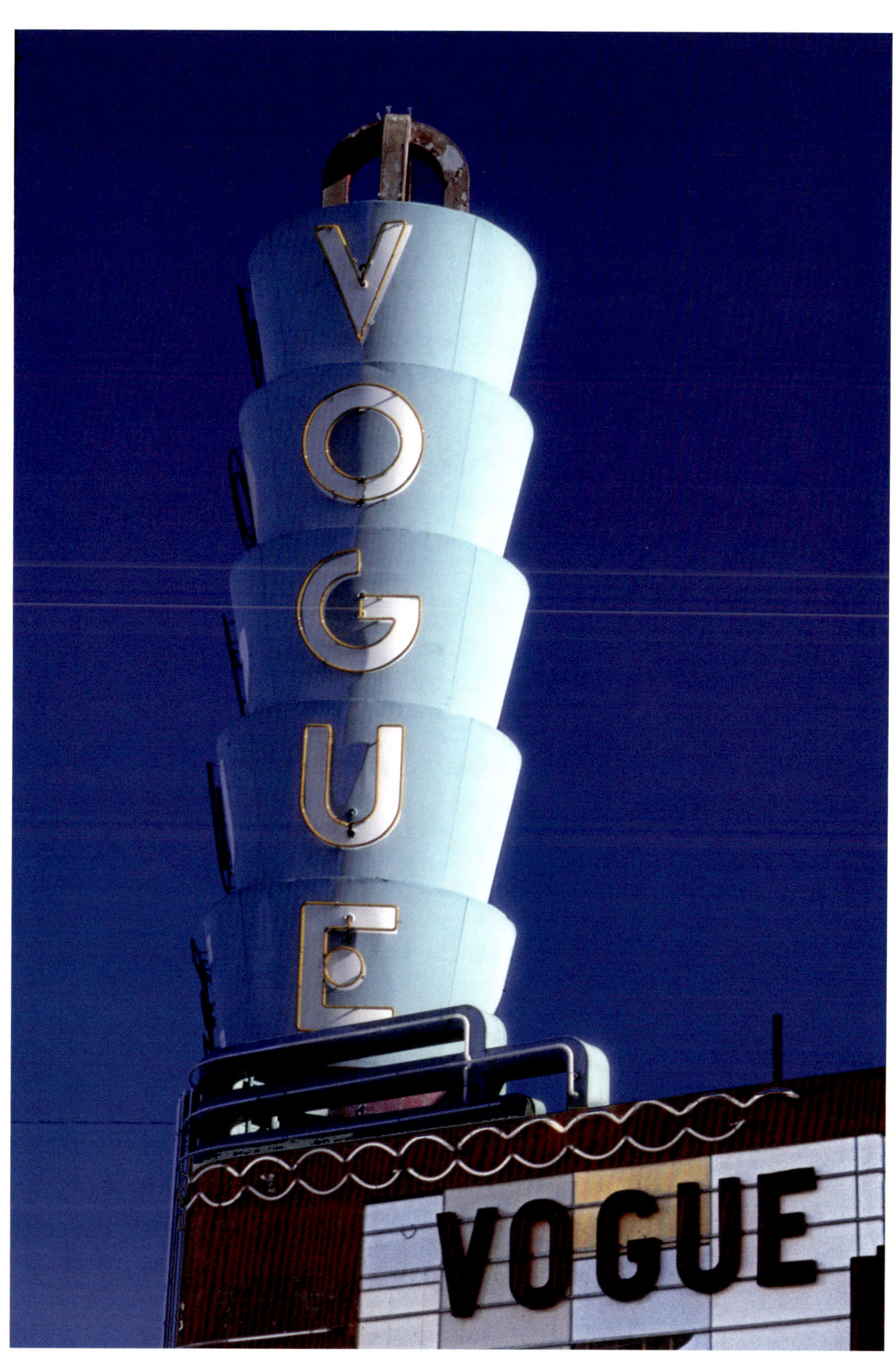

← *Cameo Theater sign (Alfred F. Rosenheim, 1910)*
528 S. Broadway, photographed 1988.

↑ *Vogue Theater, sign detail (William Glenn Blach, 1949)*
246 6th Street, Oxnard, photographed 1977.

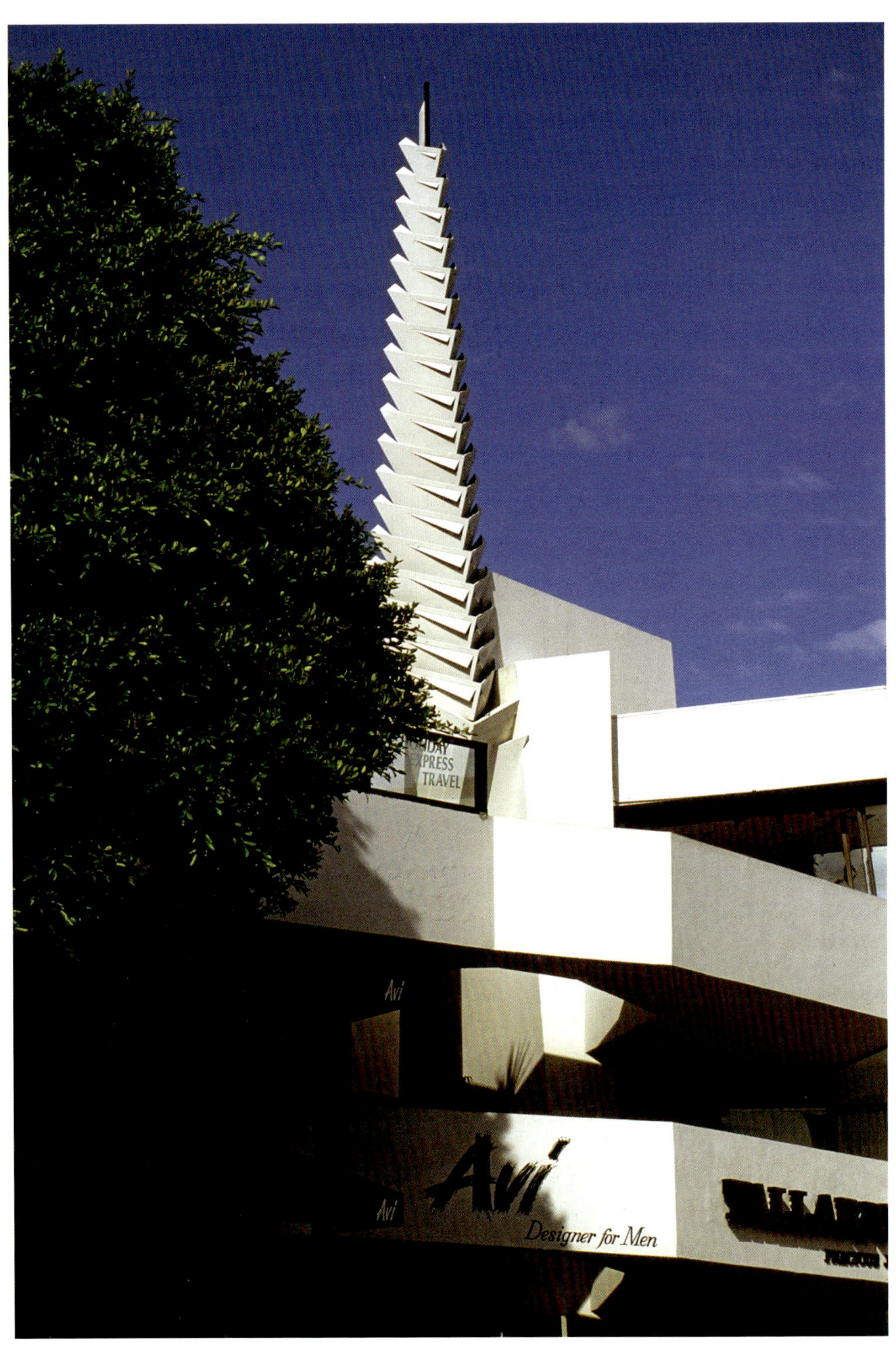

↑ *Anderton Court Shops (Frank Lloyd Wright, 1952) 332 Rodeo Dr., Beverly Hills, photographed 1988.*

→ *E. Clem Wilson Building (Meyer and Holler, 1930) 5525 Wilshire Blvd., photographed 1977 as Mutual of Omaha, now Samsung.*

OVERLEAF: *Gilmore Drive-In Theatre (William Glenn Balch and Louis L. Bryan) formerly 6201 W. 3rd St., photographed 1979.*

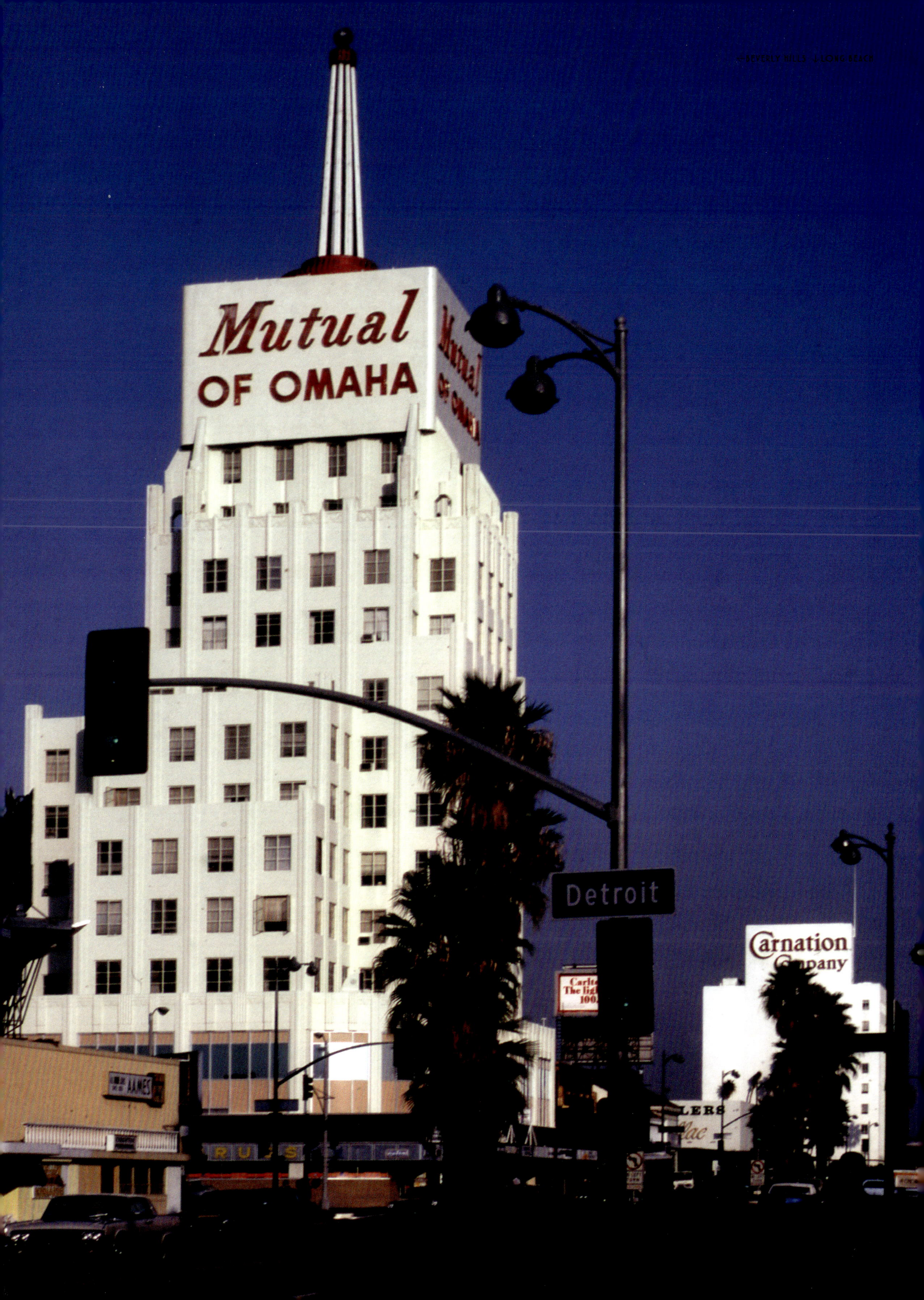
Mutual
OF OMAHA
Detroit
Carnation
AAMES

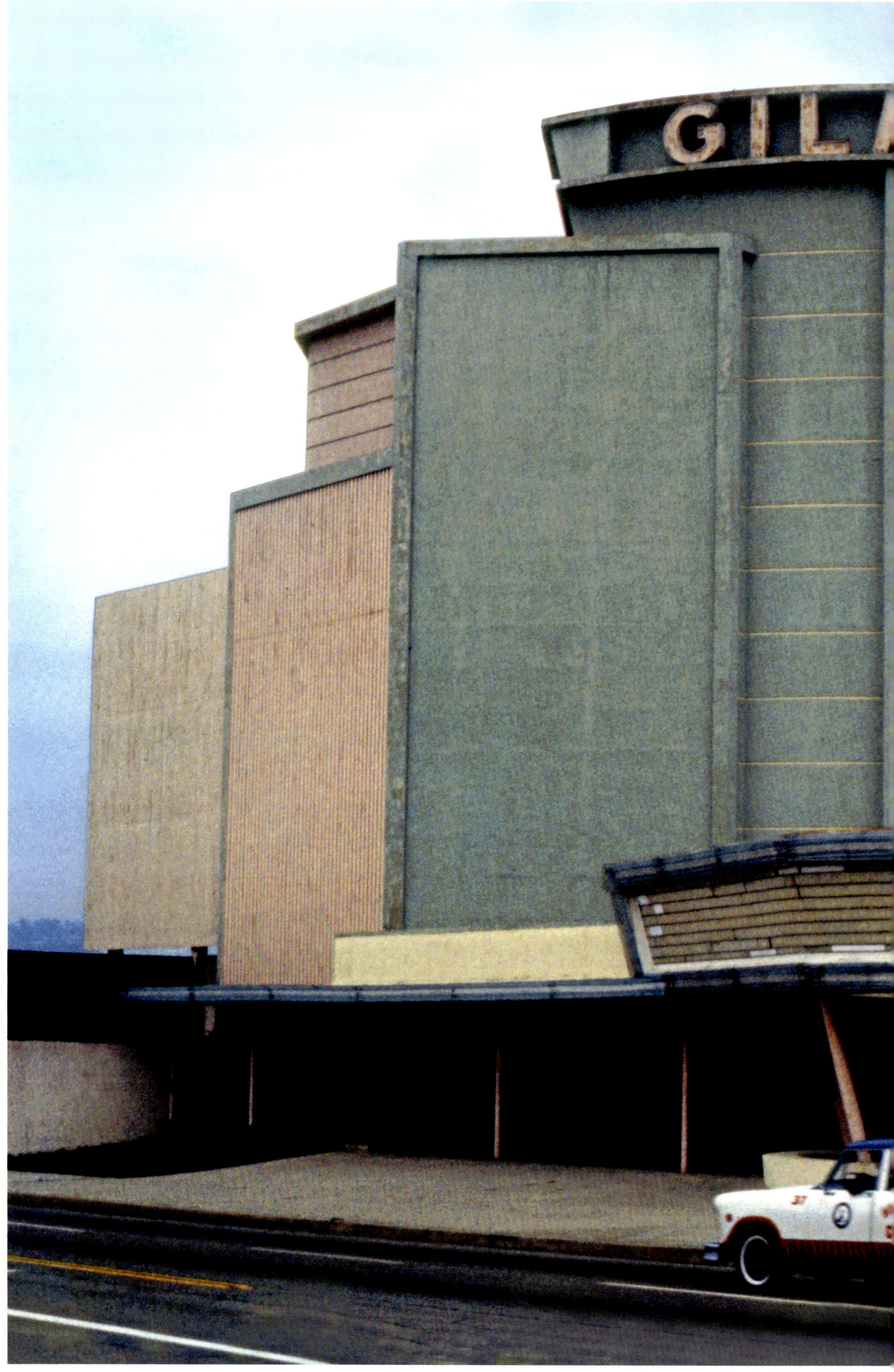
GIL

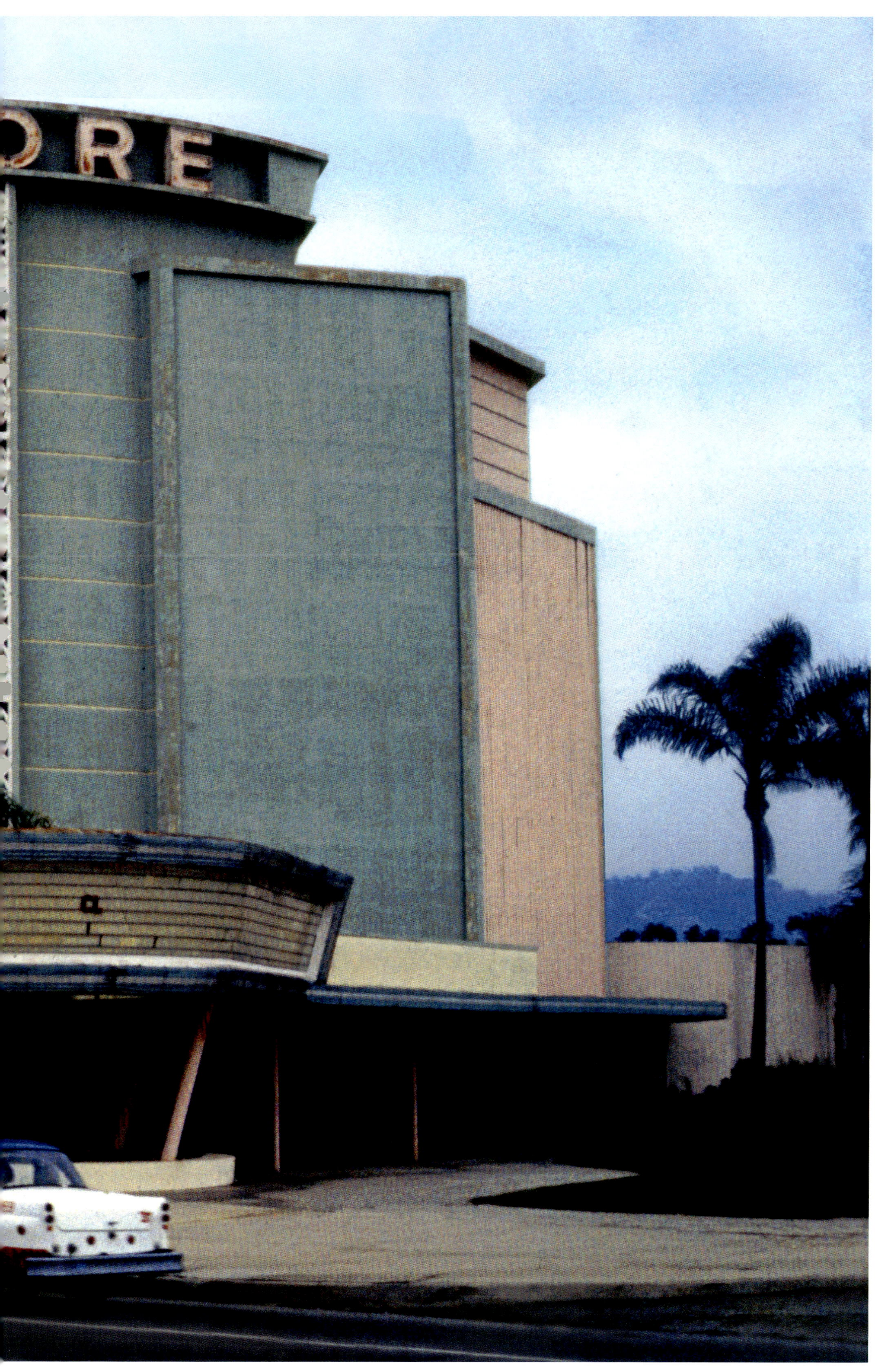
ORE

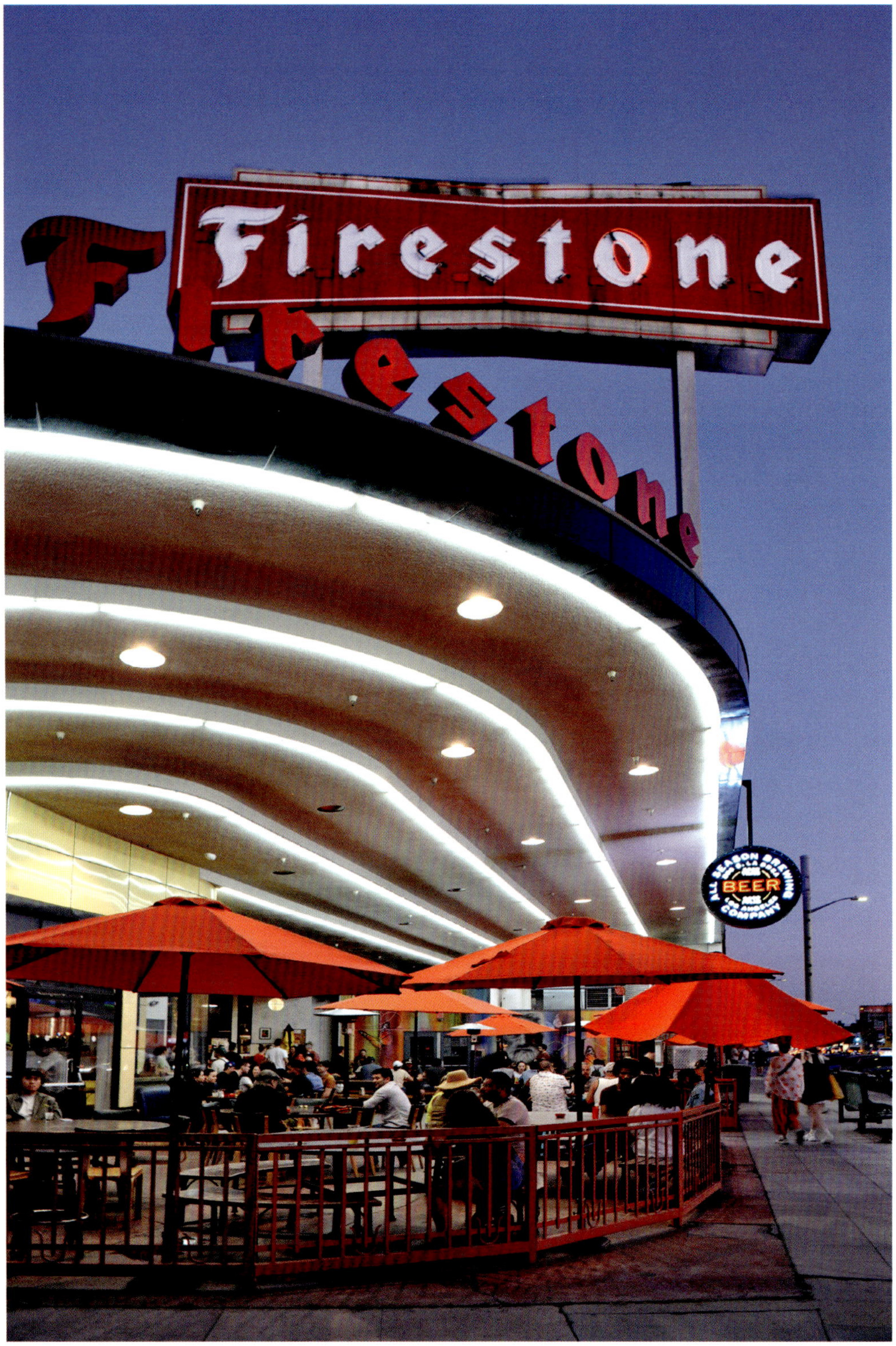

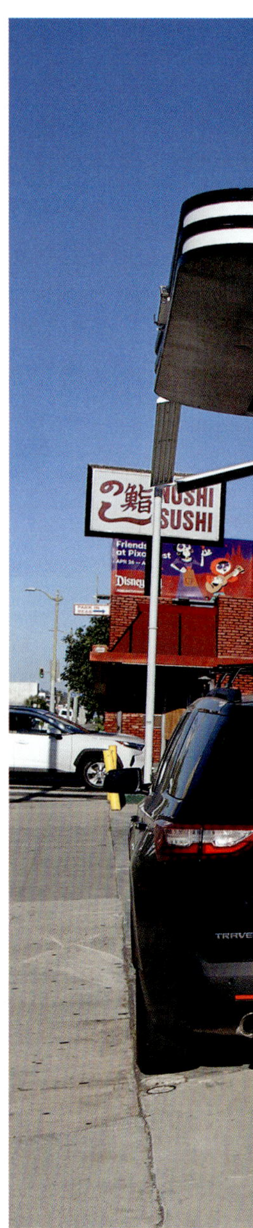

↑ Firestone Garage, now All Season Brewing Company (R.E. Ward, engineer, 1937) 800 S. La Brea Ave., photographed 2024.

→ Texaco Filling Station, now Royal Lobster (architect and year unknown) 4450 Beverly Blvd., photographed 2024.

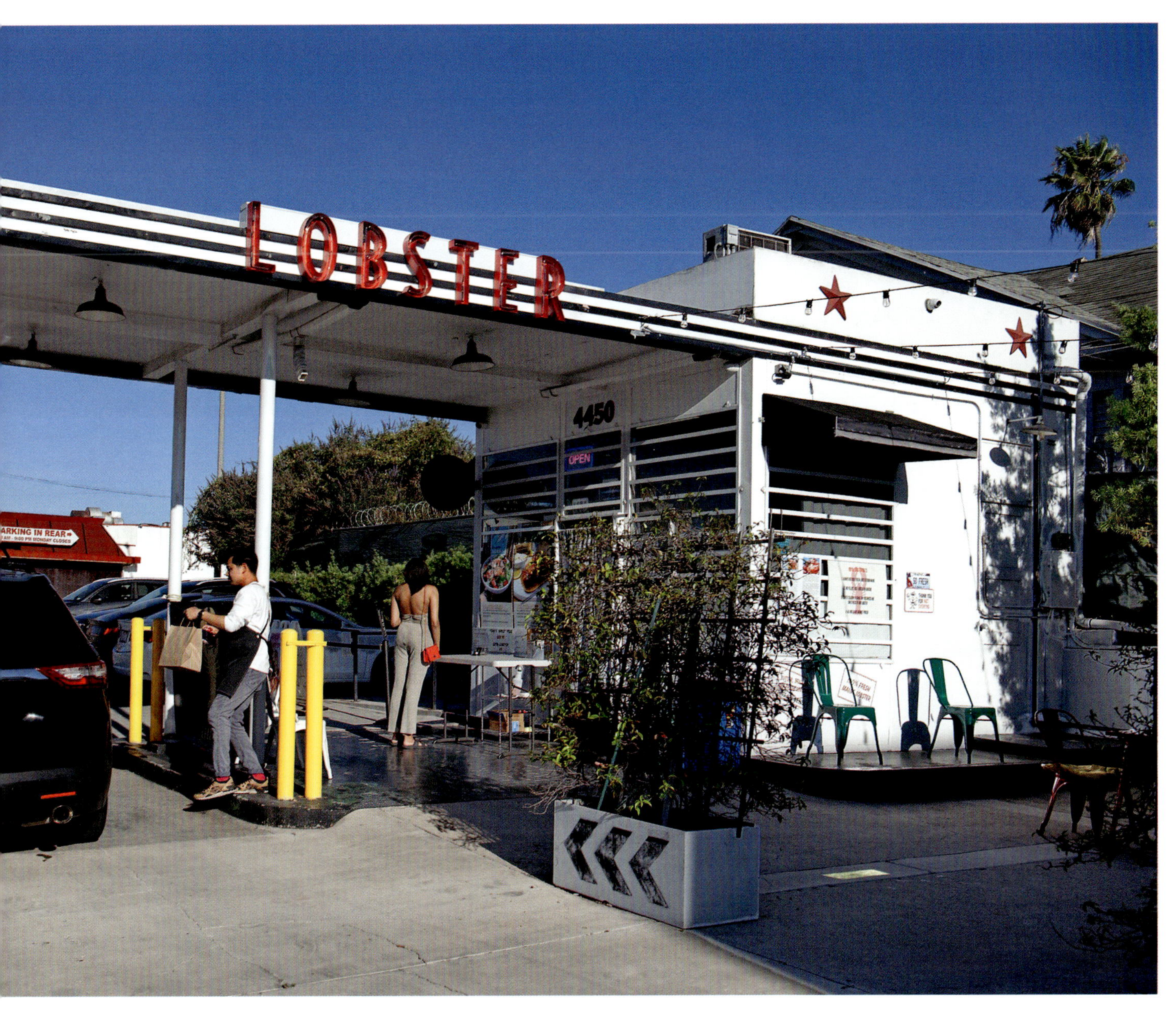
LOBSTER
4450
OPEN
PARKING IN REAR

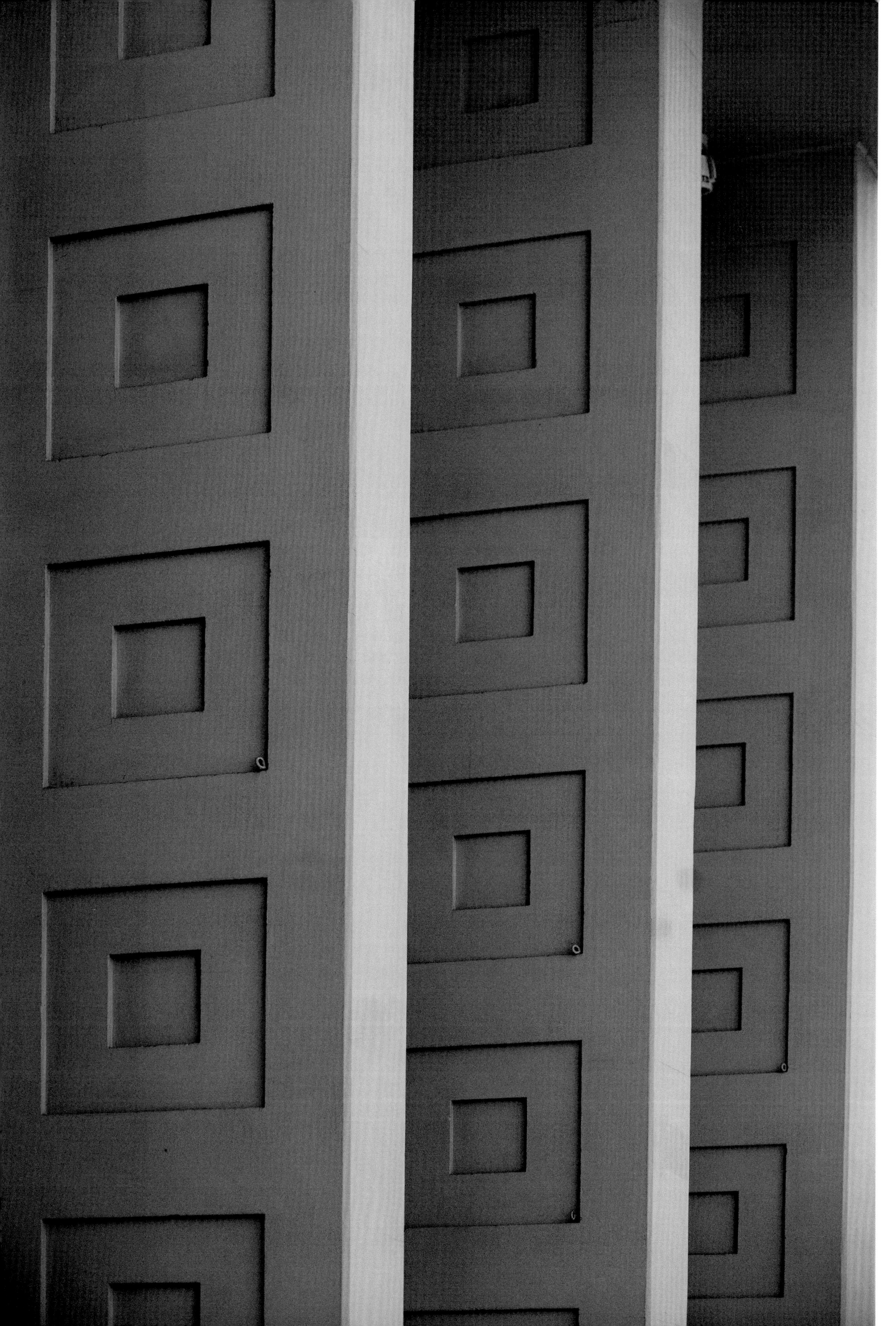

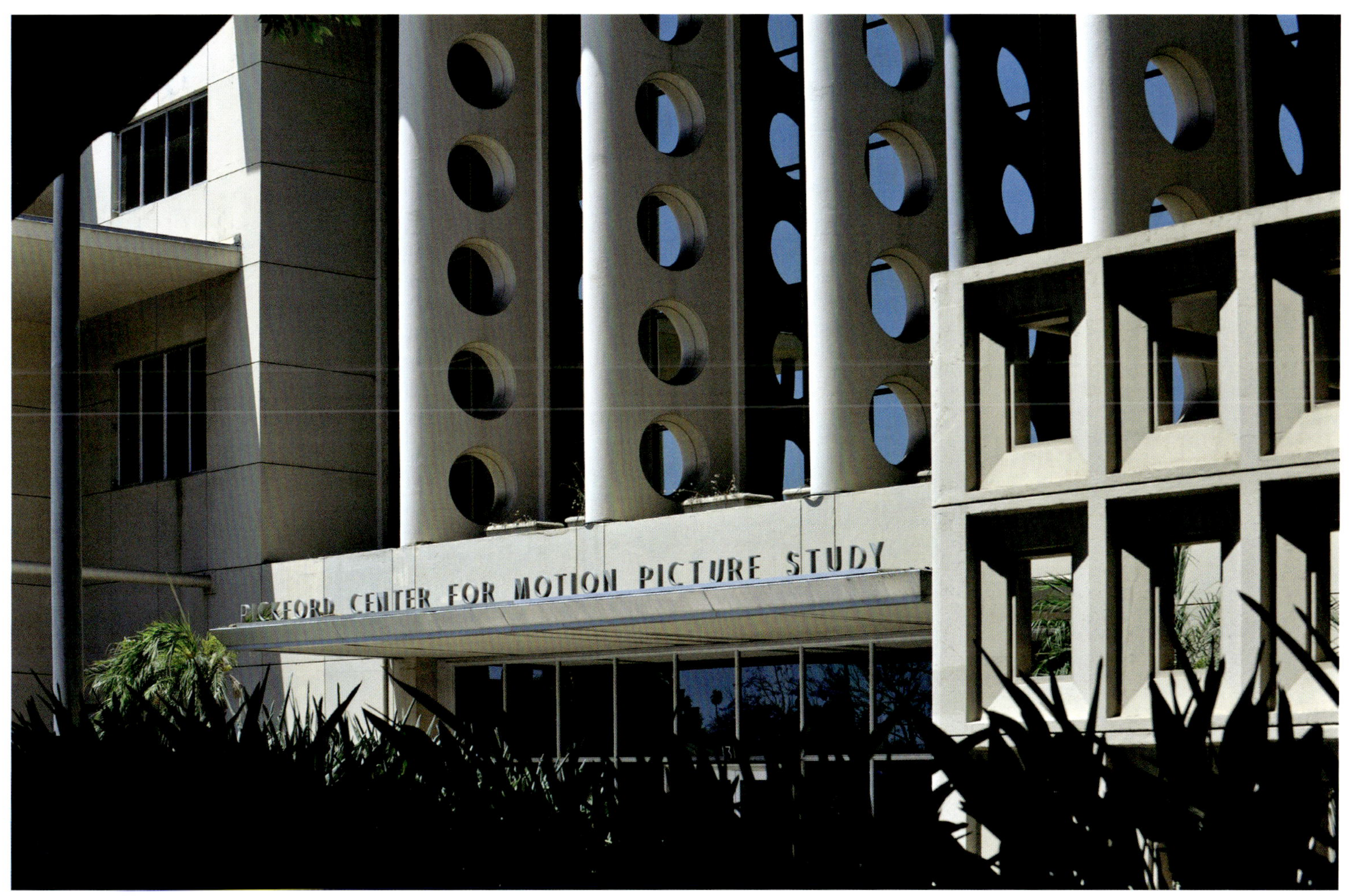

← *Burbank Water and Power, exterior detail (Daniel A. Elliott, 1949) 164 W. Magnolia Blvd., Burbank, photographed 2024.*

↑ *Don Lee Mutual Broadcast Building, now Pickford Center for Motion Picture Studies (Claud Beelman, 1948) 1313 Vine St., photographed 2024.*

OVERLEAF: *Gilmore Service Station, now Starbucks (Walter Dorwin Teague, 1935) 859 N. Highland Ave., photographed 2024.*

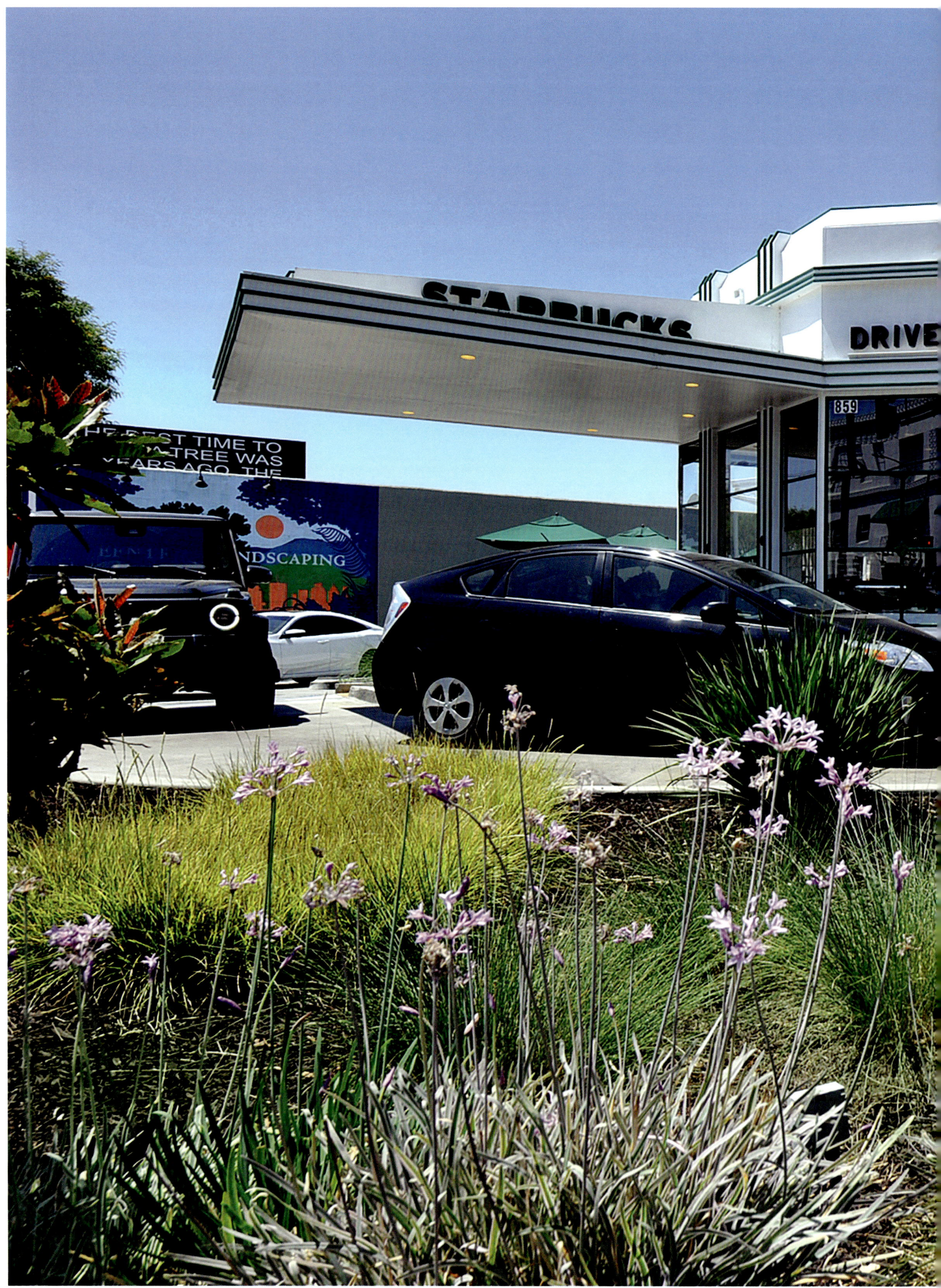
STARBUCKS
DRIVE
859
TIME TO
TREE WAS
NDSCAPING

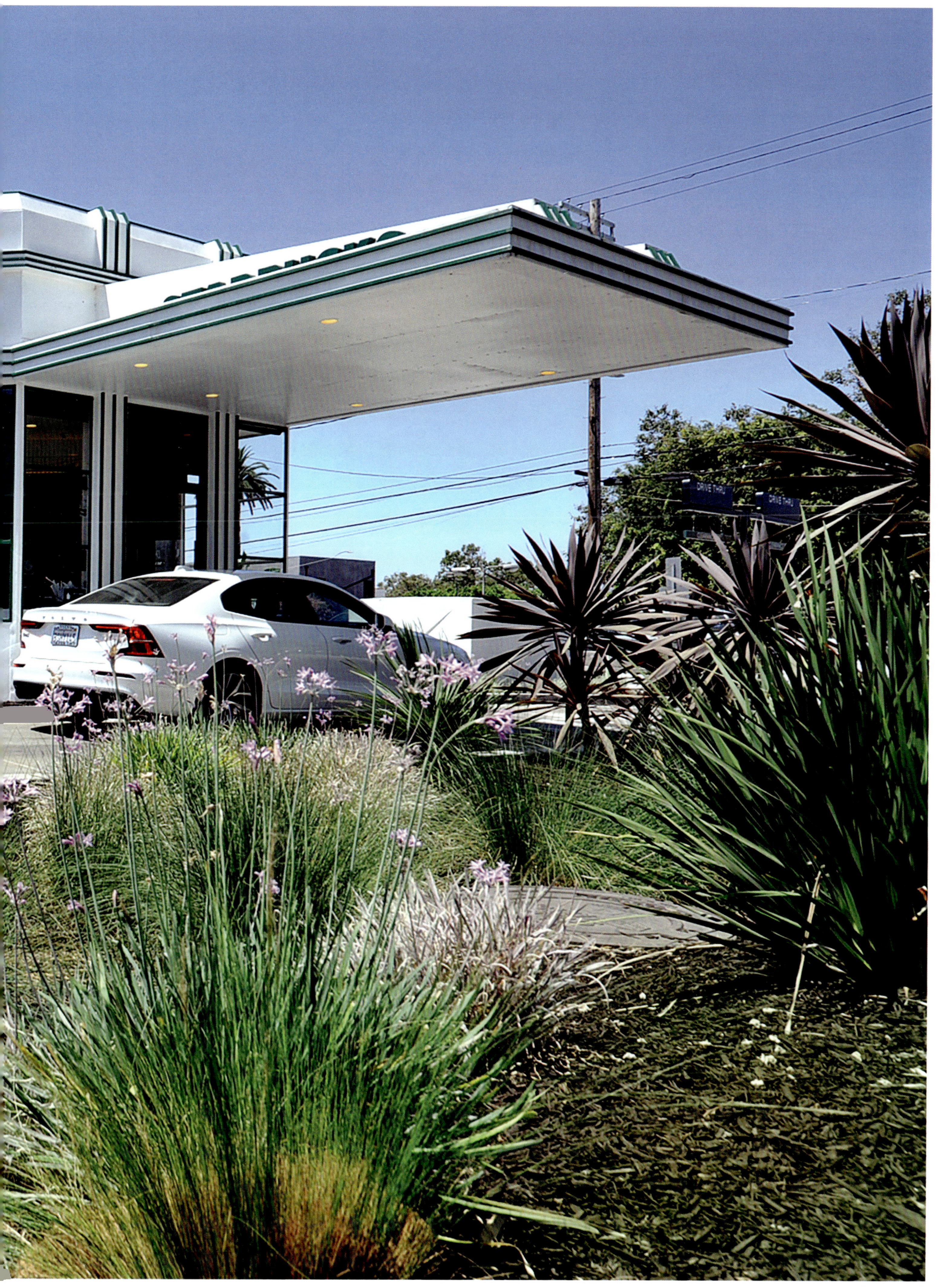
DRIVE THRU

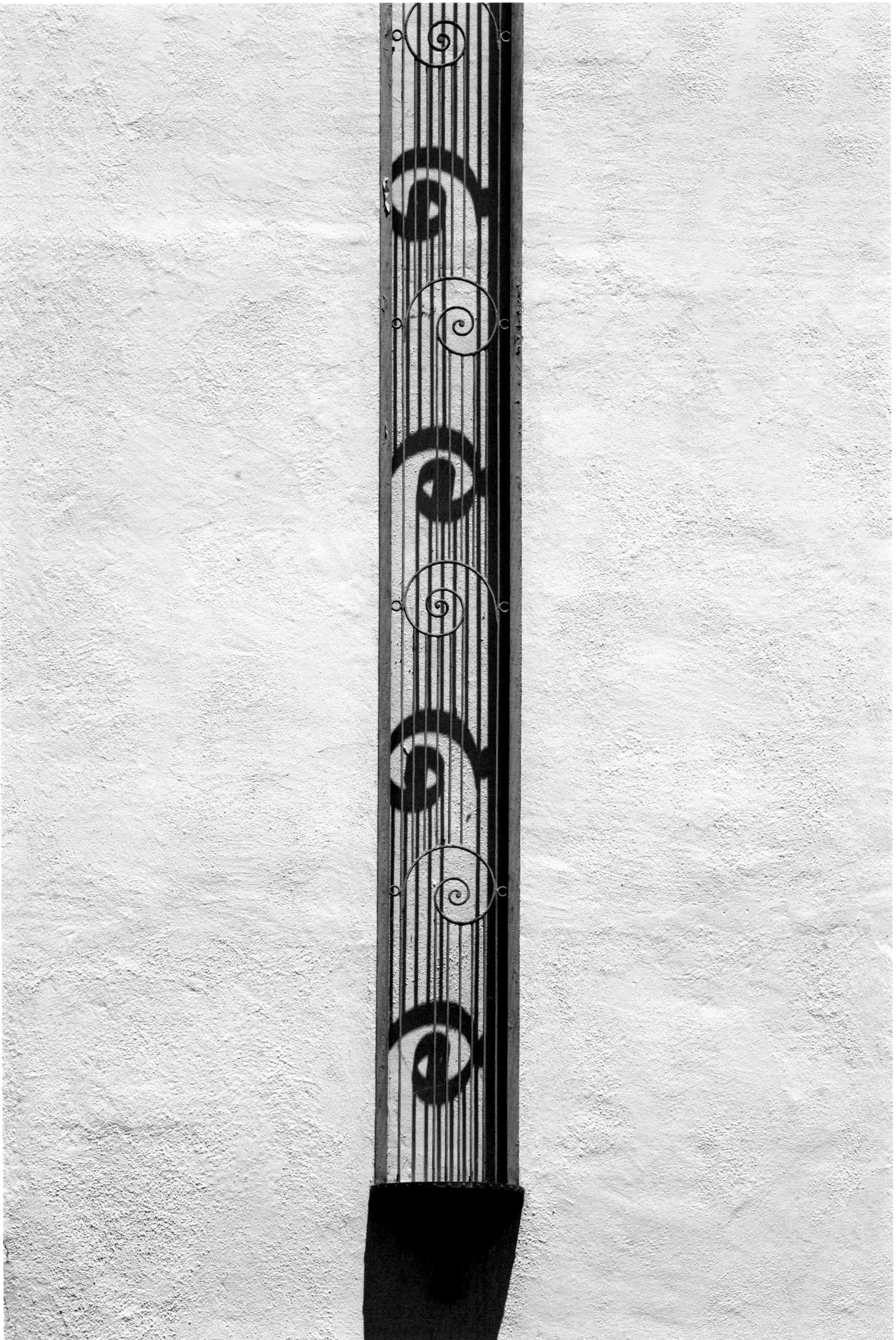

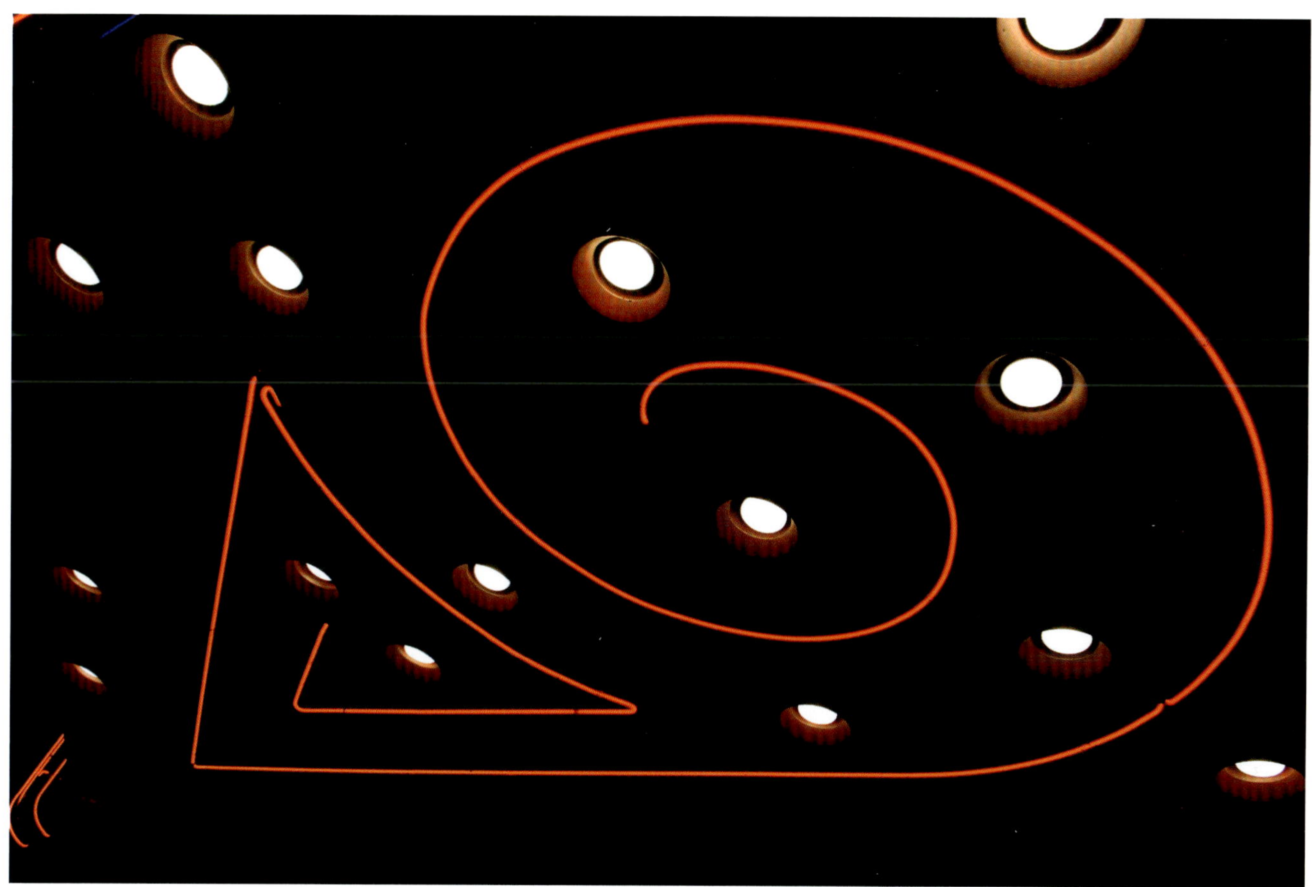

← *Moderne Apartment Building, exterior detail (H. Guthrie Thursby, 1940) 3919 W. 8th St., photographed 2024.*

↑ *Fine Arts Theater, neon detail (B. Marcus Priteca, year unknown) 8556 Wilshire Blvd., Beverly Hills, photographed 2008.*

OVERLEAF: *Saban Building, formerly May Company Department Store, now Academy Museum of Motion Pictures (A. C. Martin & Associates and Samuel Marx, 1939) 6067 Wilshire Blvd., photographed 2024.*

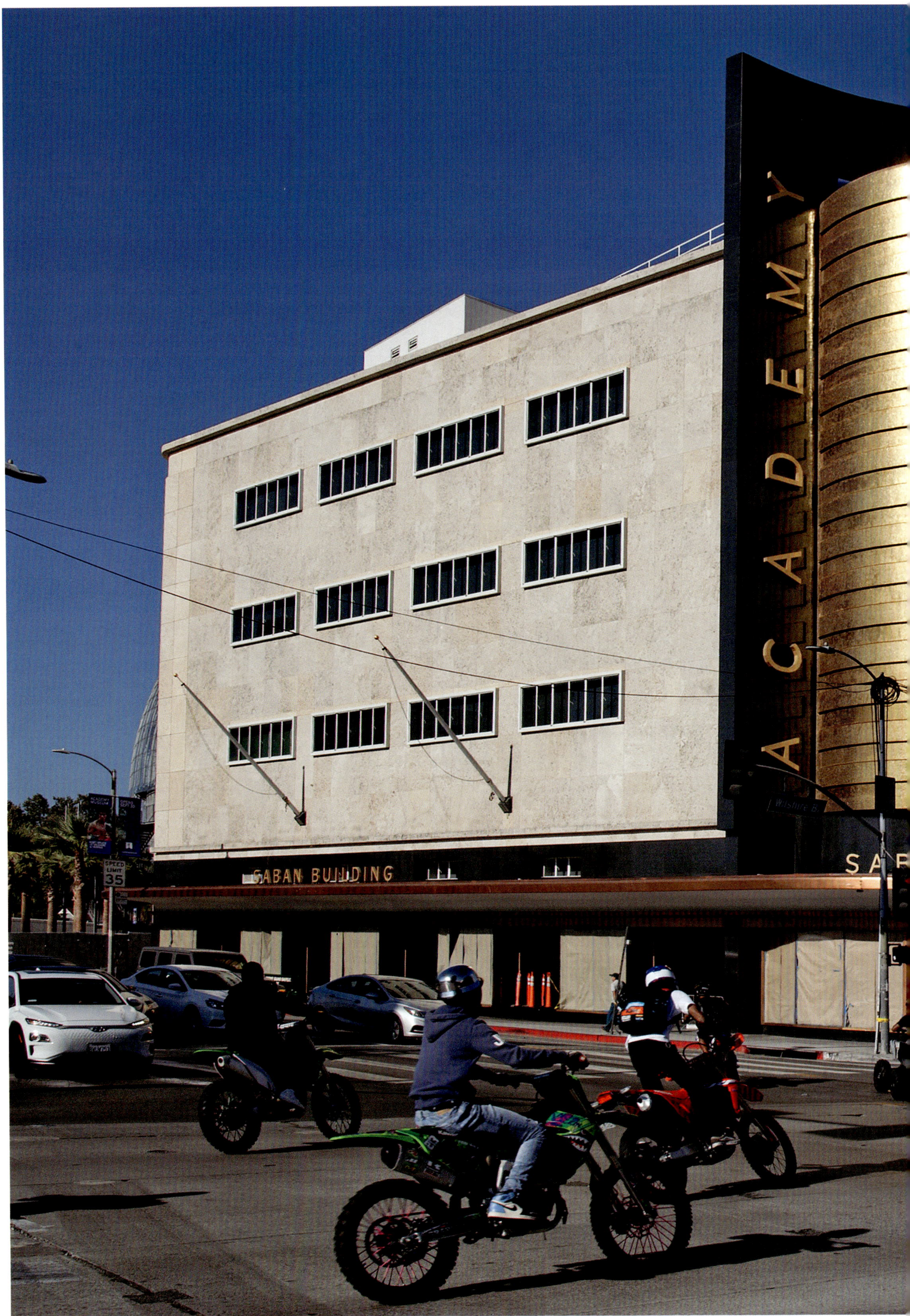
ACADEMY
SABAN BUILDING
SPEED LIMIT 35

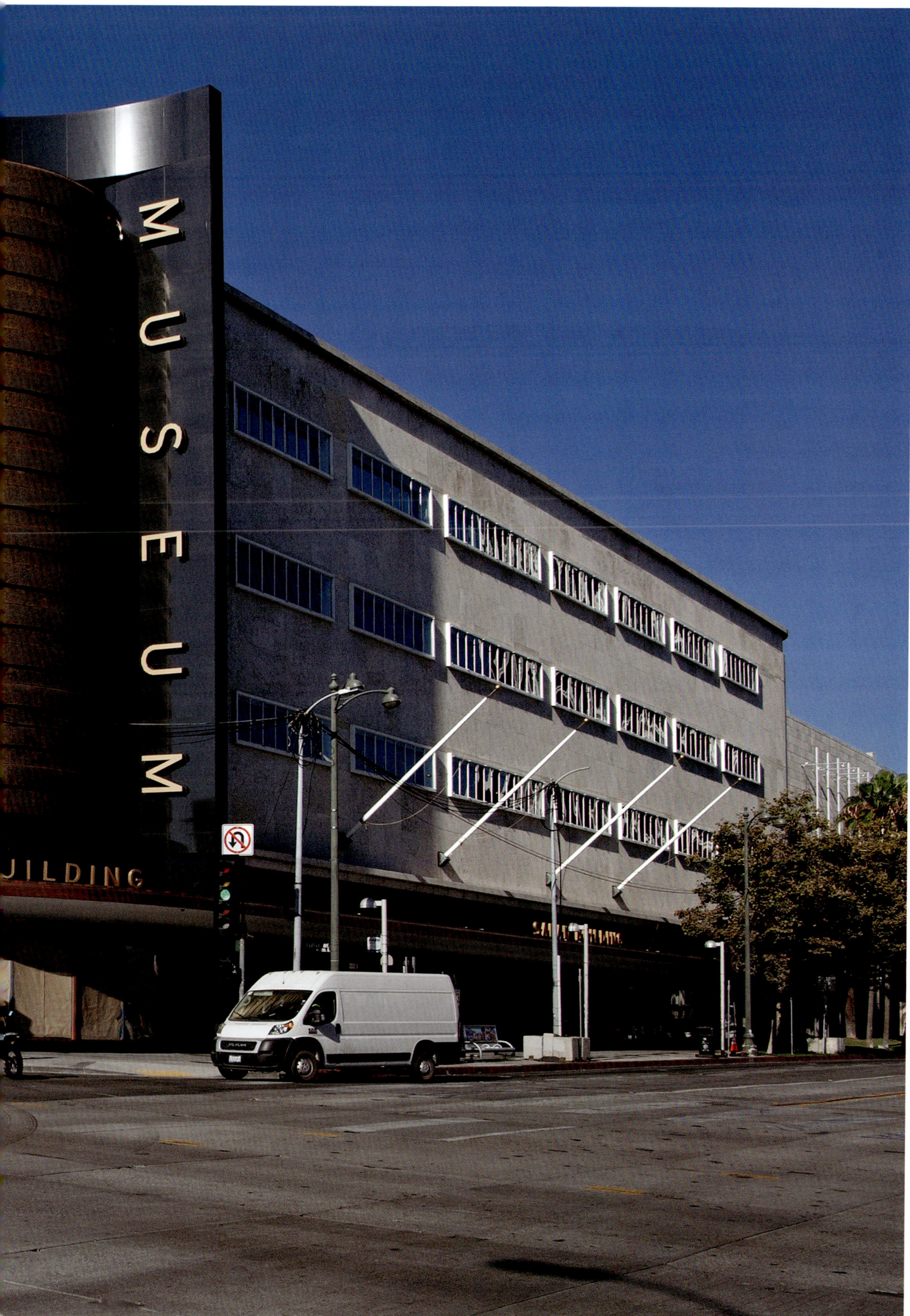
MUSEUM

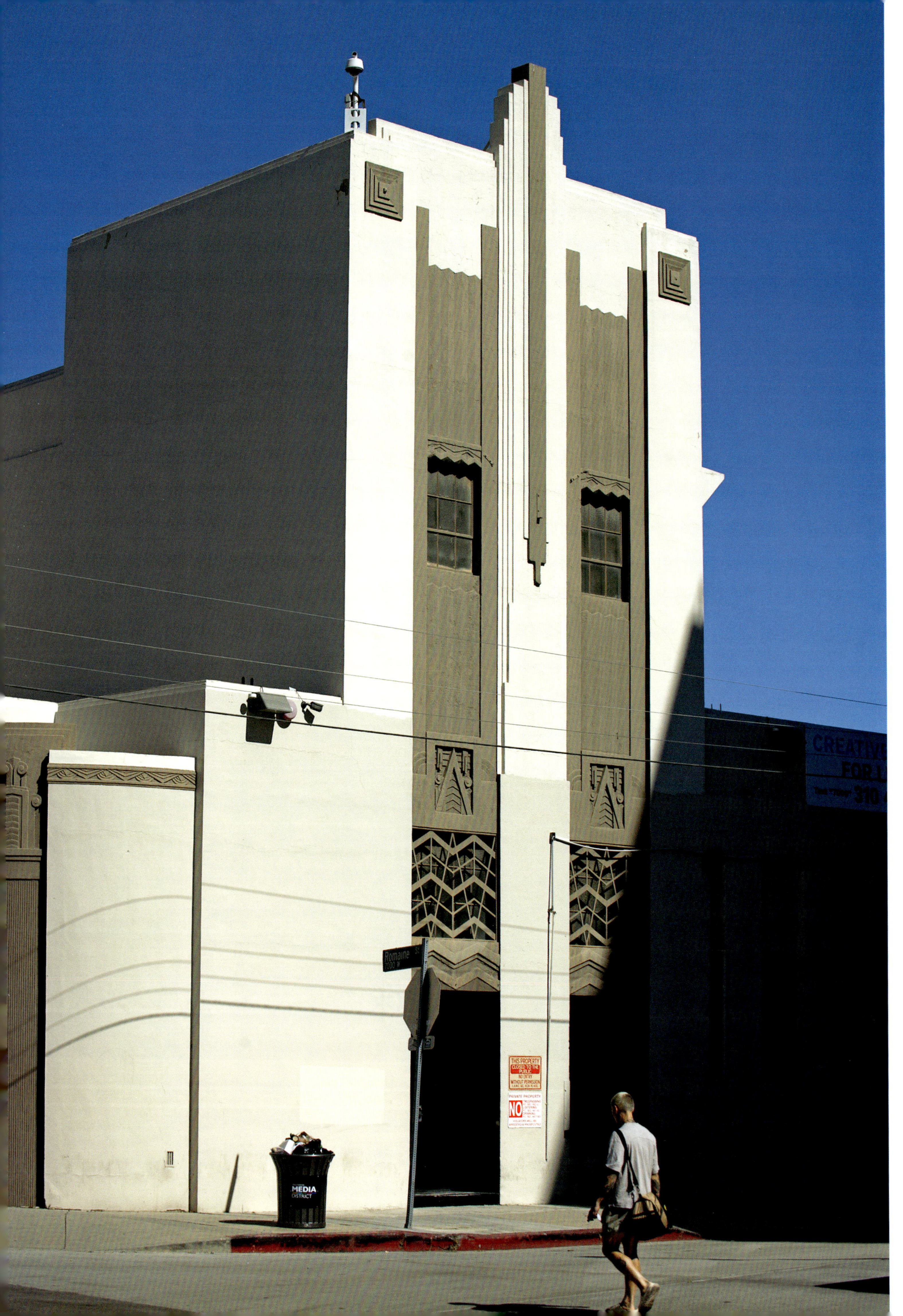
Romaine St
THIS PROPERTY
CLOSED TO THE PUBLIC
NO ENTRY
WITHOUT PERMISSION
PRIVATE PROPERTY
NO
TRESPASSING
LOITERING
DRINKING
MEDIA
DISTRICT

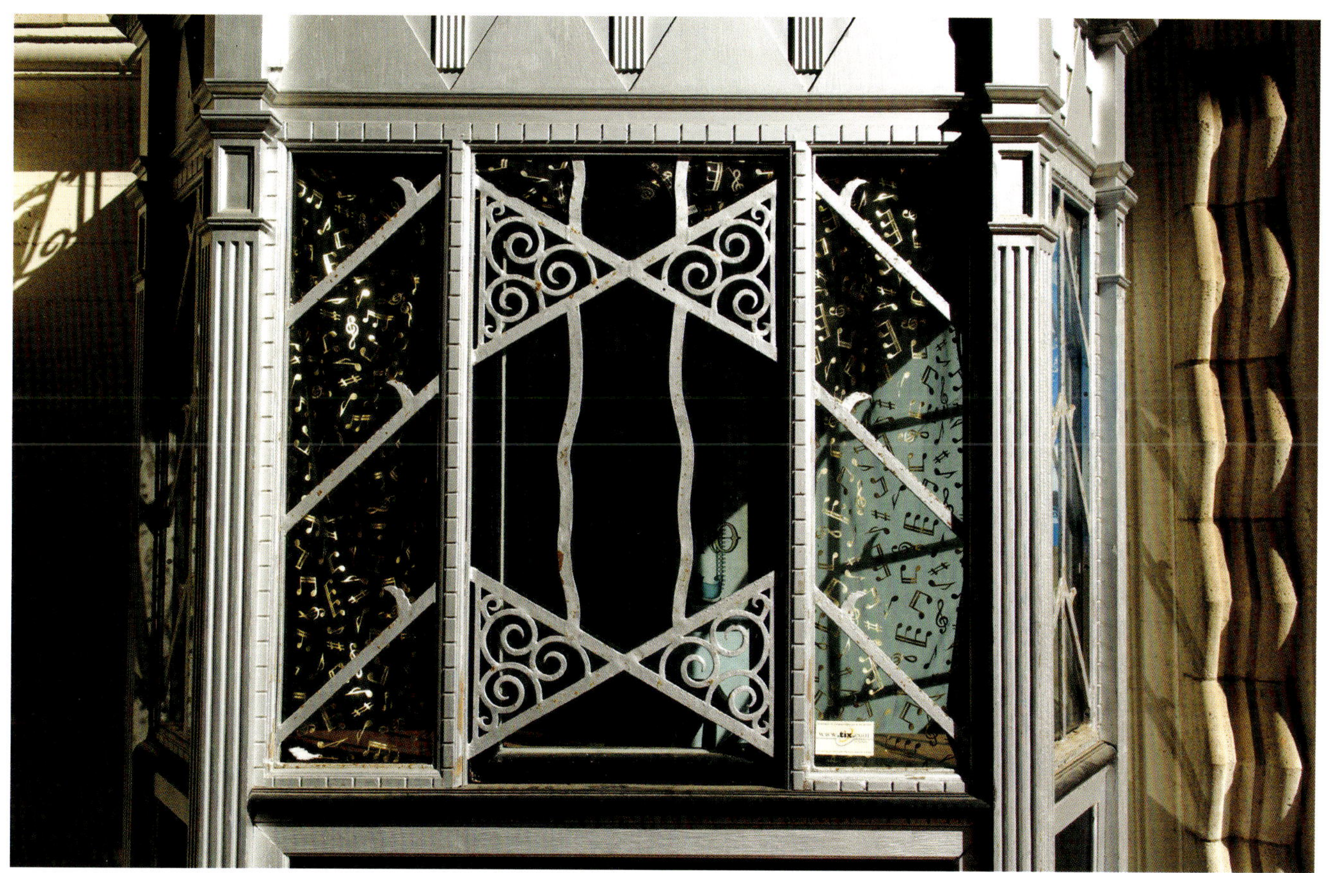

← *Howard Hughes Headquarters Building (former) (architect unknown, 1930) 7000 Romaine St., photographed 2024.*

↑ *Catalina Casino, detail (David Malcom Renton, 1929) Avalon, Catalina Island, photographed 2008.*

OVERLEAF: *Aztec Hotel (Robert Stacy-Judd, 1929) 311 W. Foothill Blvd., Monrovia, photographed 2024.*

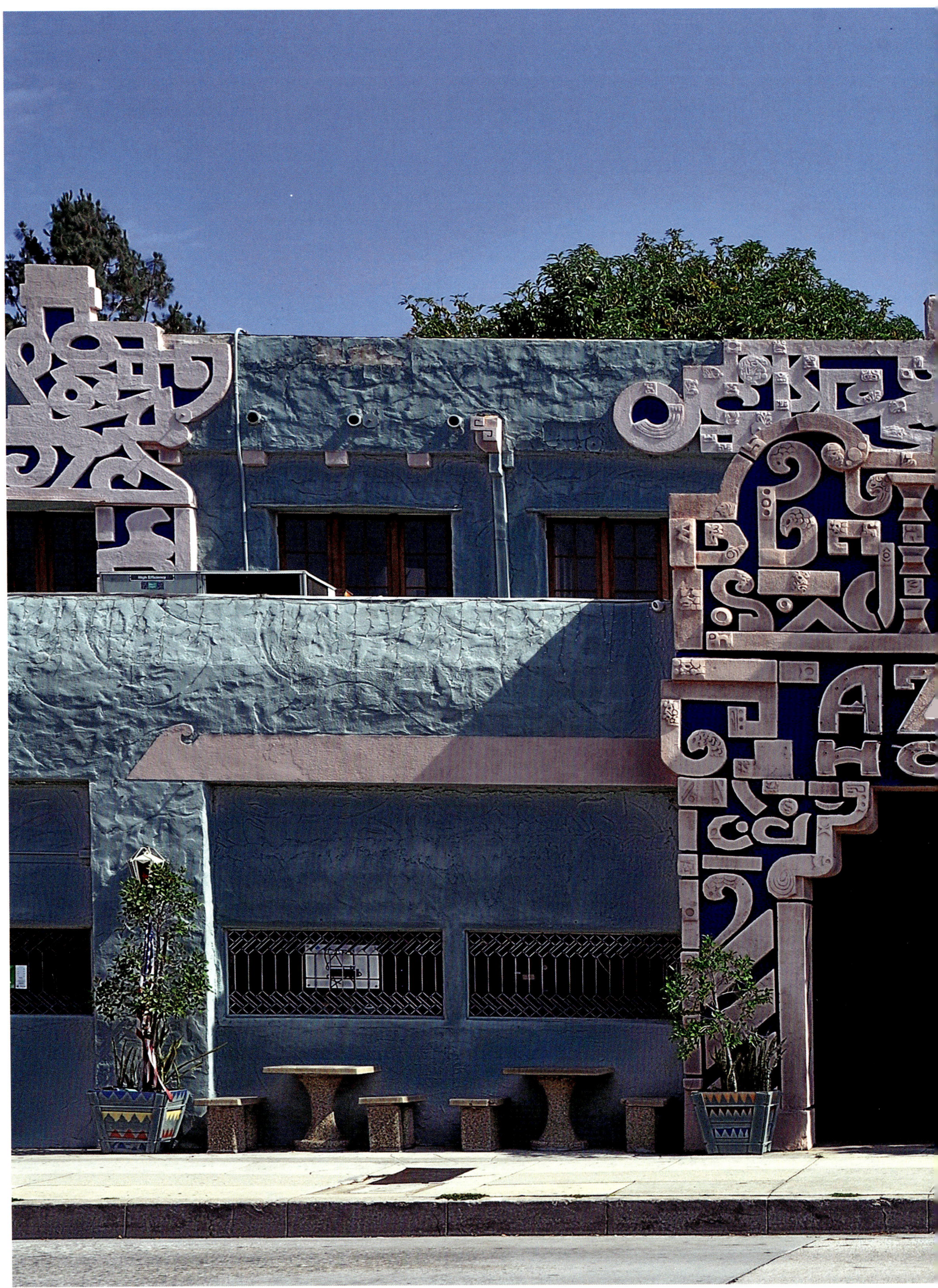

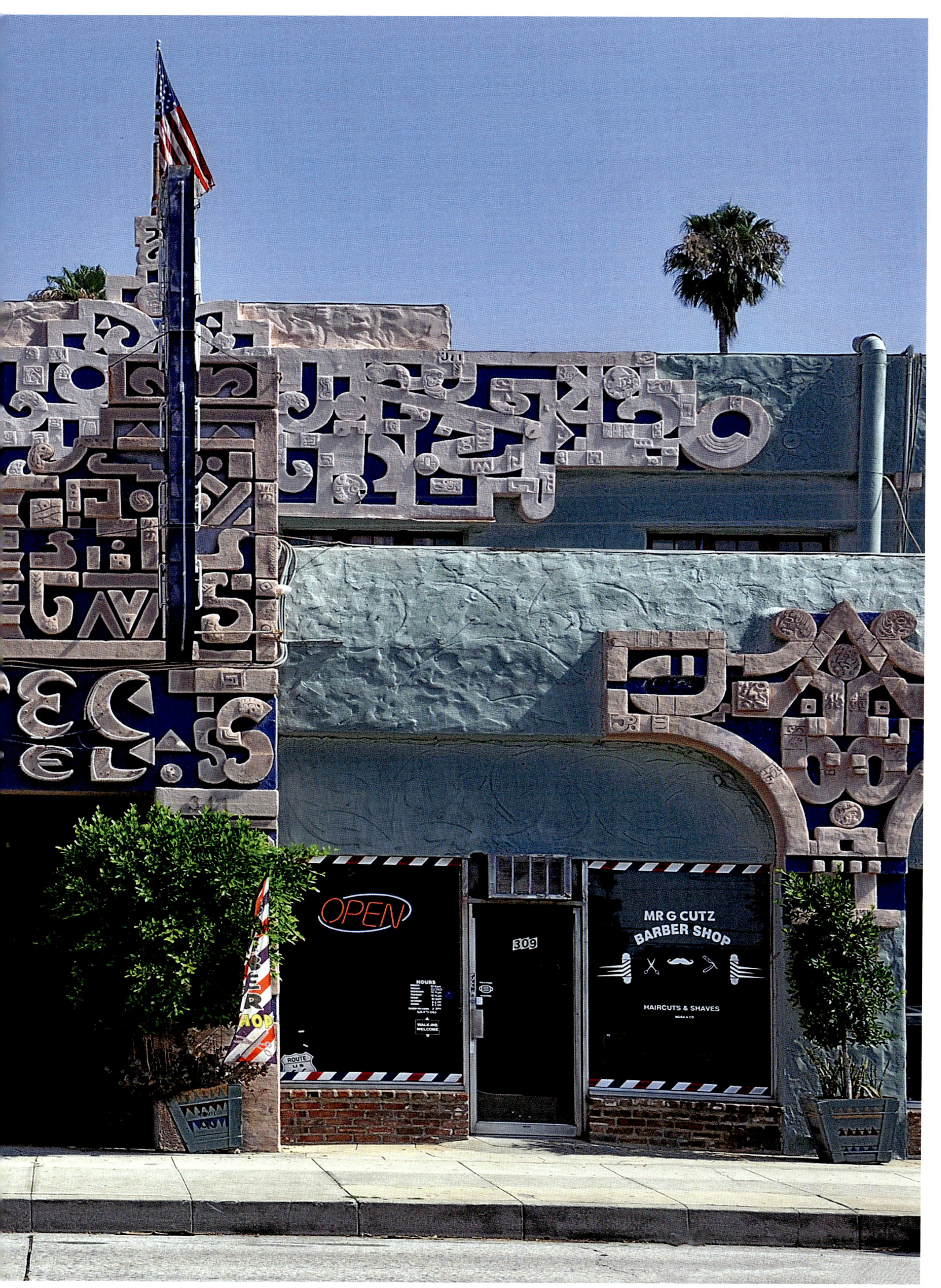
OPEN
309
MR G CUTZ
BARBER SHOP
HAIRCUTS & SHAVES

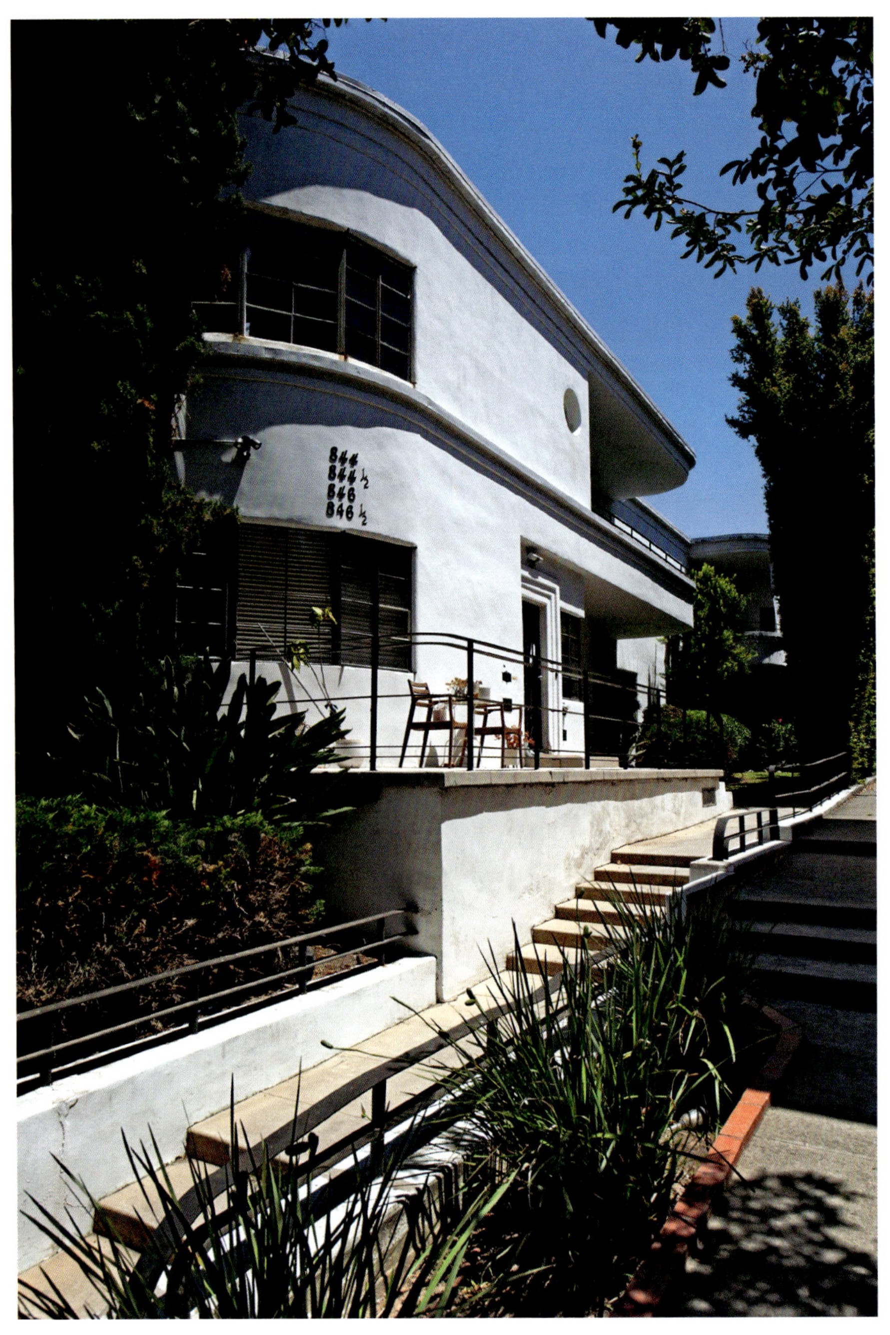

↑ *Streamline Modern Fourplex (Plummer, Wurdeman, and Becket, 1936) 844 S. Plymouth Blvd., photographed 2024.*

→ *Mauretania Apartments (Milton J. Black, 1934) 520-522 Rossmore Ave., photographed 2024.*

OVERLEAF: *Burbank Water and Power, exterior detail (Daniel A. Elliott, 1949) 164 W. Magnolia Blvd., Burbank, photographed 2024.*

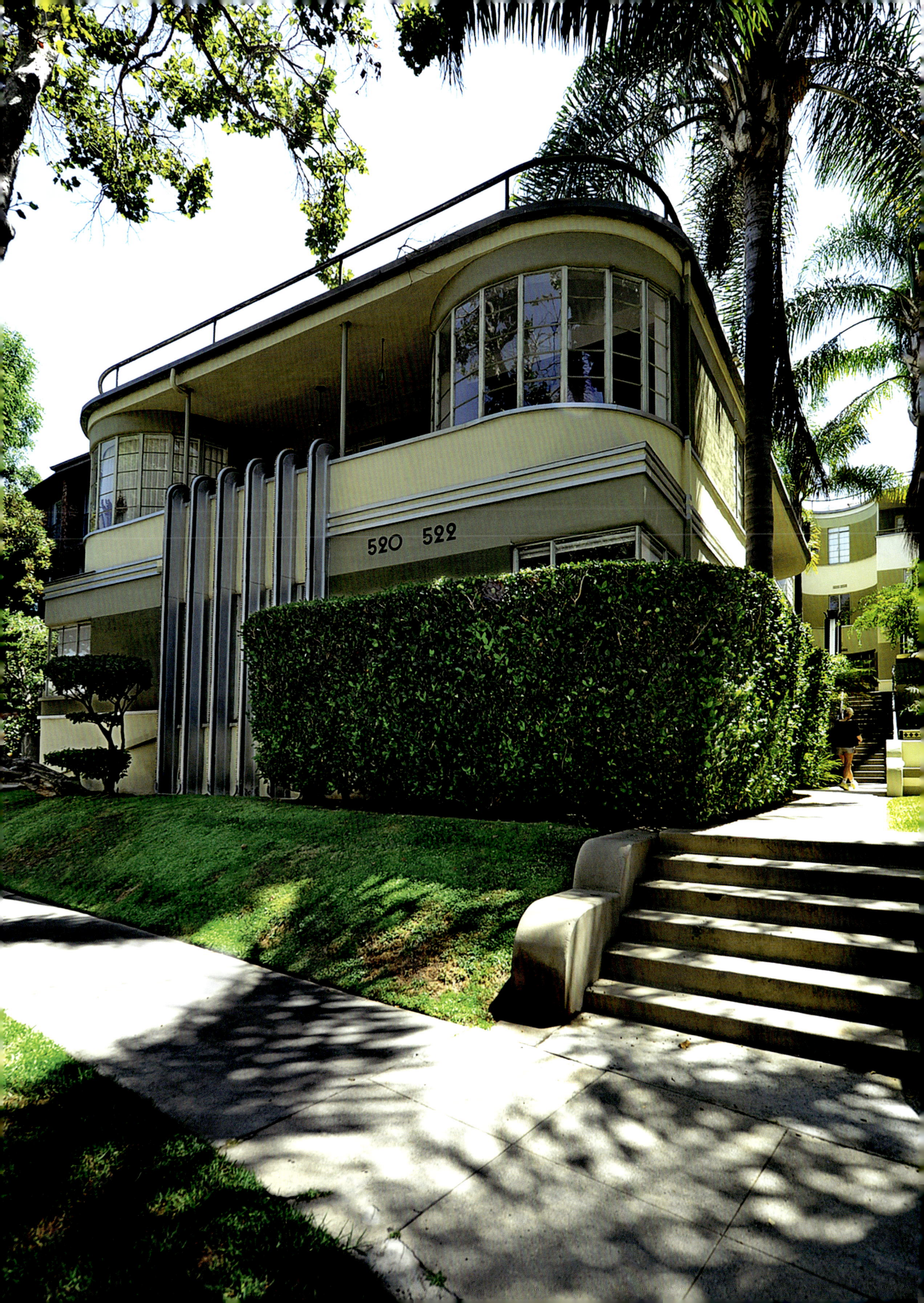
520 522

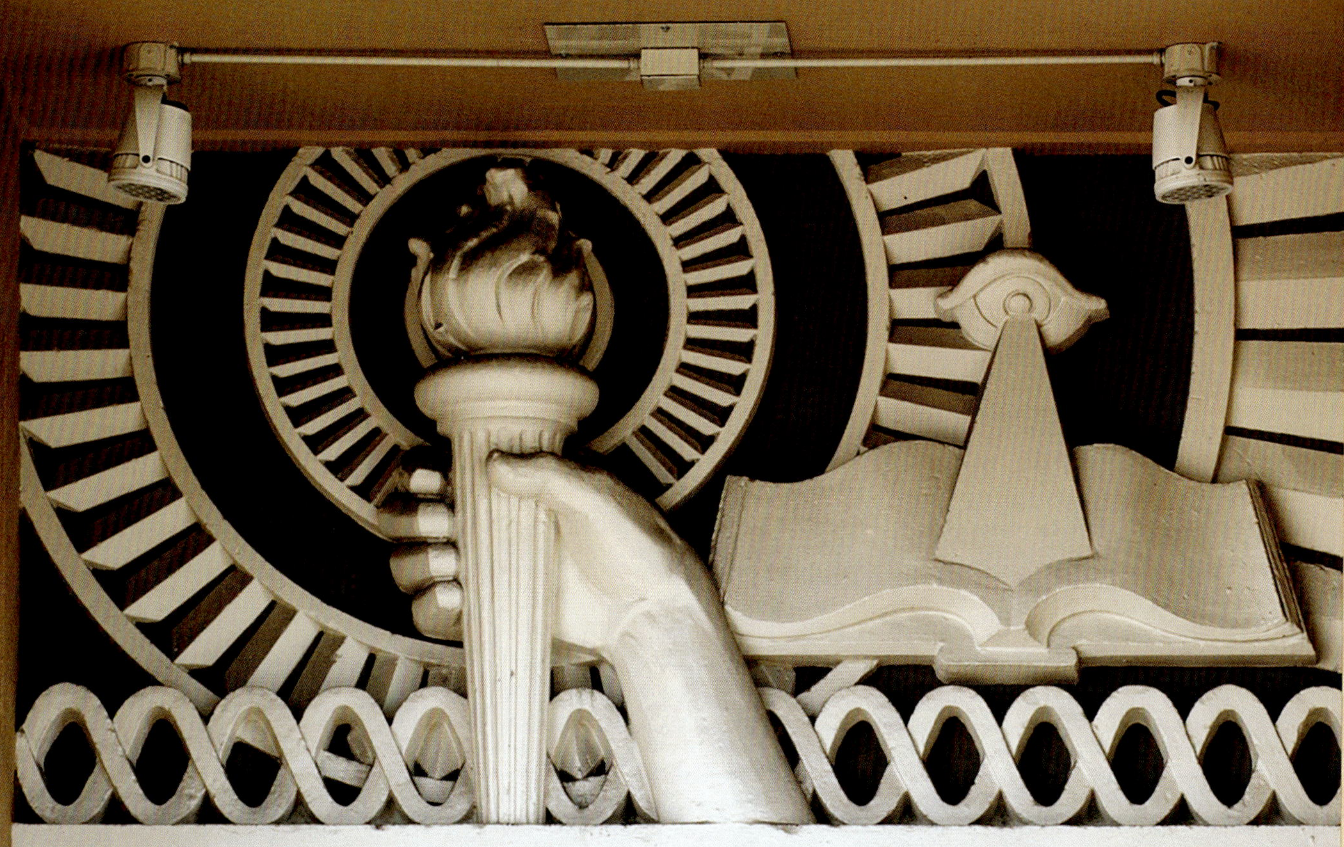
LIGHT

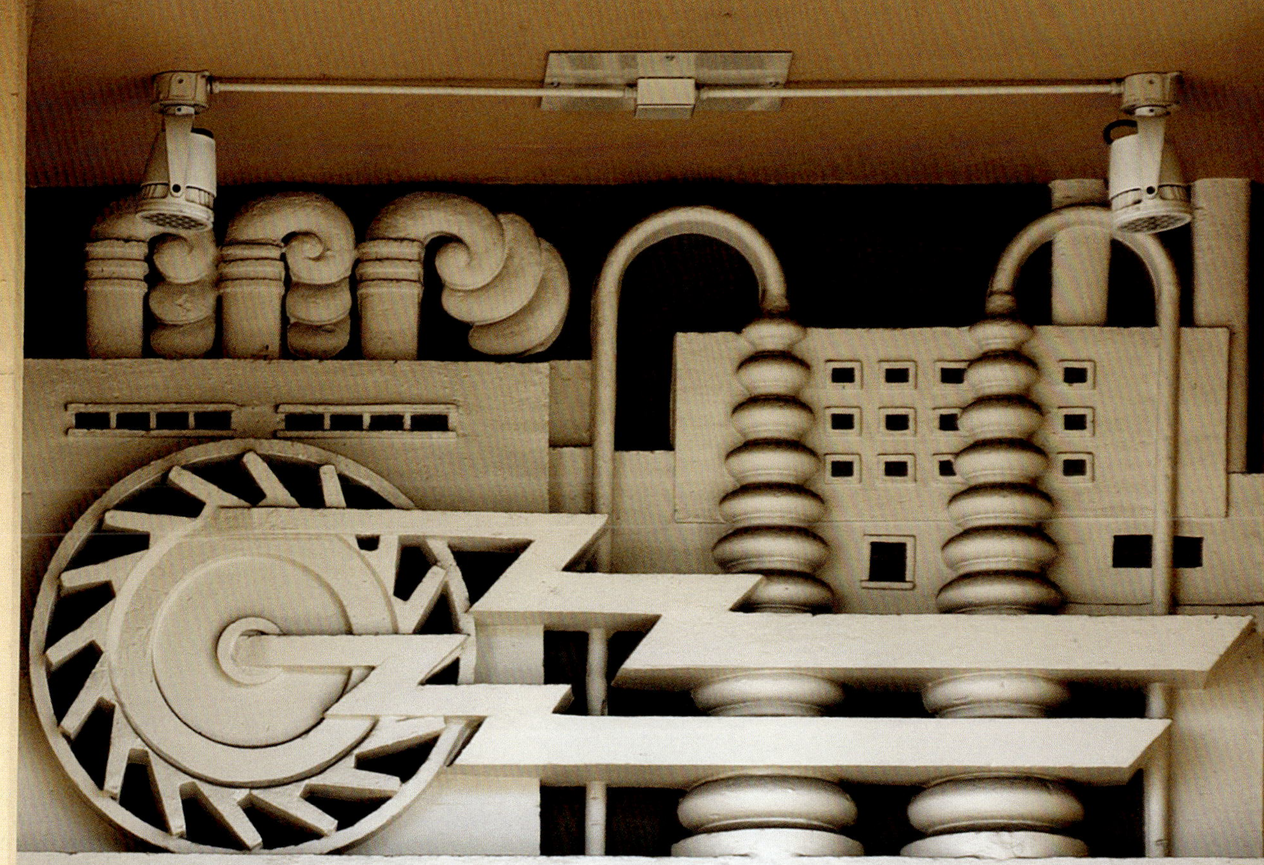
POWER

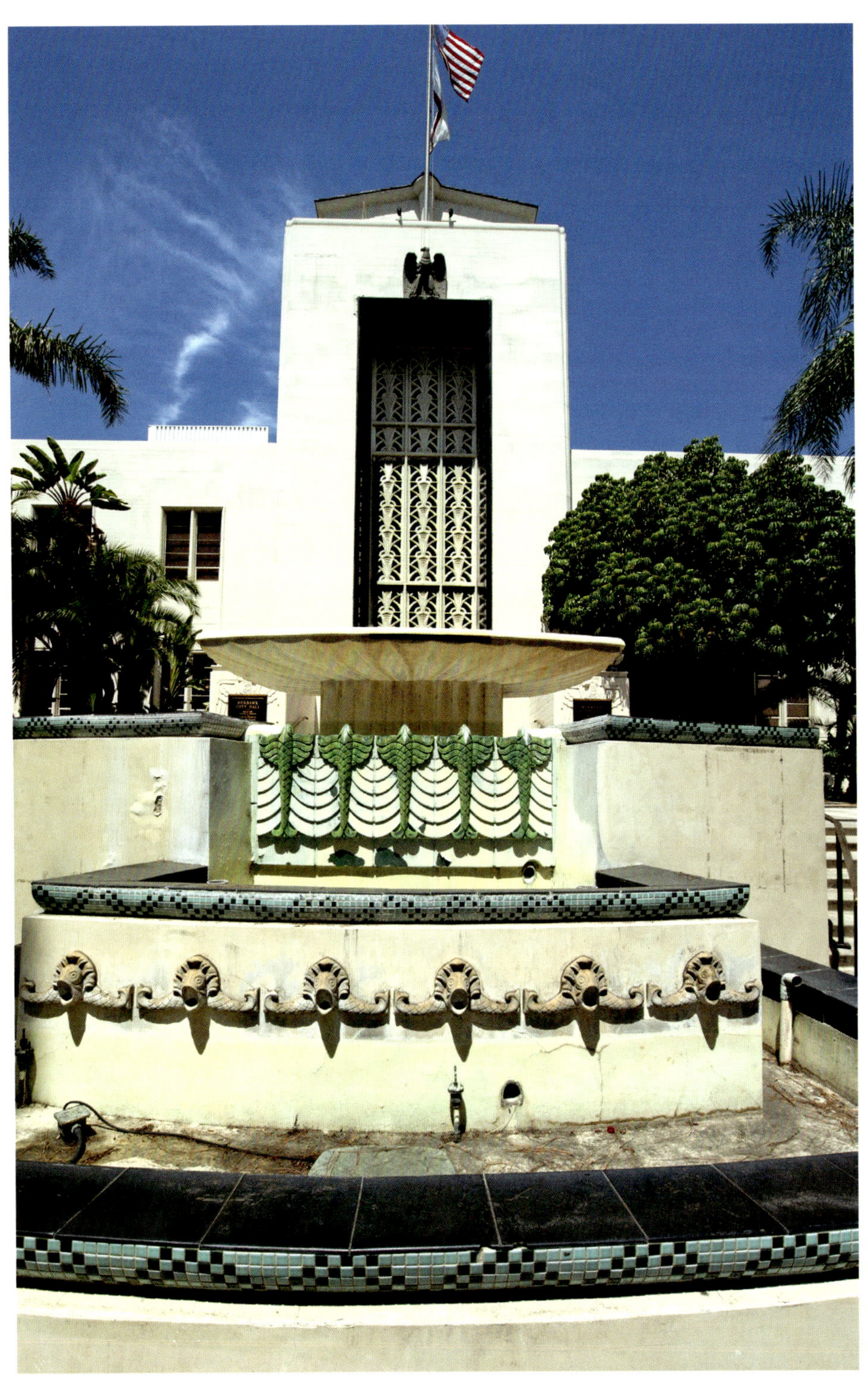

↑ *Burbank City Hall (William Allen and George Lutzi, 1943) 275 E. Olive Ave., photographed 2024.*

→ *Santa Monica City Hall (Donald B. Parkinson and J.M. Estep, 1938) 1685 Main St., photographed 2024.*

OVERLEAF: *Griffith Observatory (John C. Austin and Frederick M. Ashley, 1935) 2800 E. Observatory Rd., photographed 1992.*

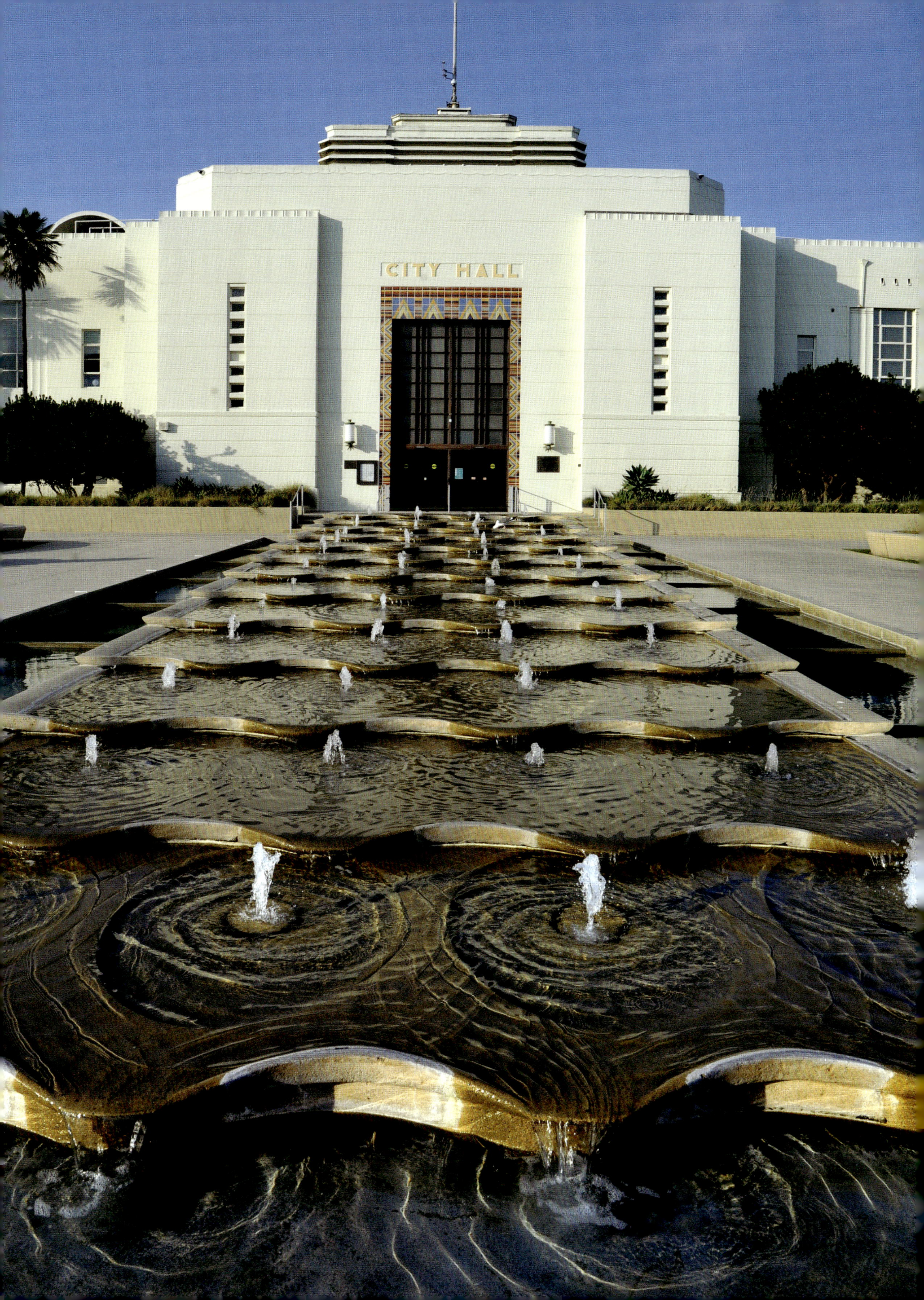
CITY HALL

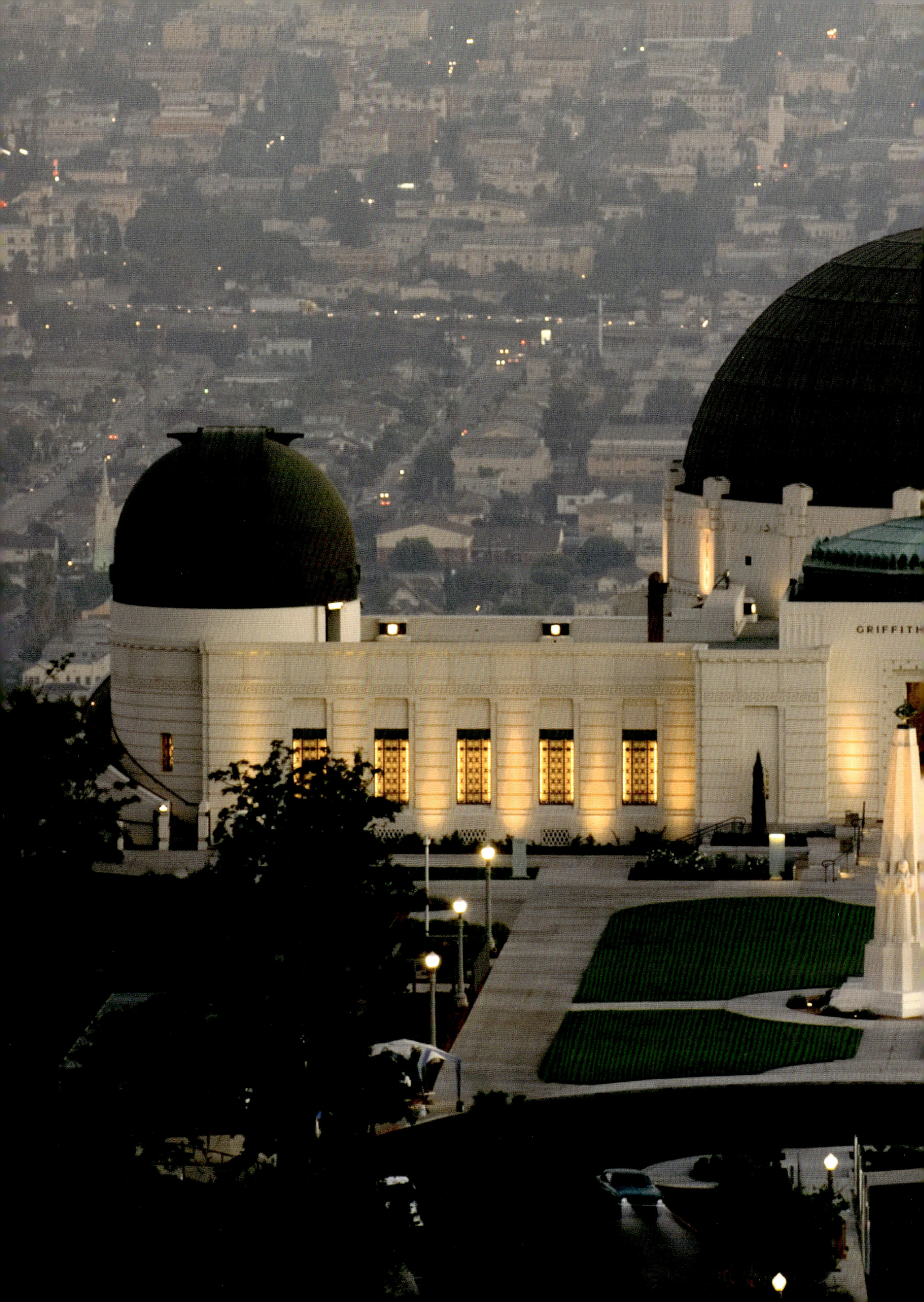
GRIFFITH

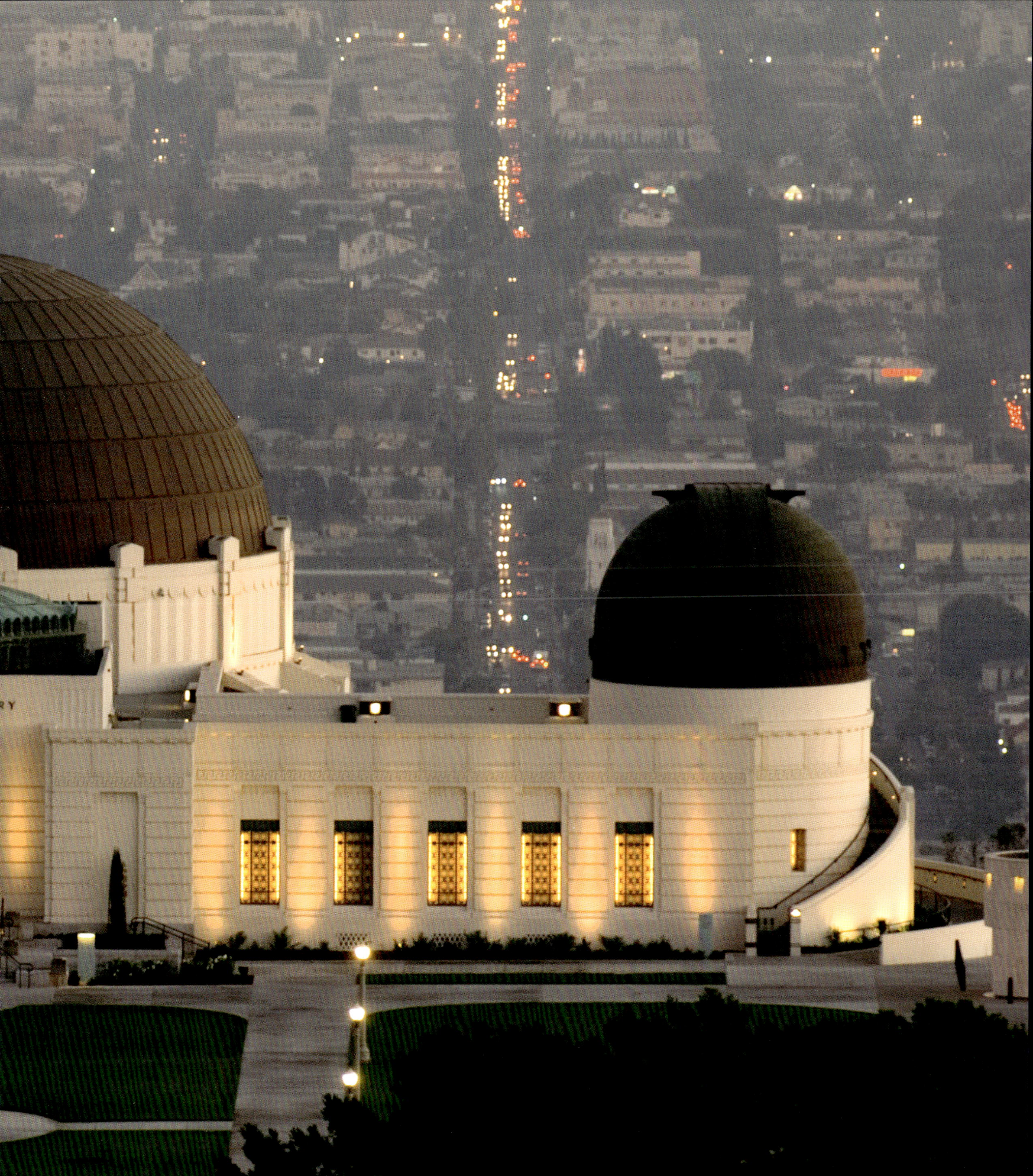

Afterword | **ROBERT LANDAU**

PHOTOGRAPHING THE L. A. CITYSCAPE

I'd like to make this clear from the start: I am first and foremost an urban landscape photographer, and sometimes I write about the things I photograph. I have no professional background in architecture, and I never consciously set out to create a book about Art Deco. You might say that the subject found me.

The first images that got me excited about becoming a photographer were made by early twentieth-century European street photographers like André Kertész and Eugène Atget, whose black-and-white pictures, particularly of the Paris cityscape, I studied in books that I found on my parents' bookshelves. My father, Felix Landau, was born in Vienna, but he and his family fled to New York in the late 1930s and became Ameran citizens. After my father's military service was over, he and my mother, Mitzi, decided to move westward, and settled in Los Angeles, where I was born. Felix borrowed some money and in 1949 opened a small frame shop on Melrose Avenue. Soon thereafter, and with some financial assistance from the GI Bill, he studied art history at UCLA and transformed the frame shop at the corner of Melrose Place and La Cienega Boulevard into an art gallery called the Felix Landau Gallery. It became an important cultural touchstone in Los Angeles throughout the 1950s and '60s. By the time Felix closed his gallery in 1970 and relocated back to Europe, he had left a mark on LA, and of course on me as well. Growing up with and around great art, both at home and in his gallery, I couldn't help but deeply believe in this maxim: art matters.

I began photographing Los Angeles in the late 1960s, usually heading out on foot with my camera loaded with black-and-white film. I could purchase a roll of Tri-X film with twenty or thirty-six exposures for a few dollars, and then develop it myself at home at night in a makeshift darkroom. This suited me fine because at first I wanted to emulate the work of my heroes. I didn't know exactly what I was looking for, but I sensed early on that Los Angeles was nothing like Paris or even, for that matter, any of the East Coast American cities I had visited. For one thing, at least in those years, there were very few people walking in the streets. Even downtown, now reinvigorated with a resident population, was at that time a business hub by day and a ghost town at night. There was a transit system made up of buses that ran infrequently, but Los Angeles was essentially a city of cars that transported people across town from destination to destination.

The city's buildings, both commercial and residential—other than downtown or along Wilshire Boulevard—were shorter and more spread out than most typical modern cities. Homes were primarily single-family structures or apartment complexes of varying capacity, and small businesses were generally one- or two-story affairs lined up side by side on long boulevards zoned for commercial use, like Pico Boulevard in between the beach and downtown, or Ventura Boulevard in the San Fernando Valley. In those days before big box mega stores, locally owned and operated grocery stores, diners, movie houses, hardware stores, and stationary stores were vital, and they brought a great deal of cultural character to their neighborhoods. All of these aspects played a part in

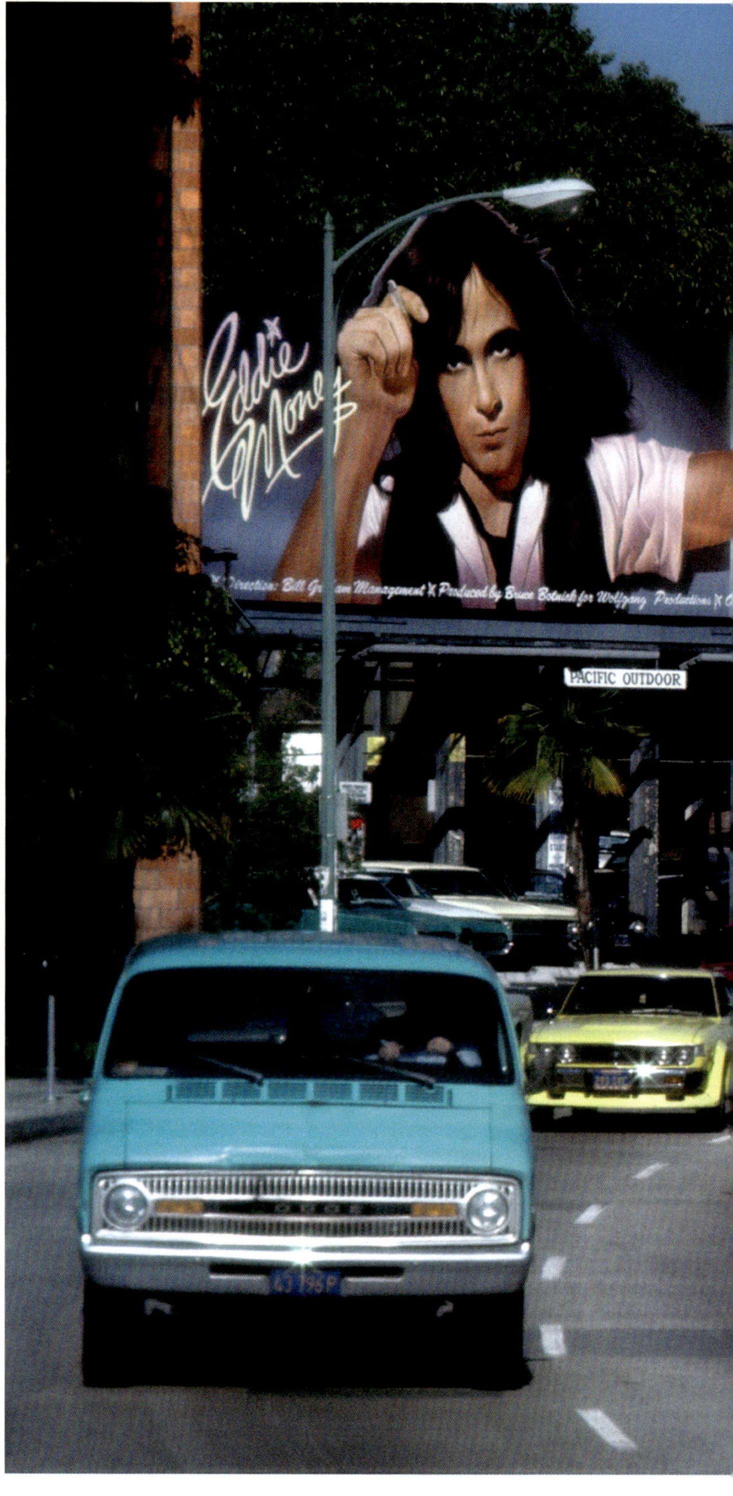

forming the physical appearance and local flavor of the city that I grew up in and wanted to portray with my camera.

It was not long into my exploration of Los Angeles that I had an epiphany and converted to making photographs in color; the city seemed to demand it. Toward the end of the 1960s and through the 1970s, I was living on a street just a block above the Sunset Strip, near to where Tower Records was located. I had become enamored with the spectacle of the enormous hand-painted billboards that lined the Strip just steps from my front door, depicting all of the great rock and roll stars of that era. I noticed that these one-of-a-kind artistic billboards would disappear within a few weeks of first being posted, be painted over, and reappear with new images; I began documenting them, at first in black and white. However, the classic rock and roll billboards, derived from cutting-edge album cover art, were painted in vivid colors, and a great deal would have been lost had they been seen only in black and white. Rolls of Kodachrome color transparency film were added to my camera kit, and I continued to pursue this uniquely L.A. advertising phenomenon with my camera into the early 1980s. Many years later, this subject became the focus of my book *Rock 'n' Roll Billboards of the Sunset Strip*.

Sunset Strip, West Hollywood, photographed 1979.

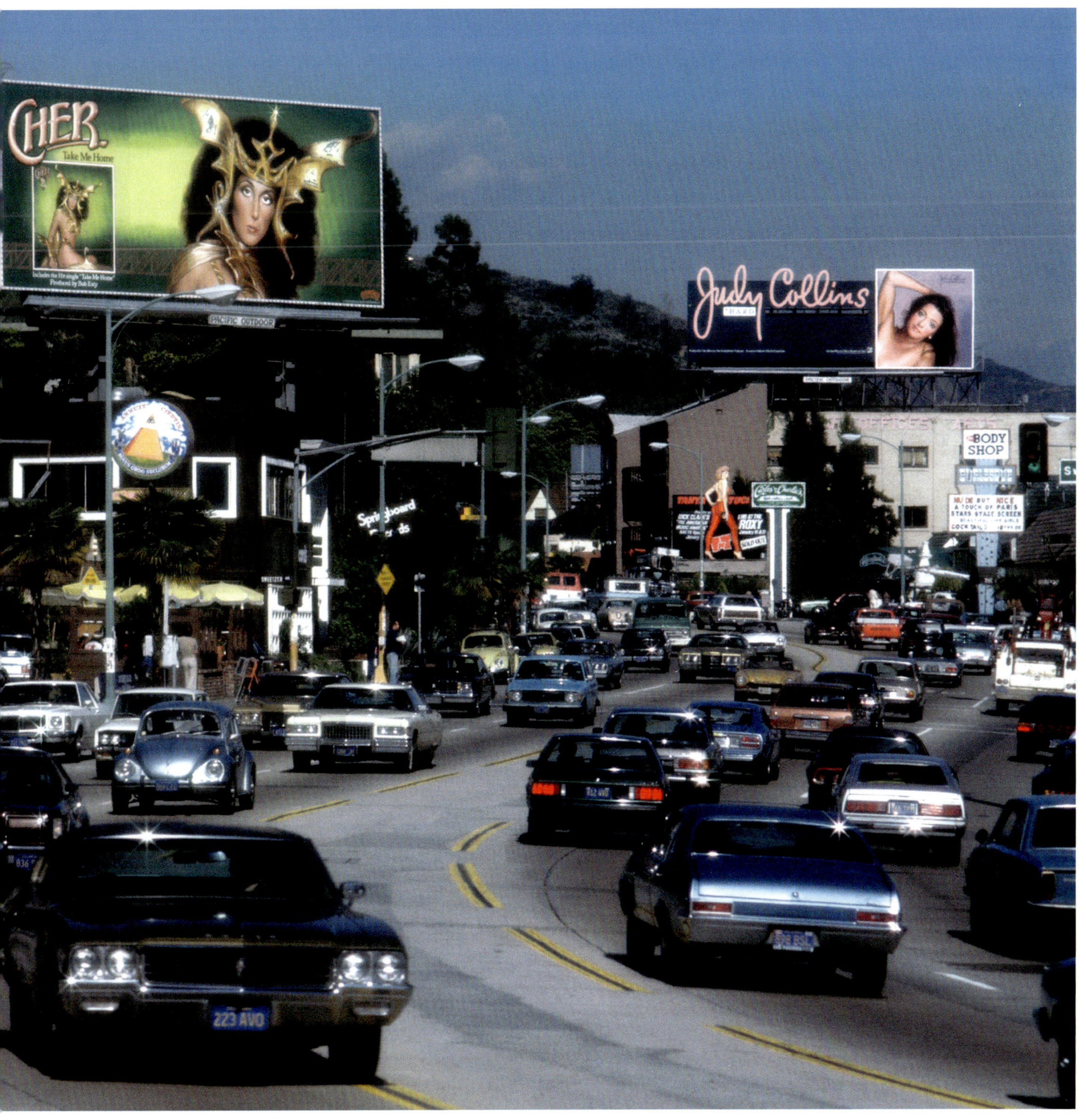

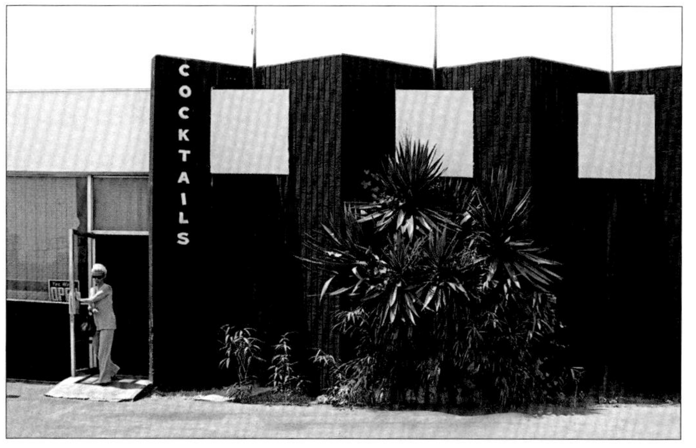

While at that point in time my interest in the billboards seemed like a diversion, and some forty years would pass before the book was published, there were some valuable lessons taken more quickly from the pursuit. Many of the external elements in the Los Angeles urban landscape, like outdoor advertising, are necessarily quite colorful as they are designed to catch the attention of, and deliver a message to, people driving by in their cars. Small businesses and shops, bars and restaurants, movie theaters and nightclubs, and even apartment buildings compete for consumer attention, relying on eye-catching shapes, colors, and signs to be noticed. In a city that came of age in the twentieth century and developed with and for automobiles, a city where signs become architecture and buildings become signs, a modern form of urban vernacular communication was created. In this new visual language color is more than an embellishment, it is part of the message. As for capturing LA in photographs, it became clear to me; Los Angeles is not a monochromatic city.

Another lesson from observing the Sunset Strip in my youth was the understanding of how quickly everything changes. Even the iconic and era-defining billboard depicting the Beatles crossing Abbey Road, which towered over the boulevard in December 1969, was taken down and replaced within weeks. All of the hip boutiques and coffee houses located near that billboard, which also seemed to reflect the spirit of those times, vanished and then reappeared with new looks and new names on Melrose Avenue in the 1980s, before yet again relocating to Silver Lake and Los Feliz and eventually to a newly gentrified downtown.

It is my opinion that the great cities that have stood over time are great because while they continue to grow and change, they respect and preserve what is great from their past. This requires both an openness to new ideas as well as an appreciation for what has come before. I believe the layering of styles and the presence of buildings from different eras, sometimes side by side, makes cities interesting, gives them texture and creates the personality that makes them unlike anywhere else. Given this outlook I was less surprised to realize, while looking back through my archives of Los Angeles imagery spanning many decades, that along with a large number of photographs of street scenes reflecting the influences of mid-century, pop culture, and postmodern scenes, I had also amassed an extensive collection of Art Deco imagery. It is worth noting that the buildings, façades, ornaments, statues, signs, and other details that appear in this book have now stood for around 100 years, which by LA standards qualifies as ancient history.

Without understanding anything about Art Deco, where it came from, or why it was there, my eye was instinctively drawn to the unique shapes, colors, materials, elegant forms, and the sheer joy of the energetic style. Whenever I encountered anything authentically Art Deco in the environment, it felt like a new discovery. And while the subjects and resulting photographs resonate with the vibrant spirit of a bygone era from the city's past, their ongoing presence and continued relevance in the Los Angeles cityscape keeps them perpetually modern…even timeless, for me.

One of the first Art Deco photographs I recall taking was a black-and-white image of a camera store on Wilshire Boulevard called The Darkroom, where I would occasionally purchase film. Along with its elegant lines and distinctive typography on the façade, I was attracted by the element of

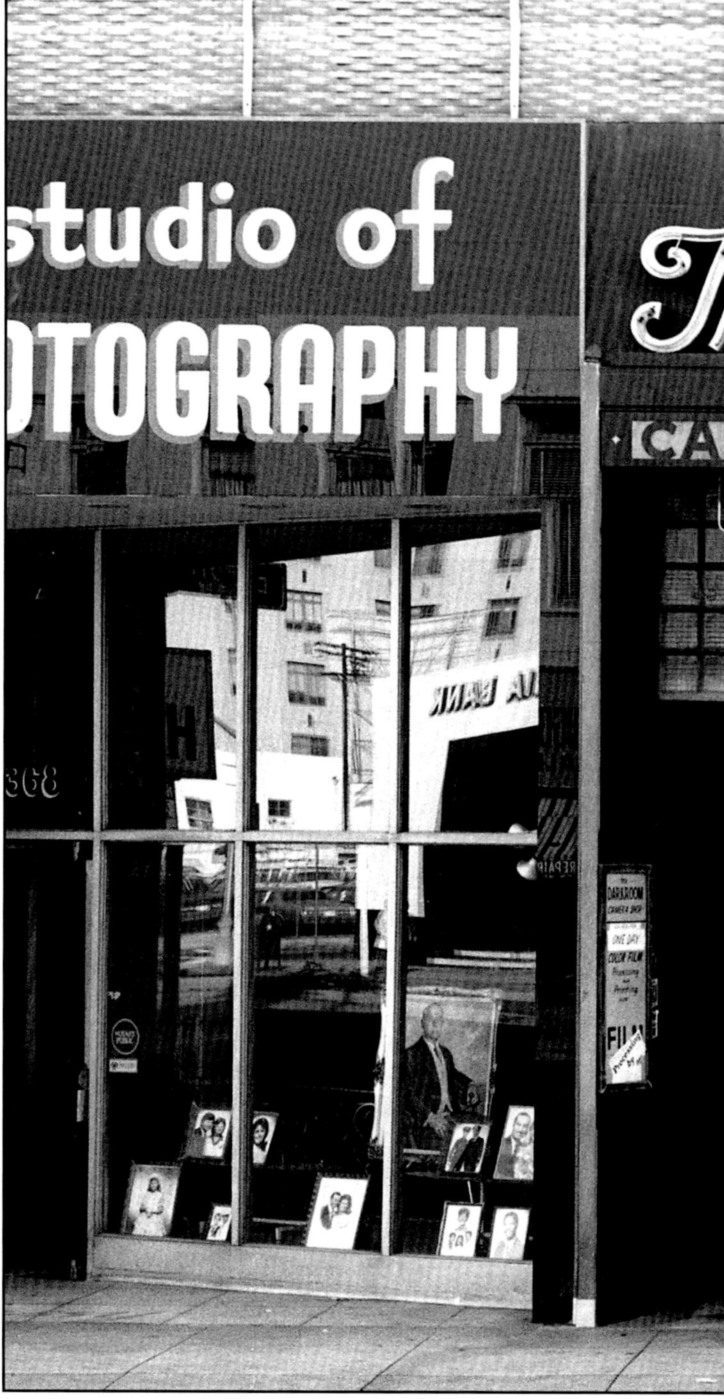

playfulness in the recreation of a 35mm camera body in the storefront's window. Another early deco image I shot, this one a few years later, and in color, was of the Eastern Columbia Building on Broadway downtown. Its elegant upward-reaching proportions and glittering turquoise blue terra-cotta exterior with gold trim would make it stand out in any city, anywhere. I have returned countless times over the years to photograph this building and it remains a favorite landmark of mine.

Once I've identified a subject that captures my interest, I like to return at different times of day to view it with different lighting. I have developed a sense about the light here in Southern California which, with all its brightness, can be quite brutal. There are times of year when the position of the sun or the presence of cloud cover can soften the intense midday overhead glare, but generally speaking the best times to see and photograph the city in color are the early hours after dawn, and the hours preceding sunset. That's when the majority of these photos were taken. Some buildings and signs that light up at night are best photographed with a tripod at sunset or dusk. Living here and focusing on particular subjects has also allowed me to return years later to see how certain scenes may have changed, such as a building on Melrose Avenue that I first photographed in the 1970s when it caught my eye as a car repair shop. Twenty years later it was a hip restaurant serving Argentinian food (p. 110-111).

← *Kingpin Lanes (Arthur Froelich, 1961) 3415 Sepulveda Blvd., photographed 1976.*

↓ *The Darkroom (Marcus P. Miller, 1936) 5370 Wilshire Blvd., photographed 1976.*

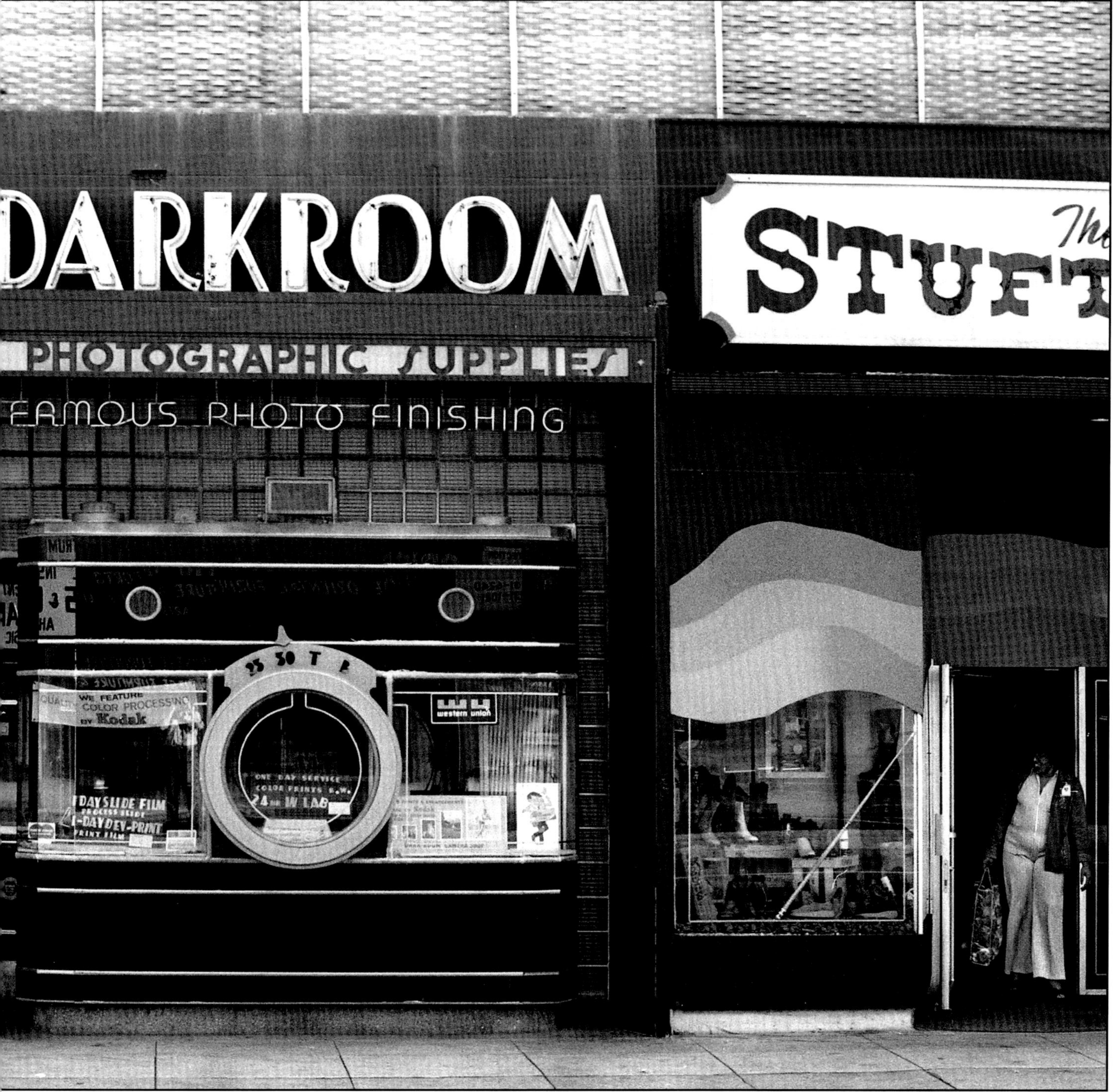

A movie theater I photographed, a drive-in, was named the Gilmore (p. 178-179) as it was part of the historic 256-acre-land parcel owned by the Gilmore family. I recalled watching the film *Easy Rider* there in 1969 from the inside of my first car. The photograph I shot some ten years later shows the fading pastel-colored exterior of the structure, built in 1948, that housed the theater's large outdoor movie screen on its inner side. I was lucky to catch a vintage taxi cab driving past the marquee that had been left blank after the venue's closing in 1977, just a few years before the structure was demolished.

In that same neighborhood stood the Pan-Pacific Auditorium, opened in 1935, where I remember attending public events and traveling shows like the Ice Capades and the Harlem Globetrotters. On one of my shooting expeditions in the 1980s I was a bit taken aback to see it fenced off and in a state of clear distress, and I was moved to take a photograph. Not long thereafter, I recall reading that the structure, having been placed on the National Register of Historic Places and being considered for a new cultural

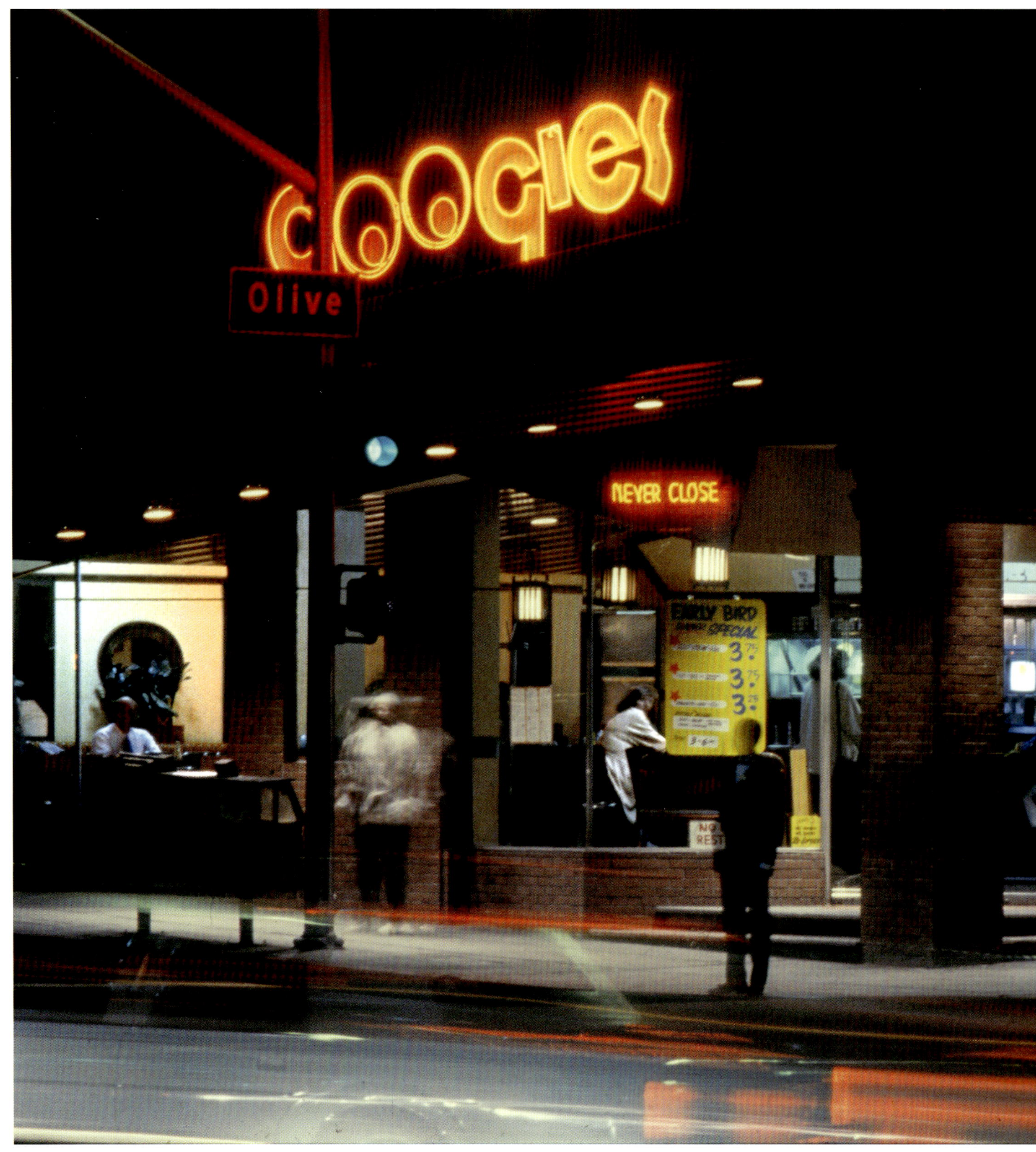

purpose, had rather mysteriously caught fire and was destroyed. Pan Pacific Park, an urban park with a recreation center, now occupies that space. A replica of the iconic building's Moderne entryway has since been recreated at the entrance to Disney California Adventure theme park and is also memorialized in the logo for the Los Angeles Art Deco Society.

Los Angeles has not had a great record when it comes to respecting and preserving its own historic past. Incredible buildings and entire culturally significant neighborhoods have

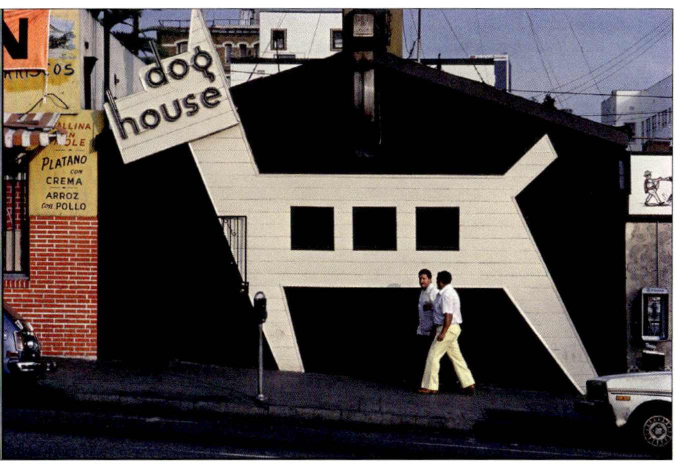

vanished under the guise of "progress." Even LA's defining industry, the Hollywood movie business, has only just recently found a museum to tell its story to the world, some 100 years after its inception. The good news is that, midway into its third century, the city finally seems more alert and willing to acknowledge and preserve its past, particularly where important and beautiful buildings are concerned. There are noble groups like the Los Angeles Conservancy and the Art Deco Society of Los Angeles leading this battle, but I think it's the realization by the general public that the style and craftsmanship of many older buildings, particularly when compared to contemporary structures of lesser quality, deserve to be restored and maintained. To that point, the Academy Museum of Motion Pictures (p.188-189)is housed in the remnant of an Art Deco department store on the Miracle Mile of Wilshire Boulevard, several vintage movie theaters around town have transformed into churches, and there are even a few repurposed vintage deco gas stations including one that became a Starbucks (p. 184-185), and another offering lobster rolls (p. 180-181) to customers who pull up in their cars to a spot where gas pumps once stood.

As a first impression, Los Angeles, seen from the seat of an aircraft approaching LAX, may look like one big sprawling mess. But then, from the wheel of a car driving out from the airport in any direction and on any freeway...it's not that different. As a photographer, taking on this city requires a commitment of time and persistence to sift through it all; the good, the bad, and the ugly. In choosing what to focus on I've had to trust my instincts, honed over the years, and go with what most grabs my eye. There are many more untold stories here capable of revealing intriguing facets of a hard-to-define city than I'll have time for. What keeps the quest interesting is the opportunity and real possibility of discovering something brand new and unforeseen, or just as satisfying, rediscovering something totally unexpected from the past like the abundant presence of historic Art Deco treasures hiding in plain sight. ■

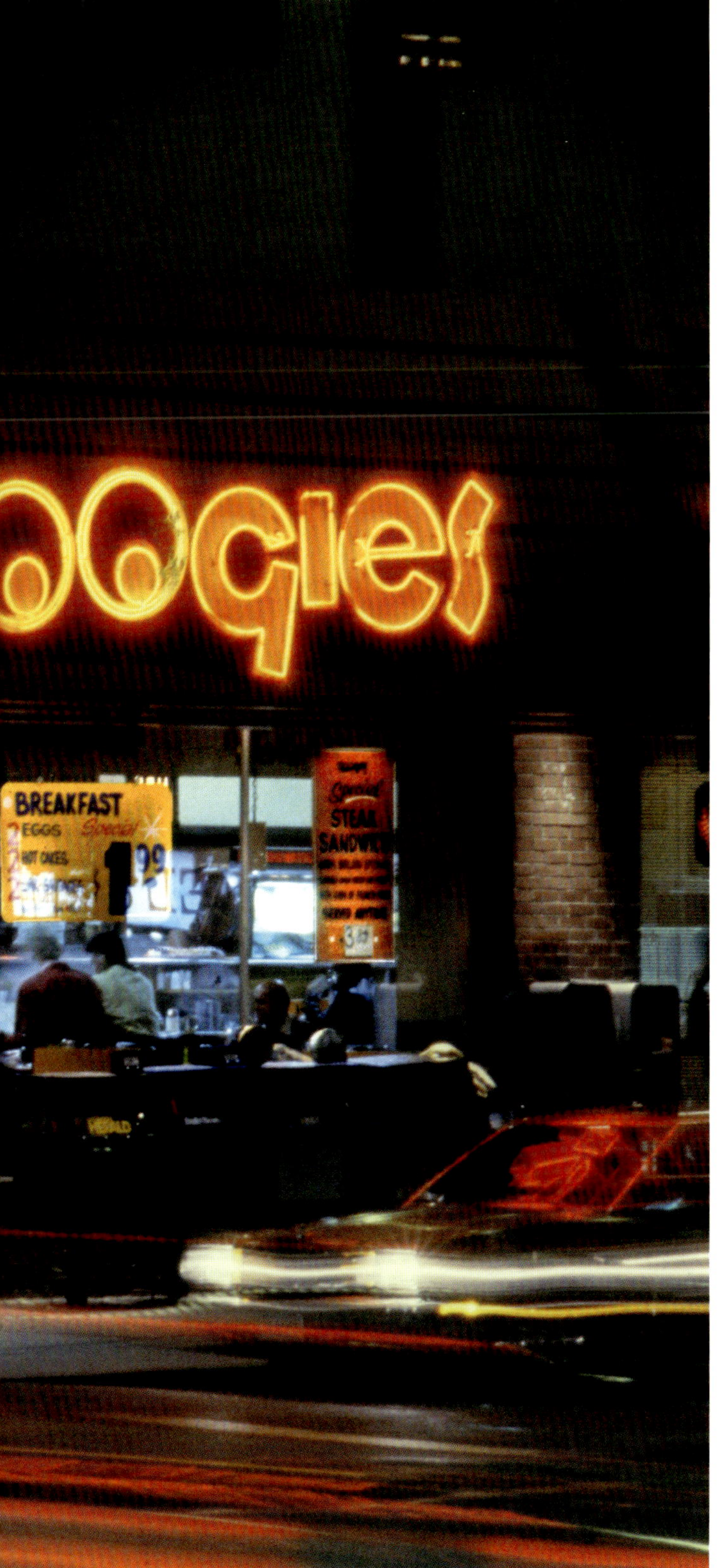

← Googies (Armet & Davis, 1955) 555 W. 5th St., photographed 1977.

↑ Dog House (architect and year unknown) 616 S. Alvarado Blvd., 1982.

ACKNOWLEDGMENTS

I want to thank Frans Evenhuis, designer extraordinaire, book partner in crime, and lifelong friend for making the work shine. I'd also like to recognize Paddy Calistro and Scott McAuley for creating Angel City Press, allowing Frans and I to get in on the fun, and for passing the torch to the steady hand of Terri Accomazzo, who suggested that we create this book. And, thanks to all of you who love books that you can hold in your hands.

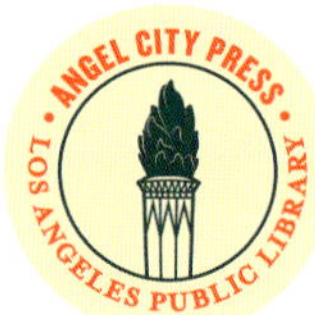

Published by Angel City Press at Los Angeles Public Library
www.angelcitypress.com

Art Deco | Los Angeles

Design by Frans Evenhuis

10 9 8 7 6 5 4 3 2 1

ISBN-13 978-1-62640-139-6

Library of Congress Cataloging-in-Publication Data is available

Printed in Canada

PHOTO CREDITS

All images by Robert Landau except where listed below:
Alamy: 26 • Alamy/Pictorial Press Ltd.: 25

Fine Art prints of the photographs in this book are available.
Contact: rlandau444@gmail.com

Footnotes | ALAN HESS

1 | David Gebhard, *Tulsa Art Deco: An Architectural Era 1925 to 1942 (Tulsa: The Junior League of Tulsa, 1980)*, 7.

2 | Sheldon Cheney, Sheldon, *The New World Architecture* (New York: Tudor Publishing Company, 1930), 79.

3 | Oliver Reagan and Lewis Mumford, American Architecture of the Twentieth Century (New York: Architectural Book Publishing Company, 1927), preface.

4 | Gebhard calls Frank Lloyd Wright's Johnson Wax Headquarters (1939) in Racine, Wisconsin "the crowning jewel of the Streamline Moderne;" see Gebhard, Tulsa Art Deco, p 22.

5 | This variation is also sometimes called PWA Moderne, from the New Deal's earlier Public Works Administration.

6 | For more on Late Moderne see Steven Keylon, *The Design of Herbert W. Burns* (Palm Springs: Palm Springs Preservation Foundation, 2018), 4-5.

7 | Kevin Lynch, *The Image of the City* (Cambridge, MA: Massachusetts Institute of Technology, 1960), 35.

8 | Sheldon Cheney, *The New World Architecture* (New York: Tudor Publishing Company, 1930), 191.

9 | See David Gebhard and Harriette Von Breton, *L.A. In the Thirties* (Salt Lake City: Peregrine Smith, inc., 1975); David Gebhard, *Tulsa Art Deco: An Architectural Era 1925 to 1942* (Tulsa: The Junior League of Tulsa, 1980); Martin Greif, *Depression Modern: The Thirties Style in America* (New York: Universe Books, 1980); Laura Cerwinske *Tropical Deco, The Architecture and Design of Old Miami Beach* (New York: Rizzoli 1981.)

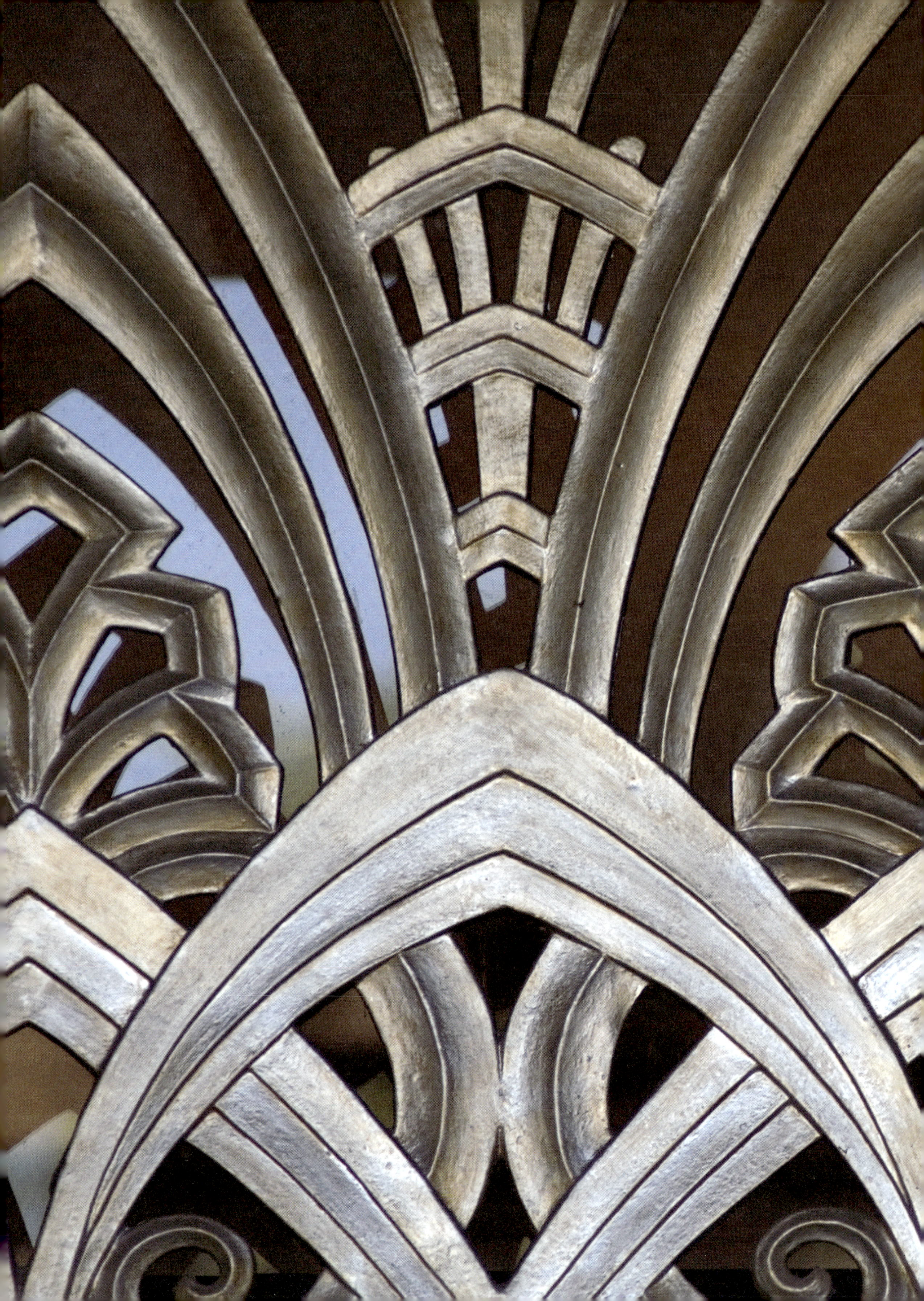